The American
Church History Series

CONSISTING OF A SERIES OF
DENOMINATIONAL HISTORIES PUBLISHED UNDER THE AUSPICES OF
THE AMERICAN SOCIETY OF CHURCH HISTORY

General Editors

REV. PHILIP SCHAFF, D. D., LL. D.   BISHOP JOHN F. HURST, D. D., LL. D.

RT. REV. H. C. POTTER, D. D., LL. D.   REV. E. J. WOLF, D. D.

REV. GEO. P. FISHER, D. D., LL. D.   HENRY C. VEDDER, M. A.

REV. SAMUEL M. JACKSON, D. D., LL. D.

VOLUME VI

A HISTORY

OF THE

PRESBYTERIAN CHURCHES
IN THE UNITED STATES

BY

ROBERT ELLIS THOMPSON, D. D.

ℕew ℤork
𝔗he 𝔠hristian 𝔏iterature 𝔠o.

MDCCCXCV

CONTENTS.

v

A HISTORY OF THE PRESBYTERIAN CHURCH IN THE UNITED STATES.

BY

Rev. ROBERT ELLIS THOMPSON, D.D.,
Philadelphia, Pa.

BIBLIOGRAPHY.

I. THE REFORMED CHURCHES OF EUROPE.

Baird, C. W., *History of the Huguenot Emigration to America.* 2 vols., 1st and 2d editions, New York, 1885.

Baird, H. M., *History of the Rise of the Huguenots of France (1512–1574).* 2 vols., New York, 1879; 2d ed., 1883.

———, *The Huguenots and Henry of Navarre.* 2 vols., New York, 1886.

Baum, G., et Cunitz, E., *Histoire Ecclésiastique des Églises Reformées au Royaume de France.* 2d ed., 2 vols., Paris, 1883–1884.

Calvini, Joh., *Opera quæ supersunt Omnia*, ed. G. Baum, E. Cunitz, et E. Reuss. In the *Corpus Reformatorum.* Brunswick, 1864 ff.

Comba, Emilio, *Histoire des Vaudois d'Italie depuis leur Origines jusq'à nous Jours.* 2 tomes.

———, *History of the Waldenses of Italy from their Origin to the Reformation.* Translated by T. E. Comba. London, 1889.

———, *Storia della Riforma in Italia.* Tom. i., Firenze, 1891.

———, *Storia dei Valdesi.* Turin, 1893.

Cunningham, William, *The Reformers and the Theology of the Reformation.* 2 vols., Edinburgh, 1862.

Dalton, Hermann, *Johannes à Lasco: Beitrag zur Reformationsgeschichte Polens, Deutschlands und Englands.* Gotha, Perthes, 1881. (English translation, London, 1886.)

Dyer, T. H., *Life of John Calvin, Compiled from Authentic Sources, and Particularly from his Correspondence.* London, 1849.

Ebrard, Joh. Heinr. Aug., *Handbuch der christlichen Kirchen- und Dogmengeschichte für Prediger und Studierende.* Vols. iii. and iv., Erlangen, Deichert, 1866.

Goebel, Max, *Geschichte des christlichen Lebens in der rheinisch-westfhälischen evangelischen Kirche.* 3 vols., Coblenz, 1849–1860.

Haag, Eug. et Em., *La France Protestante, ou Vies des Protestants Français qui se sont fait un Nom dans l'Histoire depuis les Premiers Temps de la Réformation jusq'à la Reconnaissance du Principe de la Liberté des Cultes par l'Assemblée Nationale.* Paris, 1853–1859, 10 tom., gr. 8; new edition, Paris, 1877 ff.

Henry, Paul, *Leben Johann Calvins, des grossen Reformators.* 3 vols., Hamburg, 1835–1844. (Imperfect English rendering by Dr. Henry Stebbing, London, 1849.)

Heppe, Heinrich, *Geschichte des Pietismus und der Mystik in der Reformirten Kirche, namentliche der Niederlande.* Leiden, 1879.

Herzog, Joh. Jak., *Abriss der gesammten Kirchengeschichte.* Parts iii. and iv., Erlangen, Besold, 1882; 2d ed., edited by G. Koffmane, 1892. *Leben und ausgewählte Schriften der Väter und Begründer der Reformirten Kirche.* 10 vols., Elberfeld, 1857–1863. *Johannes à Lasco,* von P. Bartels; *Wolfg. Fab. Capito und Mart. Butzer,* von J. W. Baum; *Ulrich Zwingli,* von R. Christoffel; *Joh. Oekolampad und Oswald Myconius,* von K. R. Hagenbach; *Lambert von Avignon,* von F. W. Hassenkamp; *H. Bullinger und Leo Judä,* von C. Pestalozzi; *Guillaume Farel, Pierre Viret, und P. M. Vermigli,* von Carl Schmidt; *Kaspar Olevianus und Zach. Ursinus,* von K. Sudhoff; *Johann Calvin,* von C. Stähelin; *Theo. Beza,* von Heinr. Heppe; *Bert. Haller,* von C. Pestalozzi; *Ambrosius Blaurer und Joachim Vadianus,* von T. Pressel; *John Knox,* von F. Brandes.

Lorgion, Diest, *De Nederduitsche Hervormde Kerk in Friesland.* Groningen, 1848.

Mayer, Lewis, *History of the German Reformed Church.* Vol. i., Philadelphia, 1850.

Niemeyer, Aug. Herm., *Collectio Confessionum in Ecclesiis Reformatis Publicatarum.* Leipsic, 1840.

Ritschl, Albrecht, *Geschichte des Pietismus.* Vol. i., *Der Pietismus in der Reformirten Kirche.* Bonn, Marcus, 1880.

Schaff, Philip, *Bibliotheca Symbolica Ecclesiæ Universalis: The Creeds of Christendom, with a History and Critical Notes.* New York, 1877; 3d ed., New York, 1884.

———, *The History of the Christian Church.* Vol. vii., *The Swiss Reformation.* New York, Scribners, 1892.

Smith, Henry B., *The Reformed Churches of Europe and America, in Relation to General Church History.* New York, 1855.

II. The Presbyterian Churches of Great Britain and Ireland.

Blair, Robert, *Autobiography and Life, 1593–1666.* Edited by Dr. Thomas McCrie. Edinburgh, published by the Wodrow Society, 1849.

Calderwood, David, *A History of the Church of Scotland* [to 1625]. Edited by Thomas Thomson. 8 vols., published by the Wodrow Society, Edinburgh, 1842–1849.

Killen, William Dool, *Ecclesiastical History of Ireland.* 2 vols., London, 1875.

Knox, John, *A History of the Reformation of Religion within the Realm of Scotland.* Forms vols. i. and ii. of his *Works* edited for the Wodrow Society by David Laing, Edinburgh, 1846.

McCrie, Thomas, Jr., *Annals of English Presbytery from the Earliest Period to the Present Time.* London, 1872.

Mitchell, Alexander F., *The Westminster Assembly: Its History and Standards.* London, 1883.

Reid, James Seaton, *A History of the Presbyterian Church in Ireland, comprising the History of the Province of Ulster from the Accession of James the First. With a Preliminary Sketch of the Reformed Religion in Ireland during the Sixteenth Century, and an Appendix, consisting of Original Papers.* 3 vols., Belfast, 1833–1853; new (third) edition, with additional Notes by William Dool Killen, 3 vols., Belfast, 1867.

Wodrow, Robert, *The History of the Sufferings of the Church of Scotland from the Restoration to the Revolution.* Edited by Dr. Robert Burns. 4 vols., Glasgow, Blackie & Son, 1841.

III. AMERICAN PRESBYTERIANISM IN GENERAL.

Beecher, Willis J. and Mary A., *An Index of Presbyterian Ministers, 1706–1881.* Philadelphia, 1883.

Blake, T. C., *Old Log House : History and Defense of the Cumberland Presbyterian Church.* Nashville, 1878.

Crisman, E. B., *Origin and Doctrines of the Cumberland Presbyterian Church.* Nashville and St. Louis, 1880.

Gillett, Ezra Hall, *History of the Presbyterian Church in the United States of America.* 2 vols., Philadelphia, Presbyterian Publication Committee, 1864; revised edition, Philadelphia, Presbyterian Board of Publication, 1873.

Glasgow, W. Melanchthon, *History of the Reformed Presbyterian Church in America. With Sketches of all her Ministry, Congregations, Missions, Institutions, Publications, etc., and Embellished with over Fifty Portraits and Engravings.* Baltimore, 1888.

Harper, R. D., *The Church Memorial, containing Important Historical Facts and Reminiscences Connected with the Associate and Associate Reformed Churches.* Xenia, O., 1859.

Hays, George P., *Presbyterians : A Popular Narrative of their Origin, Progress, Doctrines, and Achievements.* With special chapters by Rev. W. J. Reid, D.D., and Rev. A. G. Wallace, D. D., of the United Presbyterian Church of North America; Rev. J. M. Howard, D.D., and Rev. J. M. Humbert, D.D., of the Cumberland Presbyterian Church; Rev. Moses D. Hoge, D.D., of the Presbyterian Church in the United States; and Rev. W. H. Roberts, D.D., LL.D., American Secretary, Presbyterian Alliance. Introduction by Rev. John Hall, D.D., LL.D., and Rev. William E. Moore, D.D., LL.D. New York, 1892.

Latham, Robert, *History of the Associate Reformed Synod of the South. To which is prefixed a History of the Associate Presbyterian and Reformed Presbyterian Churches.* Harrisburg, 1882.

Lindsley, J. B., *Sources and Sketches of Cumberland Presbyterian History.* In the "Theological Medium," Nashville, 1877–1878.

McDonnold, B. W., *History of the Cumberland Presbyterian Church.* Nashville, 1888.

McGill, Alexander T., and Others, *Centennial Historical Discourses. Delivered in the City of Philadelphia, June, 1876, by Appointment of the General Assembly of the Presbyterian Church in the United States. With the Moderator's Sermon.* Philadelphia, 1876.

Miller, James P., *Biographical Sketches and Sermons of Some of the First Ministers of the Associate Church in America. To which is prefixed an Historical Introduction, containing an Account of the Rise and Progress of the Associate Church for the First Half-century of her Existence in this Country.* Albany, 1829.

Nevin, Alfred, *Encyclopedia of the Presbyterian Church in the United States of America, including the Northern and Southern Assemblies.* Philadelphia, 1884.

Rockwell, Joel Edson, *Sketches of the Presbyterian Church.* Philadelphia, 1854.

Scouller, James Brown, *Manual of the United Presbyterian Church of North America.* Pittsburg, 1888. (See also vol. xi. of this series, and Dr. Scouller's valuable historical articles in the " United Presbyterian " of Pittsburg.)

Sprague, William Buell, *Annals of the American Pulp*°*t ; or, Commemorative Notices of Distinguished American Clergymen of Various Denominations, from the Early Settlement of the Country to the Close of the Year 1855.* Vols. iii. and iv., *The Presbyterian Pulpit.* Vol. ix., *The Associate, Associate Reformed, and Reformed Presbyterian Pulpit.* New York, Carters, 1859 and 1869.

IV. THE COLONIAL PERIOD.

A Brief Account of the late Rev. Caleb Smith, Minister of the Gospel at Newark Mountains, . . . Chiefly Extracted from his Diary and Other Private Papers. Woodbridge, N. J., 1763.

A Narrative of a New and Unusual American Imprisonment of Two Presbyterian Ministers, and Prosecution of Mr. Francis Makemie ; one of them for Preaching One Sermon at the City of New York. By a Learner of Law and a Lover of Liberty. Boston, 1707 and 1755 ; Washington, 1845.

Alexander, Archibald, *Biographical Sketches of the Founder and the Principal Alumni of the Log College, together with an Account of the Revivals of Religion under their Ministry.* Princeton, 1845.

Baird, Charles W., *The Civil Status of Presbyterians in the Province of New York.* In the " Magazine of American History," New York, 1879.

Balch, Thomas, *Calvinism and American Independence.* n. d.

Barnes, Albert, *Essay on the Life and Times of President Davies.* Prefixed to the fourth edition of his *Sermons,* New York, 1851.

Beatty, Charles, *Journal of a Two Months' Tour with a View of Promoting Religion among the Frontier Inhabitants of Pennsylvania, and of Introducing Christianity among the Indians to the Westward of the Alegh-geny Mountains.* Philadelphia, 1768 ; London, 1768 ; Edinburgh, 1798.

Blair, Samuel, *A Short and Faithful Narrative of the late Remarkable Revival of Religion in the Congregation of New-Londonderry, and Other Parts of Pennsylvania.* Philadelphia, Bradford, 1744.

———, *A Vindication of the Brethren who were Unjustly and Illegally Cast Out of the Synod of Philadelphia, from Maintaining Principles of Anarchy in the Church.* Philadelphia, Franklin, 1744.

Bowen, L. P., *The Days of Makemie; or, The Vine Planted: A.D. 1680–1708.* With an Appendix. Philadelphia, Presbyterian Board, 1885.

Brainerd, Thomas, *The Life of John Brainerd, the Brother of David Brainerd, and his Successor as Missionary to the Indians of New Jersey.* Philadelphia, 1865.

Breed, William P., *An Historical Discourse on Presbyterians and the Revolution.* Philadelphia, 1876.

Briggs, Charles Augustus, *American Presbyterianism: Its Origin and Early History. Together with an Appendix of Letters and Documents, many of which have Recently been Discovered.* With Maps. New York, 1885.

Buell, Samuel, *A Copy of a Letter to the Rev. Mr. Barber, in Groton, Conn. :
A Faithful Narrative of the Remarkable Revival of Religion in the Congregation of Easthampton, on Long Island, in the Year of our Lord
1764; with Some Reflections.* London, 1764. (A new edition, to which
is added *Sketches of the Border's Life, also Revivals in Bridgehampton
and Easthampton in 1800.* Sag Harbor, 1808.)

Carruthers, E. W., *A Sketch of the Life and Character of David Cald-
well, D.D., near Sixty Years Pastor of the Churches of Buffalo and
Almance* [N. C.]. *Including Some Account of the Regulation, together
with the Revolutionary Transactions in which he was Concerned; and a
Very Brief Notice of the Ecclesiastical and Moral Condition of North
Carolina while in its Colonial State.* Greensborough, N. C., 1842.

Clyde, John C., *Life and Labors of John Rosbrugh, the Clerical Martyr
of the Revolution.* Easton, Pa., 1880.

Craighead, J. G., *Scotch and Scotch-Irish in American Soil.* Philadelphia,
1878.

Davies, Samuel, *Letters Showing the State of Religion in Virginia, Particularly among the Negroes.* Boston, 1751–1757; London, 1757 and 1761.
——, *The State of Religion among the Protestant Dissenters in Virginia;
in a Letter to Joseph Bellamy.* Boston, 1751.

Dickie, J. F., *John Witherspoon, Patriot, 1722–1794.* Detroit, n. d.

Dickinson, Jonathan, *A Display of God's Special Grace, in . . . the Con
viction and Conversion of Sinners, so Remarkably of late Begun, and Going
on in these American Parts.* Boston, 1742; 2d ed., Philadelphia, 1743.

Edwards, Jonathan, *Memoirs of the Rev. David Brainerd, Missionary to
the Indians on the Borders of New York, New Jersey, and Pennsylvania;
Chiefly Taken from his own Diary.* Boston, 1747. (New edition, by
Sereno Edwards Dwight, *including his Journal, now for the First Time
Incorporated with the Rest of his Diary in a Regular Chronological
Order.* New Haven, 1822.)

Engles, William M., *Records of the Presbyterian Church in the United
States of America, containing the Minutes of the Presbytery of Philadelphia from A.D. 1706 to 1716; Minutes of the Synod of Philadelphia
from A.D. 1717 to 1758; Minutes of the Synod of New York from A.D.
1745 to 1758; Minutes of the Synod of New York and Philadelphia
from A.D. 1758 to 1788.* Philadelphia, Presbyterian Board of Publication, 1841.

Finley, Samuel, *Letter to a Friend concerning Mr. Whitfield, Messrs. Tennents, and their Opposers.* Philadelphia, Franklin, 1740.

Gillespie, George, *A Letter to the Reverend Brethren of the Presbytery of
New York, or of Elizabethtown, in which is Shown the Unjustness of the
Synod's Protest, entered last May at Philadelphia, against Some of the
Reverend Brethren; as also Some of the Causes of the Great Decay of
Vital Religion and Practical Holiness in our Presbyterial Church. With
Proofs of God's Remarkable Appearance for the Good of Many Souls.*
Philadelphia, Franklin, 1740.

Headley, J. T., *The Chaplains and Clergy of the American Revolution.*
New York, 1864.

Hill, William, *A History of the Rise, Progress, and Character of American
Presbyterianism. Together with a Review of "The Constitutional History
of the Presbyterian Church in the United States of America," by Charles
Hodge, D.D.* Washington, 1839.

Hodge, Charles, *The Constitutional History of the Presbyterian Church in the United States of America. Parts i. and ii., 1705–1788.* Philadelphia, 1839–1840.

Life of the Rev. William Tennent [Jr.]. *With an Account of his being Three Days in a Trance.* New York, 1847 and 1858.

Patillo, Henry, *Sermons, etc.: I. On the Divisions among Christians; II. On the Necessity of Regeneration to Future Happiness; III. The Scripture Doctrine of Election; IV. Extract of a Letter from Mr. Whitfield to Mr. Wesley; V. An Address to the Deists.* Wilmington, N. C., 1788.

Prince, Thomas, Jr., *The Christian History, containing Accounts of the Revival and Propagation of Religion in Great Britain and America in 1743 and 1744.* 2 vols., Boston, 1744–1745. (Contains contributions from Gilbert Tennent and others of the New Brunswick party.)

Rice, John H., *A Memoir of President Davies.* In his " Literary and Evangelical Magazine " (Vol. II., Richmond, Va., 1819).

Smith, Samuel Stanhope, *Life of John Witherspoon, D.D. With the Sermon Preached at his Funeral by John Rodgers, D.D.* Prefixed to his *Works,* 4 vols., New York, 1800–1807.

Smucker, J. A., *The Great Awakening.* In the *Proceedings of the American Antiquarian Society,* Worcester, Mass., 1874.

Spence, Irving, *Letters on the Early History of the Presbyterian Church in America. With a Sketch of the Life of the Author.* Philadelphia, 1838.

Spencer, Elihu, *The State of the Dissenting Interest in the Middle Colonies of America.* 1759. Reprinted in the *Collections of the Massachusetts Historical Society,* second series, vol. i.

Tennent, Gilbert, *The Danger of an Unconverted Ministry Considered in a Sermon on Mark vi. 34, Preached at Nottingham, Pa.* Philadelphia, Franklin, 1740. (German translation, Germantown, Saur, 1740.)

The Case of the Scotch Presbyterians of the City of New York. New York, 1773.

Thornton, J. W., *The Pulpit of the American Revolution; or, The Political Sermons of the Period. With an Historical Introduction, Notes, and Illustrations.* Boston, 1860; 2d ed., 1876.

Tracy, Joseph, *The Great Awakening: A History of the Revival of Religion in the Time of Edwards and Whitfield.* Boston, 1842.

Webster, Richard, *A History of the Presbyterian Church in America, from its Origin until the Year 1760. With Biographical Sketches of its Early Ministers. With a Memoir of its Author by the Rev. C. van Rensselaer, D.D., and an Historical Introduction by the Rev. William Blackwood, D.D.* Philadelphia, Joseph M. Wilson, 1858.

Whitefield, George, *A Continuation of the Rev. Mr. Whitefield's Journal from a Few Days after his Arrival at Georgia to his Second Return Thither from Pennsylvania.* Philadelphia, Franklin, 1740.

V. From Independence to Division.

A Brief Account of the Associated Presbyteries. With a General View of their Sentiments concerning Religion and Ecclesiastical Order. New York, 1796.

Adair, Robert, *Memoir of Rev. James Patterson, late Pastor of the First Presbyterian Church, Northern Liberties, Philadelphia. With an Introduction and Chapter on Field Preaching by Rev. D. L. Carroll, D.D.* Philadelphia, Perkins, 1840.

Alexander, James W., *The Life of Archibald Alexander, D.D., First Professor in the Theological Seminary at Princeton, N. J.* New York, Scribners, 1854.

Anderson, T. C., *Life of Rev. George Donnell, First Pastor of the Cumberland Presbyterian Church in Lebanon. With a Sketch of the Scotch-Irish Race.* Nashville, Tenn., 1859.

Baird, Robert, *Memoir of the Rev. Joseph Sanford, Pastor of the Second Presbyterian Church, Philadelphia.* Philadelphia, Perkins, 1836.

Beard, Richard, *Brief Biographical Sketches of Some of the Early Ministers of the Cumberland Presbyterian Church.* Nashville, 1867.

Beasley, Fr., *A Brief Memoir of the Life and Writings of Dr. Samuel Stanhope Smith, President of Princeton College.* Prefixed to his *Sermons.* Philadelphia, 1821.

Birch, Thomas Ledlie, *Seemingly Experimental Religion, Instructors Unexperienced, Converters Unconverted, Revivals Killing Religion, Missionaries in Need of Teaching; or, War against the Gospel by its Friends. Being the Examination and Rejection of Thomas Ledlie Birch, a Foreign Ordained Minister, by the Rev. Presbytery of Ohio, under the Very Rev. General Assembly's Alien Act.* Washington, Pa., 1806.

Brown, Isaac V., *Biography of the Rev. Robert Finley, D.D., Author of the American Colonization Society.* Philadelphia, 1857.

Brown, Matthew, *A Memoir of the Rev. Obadiah Jennings, D.D., of Nashville, Tenn.* Pittsburg, 1832.

———, *A Memoir of the Rev. John Macmillan, D.D.*

Cossitt, F. R., *The Life and Times of Rev. Finis Ewing, one of the Fathers and Founders of the Cumberland Presbyterian Church. To which are added Remarks on Dr. Davidson's History; or, A Review of his Chapter on the Revival of 1800, and his History of the Cumberland Presbyterians.* Louisville, 1853.

Dana, Daniel, *A Discourse Preached on the Fiftieth Anniversary of the Author's Ordination.* Newburyport, 1845.

Elliott, David, *Biographical Sketch of the Rev. Samuel Porter.* Prefixed to his *Discourses and Dialogues.* Pittsburg, 1853.

———, *The Life of the Rev. Elisha Macurdy. With an Appendix containing Brief Notices of Various Deceased Ministers of the Presbyterian Church in Western Pennsylvania.* Alleghany, 1848.

Ely, Ezra Stiles, *A Contrast between Calvinism and Hopkinsianism.* New York, 1811.

———, *History of the Ecclesiastical Proceedings Relative to the Third Presbyterian Church in Philadelphia, the Rev. E. S. Ely, and the Judicatories of the Church with which they are Connected.* Philadelphia, 1814.

Green, Ashbel, *Historical Sketch of Domestic and Foreign Missions of the Presbyterian Church of the United States.* Philadelphia, 1838. (*A new edition, with Supplementary Notes* by John C. Lowrie, D.D. 1855 and 1868.)

———, *Memoirs of the Rev. Joseph Eastburn, Stated Preacher in the Mariners' Church, Philadelphia.* Philadelphia, 1828.

Gridley, Samuel H., *A Sketch of the Life of Professor James Richards, D.D.,* *of Auburn Theological Seminary.* Prefixed to his *Lectures on Mental Philosophy and Theology.* New York, 1846.

Griffin, Edward Dorr, *A Sermon Preached at the Funeral of the Rev. Alexander McWhorter, D.D., of Newark, N. J.* New York, 1807.

Gurley, R. R., *Life and Eloquence of Sylvester Larned.* New York, 1844.

Hall, James, *A Narrative of a Most Extraordinary Work of Religion in North Carolina.* Philadelphia, 1802.

———, *Report of a Missionary Tour through Mississippi and the Southwestern Country in 1801.*

Humphrey, Edward P., and Cleland, Thomas H., *Memoirs of the Rev. Thomas Cleland, D.D., Compiled from his Private Papers.* Cincinnati, 1859.

Jones, Joseph H., *The Life of Ashbel Green, V.D.M., Begun to be Written by Himself in his Eighty-second Year, and Continued to his Eighty-fourth.* New York, 1849.

Kirk, Edward N., *Memorial of the Rev. John Chester, D.D.* Albany, 1829.

Kollock, S. K., *Biography of the Rev. Henry Kollock, of Savannah.* Prefixed to his *Sermons.* Savannah, 1822.

Lacy, Drury, *An Account of the Great Revival in Kentucky.*

Lundie, Mrs. M. G., *Memoirs of the Life and Character of the Rev. Matthias Bruen, late Pastor of the Presbyterian Church in Bleecker Street, New York.* New York, 1831.

McNemar, Richard, *The Kentucky Revival; or, A Short History of the late Extraordinary Outpouring of the Spirit of God in the Western States.* Pittsfield, 1808.

Mason, John M., *A Plea for Sacramental Communion upon Catholic Principles.* New York, 1816.

Maxwell, William, *A Memoir of the Rev. John H. Rice, D.D., First Professor of Christian Theology in Union Theological Seminary, Virginia.* Philadelphia, J. Whetham, 1835.

Miller, Samuel, *Memoir of the Rev. Charles Nisbet, D.D., late President of Dickinson College.* Philadelphia, 1840.

———, *Memoirs of the Rev. John Rogers, D.D., late Pastor of the Wall Street and Brick Churches, New York.* New York, 1813; abridged edition, Philadelphia, Presbyterian Board, 1840.

———, *The Life of Samuel Miller, D.D., Second Professor in the Theological Seminary of the Presbyterian Church at Princeton, N. J.* 2 vols., Philadelphia, Claxton, Remsen & Haffelfinger, 1869.

Patterson, Robert, *Biography of the Rev. John Ewing, D.D., First Provost of the University of Pennsylvania.* Prefixed to his *Lectures.* Philadelphia, 1809.

Paxton, W. M., *A Memorial of Francis Herron, D.D.* Pittsburg, 1860.

Plumer, William S., *Memoir of Rev. William Nevins.* Prefixed to his *Select Remains.* New York, 1836.

Rice, J. H., *Memoir of the Rev. J. B. Taylor.* New York, 1830.

Speer, William, *The Great Revival of 1800.* Philadelphia, Presbyterian Board, 1872.

Sprague, William B., *Life of Daniel Dana, D.D.* Boston, 1866.

Spring, Gardiner, *Memoirs of the Rev. Samuel J. Mills, late Missionary to the South Western Section of the United States.* New York, 1820.

Van Vechten, Jacob, *Memoirs of John M. Mason, D.D., S.T.P. With Portions of his Correspondence.* New York, 1856.

Whelpley, S., *The Triangle : A Series of Numbers upon Three Theological Points Enforced from Various Pulpits in the City of New York.* By Investigator. New York, 1816 and 1831.

Wilson, James P., *Life of the Rev. John Ewing, D.D.* Prefixed to his *Sermons.* Easton, 1812.

Wood, James, *Memoirs of the late Sylvester Scovel, D.D., President of Hanover College, Indiana.* New Albany, 1851.

Wylie, Samuel Brown, *Memoir of Alexander McLeod, D.D., New York.* New York, 1855.

VI. THE ERA OF DIVISIONS.

A Report of the Debates in the Presbytery of Philadelphia at a Special Meeting held in the City of Philadelphia on the 30th of November, and Continued on the 1st and 2d of December, 1830. Philadelphia, 1830.

Baird, Samuel J., *A History of the New School, and of the Questions Involved in the Disruption of the Presbyterian Church in 1838.* Philadelphia, Claxton, Remsen & Haffelfinger, 1868.

Barnes, Albert, *The Way of Salvation : A Sermon Delivered at Morristown, N. J., February 8, 1829. Together with Mr. Barnes's Defense of the Sermon, Read before the Synod of Philadelphia, at Lancaster, October 29, 1830, and his "Defense" before the Second Presbytery of Philadelphia, in Reply to the Charges of the Rev. Dr. George Junkin.* New York, Leavitt, Lord & Co., 1836.

Beecher, Charles, *Autobiography, Correspondence, etc., of Lyman Beecher, D.D.* With Illustrations. 2 vols., New York, 1866.

Beecher, Edward, *Narrative of the Riots at Alton, in Connection with the Death of Rev. Elijah P. Lovejoy.* Alton, 1838.

Beecher, Lyman, *Views in Theology.* Published by Request of the Synod of Cincinnati. Cincinnati, 1836.

Brown, Isaac V., *A Historical Vindication of the Abrogation of the Plan of Union by the Presbyterian Church in the United States of America.* Philadelphia, 1854.

Cheeseman, Lewis, *Differences between Old and New School Presbyterians.* Rochester, N. Y., 1848.

Crocker, Zebulon, *The Catastrophe of the Presbyterian Church in 1837, including a Full History of the Recent Theological Controversies in New England.* New Haven, Noyes, 1838.

Duffield, George, *Spiritual Life ; or, Regeneration Illustrated in a Series of Disquisitions Relative to its Author, Subject, Nature, Means.* Carlisle, Pa., 1832.

———, *The Principles of Presbyterian Discipline Unfolded and Illustrated in the Protests and Appeals of Rev. George Duffield, Entered during the Process in the Presbytery of Carlisle.* Carlisle, 1835.

History of the Division of the Presbyterian Church in the United States of America. By a Committee of the Synod of New York and New Jersey. New York, 1852.

Junkin, George, *The Vindication, containing a History of the Trial of the Rev. Albert Barnes by the Second Presbytery and by the Synod of Philadelphia. To which are appended New-Schoolism in the Seventeenth Compared with New-Schoolism in the Nineteenth Century.* Philadelphia, Martien, 1836.

Lovejoy, Joseph C. and Owen, *Memoir of the Rev. Elijah P. Lovejoy, who was Murdered in Defense of the Liberty of the Press, at Alton, Ill., Nov. 7, 1837. With an Introduction by John Quincy Adams.* New York, 1838.

McCalla, W. L., *A Correct Narrative of the Trial of the Rev. Albert Barnes.* Philadelphia, 1835.

Miller, Samuel, *Letters to Presbyterians on the Present Crisis in the Presbyterian Church in the United States.* Philadelphia, 1833.

Miller, Samuel, Jr., *Report of the Presbyterian Church Case: The Commonwealth of Pennsylvania, at the Suggestion of James Todd and Others, vs. Ashbel Green and Others.* Philadelphia, Martien, 1839.

Phillips, W. W., and Others, *An Address to the Ministers, Elders, and Members of the Presbyterian Church in the United States.* New York, 1836.

The Trial and Acquittal of Lyman Beecher, D.D., before the Presbytery of Cincinnati, on the Charge of Heresy. Cincinnati and New York, 1835.

Trial of the Rev. Albert Barnes before the Synod of Philadelphia, in Session at York, October, 1835, on a Charge of Heresy Preferred against him by the Rev. George Junkin. With all the Pleadings and Debate. As reported for the New York " Observer" by Arthur J. Stansbury. New York, Van Nostrand & Dwight, 1836.

Van Rensselaer, Cortlandt, *Historical Contributions relating to the Founders, Principles, and Acts of the Presbyterian Church. With Special Reference to the Division of 1837–1838.* In his *Essays and Discourses, Practical and Historical,* pp. 205–410. Philadelphia, Presbyterian Board of Publication, 1861.

Wilson, J. L., *The Plea in the Case of Lyman Beecher, D.D., before the Synod of Cincinnati.* Cincinnati, 1837.

Wood, James, *Facts and Observations concerning the Organization of Churches in the Three Synods of Western New York and the Western Reserve.* Saratoga, 1837.

———, *Old and New Theology.* Philadelphia, 1845. Second edition, 1853.

VII. From Division to the War.

A Memoir of J. D. Paxton, D.D., late of Princeton, Ind. Philadelphia, 1870.

Adger, James B., *The Collected Writings of the Rev. James Henley Thornwell, D.D.* 4 vols., Richmond, 1871–1873.

Alexander, Henry Carrington, *The Life of James Addison Alexander, D.D., Professor in the Theological Seminary at Princeton, N. J.* 2 vols., New York, Scribners, 1870.

Alexander, James W., *Forty Years' Familiar Letters, constituting, with the Notes, a Memoir of his Life.* Edited by the Surviving Correspondent, John Hall, D.D. (of Trenton). 2 vols., New York, Charles Scribner, 1860.

Armstrong, George Dodd, *The Christian Doctrine of Slavery.* New York, 1858.

Baird, Henry M., *The Life of the Rev. Robert Baird, D.D.* New York, Randolph, 1866.

Baker, William M., *The Life and Labors of the Rev. Daniel Baker, Pastor and Evangelist.* Philadelphia, Martien, 1859.

Barnes, Albert, *The Church and Slavery.* Philadelphia, 1857.

———, *Life at Threescore.* Philadelphia, 1858.

———, *Life at Threescore and Ten.* Philadelphia, 1868.

Baxter, George Addison, *An Essay on Slavery.* Richmond, 1836.

Birney, W., *James G. Birney and his Times.* New York, 1890.

Brainerd, Mrs. M., *Life of Rev. Thomas Brainerd, D.D., for Thirty Years Pastor of Old Pine Street Church, Philadelphia.* Philadelphia, Lippincott, 1870.

Dabney, R. L., *Memoir of the Rev. F. S. Sampson, D.D., Professor in Union Theological Seminary.* Richmond, 1854.

Halsey, Leroy J., *A Sketch of the Life and Educational Labors of Philip Lindsley, D.D.* Hartford, 1859. Also prefixed to his *Works,* 3 vols., Philadelphia, 1866.

———, *Memoirs of the Life and Character of Rev. Lewis Warner Green, D.D. With a Selection from his Sermons.* New York, Scribners, 1871.

Hatfield, Edwin F., *Patient Continuance in Well-doing: A Memoir of Elihu Baldwin, D.D., First Pastor of the Seventh Presbyterian Church, New York, and First President of Wabash College.* With an Introduction by Samuel Hanson Cox, D.D. New York, Leavitt, 1843.

Hodge, Archibald Alexander, *The Life of Charles Hodge, D.D., LL.D., Professor in the Theological Seminary, Princeton, N. J.* New York, Scribners, 1880.

Hodge, Charles, and Others, *Memorial of Cortlandt Van Rensselaer.* Philadelphia, 1860.

Janeway, T. L., *Memoir of the Rev. Jacob J. Janeway, D.D.* Philadelphia, 1860.

McCullagh, Joseph H., *The Sunday-school Man of the South: Memoirs of the Rev. John McCullagh.* Philadelphia, 1889.

Palmer, Benjamin M., *Life and Letters of Rev. James Henley Thornwell, D.D.* Richmond, 1875.

Prime, Samuel Irenæus, *Autobiography and Memorials.* Edited by his Son, Wendell Prime. New York, Randolph, 1888.

———, *Memoirs of the Rev. Nicholas Murray, D.D.* ["Kirwan"]. New York, Harpers, 1863.

Rankin, John (of Strait Creek, Ohio), *Letters on American Slavery Addressed to Thomas Rankin at Middlebrook, Va.* Newburyport, 1836.

Robinson, John, *The Testimony and Practice of the Presbyterian Church in Reference to American Slavery. With an Appendix containing the Position of all the Other Churches in Relation to the Same Subject.* Cincinnati, 1852.

Schenck, W. E., *A Discourse on the Death of Benjamin Holt Rice.* Philadelphia, 1856.

Sherwood, J. M., *Sketch of the Life of Ichabod S. Spencer, D.D.* Prefixed to his *Sermons.* 2 vols., New York, 1855.

Smith, Mrs. E. L., *Henry Boynton Smith: His Life and Work.* Edited by his Wife. New York, A. C. Armstrong & Son, 1881.

Smith, Henry B., *Memoir of Anson G. Phelps.* New York, 1858.

Smith, Henry B., and Hitchcock, Roswell D., *Life, Writings, and Character of Edward Robinson.* New York, 1863.

Sprague, William B., *Memoirs of the Rev. John McDowell, D.D., and the Rev. William A. McDowell, D.D.* New York, Robert Carter, 1864.

Spring, Gardiner, *Personal Reminiscences of the Life and Times of.* 2 vols.,
	New York, Charles Scribner, 1866.
Stearns, L. F., *Life of Henry B. Smith.* Boston and New York, 1892.
The Life and Writings of Rev. Joseph Gordon. Written and Compiled by a
	Member of the Free Presbyterian Synod. Cincinnati, 1870.
(Torrey, David), *Memorial Sketch of Zephaniah Moore Humphrey.* Phila-
	delphia, 1883.
Wisner, William, *Incidents in the Life of a Pastor.* New York, 1857.
Wood, Charles, *A Memorial of Dr. John C. Lord.* Buffalo, 1877.
Wood, Jeremiah, *The Model Pastor: The Life and Character of the Rev.
	Elisha Yale, D.D., late of Kingsboro* [N. Y.], *Drawn Chiefly from his
	own Diary and Correspondence. Together with the Discourse Preached
	at his Funeral.* Albany, Munsell, 1854.

VIII. DURING AND SINCE THE WAR.

*Addresses Delivered at the Centennial Celebration of the General Assembly of
	the Presbyterian Church, Philadelphia, May 24, 1888.* Philadelphia, 1888.
Boardman, Henry A., *The General Assembly of 1866.* Philadelphia, 1867.
Briggs, Charles Augustus, *Whither? A Theological Question for the
	Times.* New York, 1889.
Carter, R., *Robert Carter: His Life and Work.* New York, 1891.
Craven, E. R., *Speech on the Revision of the Confession of Faith.* Phila-
	delphia, 1890.
Dabney, R. L., *The Life and Campaigns of Lieutenant-General Thomas J.
	Jackson.* New York, 1866.
Dodge, D. Stuart, *Memorial of William E. Dodge.* New York, Ran-
	dolph, 1887.
Eaton, S. J. M., *Memoir of the Rev. Cyrus Dickson, D.D., late Secretary
	of the Board of Home Missions.* New York, 1882.
Edgar, G. P., *Dr. Talmage Vindicated by Presbytery and Synod.* New
	York, 1880.
Grasty, John S., *Memoir of Rev. Samuel B. McPheeters, D.D.* With an In-
	troduction by Rev. Stuart Robinson, D.D. St. Louis, Southwestern
	Book & Publishing Company, 1871.
Hodge, A. A., and DeWitt, John, *Funeral Address and Commemorative
	Discourse* [on] *Henry A. Boardman, D.D.* Philadelphia, 1881.
Hodge, Charles, *Reunion of the Old and New School Presbyterian Churches.*
	New York, 1867.
How Shall We Revise? A Bundle of Papers. By Drs. Briggs, Evans,
	White, Vincent, Parkhurst, Hamilton, and Thompson. New York, 1890.
Hutchinson, J. R., *Reminiscences, Sketches, and Addresses from my Papers,
	during a Ministry of Forty-five Years in Mississippi, Louisiana, and
	Texas.* Houston, 1874.
Jackson, Sheldon, *Alaska and Missions on the North Pacific Coast.* New
	York, n. d.
McCosh, James, *Whither? Oh, Whither?* New York, 1889.
Martyn, Carlos, *William E. Dodge.* New York, 1890.
(Prentiss, G. L.), *Life and Letters of Elizabeth Prentiss.* New York, Ran-
	dolph, 1882.
Presbyterian Reunion: A Memorial Volume, 1837–1871. New York, 1871.

Proceedings of Presbyterian Reunion at Pittsburg, November 12, 1869. Pittsburg, 1869.

Salmond, C. A., *Princetoniana: Charles and A. A. Hodge. With Class and Table Talk of Hodge the Younger.* By a Scottish Princetonian. New York, Scribner & Welford, 1888.

Sample, Robert F., *Memoir of the Rev. John C. Thom, Pastor of Pine Street Church.* St. Louis, 1865.

Schaff, Philip, *Creed Revision in the Presbyterian Churches.* New York, 1890.

———, *Berlin, 1842—New York, 1892: The Semi-Centennial of Philip Schaff.* With Portrait. New York (privately printed), 1892.

Shedd, W. G. T., *The Proposed Revision of the Westminster Standards.* New York, 1890.

Smith, Henry B., *Reunion of the Presbyterian Churches.* New York, 1867.

Steele, David, *Reminiscences, Historical and Biographical.* Philadelphia, 1885.

The Case against Professor Briggs. 2 parts, New York, Scribners, 1893.

The Life of George Hay Stuart, Written by Himself. Edited by Robert Ellis Thompson, D.D. Philadelphia, J. M. Stoddart & Co., 1890.

The Presbyterian Union Convention, held in Philadelphia, November 6, 1867: Minutes and Phonographic Report. Philadelphia, 1868.

The Trial of the Rev. David Swing before the Presbytery of Chicago. Edited by a Committee of the Presbytery. Chicago, 1874.

Van Dyke, Henry, *Historic Presbyterianism: Three Sermons for the Times.* New York, Randolph, 1893.

Williams, Albert, *A Pioneer Pastorate and Times, embodying Contemporary Local Transactions.* San Francisco, 1879.

Wilson, Joseph M., *The Presbyterian Historical Almanac, and Annual Remembrancer of the Church.* 10 vols., Philadelphia, 1859–1868.

Wilson, Samuel R., *Reply to the Attack of Rev. R. J. Breckinridge, D.D., LL.D., upon the Louisville Presbytery; and Defense of the "Declaration and Testimony" made in the Synod of Kentucky.* Louisville, 1865.

IX. LOCAL CHURCH HISTORY.

A History of the Independent or Circular Church, Charleston, S. C. Charleston, 1853.

Alexander, S. D., *Princeton College during the Eighteenth Century.* New York, 1872.

———, *The Presbytery of New York, 1738–1888.* New York, Randolph, 1888.

Backus, John C., *An Historical Discourse: On Taking Leave of the Old Church Edifice of the First Presbyterian Congregation in Baltimore.* Baltimore, 1860.

Baird, Charles W., *History of the Bedford Church* [N. Y.]. New York, 1882.

Barrows, John H., *Jubilee Services, June 24-27, 1883: An Account of the Celebration of the Fiftieth Anniversary of the Organization of the First Presbyterian Church of Chicago.* Chicago, 1883.

Bayless, John C., *Historical Sketch of the Presbyterian Church of Ashland, Ky., with Some Notice of the Educational Efforts in the Town.* Ashland, 1871.

Beadle, E. R., *The Old and the New, 1743–1876: The Second Presbyterian Church of Philadelphia; its Beginning and Increase.* Philadelphia, 1876.

Berry, T. C., *An Historical Survey of the First Presbyterian Church, Caldwell, N. J.* Newark, 1871.

Blaikie, Alexander, *A History of Presbyterianism in New England: Its Introduction, Growth, Decay, Revival, and Present Mission.* Boston, 1882.

Brick Church Memorial, containing the Discourses Delivered by Dr. Spring on the Closing of the Old Church in Beekman Street and the Opening of the New Church on Murray Hill; the Discourse Delivered on the Fiftieth Anniversary of his Installation as Pastor of the Brick Church. With the Proceedings of the Memorial Meeting, and the Discourse Preached on the Occasion of Mrs. Spring's Death. New York, 1861.

Brown, Allen H., *An Outline History of the Presbyterian Church in West or South Jersey from 1701 to 1865. With an Appendix from 1865 to 1869.* Philadelphia, Martien, 1869.

Catto, W. T., *A Semi-Centenary Discourse in the First African Presbyterian Church, Philadelphia. With a History of the Church from its First Organization, including a Brief Notice of Rev. John Gloucester, its First Pastor. Also an Appendix of Sketches of All the Colored Churches in the City.* Philadelphia, 1857.

Centenary Memorial of the Planting and Growth of Presbyterianism in Western Pennsylvania and Parts Adjacent, containing the Historical Discourses Delivered at a Convention of the Synods of Pittsburg, Erie, Cleveland, and Columbus, held at Pittsburg, December 7–9, 1875. With Appendices and Illustrations. Pittsburg, 1876.

Centennial Memorials of Presbyterianism in Western Pennsylvania. Harrisburg, 1869.

Chambers, George, *A Tribute to the Principles, Virtues, Habits, and Public Conduct of the Irish and Scotch Early Settlers of Pennsylvania.* Chambersburg, 1856.

Chase, F., *A History of Dartmouth College and the Town of Hanover.* Edited by T. K. Lord. Vol. i., Cambridge, 1891. (Tells what is known of the Presbytery of Grafton.)

Clyde, J. C., *History of the Allen Township Presbyterian Church, and of the Community which Sustained it, in what was Formerly Known as the Irish Settlement, Northampton County, Penna.* Philadelphia, 1876.

Coffin, Joshua, *History of Newbury, Newburyport, and West Newbury from 1685 to 1845.* Boston, 1845.

Creigh, Alfred, *Discourse at the Reunion of Presbyterians in the Cumberland Valley, 1874.*

———, *History of Washington County, Pennsylvania, from its First Settlement to the Present Time.* Pittsburg, 1870.

Cuyler, Theodore Ledyard, *Lafayette Avenue Church: Its History and Commemorative Services, 1860–1885.* New York, 1885.

Dales, J. B., *A Memorial Discourse: 1830–1880. By the Pastor of the Second United Presbyterian Church, Philadelphia.* Philadelphia, 1881.

Davidson, Robert, *History of the Presbyterian Church in the State of Kentucky. With a Preliminary Sketch of the Churches in the Valley of Virginia.* New York, 1847.

———, *Historical Sketch of the First Presbyterian Church of New Brunswick, N. J.* New Brunswick, 1852.

Dickey, John McElroy, *A History of the Presbyterian Church in the State of Indiana.* 1828.

Disosway, G. P., *Earliest Churches of New York and its Vicinity.* New York, 1865.

Donaldson, Alexander, *A History of the Churches in Blairsville Presbytery. Prepared at its Request and Read before it in Blairsville, January 28, 1874.* Pittsburg, 1874.

Duffield, George, *An Historical Discourse Delivered during the Centennial Celebration of the First Presbyterian Church of Carlisle, July 1, 1857.* Carlisle, 1857.

Duffield, J. T., *Discourse on the History of the Second Presbyterian Church of Princeton, N. J.* Princeton, 1876.

Eaton, S. J. M., *History of the Presbytery of Erie.* New York, 1868.

Edgar, George P., *History of the Second Presbyterian Church in Rahway, N. J.* Rahway, 1887.

Ewing, R. C., *Historical Memoirs: Brief History of the* [Cumberland Presbyterian] *Church in Missouri, and Sketches of Ministers Engaged in the Work.* Nashville.

Foote, William Henry, *Sketches of Virginia, Historical and Biographical.* Philadelphia, Martien, 1849. Second series, Philadelphia, Martien, 1855.

———, *Sketches of North Carolina, Historical and Biographical, Illustrative of the Principles of a Portion of her Early Settlers.* New York, Carters, 1846.

Fowler, Henry, *History of the Church of Christ in Auburn: A Discourse.* Auburn, N. Y., 1868.

Fowler, P. H., and Mears, John W., *Historical Sketch of Presbyterianism within the Bounds of the Synod of Central New York. Prepared and Published at the Request of the Synod.* Utica, 1877.

Futhey, J. Smith, *Historical Discourse Delivered on the Occasion of the One Hundredth Anniversary of the Upper Octorara Presbyterian Church, Chester County, Pa., September 14, 1870. With an Account of the Celebration and Appendix.* Philadelphia, 1870.

Gayley, Samuel A., *An Historical Sketch of the Lower West-Nottingham Presbyterian Church.* Philadelphia, Martien, 1865.

Green, Ashbel, *A History of the College of New Jersey.* Appended to his *Discourses Delivered in the College.* Philadelphia, 1822.

Greenleaf, Jona, *Sketches of the Ecclesiastical History of the State of Maine.* Portsmouth, 1821.

———, *A History of the Churches of All Denominations in the City of New York, from its First Settlement.* New York, 1846.

Hageman, J. F., *History of Princeton and its Institutions.* 2 vols., Philadelphia, 1879.

Hall, John, *History of the Presbyterian Church in Trenton, N. J., from the First Settlement of the Town.* New York, Randolph, 1859.

Halsey, Le Roy J., *A History of the McCormick Theological Seminary of the Presbyterian Church.* Chicago, 1893.

Hatfield, Edwin F., *The Early Annals of Union Theological Seminary.* New York, 1876.

———, *The History of Elizabeth, N. J., and Early History of Union County.* New York, 1868.

Hawley, Charles, *History of the First Presbyterian Church of Auburn, N. Y.* Auburn, 1876.

Hazen, H. A., *The Pastors of New Hampshire, Congregational and Presbyterian.* Bristol, N. H., 1878.

Hervey, H. M., *Historical Sketches of the Presbyterian Church in Licking County, Ohio.* Newark, O., 1869.

Hewat, Alexander, *Historical Account of the Rise and Progress of the Colonies of South Carolina and Georgia.* 2 vols., London, 1779.

Historical Sketch of the [New School] *Synod of Ohio from 1838 to 1868. Prepared and Published under Synodical Authority.* Cincinnati, 1870.

Hotchkin, James H., *A History of the Purchase and Settlement of Western New York, and the Rise, Progress, and Present State of the Presbyterian Church in that Section.* New York, 1848.

Howe, George, *Early History of Presbyterianism in South Carolina: A Sermon Preached at Charleston, November 15, 1854.* Columbia, 1855.

———, *Early Presbyterian Immigration into South Carolina: A Discourse Delivered before the General Assembly, May 17, 1858.* Columbia, 1858.

———, *The Scotch-Irish and their First Settlement on the Tyger River, S. C.: A Centennial Discourse.* Columbia, 1861.

———, *History of the Presbyterian Church in South Carolina.* Vol. i., Columbia, 1870.

Hoyt, J., *The Mountain Society: A History of the First Presbyterian Church of Orange, N. J., Organized about 1719.* New York, 1860.

Johnson, William M., *Presbyterianism in Cohoes, N. Y.* Cohoes, 1876.

Johnston, John, *Early Presbyterianism East of the Hudson.* n. d.

Junkin, D. X., *A Discourse Delivered on the Centenary of the First Presbyterian Church, Greenwich, N. J.* Easton, Pa., 1875.

Kennedy, William S., *The Plan of Union; or, A History of the Presbyterian and Congregational Churches of the Western Reserve* [Ohio]. *With Biographical Sketches of the Early Missionaries.* Hudson, O., 1856.

Lawrence, Robert F., *The New Hampshire Churches, comprising Histories of the Congregational and Presbyterian Churches in the State, with Notices of Other Denominations; also containing Many Interesting Incidents Connected with the First Settlement of Towns.* Claremont, 1856.

Lincoln, W., *The History of Worcester from its First Settlement to 1836. Continued from 1836 to 1861 by Charles Hessey.* Worcester, Mass., 1862.

McAllister, David, *The National Reform Movement: Its History and Principles.* Philadelphia, 1890.

McClune, James, *History of the Presbyterian Church in the Forks of Brandywine, Chester County, Pa. (Brandywine Manor Presbyterian Church), from 1735 to 1835.* Philadelphia, 1885.

McDermott, C., *History of the First Presbyterian Church of Dayton, O.* Dayton, 1880.

Macdonald, J. M., *Two Centuries in the History of the Presbyterian Church, Jamaica, L. I.* New York, 1863.

McIlwain, J. W., *Early Presbyterianism in Maryland.* Baltimore, 1890.

Mack, R. C., *"Old Nutfield": The Celebration of the One Hundred and Fiftieth Anniversary of the Settlement of Londonderry, Derry, Windham, etc.* Portraits. Concord, 1870.

MacLean, Rev. John, *History of the College of New Jersey, from its Origin in 1746 to the Commencement of 1854.* 2 vols., Philadelphia, 1877.

Maclise, D. M., *Historical Discourse at Montgomery, N. Y., on the Anniversary of the Goodwill Presbyterian Church.* New York, 1865.

McMaster, Samuel, *History of the Presbyterian Church of Rehoboth, Md.*

Mitchell, J. Y., *History and Directory of Temple Presbyterian Church.* Philadelphia, 1873.

Montfort, J. G., *Presbyterianism North of the Ohio: An Historical Discourse Delivered April 9, 1872, being the Fiftieth Anniversary of the Presbytery of Cincinnati. Containing a Statement of the Planting and Progress of the Presbyterian Church in Ohio . . . from 1790 to 1822.* Cincinnati, 1872.

Moore, William E., and Awl, William M., *History of the Presbytery of Columbus from 1823 to 1876.* Columbus, 1876.

Morris, E. D., *Five Years of Ministerial Life.* Columbus, 1851.

——, *God Merciful to His Church: An Historical Discourse.* Columbus, 1866.

Mott, George S., *History of the Presbyterian Church of Flemington, N. J.* Flemington, 1876.

Murphy, Thomas, *One Hundred Years of the Presbyterian Church of Frankford.* Philadelphia, 1872.

——, *The Presbytery of the Log College; or, The Cradle of the Presbyterian Church in America.* Philadelphia, Presbyterian Board, 1889.

Murray, Nicholas, *Notes, Historical and Biographical, concerning Elizabethtown, N. J.: Its Eminent Men, Churches, and Ministers.* Elizabethtown, 1844.

Nevin, Alfred, *Churches of the Valley ;. or, An Historical Sketch of the Old Presbyterian Congregations of Cumberland and Franklin Counties, in Pennsylvania.* Philadelphia, Joseph M. Wilson, 1852.

——, *History of the Presbytery of Philadelphia, and of the Philadelphia Central.* Philadelphia, Fortescue, 1888.

Niven, Archibald C., *Centennial Memorial: A Record of the Proceedings on the Occasion of the One Hundredth Anniversary of the Associate Reformed Presbyterian Church of Little Britain* [in Lancaster County, Pa.]. New York, 1857.

Norcross, George, *Centennial Memorial; or, History of the Presbytery of Carlisle.* 2 vols., Harrisburg, 1889.

Norton, A. T., *History of the Presbyterian Church in the State of Illinois.* Vol. i., St. Louis, 1879.

Ohio: Historical Addresses on the history of the Presbyterian churches in Ashtabula (by J. N. McGiffert); Blendon Township, Franklin County (by H. M. Robertson); Chillicothe (by Henry W. Biggs); Cincinnati 2d (by Nathaniel Wright); Clairsville (by Robert Alexander); Columbus 2d (by William E. Moore); Jersey (by D. R. Colmery); Loveland (by Henry A. Rossiter); Putnam (by Addison Kingsbury); Mansfield (by S. W. Miller); Mount Gilead (by D. B. Hervey and H. Shedd); Reading and Lockland (by W. A. Hutchinson); South Salem (by Robert K. Campbell); Springdale (by William H. Jones); Xenia (by T. M. Hopkins). Cincinnati, Columbus, etc., 1874–1877.

Parker, Edward L., *History of Londonderry, N. H.* Boston, 1851.

Patten, J. A., *Lives of the Clergy of New York and Brooklyn.* With Portraits. New York, 1874.

Patterson, R. M., and Davidson, R., *Historical Sketch of the Synod of Philadelphia. Biographical Sketches of Distinguished Ministers of the Synod.* Philadelphia, Presbyterian Board, 1876.

Patton, Jacob Harris, *The Triumph of the Presbytery of Hanover; or,*

The Separation of Church and State in Virginia. With a Concise History of the Presbyterian Church in the United States from 1705 to 1888. New York, Randolph, 1887.

Peet, Stephen, *History of the Presbyterian and Congregational Ministers and Churches in Wisconsin.* Milwaukee, 1851.

Petrie, George, *Church and State in Early Maryland.* Baltimore, 1892.

Prentiss, George L., *Union Theological Seminary in the City of New York: Historical and Biographical Sketches of its First Fifty Years.* New York, 1889.

Presbyterianism in Cincinnati: Its History, Position, and Duty. Cincinnati, 1871.

Prime, N. S., *Ecclesiastical History of Long Island, from its First Settlement to 1845. With Special Reference to its Ecclesiastical Concerns.* New York, 1845.

——, *History of the Secession from the Synod of New York and Philadelphia in 1780, which Assumed the Name of " The Associated Presbytery of Morris County."* (Manuscript: see Gillette, vol. i., pp. 207–214.)

Proud, Robert, *The History of Pennsylvania, in North America, from the Original Institution and Settlement of that Province, in 1681, till 1742.* 2 vols., Philadelphia, 1797–1798.

Record of the Twenty-fifth Anniversary of the South Park Presbyterian Church, Newark, N. J., Oct. 27, 1876. Illustrated. Newark, 1878.

Records of the Synod of Pittsburg, from its First Organization, September 29, 1802, to October, 1832, inclusive. Printed by the Approbation of Synod, at their Meeting in Alleghany City, 1850. Pittsburg, 1852.

Sample, Robert F., *Historical Sketch of the Presbyterian Church of Bedford,* [Penna.]. Philadelphia, Claxton, 1866.

Schenck, William Edw., *Historical Account of the First Presbyterian Church of Princeton, N. J.* Princeton, 1851.

Scott, John Welwood, *An Historical Sketch of the Pine Street or Third Presbyterian Church in the City of Philadelphia. With an Introduction by the Present Pastor.* Philadelphia, Lydia R. Bailey, 1837.

Scouller, J. B., *History of the Big Spring* [U. P.] *Presbytery.* Harrisburg, 1881.

——, *History of the* [U. P.] *Presbytery of Argyle* [N. Y.]. 1880.

——, *History of the United Presbyterian Church of Big Spring, Newville, Pa., 1764–1878.* Carlisle, Pa., 1878.

Scouller, J. B., and Harper, James, *History of the Associate Reformed Synod of New York, and of the United Presbyterian Synod.* Philadelphia, 1877.

Shedd, Henry, *Home Missionary Life: An Autobiographical Discourse.* Mount Gilead, O., 1872.

Shepherd, Thomas J., *The Days that are Past: A History of the First Presbyterian Church, Northern Liberties, Philadelphia.* Philadelphia, 1864; enlarged edition, Philadelphia, 1881.

Sloan, D. H., *A History of the Presbytery of Kittanning, . . . with its Churches and Schools.* Pittsburg, 1888.

Smith, E. V., *History of Newburyport, Mass., from its Earliest Settlement. With a Biographical Appendix.* Newburyport, 1854.

Smith, Joseph, *History of Jefferson College, Cannonsburg, Penna., including an Account of the Early Log-cabin Schools and the Cannonsburg*

Academy. With Biographical Sketches of Matthew Brown, Samuel Ralston, Matthew Henderson, and Others. Pittsburg, 1857.

———, *Old Redstone ; or, Historical Sketches of Western Presbyterianism, its Early Ministers, Perilous Times, and its First Records.* Philadelphia, 1854.

Smith, William, *History of the late Province of New York, from its Discovery to the Appointment of Governor Colden in 1762.* 2 vols., New York, 1829.

Sprague, William B., *A Discourse to the Alumni of the Princeton Theological Seminary on the Occasion of the Completion of its First Half-century. With an Appendix.* Albany, 1862.

Stearns, Jonathan F., *The First Church in Newark: Historical Discourses relating to the First Presbyterian Church in Newark.* Illustrated. Newark, 1853.

The Mountain Whites of the South. By a Scotch-Irishman. Pittsburg, 1893.

The Wylie Memorial Presbyterian Church : Commemorative Services on the Fiftieth Anniversary of the Ordination and Installation of Rev. T. W. J. Wylie, D.D. Philadelphia, 1893.

Turner, D. K., *History of Neshaminy Presbyterian Church of Warwick, Hartsville, Bucks County, Pa., 1726–1876.* Philadelphia, 1876.

Tuttle, Samuel L., *A History of the Presbyterian Church in Madison, N. J.* New York, 1855.

Vass, L. C., *History of the Presbyterian Church of New Berne, N. C. With a Résumé of Early Ecclesiastical Affairs in Eastern North Carolina, and a Sketch of Early Days of New Berne, N. C.* Richmond, 1886.

Watson, Samuel L., *History of Bethel (S. C.) Presbyterian Church.* In the Yorkville, S. C. "Enquirer," November, 1855.

Weeks, S. B., *The Religious Development in the Province of North Carolina.* Baltimore, 1888.

White, Erskine N., *History of the West Twenty-third Street Presbyterian Church, New York.* New York, 1876.

Willey, S. H., *Discourse at the Closing Exercises of the Howard Presbyterian Church, January 6, 1867.* San Francisco, 1867.

Williams, J. L., *Historical Sketch of the First Presbyterian Church of Fort Wayne, Indiana.* Fort Wayne, n. d.

Williams, Samuel Porter, *Historical Account of the First Presbyterian Church and Society in Newburyport.* Newburyport, 1826.

Willis, William, *Genealogy of the McKinstry Family. With a Preliminary Essay on the Scotch-Irish Immigration into America.* Boston, 1856.

———, *The Scotch-Irish Immigration into Maine, and Presbyterianism in New England.* In the *Collections of the Massachusetts Historical Society,* vol. vi.

Wing, Conway P., *A History of the First Presbyterian Church of Carlisle, Pa.* Carlisle, 1877.

———, *History of the Presbyteries of Donegal and Carlisle.* Carlisle, 1876.

X. Presbyterian Polity and Law.

Alexander, W. A., *A Digest of the Acts of the General Assembly of the Presbyterian Church in the United States, from its Organization to the Assembly of 1887, inclusive. With certain Historical and Explanatory Notes.* Richmond, Presbyterian Committee of Publication, 1888.

Baird, Samuel J., *A Collection of the Acts, Deliverances, and Testimonies of the Supreme Judicatory of the Presbyterian Church, from its Origin in America to the Present Time.* Philadelphia, Presbyterian Board, 1855.

Hodge, Charles, *Discussions in Church Polity. From the Contributions to the "Princeton Review." Selected and Arranged by Rev. W. Durant. With Preface by A. A. Hodge, D.D.* New York, 1878.

Hodge, J. Aspinwall, *What is Presbyterian Law as Defined by the Church Courts?* Philadelphia, Presbyterian Board, 1882 ; 3d ed., with *Decisions of Assemblies,* Philadelphia, 1884.

Macleod, Alexander, *An Ecclesiastical Catechism.* New York, 1807. Frequently reprinted in America and Scotland.

Miller, Samuel, *An Essay on the Warrant, Nature, and Duties of the Office of the Ruling Elder in the Presbyterian Church.* New York and Boston, 1831 ; Glasgow, 1835 ; Philadelphia, Presbyterian Board, 1840.

Moore, William E., *New Digest of the Acts and Deliverances of the Presbyterian Church.* Philadelphia, Presbyterian Publication Committee, 1861.

———, *The Presbyterian Digest : A Compend of the Acts and Deliverances of the General Assembly of the Presbyterian Church in the United States of America. Compiled by the Order and Authority of the General Assembly.* Philadelphia, Presbyterian Board, 1873.

Smyth, Thomas, *Ecclesiastical Catechism of the Presbyterian Church.* Boston, 1841.

———, *Ecclesiastical Republicanism.* Boston, 1843.

———, *The Name, Nature, and Functions of the Ruling Elder.* New York, 1845.

Steuart, Walter, of Pardovan, *Collections and Observations, Methodized, concerning the Worship, Discipline, and Government of the Church of Scotland. In Four Books.* Edinburgh, 1709. Frequently reprinted.

United Presbyterian Digest of the General Assembly, 1859–1878. Pittsburg, 1879.

XI. Subsidiary Literature.

Baird, Robert, *Religion in America ; or, An Account of Origin, Relation to the State, and Present Conditions of the Evangelical Churches in the United States. With Notices of the Evangelical Denominations.* New York, 1844 ; 2d ed., 1856.

Beecher, Thomas K., *Our Seven Churches.* New York, 1870.

Dorchester, Daniel, *Christianity in the United States, from the First Settlement down to the Present Time.* New York, 1888.

Hurst, John F., *Short History of the Church in the United States.* New York, 1890.

Reed, Andrew, and Matheson, James, *Narrative of the Visit to the American Churches by the Deputation of the Congregational Union of England and Wales.* New York, 1835.

Rupp, Israel Daniel, *He Pasa Ecclesia : An Original History of the Religious Denominations at Present Existing in the United States, containing Authentic Accounts of their Rise, Progress, Statistics, and Doctrines.* Written expressly for the Work by eminent Theological Professors, Ministers, and Lay Members of the Respective Denominations. Philadelphia, 1844.

Winebrenner, John, a second enlarged edition of the same work, with a somewhat different title-page. Harrisburg, 1848.

Schaff, Philip, *America: A Sketch of the Political, Social, and Religious Character of the United States of North America, in Two Lectures Delivered at Berlin. With a Report Read before the German Church Diet at Frankfort-on-the-Main, September, 1854.* Translated from the German. New York, 1855.

———, *Church and State in the United States; or, The American Idea of Religious Liberty and its Practical Effects. With Official Documents. (Papers of the American Historical Association,* vol. ii., No. 4.) New York, Putnams, 1883.

Shiells, Robert, *The Story of the Token as Belonging to the Sacrament of the Lord's Supper.* New York, 1891.

Thompson, Joseph P., *Church and State in the United States.* Boston, 1873.

Zahn, Adolph, *Abriss einer Geschichte der Evangelischen Kirche in Amerika im Neunzehnten Jahrhundert.* Stuttgart, 1889.

THE PRESBYTERIAN CHURCH IN AMERICA.

CHAPTER I.

INTRODUCTION: THE HISTORIC ANTECEDENTS IN THE OLD WORLD.

THE group of ecclesiastical bodies which constitute the Presbyterian family in America hold a place of great importance in the religious life of the nation. American Presbyterianism has been of weight beyond its numerical strength through the services it has rendered to theological science, the interest it has maintained in Christian doctrine, the high standard of intelligence it has set up for both its ministry and its people, its capacity to develop strength of character, its superior family discipline, and its conservative influence upon the national life. In the sphere of church organization it was the pioneer in the creation of that synodical type of government which now constitutes the actual polity of nearly all our churches, even of those which hold to the theory of congregational independency on the one side, or of diocesan episcopacy on the other.

Presbyterianism claims to be substantially the method of church organization indicated in the New Testament. It holds middle ground between systems which eliminate the Christian people from any direct share in the control

of church affairs, and those which offer little or no safeguard against popular prejudice or passion. It knows of
no higher work, and it recognizes no higher calling, than
that of the pastor of the Christian congregation, in whom
it sees the bishop of the first churches. Yet it also recognizes a church whose extent transcends the Christian
congregation, and takes shape in provincial, national, and
ecumenical synods, councils, or assemblies, vested with
authority to speak for the larger unities they represent.

The claims which have been put forward, that this order
of church government was perpetuated from the days of
the Apostles in the Scotch Culdees or the Italian and
French Waldenses, will not stand the test of historical
criticism. The Culdees represented the strange tribal
organization of the Scottish (i.e., Irish) Church founded
by Patrick—an organization as alien to modern Presbyterianism as it was to medieval Romanism. The Waldenses
grew out of a comparatively recent protest against the
scholastic development of the Church of Rome, and received from the Swiss Reformers far more than they had
to impart. Those Reformers, equally with Luther and
Cranmer, were obliged, in effecting the emancipation of
the Protestant nations from the usurped authority of the
Bishop of Rome, to make radical changes in the system
they found in existence. All three types of Protestantism,
however, started from elements of doctrine, worship, and
organization they found already at hand, and which they
found in harmony with their reading of the New Testament. To these they gave a new weight, setting them in
a new perspective, but claiming to be reformers, and not
revolutionists, as were the Anabaptists. The reformers
of the churches called Reformed on the Continent, and
Presbyterian in the British Islands, did the work more
thoroughly and with less regard to historic tradition than

either of the others. They took as the official unit the pastorate exercised by the parish priest of the Latin Church, whom they accepted as bishop in the apostolic sense, and as amply empowered to transmit his own office by ordination.

It was in Geneva, in the days of Calvin's influence, that the Presbyterian polity was set up; but it was in northern Holland, under the guidance of John à Lasco, that it was developed beyond what was needed in a city church and adapted to the use of a nation. It became the church government of the French Huguenots, of the Protestants of Switzerland and the Palatinate, of the Reformed of Hesse, Brandenburg, and other parts of Germany, and of the national churches of Holland and Scotland. By the earlier Puritans in the Church of England it was regarded as the ideal order for a church. Dr. Thomas Cartwright of Cambridge University defended it as such in 1583–84, and in 1588 it was set up in secret in several English localities, but suppressed by Archbishop Whitgift in 1591.

In Scotland the polity established by John Knox in 1560, and developed by Andrew Melville in 1578, was hated by the Stuart dynasty because of its claim to independence of state control. James VI. found the complaisant episcopacy of his English kingdom so much more to his mind that in 1610–12 he forced that polity upon his Scottish subjects, and in 1617–21 introduced a number of Anglican usages, which were repugnant to Scottish feeling. The attempt of his son, in 1637, to supersede John Knox's liturgy by a service book like that of the Church of England came close upon the publication of a Book of Canons, which had established the ecclesiastical supremacy of the king and his bishops, and set aside the synodical government of the church. The two measures precipitated the revolt against the Stuart tyranny, which spread throughout the two kingdoms, and awakened hopes of a uniformity in doctrine, worship, and government in the national churches of both. The Westminster Assembly of Divines, which was in no sense a church synod, planned a polity such as "the example of the best Reformed Churches" suggested. But the revolt against the prelatic tyranny of Laud and his associates had produced a restlessness under all authority, resulting in a demand for the democratic independency of the churches. This in turn produced a counter-reaction to prelacy as an escape from anarchy, with the return of the Stuarts. In a few localities the polity outlined by the Westminster divines had been set up, but it disappeared entirely with the Restoration, although one section of the English dissenters retained the name Presbyterians, while in fact they were Independents.

In Scotland the Stuarts again set up prelacy, but without attempting to force a liturgy upon the people. Their tyranny and intolerance made the rule of their bishops loathsome to the nation, to whom it was equally unnational and unscriptural. The revolution of 1688–90 gave them the opportunity to return to a polity which persecution had made doubly dear to them. A small body of the most pronounced Presbyterians, especially in the western parts of the Lowlands—the Cameronians or Hill men—refused to accept this Revolution Settlement as adequate. As dissenting from both church and state, they organized themselves into lay societies for mutual edification, until in 1706 the accession of Rev. John Macmillan furnished them with ministry and ordinances. For a long time they erected no houses of worship, as claiming the parish churches as theirs by rights; and even after the discomforts of hill-side services drove them under roof, they continued to observe the semi-annual communions in the open air. A second secession from the Kirk took place in 1737, and a third in 1752, consequent partly upon the introduction of patronage into the church in 1712, in violation both of the Revolution Settlement of 1688, and of the Treaty of Union with England of 1707 ; and partly upon the growing indifference to doctrinal beliefs under the influence of the eighteenth-century culture. The three constitute the Reformed Presbyterian (or Covenanter), the Associate (or Seceder), and the Relief Churches. The two former play their part in American church history.

But it was not directly from either Scotland or England that the Presbyterian Church of America received its principal inflow of members, or took its character mainly. The forfeiture of the estates of the Earls of Tyrone and of Tyrconnell in the Irish province of Ulster in 1607 placed at the disposal of the crown a large area of land in the north of Ireland, which was planted in 1610 and the years following with English but especially with Scotch settlers, the "undertakers," to whom grants were made, being forbidden to rent or sell lands to the native Irish. Through this and subsequent confiscations and plantations of that century, Ulster became a Scottish colony in the main, four fifths of its Protestant people being attached to the Presbyterian polity, and many of them refugees from Scotland during "the killing time" which followed the Stuart Restoration. Yet the prelatic system was established throughout all Ireland, Presbyterians and Catholics being forced to pay for the support of the English Church system, and being subjected to the jurisdiction of the bishops' courts in all matters relating to wills, marriages, and divorces. And while the Presbyterian colonists never were subjected to the atrocity of the penal laws against the Catholic natives, and, after the Revolution, were permitted the exercise of their worship and of their church government, they were still excluded from office, including Parliament, required to have their marriages solemnized by

Anglican ministers, and otherwise ill-treated and insulted. This, along with the breaches of contract on the part of the Irish landlords, drove them to America in such numbers as both depleted the Ulster colony and greatly strengthened those of America. To this Scotch-Irish immigration was due the firm establishment and rapid growth of the Presbyterian Church in the colonial period of American history.

From this rapid historical sketch I pass to some of the distinctive features of the Reformed Church. Its polity was by no means its most noteworthy characteristic. Taking an impress from the strong, logical intellect of John Calvin, it always has put theological doctrine into its foreground. It has laid a stress upon doctrinal soundness as an element of wholesome church life, which differentiates it from both Lutheran and Anglican Protestantism. Its weaker side, in this respect, has been an over-confidence in the adequacy of human logic to bring the truth of the Scriptures into a systematic form, and to present it in a coherent sequence which the Bible does not seek to furnish. This tendency naturally reached its culmination in the seventeenth century, the scholastic middle age of Protestant history. From the meeting of the Synod of Dort in 1618 till the drafting of the Helvetic Consensus in 1675, the Reformed Church of Europe passed through a development of theological definition, whose confessions of theology, through their increasing stringency, stand in sharp contrast to the freer, more popular, and more devout confessions of faith of the century of the Reformation. The Confession and Catechisms drafted by the Westminster Assembly, and accepted afterward as the standards of Presbyterian orthodoxy in Scotland, Ireland, and America, surpassed in systematic elaborateness and logical precision nearly every other Protestant symbol. Their sub-

stitution by the Scotch Assembly of 1648 for John Knox's
spirited Scottish Confession of 1562 was in the vain hope
of attaining ecclesiastical uniformity with England. It
had the effect of carrying the requirement of theological
agreement to niceties not before prescribed.

When the teaching of the Reformed Church, in the
age before the Synod of Dort, was called Calvinism, the
reference was not to its view of predestination, but to its
teaching as to the sacraments. In that era there was a
substantial agreement among the Protestant churches in
accepting the Augustinian view that man's will is in bondage through sin, and must be set free by divine grace.
This is asserted against the more than half Pelagianism of
the Church of Rome, by Luther in his controversy with
Erasmus (1524–26), and by the Lutheran divines who compiled the "Formula of Concord" (1579), no less than by
Calvin or by Knox. Indeed, Knox probably would have
shrunk from the extreme statements of the Lambeth
Articles, drafted in 1579 by Archbishop Whitgift and four
other Anglican divines, formally approved by Archbishop
Hutton of York, and incorporated by Archbishop Ussher
into the Articles of the Established Church of Ireland.
It is therefore a mistake to give Calvin's name to teach-
ing he shared with Augustine and Aquinas, Luther and
Andreä, Cranmer and Whitgift; and the mistake has been
possible only because the Reformed Church adhered to the
Augustinian teaching, while the Lutheran and Anglican
Churches, in spite of their own formulas, have approximated to that of the Church of Rome.

With the exception of the school of Zwingli, which soon
ceased to exert an appreciable influence, the Reformed
theologians held to the objective reality of sacramental
grace, but expressed this in terms which placed the assertion of it on Protestant ground. They recognized a gift of

regenerating grace in baptism, bestowed even upon the unconscious child, while they maintained that his membership in the church was his birthright as a child of Christian parentage. Following the Old Testament analogy, they taught that the children of Christians are " born within the covenant," and are baptized because this natural descent is accompanied by spiritual privilege. And when such children had come to years of discretion, and had been taught catechetically the " saving knowledge " of the gospel, if their lives were free from reproach, the Reformed Church acknowledged their right to the sacrament of the Lord's Supper. In this also it saw no " bare and empty sign," but an appointed channel of grace, through the presence in it of the divine-human person of our Lord to the faith of those who worthily participate. This presence, however, is in the ordinance, and not " in, with, or under " the elements—a gift of grace received by faith, not by the mouth, and by the believing communicant alone. It is this which is Calvinism, in the historic sense of the term.

In its forms of worship the Reformed Church was liturgic, yet with a striving after simplicity and an indifference to the older liturgic traditions, which distinguishes it from both the Lutheran and the Anglican. In Hesse it approached its sister-churches most nearly in these things, while in other parts of Germany, in Switzerland, France, Holland, Scotland, and Ulster, the divergence was wide. As we have seen, it was the attempt to force elaborate Anglican forms on the Scottish Kirk which proved " the last straw " in the burden the Stuarts were laying upon Scotland. By a natural tendency this Reformed love of simplicity, by force of opposition, became a Puritan indifference to form; and the Westminster Assembly found no difficulty in setting aside all prescribed forms, including John Knox's " Book of Common Order," and substituting the general directions of the Directory for Worship, with merely exemplary forms, which fell into desuetude.

In contrast to this informality of the church's prayers was the strictness of prescription in the matter of praise. The Psalms in metrical versions were the handbook of every national church of the Reformed faith, from Warsaw to Rochelle, and from Geneva to Edinburgh, and through Puritan influence they attained the same use in the Anglican Church, while the Lutherans were the hymn-writers and hymn-singers of earlier Protestantism. As the Reformed psalters supplemented the Psalms with metrical versions of other passages of Scripture, and even with metrical doxologies and a few hymns, it cannot be said that the exclusive use of the Book of Psalms was a principle they accepted.

The most characteristic element in the life of the Reformed Church, and that by which it influenced European history the most profoundly, was neither its polity, nor its type of doctrine, nor its forms of worship, but its ethical and social discipline. Under John Calvin's rule Geneva became one of the world's wonders—a city in which all that Savonarola had dreamed and hoped for Florence was actually realized. In Geneva Christian living was the first concern of laws and of magistracy. Offenses against the moral law of God were treated as crimes, and the Christian conception of duty was assumed as part of the public policy. The impression of Calvin's influence on the city was lasting as well as deep. Even Lutherans, like John Valentine Andreä (1614) and Philip Jakob Spener (1660), came back from a visit to Geneva with a lofty envy of the orderliness, the moral correctness, the show of reverence for sacred things, and the deference to authority, which still characterized the city by Lake Leman.

We now see the imperfection of Calvin's method, and therefore of his achievement. We draw the line of discrimination between sins and crimes, as that age did not. We see in the Genevan administration an extension of legal methods into a province where they have no fitness, and which must provoke a reaction. Our Reformed fathers made nothing of such distinctions. They accepted, with hearty enthusiasm, the Genevan ideal of a community binding upon itself the law of God, entering into covenant with him for the consecration of public and social life to his glory, and aiming at the immediate realization of his kingdom through the repression of all base and unchristian habits and instincts by the whole weight of collective authority. It was this that fired the imaginations and strengthened the wills of the great reformers and statesmen of the Reformed faith: of William the Silent and Admiral Coligny, of Latimer and Knox, of Marnix de Aldegonde and Agrippa d'Aubigne. It was this purpose to establish the direct rule of God upon earth—a theocracy in the true sense—that found expression in the poetry of Edmund Spenser and John Milton, and that sent the Pilgrims and the Puritans across the ocean to seek a freer field for its realization. It was this that plunged Presbyterian Scotland and Puritan England into the struggle with the Stuarts, against whose low and demoralizing influence Milton directed the scorn of his " Comus." This theocratic ideal played a primary part in the public life of Europe in the great struggle with the Counter-Reformation.

In Scotland the Genevan ideal was embraced with a fervor that might have been expected from the mixture of Celtic and Scandinavian in the nation's make-up. In Wordsworth's phrase,

> The Scottish Church . . . had held
> The strong hand of her purity

upon a nation in whom willfulness and lawlessness had been fostered by centuries, and whose worst vices had had the sanction of the example of the ecclesiastics highest in place. Through defeat and through victory, through periods of popular support and times of royal or aristocratic antagonism, the Knoxes, the Melvilles, the Bruces, the Hendersons, the Guthries, and the Rutherfords of the Kirk labored to make their Scotland a holy nation, a people in covenant with their God. The continuous pressure of session and presbytery, synod and assembly, was exerted for the extirpation of vice, and the elevation of social life to the level of their own spiritual vision. At times, indeed, this was employed against usages we have learned to regard as innocent; at others it was intruded into a political sphere in which it had no proper exercise. On the whole, however, the Kirk's claim " to treat in an ecclesiastical way of greatest and smallest matters, from the king's throne, that should be established in righteousness, to the merchant's balance, that should be used in faithfulness," was not only recognized in fact, but was directed to the best interests of the nation. It was this discipline which created those cottage homes, which Burns has immortalized in his most gracious verse, and of which Wordsworth writes:

> A virtuous household, though exceeding poor!
> Pure livers were they all, austere and grave,
> And fearing God: the very children taught
> Stern self-respect, a reverence for God's Word,
> And an habitual piety, maintained
> With strictness scarely known on English ground.

It is noteworthy that in later times if the people complained of the Kirk, or withdrew from her communion, it always was because she fell short of the theocratic vigor and rigor they had learned to demand of her. In their hearts the nation knew that it was just their faithfulness to the ideal of Knox and of Henderson which made them a great people—a people capable of binding on itself the yoke of service and of self-denial, and of foregoing the satisfactions and enjoyments of the present for some greater good.

In the Reformed, as distinguished from the Anabaptist and Independent conception, the proper subjects of such a discipline are a whole nation embracing the faith and order of the gospel by their collective act. Accepting "the judgment of charity," they took for granted the Christian standing and character of all who had been born and brought up in such a nation, and taught the truths and subjected to the discipline of the gospel, and kept by God's grace from profaning the Christian name by any scandal. Such they accepted as entitled to the ordinances of the church, for both themselves and their children. In practice, however, they treated this as merely the minimum of a Christian profession, and urged upon all to "go on to perfection."

The daughter-church in Ulster preserved in great measure the theological and theocratic character of the Scottish Kirk. Its social position, however, was very different, and its environment reacted upon its character. Its Presbyterianism was not the creed and order of a whole people. It must recognize as in its membership only those who gave it their voluntary adherence, in the face of legal proscriptions and of the attractions of the Anglican establishment, and even of Irish Romanism. This made it less theocratic in itself, and caused a less theocratic tone in the preponderant influence Ulster exercised upon the Presbyterianism of America.

CHAPTER II.

THE DAY OF SMALL THINGS, 1629–1713.

IN view of the extensive acceptance of the Presbyterian theory of church order in the British Islands, it is surprising that so long a period elapsed before it took root in any of the British colonies in America. Up to the time of Cromwell's accession to power, and even after that event, the central and probably the largest body of the English Puritans were Presbyterians, with moderate Episcopalians like Ussher and Reynolds forming the right wing, while Independents and Baptists were the left. While the Pilgrim Fathers, who settled the Plymouth colony, were Independents on principle, the Puritans of the Massachusetts Bay colony were largely Presbyterians in theory before their emigration. But the suppression of the attempts to set up the Genevan order in England in 1591 through the hostility of Archbishop Whitgift, and its partial suspension in Scotland by the Compromise of 1586, and by the Articles of Perth in 1618, had prevented any practical application of Presbyterian principles within Great Britain. It was merely a theory, and in the case of the English Puritans it was subject to the influence of that general tendency to pure individualism which dominated the whole Puritan movement. From Anglican to Presbyterian, from that to Independent, and from that to Baptist, ending often in Seekerism or Quakerism, is the gamut through which the active spirits of the time easily ran.

In laying the foundations of church order in the absence of precedence and traditions, and not uninfluenced by the proximity of the pronounced Independents of Plymouth, the Puritans of New England drifted into arrangements which were midway between Presbyterianism and Independency, with a strong leaning toward the latter. Not that there was no resistance to this. "The New England way," as it was called, excited some sharp criticism among the Puritan divines in England, and in 1637–39 there was a prolonged correspondence between them and their brethren on the subject, not entirely to their satisfaction. But the two tendencies struggled for the mastery for nearly seventy years, the Presbyterian finding able supporters in John Eliot ("The Divine Ordinance of Councils," 1665) and the Mathers. Dr. H. M. Dexter felicitously describes "the New England way" as "a Congregationalized Presbyterianism" which "had its roots in one system and its branches in another," and says that the Massachusetts churches differed locally "from the almost Presbyterianism of Hingham and Newbury[port]" to the pronounced Independency of Plymouth. But he is not so happy in his statement that the system was "essentially Genevan within the local congregation, and essentially other outside it." The absence of regularly constituted sessions for the administration of church discipline, and the refusal of baptism to the children of baptized persons who were not communicants, marked the local congregation as un-Presbyterian. The latter rule was a rejection of the "judgment of charity" accepted by all the Reformed churches. It was one of the moot-points between the two parties in the Westminster Assembly, and in 1662 the severer rule had to be relaxed even in New England by the Half-Way Covenant. On the other hand, the high authority claimed and exercised by synods called by the civil magistrate, of which six met during the seventeenth century, shows that, even outside the local congregation, "the New England way" was not so entirely other than Genevan. We hear of no more such synods when the Congregational principle had attained supremacy in Massachusetts, and the church order had taken the shape indicated in the writings of Rev. John Wise ("The Churches' Quarrell Espoused," 1710), who completed what John Cotton and his associates had begun.

In the sister-colony of Connecticut the movement was in the opposite direction. The Saybrook Platform (1708) gave jurisdiction over the local churches to the consociations consisting of the ministers and the "messengers of the churches" in an assigned district. Under its operation the churches of Connecticut grew more conscious of their relation to the Presbyterianism of the Middle States than to the Congregationalism of Massachusetts, and they freely used the name Presbyterian as the briefest description of their ecclesiastical position.

On the other hand, we shall see that the Congregationalism of Massachusetts and the States north of it proved itself strong enough to absorb and assimilate an Ulster immigration, which came with the purpose of establishing the Scottish order on New England soil.

From 1640 onward we find a certain amount of migration from New England into the Dutch settlements on Long Island and the mainland. Mostly this was Congregationalist, but two of the ministers who made this transfer—Francis Doughty to Long Island in 1642, and thence to New Amsterdam the next year, and Richard Denton to Long Island in 1643—were distinctly Presbyterians. They both had trouble with their Congregationalist neighbors as to the extent of the Abrahamic covenant in the matter of baptizing the children of those who were not communicants. Both were welcome to the Dutch, who adhered stoutly and somewhat intolerantly to their Reformed faith and order. And in New York the atmosphere tended to make the transformation of Puritan into Presbyterian an easy one, as the subsequent history will show.

The Scotch never have been a colonizing people, the settlement of the Irish province of Ulster in the reign of James I. being their only national achievement of that kind. Up to their ill-fated experiment at Darien (1698) they made no large effort at establishing a colony in the New World. In South Carolina, Maryland, and East Jersey were small bodies of Scotch immigrants who sought a home in America during the religious troubles of the period between the Restoration and the Revolution, the first having been deported after the defeat at Bothwell Brig (1684) by way of punishment. Both their deportation and the Darien failure did so far contribute to the Presbyterian element in the colonies, that in South Carolina Presbyterian churches grew up, and a Presbytery was organized in 1722–23, but partly of New England Puritans.

The Scotch-Irish colony in Ulster far exceeded the mother-country in colonizing energy. Large sections of that province had been granted by James I. to royal favorites in Scotland, who held out great inducements to their countrymen to become their tenants in Ireland. Unfortunately, these pledges had not the force of a law, and were generally broken. Besides this, as the century advanced, and the prelatizing policy of the Stuarts became pronounced, the religious difficulty became more acute. As early as 1636 a ship-load of the Scotch of Ulster set sail for New England, having been invited by the authorities of that province to settle on the Merrimac River. The ministers on board were Robert Blair and John Livingston, who both were to play a prominent part in the impending troubles in Scotland. The ship was driven back by contrary winds, and the undertaking abandoned.

After the Restoration the Irish Presbyterians felt the weight of prelatic intolerance only less than did their Scotch brethren. Even Jeremy Taylor, now an Ulster bishop, retracted the bold arguments of his " Liberty of Prophesying " (1647), and both defended and practiced the persecution of the Scotch colonists for nonconformity to the established church. So before a decade elapsed emigration set in from Ulster to America, seeking the Barbadoes, Maryland, and Virginia as their new homes. To Maryland, indeed, Francis Doughty had come from New Amsterdam as early as 1659, his brother-in-law Captain William Stone having been made governor of the colony by the Calverts, as a safeguard against interference on the part of the Commonwealth government at home. We hear of Doughty as preaching on both sides of the Potomac, but there is no record of his death, or of any permanent result of his labors. To Maryland also Fifeshire colonists had been brought by Captain Vivian Beale to escape the persecution in Scotland.

With the first immigration of the Scotch-Irish it may be said that Presbyterianism had come to stay. Prelatic intolerance in Ireland had had the natural effect of intensifying their attachment to their own church and its order. The tenacity of will for which they always have been famous came into play in planting the Presbyterian order and doctrine in a new environment. As but one minister, probably Richard Salwey by name, shared in the earlier migration, they were indebted to the ministrations of an English Presbyterian, Matthew Hill, who had been induced by Richard Baxter to make his home in Maryland. In 1669 he writes to Baxter: " We have many of the Reformed religion, who have a long while lived as sheep without a shepherd, though last year brought in a young man from Ireland, who hath already had good success in his work. We have room for more ministers." In 1680 the Scotch-Irish in the colony applied to the Irish Presbytery of Laggan for another minister. The arrest and deportation of the members of that Presbytery for keeping a public fast prevented a response in the ordinary fashion, but probably was the means of sending to Maryland its former moderator, William Traill, in 1682, and Francis Makemie in 1683.

It is to Francis Makemie rather than to Matthew Hill or William Traill that the American Presbyterian Church has been accustomed to look back as to her founder. The others preceded him and were men of ability. But William Traill returned to Scotland at the Revolution, and Makemie was the more energetic nature. His ordination seems to have been among the last acts of the Presbytery of Laggan before its dispersion by official violence. In America at first he went to and fro as an evangelist, ranging from South Carolina to New York, combining commerce with preaching, and making Rehoboth, on the eastern shore of Maryland, the center of his labors at least as early as 1691. He came forward as the literary champion of his church when it was attacked by either Quakers or prelatists. In New York, on the ground preëmpted by Doughty and Denton, he suffered arrest and imprisonment in 1706 for the offense of preaching without a license, as the Episcopal Church had been established in that colony by a legislative trick in 1693, and Governor Cornbury, the Queen's cousin, was ruling the people after the Stuart fashion in the matter of suppressing dissent. Makemie's vigorous defense and acquittal in the next year fixed attention on Cornbury's conduct, and thus contributed to his recall in 1709.

Altogether, Francis Makemie, although not a man of the first order, and unable to stand comparison with many of the later leaders of the church he " founded," was a person of such vitality and energy, such excellent judgment and genuine piety, as made him greatly useful in his day, and entitles him to the gratitude of all who believe that Presbyterianism has been of eminent service in the religious life of the nation.

Up to this time, while there had been separate congregations of Presbyterian structure, no Presbytery had ever met to exercise control over their governing sessions. Some kind of informal conference or council must have been held in 1701, when Jedediah Andrews was ordained to the pastorate in Philadelphia. " The Presbyterians," writes Rev. John Talbot, missionary of the S. P. G., " have come a great way to lay hands on each other." In 1705, presumably in the same young and growing city, a regular Presbytery met, and chose Francis Makemie to the moderatorship. Five other ministers were enrolled as members. Philadelphia was the most northern point represented, until the ordination of John Boyd as pastor at Freehold, in the year following. The other churches lay in Delaware and Maryland, Snow Hill in the latter State being probably the oldest in date of organization.

From 1705 until 1716 inclusive, the Presbytery of Philadelphia was the only judicature of the church, and in the twelve years it had increased from five to seventeen ministers, chiefly by arrivals from New England and the British Islands. From Philadelphia northward to Long Island, the pastors were generally from Old or New England; in Maryland, either Scotch or Irish; while Delaware was the meeting-ground of the two elements.

As the church of the new immigration it had great difficulties to encounter. The people were extremely poor,

and sparsely settled; and in their disheartening battle
for the conquest of nature, they tended to sink into mere
animalism through the neglect of spiritual interests.   The
supply of ministers was far below the need, and there was
a temptation to accept as such men poorly fitted in point
of learning or of character.   But the Presbytery exacted
adequate credentials and assurance of orthodoxy and good
character from all applicants.   When a young Welshman
in 1710 undertook to preach to the people of the Welsh
Tract without a license, he was rebuked, and required to
place himself under competent direction that he might be
educated for the sacred office; and it was not until 1715
that he was ordained.   The number of cases of discipline
for moral offenses was excessive among both ministers and
people; and to these were added disputes and uncertainties
as to the degrees within which marriage was forbidden, as
might be expected in small and isolated settlements, where
the range of choice was very limited.

The forms of Presbyterian government used in Scotland
and Ireland were followed as far as possible.   There was
some difficulty in bringing the Welsh and English Congregationalists, who had united with Presbytery, to see
the expediency of the authority exercised over the several congregations.   They generally acquiesced, however,
in accepting the Presbyterian Church as the representative
of the Puritan principle in the Middle States.   The fervor
of the earlier strife over the two methods of church government had died out on both sides, probably through
exhaustion.   They were united against prelacy, tolerant
of each other.

Nothing, indeed, could be more friendly than the relations of the Presbytery to the New England churches.   It
was in correspondence with the union of the Presbyterians
and Congregationalists of London, asking for additional

ministers. It had a friend and adviser in the indefatigable Cotton Mather, who worked for its growth and prosperity, as he was working vainly for the establishment of a somewhat similar plan of government in Massachusetts. In the ministers and churches of Connecticut, newly reorganized on the Saybrook Platform, it had helpful and sympathetic neighbors. Indeed, there was no sharp line of sectarian severance between the two bodies until the present century.

CHAPTER III.

GROWTH AND DISSENSION, 1713–41.

OF the Scotch colony planted in Ulster in the seventeenth century there are probably three descendants in America for one left at home. Disappointed in the expectations raised by the offers of the new landlords at the time of the plantation, and oppressed by the established Episcopal Church, they turned their eyes to America as a possible home. Of their first immigration, that to Maryland in the seventeenth century, I have spoken already. The second began in 1713, and continued until the eve of the War for Independence. It entered the colonies on three lines. The first followed the course originally proposed by Robert Blair and John Livingston in 1636, and sought New England. It was spread over a large part of Maine and several districts of New Hampshire; and it also found a home in the larger towns of Massachusetts, especially Boston, Worcester, and Pelham. Those who see nothing in the New England history but the doings of Puritans and Pilgrims ignore a large indebtedness to this strenuous and vertebrate stock, from which sprang her Websters, Greeleys, Greys, Starks, Andersons, and others who hold no mean place in her annals.

At first the new immigrants were anything but welcome. They were "a parcel of Irish," and that of itself carried with it an idea of wildness. Their intense Presbyterianism was supposed to imperil the "standing order" of the New England churches. In 1718–19 we find the selectmen of Boston taking measures to clear the town of these "passengers lately arrived from Ireland," and warning them to depart. It was not until 1730 that they were able to gather a church, under the pastorate of John Moorehead. When those who had settled in Worcester, in 1718, took measures to build themselves a church, the people "gathered by night, hewed down and demolished the structure," and "persons of consideration and respectability aided in the riotous work," we are told in W. Lincoln's "History of Worcester" (1837). This intolerance caused the greater part to migrate to New York about 1740; and in other instances the churches were weakened by removals for a like reason. They were compelled to pay taxes for the support of the Congregationalist churches, while they also maintained their own.

Their position was much more favorable where, as in Londonderry and other newly established towns of New Hampshire or Maine, they themselves constituted the town, and levied the tax for the support of their own minister. Their first Presbytery was constituted before 1729, and was called the Presbytery of Londonderry, or, by their neighbors, "the Irish Presbytery." It had some sixteen ministerial members during this period, with a still larger number of feeble churches looking to it for supplies.

The great body of the immigrants from Ulster sought the middle colonies, especially Pennsylvania, attracted by the reports of the toleration practiced in that colony and of its great natural wealth. The historian Proud estimates that six thousand had arrived by 1726. The failure of the grain crops of Ulster in that and the following years increased the volume of immigration, so that Proud estimates it at twelve thousand a year until 1750. While mixed a good deal with the people of the older settlements, these newcomers naturally took the western frontier, which exposed them to the brunt of Indian warfare, and led them to an estimate of the red man very different from that accepted by the Friends. On their obtaining control of the provincial legislature, therefore, they reversed Penn's policy of peaceful conciliation, and sought precedents for a new Indian policy in the Book of Joshua. It was this exposure to the French, and the Indians influenced by them, which turned their attention to more southern valleys of the Appalachian chain, and gave them a southward impetus which carried them as far as what is now northern Alabama. Here they joined the third stream of Ulster immigration, which entered the Carolinas by Charleston. To the two it is due that West Virginia, North Carolina, eastern Kentucky and Tennessee, and adjacent parts of South Carolina, Georgia, and Alabama constitute, with Pennsylvania, an American Ulster, far more extensive and populous than King James's Irish "plantation."

It is no longer thought sufficient to enumerate Puritan, Cavalier, and Quaker as the elements which made up America in colonial times, and directed the struggle for independence. It is now recognized that even thus early the Scotch-Irish of Ulster contributed no less than any of these to the make-up of the young nation. If the Puritan might be regarded as the thinking brain and the Quaker as the sympathetic heart of the new nation, the Scotch-Irish have been the backbone of its nationality. Deficient alike in comprehensive philanthropy and in speculative intellect, they possess in their volitional energy a quality of not less importance, as it has made them the element of persistence and of conservatism. They thus recall the part played by the Aaronic priesthood in Jewish history, which was less brilliant and attractive than the prophetic order, but not less useful as the vertebral link which bound generation to generation, and secured the continuity of the nation's life. " Grant that I may always be right, for Thou knowest I am hard to turn," is the recorded prayer of one old Presbyterian elder of this stock. His prayer might be adopted by the whole church—at any rate, by the whole Scotch-Irish stock.

Especially they have served the country as educators of the Middle States, and of those which lie west of them. Their early ministers were generally graduates of Glasgow, and it was they who established the many academies of those States, in which young men were given an education which would at least have fitted them to enter any American college. This threw the Presbyterian clergy into contact with others than their own people, enlarged their influence for good, and caused their church to be more highly esteemed. In view of the church's requirement that none but educated men should be regarded as candidates for the ministry, this combination of the schoolmaster with the pastor was regarded as natural and proper, as indeed their every seminary was a seed-plot for the ministry. They thus rendered a great service in maintaining a high educational standard at a time when the poverty of the country, the general indifference to whatever was " unpractical," and the active hostility of many sects to literary culture, made this very much harder to do than it is to-day.

At the time now under consideration the Scotch-Irish settlers were most numerous in Delaware and eastern Pennsylvania. It was through their coming that the Presbyterian Church outgrew the Presbytery and was obliged to establish a Synod with four subordinate Presbyteries, being one each in New York—which then included New Jersey—Pennsylvania, Delaware, and Maryland. At its constitution in 1717 the Synod consisted of all the ministers, with one elder from each church. But in 1724 this provisional arrangement was set aside, and the Presbyteries were directed to choose delegates equal to half their number, yet with the proviso that every third year all should attend. This arrangement for delegation, however, lasted for but two years, and then " the full Synod " was restored as a permanent institution.

A more important change in the constitution of the church was the Adopting Act of 1729, by which its ministers and licentiates, present and future, were required to subscribe to the Westminster Confession and Catechisms, " as being, in all essential and necessary articles, good forms of sound words and systems of Christian doctrine."

It had not been the purpose of the Westminster Assembly that subscription should be required to these " standards." Subscription never was introduced into the Presbyterian Church of England, as organized in various neighborhoods largely through the labors of members of the Assembly. Nor in Scotland was it required until it was enacted by Act of Assembly in 1690 to secure the ejection of the Episcopalian party from the parishes they still held in the northern shires. In Ireland the Synod of Ulster introduced it in 1698, but required it only of licentiates. It reënacted it in 1705, for all its ministers, as a safeguard against the growing tendency to Arianism. This in 1726 resulted in a division of the Irish Synod.

In America the Presbytery of New Castle had exacted a subscription to the Confession as early as 1724, and it was John Thomson, of that Presbytery, who first memorialized the Synod of Philadelphia to do the same. In 1728 the Presbytery itself renewed the memorial. The proposal met with opposition from the New England and from the Welsh ministers. Jonathan Dickinson, of Elizabethtown, pointed to the rupture of the Irish Church through requiring it, and declared that while subscription might exclude those who were scrupulous as to what they signed, it would neither "detect hypocrites, nor keep concealed heretics out of the church." He and his friends suspected a design on the part of the Scotch and Irish ministers to get rid of the Welsh and the native American element.

In the Synod of 1729, after the question had been fully handled in a committee containing the ablest men of both parties, an agreement was reached through mutual concessions. The concession to the opponents of subscription was the freedom extended to ministers and licentiates to express to Presbytery or Synod the scruples they felt as to any article in the standards, leaving the body to judge whether or not these scruples touched the "essential and necessary articles of faith." This followed the precedent set by the Irish Synod in its "Pacific Act" of 1720. With this proviso, all the ministers of the church subscribed, "after proposing all the scruples that any of them had against any articles or expressions." As a matter of fact these scruples related only to "some clauses in the 20th and 24th chapters" of the Confession, which treated of the power of the civil magistrate in matters of religion. Yet "many persons were offended" at this qualification, and desired that the Synod should require unconditional subscription; and some petitioned the Associate (or Seceder) Synod of Scotland to establish their church in America on that basis.

How well justified were Dickinson's apprehensions as to the futility of this safeguard against heretics was seen within a few years. Samuel Hemphill applied for membership in 1734, bringing credentials from the Irish Presbytery of Strabane, and then, for the second time within a year, subscribed the standards without the statement of either "scruple" or objection. A year later we find him arraigned before the Synod for preaching something like

Deism, and, in his contumacious absence, declared " unqualified for any future exercise of his ministry " within
its bounds.   This first heresy case led the Synod to protest against the practice of Irish Presbyteries in " ordaining
men to the ministry *sine titulo,* immediately before they
come over hither, thereby depriving us of our just rights,"
and to suggest that in addition to " their Presbyterial credentials," they should be furnished with " private letters
of recommendation," showing them to be " firmly attached
to our good old principles and schemes."   This implies
the admission that subscription was not the safeguard its
friends had supposed it.

Of much graver import was the dissension which arose
between the two elements of the Synod with regard to the
religious movement known in American church history
as the Great Awakening—a movement which made itself
felt from Maine to Georgia, and gave a new direction to
the religious life of the country.

To appreciate fully its significance it must be remembered
that one of the effects of emigration upon great bodies of
men is almost invariably their spiritual declension.   Just
as plants hardly can be transplanted without the sacrifice
of those fine fibrous roots on which so much of their vitality depends, so the human transplantation involves the
sacrifice of those fibers of sacred local and personal associations upon which the life of the spirit depends so much.
The old home, the traditional place of worship, the opinion
of hereditary neighbors, the wholesome routine of religious
usage, all are foregone ; and no one knows how much he is
dependent on these until he has parted with them.   Even
in New England, with all the fervor of the piety of Pilgrim
and Puritan settlers, the symptoms of spiritual decay were
speedily felt, especially in the younger generation.   The
Half-Way Covenant, with its frank defiance of Congrega-

tionalist principle, was a device to make it possible that the grandchildren of the first settlers should not be excluded from baptism and visible connection with the church. With each decade there was a palpable cooling of devotional fervor; and in spite of the Reforming Synods held in Boston in 1679 and 1680 to correct the growing laxity, it seemed probable that the sons of the Puritans would sink into shrewd money-getters, with little interest in either religion or the higher culture. In the words of Dr. Bushnell, " barbarism was the next danger."

The Scotch-Irish immigration represented a class which had already lost some ground by migration to Ireland, and it undoubtedly suffered spiritually by its second migration to America, first of all through the want of a regular ministry and worship. Matthew Hill writes of them to Baxter as scattered widely in Maryland, " as sheep without a shepherd." Where they made the attempt to gather into congregations they were generally too few and too poor to support a minister: and we find the Synod, in 1718, writing to the Presbytery of Dublin of their spiritual destitution, and of " a deplorable necessity of still continuing in the same circumstances of darkness, which may render both themselves and posterity miserable Pagans." Even where it was possible to obtain preachers, these in many cases were not of a character to weigh heavily on the side of a stricter life. The number of cases in which ministers were arraigned before the Presbytery and the Synod for grave moral offenses was very large in proportion; and in some cases the penalties imposed were very inadequate to the offense proven or confessed.

As the Presbyterian Church was not exceptional in any of these unhappy respects, an awakening to a larger measure of spiritual life was needed for the salvation of the whole country. It came almost parallel with the great

Methodist awakening in the British Islands, and it was powerfully promoted by George Whitefield, the preacher of that movement. But it had a somewhat different character and originated independently of that, and even earlier, in the labors of Jacob Frelinghuysen, who, in 1719, was settled as pastor of the Dutch Reformed Church in Raritan, N. J., where he remained until 1746. He was a native of Holland, and there had been affected by that Pietist movement which was to influence so markedly Whitefield and the Wesleys. He preached " awakening " sermons, insisted on evidences of regeneration in those he admitted to the Lord's table, and saw much fruit of his labors.

Four miles from Raritan lay New Brunswick, whose Presbyterian Church in 1726 called to its pastorate young Gilbert Tennent, who soon came under the personal influence of Dominie Frelinghuysen. Gilbert Tennent's father, William Tennent, had emigrated from Ireland to America in 1716. He was in Episcopal orders, but was of Scotch-Irish stock, and had married Catherine Kennedy, the daughter of an eminent Presbyterian minister. In 1718, possibly through her influence, he renounced the prelatic forms of government and worship, and was admitted without reordination into the Synod. He established himself in 1726 on the Neshaminy, north of Philadelphia, and opened an academy, which its enemies nicknamed " the Log College." His son Gilbert he had already educated for the ministry, and from the Neshaminy academy went forth others—including three of the principal's younger sons, Samuel Blair, and John Rowland—whose eminent usefulness was proof of the spiritual energy of their teacher.

At New Brunswick Gilbert Tennent at first had but a barren ministry. The gift of power came to him after a severe illness, and a loving letter from Dominie Frelinghuysen. He now preached the necessity of a conscious conversion from sin to God, and dealt pungently with the barren professors he found in his charge. From 1728 onward there was a notable harvest of conversions in his own flock and the adjacent districts to which he extended his labors. Other ministers—such as Jonathan Dickinson at Elizabethtown, and William Tennent the younger at Freehold—had the same joyful experience of seeing the ice of indifference broken and the message of the gospel come home in fresh power to the hearts of their people.

All this was much before the arrival of George Whitefield for his great evangelistic tour of November, 1739, to December, 1740, and even before the Awakening in New England, which began in 1734 under the preaching of Jonathan Edwards. Indeed, to say nothing of Dominie Frelinghuysen, Gilbert Tennent's ingathering began at New Brunswick a year before the " Holy Club " was formed at Oxford, and had spent its force before the date assigned by John and Charles Wesley as that of their conversion. Yet the two movements were so much alike in character that Whitefield found himself entirely at home among the Tennents and their co-workers; and in 1740 he persuaded Gilbert Tennent to continue his own work in Boston, where he labored for months with great impression. From Whitefield's comments we may infer that Tennent's preaching was more severe and inculpatory than his own. " He is a son of thunder, whose preaching must either convert or enrage hypocrites." In this Tennent reflected the manner of the Pietists, without the alleviating tinge of cheerfulness which the Methodists got from the Moravians.

But the treasure came in earthen vessels. Its presentation was affected by the personal weaknesses and the mental limitations of those who bore it, and by the spirit of their age. Not content with speaking the truth it had been given him to see, Gilbert Tennent undertook to sit in judgment upon those who did not see as he did.   He and his friends denounced " unconverted ministers " as " blind leaders of the blind " ; they also preached within the bounds of the charges of the ministers so described, as they had opportunity, without leave asked, and refusing recognition of their ministerial character.

In the Synod of 1740 Tennent and Blair presented papers which drew a black picture of the character of the ministry as a body, and, when challenged to substantiate their charges, they had to admit that they had not investigated the reports they accepted, nor had they spoken privately, as Christ requires, to these alleged offenders.

At last, by a famous sermon, preached March 8, 1740, at Nottingham, Pa., on " An Unconverted Ministry," Gilbert Tennent brought matters to a head.   It was such a public indictment of those who had stood aloof from the Awakening, that, even without the naming of names, it seemed to be meant to make it impossible for the ministers described to remain in synodical communion with him and his friends.

At the next meeting of the Synod a protest signed by twelve ministers and eight elders was presented by Robert Cross, of Philadelphia, which the majority of the Synod adopted as its own.   This arraigned the party represented by Tennent and Blair for overthrowing the authority of Synod by confining its powers to advice; for disorderly irruptions into other men's congregations; for censorious judgments of those who did not walk with them, resulting in the disturbance and division of congregations; for making the call to the ministry a matter merely of personal feeling; for preaching the terrors of the law " in such a manner and dialect as has no precedent in the Word of God " ; and for asserting that truly gracious persons are able to judge with certainty both of their own state and that of others. On these grounds they denied the right of the offenders to sit as members of that judicatory. As the Presbytery of New York was not represented, while the Southern Presbyteries were present in strength, that of New Brunswick had but small support. Only twenty-five out of the forty-seven ministers of the Synod were in attendance, and the measure was carried by a vote of twelve to ten, three not voting. The ministers and elders of the New Brunswick Presbytery, in great surprise at this result, accepted the decision and withdrew.

The very next step of the majority was to alter the terms of subscription to the Westminster standards, making it unconditional, with no liberty to state scruples and have Presbytery or Synod pass upon them as to whether they touched essential doctrines. Two of the Presbyteries, indeed, had already anticipated this action.

CHAPTER IV.

FROM THE SCHISM TO THE REUNION, 1741–58.

THE division of the Presbyterian Church in 1741, whatever elements of human weakness entered into it, was the result of forces working widely in the life of the colonies and of Great Britain. It was an indirect result of the Great Awakening which terminated the Puritan and inaugurated the Pietist or Methodist age of American church history.

During the period of division it was the progressive or New Side of the church which made the greater progress. After a friendly attempt to effect a reconciliation in 1742–43 the Presbytery of New York declined to sit in Synod on the ground that the New Brunswick Presbytery had as good right as themselves. They also desired the good-will of the Synod of Philadelphia in establishing a Synod of New York, and this was accorded with some reluctance. The body thus organized embraced the New Brunswick Presbytery, and increased from 22 members in 1745 to 72 in 1758, while the Synod of Philadelphia had fallen from 24 to 23. This was due to several causes, the first being the establishment in 1746 of the College of New Jersey, finally located at Princeton in 1757.

The education question had been a matter of controversy between the two parties until the Nottingham sermon turned the waters of strife into a new channel. The conservative party, in their anxiety to maintain a high standard of ministerial culture, were disposed to insist that none but the graduates of British universities or New England colleges should be accepted as candidates. The

34

friends of the Awakening insisted on the right of Presbyteries to license the graduates of such academies as Neshaminy, in view of the urgent need of preachers and pastors. And they insisted that the Presbyteries should lay less stress on college training and more on the evidence of the candidate being a regenerate man, called by the Holy Ghost to the ministry. To overcome the former difficulty the Synod of Philadelphia attempted to establish a college of its own, there being none at that time in the Middle Colonies. Failing in this, they voted, in 1739, to create a committee to examine the students and graduates of private seminaries, and to give those whose proficiency merited it a certificate which would serve as a diploma in their application to Presbytery. To this the friends of Neshaminy Academy objected for reasons told us only by their enemies, viz., "that it was to prevent that school from training gracious men for the ministry."

After the division, the Synod of Philadelphia took under its care the academy at New London taught by Francis Alison, an Irish graduate of Glasgow, described as "the best Latin scholar in America"; and tried to make an arrangement with Yale College for the further training of its graduates. "As learning," they write, "is not in the same esteem in this government as in New England, we beg all the indulgence your constitution can allow us, lest parents grudge expenses if they run high." But this does not seem to have accomplished much, and in 1749 Alison removed to Philadelphia to accept a post in the academy newly established by Franklin's influence.

The New York Synod did much better in applying for a charter for a college, and in placing it, in 1745, under the direction of Jonathan Dickinson, of Elizabethtown, the best scholar, the most effective writer, and the soundest judgment in the church. At his death, in 1747, Aaron

Burr was chosen to succeed him, and the college removed accordingly to Newark, where he was pastor. In 1755 both it and Burr were transferred to Princeton; and on his death, in 1757, he was succeeded by his father-in-law, Jonathan Edwards, who hardly lived to enter upon the office, and was followed in the year of the reunion by Samuel Davies. It was this young institution which poured into the Presbyterian ministry a stream of young men, imbued with sympathy with the Awakening and zealous for its objects.

Next to this, it was the sympathy of the Synod of New York, with the revival of religious interest, which aided its growth. The spirit of the time in the colonies was revivalist. Here and there resistance was offered: Harvard and Yale, after favoring Whitefield, turned against him; Connecticut enacted arrest and expulsion for " vagrant preachers," and applied the law to Samuel Finley, who had gone to New Haven to preach to a congregation of " Separates." But these were side-eddies, and the main current of the country's religious life flowed in the new channel, to the advantage of all the larger social interests. Even in a political sense the Great Awakening was a decisive influence. It broke the barriers of colonial reserve, as well as of sectarian isolation, and gave the American people, for the first time, a common intellectual interest in the movement, and personal interest in its leaders. Whitefield, Edwards, and Tennent preceded Franklin and Washington as rallying names for Americans, irrespective of local distinctions.

All this, however, does not require us to regard the Awakening as an unmixed good, or to refuse a relative justification to those who opposed it. Nor need this relative justification be based upon the extravagance of men like James Davenport and Jonathan Barber, or the uncharitableness of Tennent and Blair. Indeed, these excesses were quickly sloughed off, and the Synod of New York, under the sober leadership of Jonathan Dickinson, was animated by a different spirit from that of its Presbytery of New Brunswick. Gilbert Tennent himself laid aside his asperity, labored for the reunion of the two bodies, abandoned his oddities in dress, and donned a wig. As pastor of the Second Church in Philadelphia, in avowed opposition to the view of Jonathan Edwards, he maintained that persons of blameless life, properly instructed in the principles of Christianity, should be admitted to the Lord's table. Like Whitefield and Wesley, he lived to repent and retract the hasty and censorious judgments he had pronounced on his brethren in the ministry.

The real faults of the Awakening lay deeper than these superficial matters. One of them is indicated by the very name Methodism, by which the movement has been so generally known. It set out with the assumption that there is one method of grace, by which all God's true people are made alive unto him through his Son; and it exacted of all much the same evidences of this uniform Christian experience. Instantaneous, conscious conversion, preceded by an overwhelming sense of personal guilt, and followed by a joyful assurance of acceptance with God, was the only *ordo salutis* it recognized. Religion must thus come into the man like " a bolt from the blue," and with no conceivable relation to the past providences of his life, the human relationships in which he had been placed by God, and the Christian nurture in divine things he had received from his childhood. Mankind were classified broadly into those who knew they were converted and those who were not. The " judgment of charity " of the Reformed churches was displaced by the Anabaptist demand for a church-membership giving " credible evi-

dence " of regeneration; and the Christian nurture of the
family, along with the catechetical instruction of the young
by their pastors, came to be regarded as relatively unim-
portant.

The resultant type of Christian experience was one isolated from the relationships and relative duties of life in a
very un-Protestant fashion; and the energy of attention
was concentrated upon the succession of inward emotions
and feelings. An age of introspection and consequently
of spiritual gloom was one result, while the direct application of Christian principle to the whole life of Christian
society, and the realization of God's kingdom in this present world, were hardly contemplated as Christian duties.
The theocratic element in the life of the Reformed Church,
notably reflected in Makemie's New York sermon, gave
way before an introspective pietism, which had much in
common with the monasticism of the Church of Rome.

But in the period we are considering Presbyterian pietism
was in the heyday of youth, with all the charm of novelty
and of earnestness. It was its internal vigor, and the zeal
it was able to elicit in the young men it drew into the ministry, that made possible the rapid increase of the church
within the New Side Synod.

One sign of this vigor was the organization of the Presbytery of Hanover, the mother-Presbytery of most of the
churches and Presbyteries south of the Potomac. As early
as 1719 the Scotch-Irish migration began to flow down
the Shenandoah Valley, occupying fertile districts still un-
touched by the tobacco-planters of the eastern counties,
and bearing the brunt of Indian hostility. In view of these
services the intolerant ecclesiastical laws of the colony were
allowed to remain a dead letter beyond the Blue Ridge,
and the people were visited from time to time by Presbyterian preachers from the North, generally of the Old

Side. It was different when Presbyterianism struck root in Hanover County, built its meeting-houses in the parishes of the Established Church, and sent zealous preachers like William Robinson, Samuel Davies, John Rodgers, and John Todd to do the work neglected by the sleepy and worldly rectors of the Virginian establishment. They did not come uncalled. The reading of a few religious works by some planters of the county had produced a religious awakening independent of church or clergy. At first they met only to hear such books read, and buildings had to be erected for the accommodation of the crowds who came. Hearing of William Robinson, who was traveling toward North Carolina for his health and preaching as he went, they sent for him, satisfied themselves of his orthodoxy and piety, and put the direction of affairs into his hands. Through their labors and his, Presbyterianism struck root in a community English and Episcopalian by its traditions. Thanks to the eloquence and the administrative ability of Davies, as well as to the favor of a Scotch governor, it was protected from the legalized intolerance of the established clergy, and had time and room to grow. On hearing of Jonathan Edwards's removal from Northampton in 1749, Samuel Davies wrote to urge his coming to Virginia, but was too late, as he had consented to take charge of the Indian mission at Stockbridge. In 1755 the Synod of New York organized the Presbytery of Hanover, which embraced all the ministers who were resident in Virginia and the Carolinas, except the Presbytery of Charleston, and one minister who adhered to the Synod of Philadelphia.

The Awakening bore fruit also in the mission-work among the Northern Indians, begun in 1743 by David Brainerd. With the forks of the Delaware as his center, he extended his labors from Freehold on the east to the

Susquehanna on the west. His saintly fervor, which made him willing to forego all the comforts of civilized life, touched the heart of the red man as it had not been since the days of John Eliot, if even then; and a large harvest of converts was gathered. After his early death, in 1747, his brother John stepped into his place, and carried on the work with some interruptions until his death, in 1781, but with less fruit of his labor. So in 1748–50 Elihu Spencer labored among the Oneidas of New York. In 1757 the Presbytery of Suffolk ordained a Connecticut Mohegan, Samson Occom, to labor among his own people, which he did until his death, in 1791. He and President Davies were the two first hymn-writers of the American Presbyterian Church.

It was during this time that two other types of British Presbyterianism found a home in America. The Revolution Settlement of 1688–90 had been accepted by all the surviving ministers, of whatever shade of Presbyterianism. Many, however, of the Cameronians, or Hill People, who formed the extreme right wing of the church and who had disowned all who had accepted the Indulgence of 1670, no less than the Scottish and Irish prelates and their " curates," objected to the settlement as dealing too gently with " the indulged," and as making no proper recognition of the binding obligation of the national Covenants of 1638 and 1643. They in fact continued to renounce allegiance to both church and state as established in Scotland. As they had no ministers, they sought to edify one another in " corresponding societies " until the accession of John Macmillan, a minister of the Scottish Kirk, in 1706, enabled them to obtain the sacraments in an orderly way. That of Mr. Nairn, a minister of the Seceder Church, in 1743, made possible the constitution of a Reformed Presbytery.

Three ministers of the American Synod—Alexander Craighead and David Alexander, both of Donegal Presbytery, and John Cross, of New Brunswick Presbytery— were in agreement with the Reformed Presbyterians (or Covenanters) as to the perpetual obligation of the Covenants, while the rest, in so far as they had any distinct opinion in the matter, were satisfied with the Revolution Settlement. In 1740 Craighead was suspended for making the Covenants a term of communion in his congregation at Middle Octorara, Pa., and for other matters growing out of his zealous advocacy of the Awakening. After the exclusion of the Presbytery of New Brunswick from the Synod of Philadelphia he pleaded with them to renew the Covenants, and when they refused he turned to the Scottish Reformed Presbytery, and asked helpers for America. At Octorara in 1743 he and his adherents solemnly renewed the Covenants, with swords pointed to the four quarters of the heavens, as though to defy opposition from whatever quarter it might come. In 1751 the Scotch Presbytery sent John Cuthbertson, but two years before this Craighead had joined the Synod of New York. Some at least of his followers were more tenacious, and at Middle Octorara Cuthbertson made his home, ministering to the scattered societies of the Covenanters of Pennsylvania, until the union of 1782.

It is said, but probably not correctly, that Craighead, when tired with waiting for a response from the Reformed Presbytery, made application to the Associate (or Seceder) Synod of Scotland. This was the second body of conservative Presbyterians which declared their separation from the Kirk of Scotland, charging it with unfaithfulness to its own principles. It was in 1733 that Ebenezer Erskine and three other ministers of the Synod of Perth, who had been condemned for holding and teaching the doctrines of

Edward Fisher's book, "The Marrow of Modern Divinity" (1644), organized the first Associate Presbytery. In 1746–47 they had divided as to the lawfulness of the oath exacted of burgesses in the Scottish burghs, into Burghers and Antiburghers. To them, as representing all that was pronounced in Calvinism and strict in Presbyterianism, and yet not breaking with the civil government over Scotland and America—as Craighead and the Covenanters did—an appeal was made by those Presbyterians in Pennsylvania who objected to the qualified subscription exacted in 1729 by the Synod of Pennsylvania. In 1753 the Antiburgher Synod responded by sending Alexander Gellatly and Andrew Arnot to America, with authority to organize congregations and to constitute a Presbytery. In the meantime the division of 1741 had enabled the Old Side to alter the terms of subscription in the Synod of Philadelphia to such as ought to have satisfied the most orthodox. On the other hand, the New Side Presbytery of Newcastle issued "a judicial warning" against the newcomers, denouncing them as schismatics, and "the Marrow doctrines" as unsound. To this Messrs. Gellatly and Arnot naturally published a reply; and the relations of the two wings of the Presbyterian host were involved in an atmosphere of unhappy and unprofitable controversy as to the obligation of the Covenants, the nature of faith, and the extent and manner of "the gospel offer." Each party naturally tended to lay stress on that which sundered it from the other.

A fresh ground of difference showed itself in New York. Here a Presbyterian church had been organized in 1716, but as the Episcopalian influence defeated its repeated efforts to obtain a charter, it had been forced to vest its property in the Church of Scotland. The Scotch and Scotch-Irish element in the congregation always had had some friction with the Puritans from New England, and this came to a head in 1752, when the attempt was made to substitute Dr. Watts's paraphrastic version of the Book of Psalms for the less smooth but more faithful version based on that of Francis Rous (1643), and adopted after revision by the Westminster divines in 1645, and by the Scottish Assembly in 1649. This Scottish psalter was repugnant to the tastes of the eighteenth century through its strong no less than its weak points; and the Great Awakening had affected the taste in psalmody as much as in anything else. The Synod of New York in 1756 refused to condemn the use of Watts, as it was orthodox, and " as no particular version is of divine authority." So in that year the disaffected withdrew and organized a " Scotch church," which next year was taken under the care of the Associate Presbytery. The Synod of Philadelphia had not sanctioned any innovation in psalmody; and in the Synod of New York we hear of it only in this one church, and even in that no hymns were sung. In this way, however, arose the great dispute as to the proper " matter of praise," which still divides the lesser and more conservative Presbyterian bodies from the greater.

Throughout the whole period of the separation of the two Synods, that of New York had labored for reconciliation and reunion, with increasing weight as its numbers grew, and its management of its affairs gave evidence of its sobriety and orthodoxy. At first the personal irritation on the side of the Synod of Philadelphia was naturally very considerable, but only against the eight Irish ministers of the Tennent group. For Dickinson and his New York associates, New England Puritans chiefly, they always avowed their high regard. At last, in 1758, a plan of union was reached which both could adopt. As regards both subscription to the standards and the authority of Synod

and the Presbyteries, the Old Side carried their point.
Arrangements for stating scruples and leaving the church
court to judge of their importance were dropped. Those
who dissented from synodical or presbyterial action might
withdraw or protest, but nothing more. Intrusion into
other men's congregations and wholesale indictments of
brother-ministers were forbidden as irregular. As to the
questions growing out of the Awakening, a compromise
was reached. It was provided that candidates for the
ministry should be examined as to their "experimental
acquaintance with religion," no less than their learning
and orthodoxy. As to the Awakening itself, instead of
pronouncing upon it, the basis defines *in thesi* what is "a
work of grace," in terms far more natural to the new theology than the old; and while repudiating the extravagances of visionaries, it pledged the united Synod to work
for the promotion of what was thus described.

On this basis the reunited church entered upon a new
period of activity. The stricter view of Presbyterianism
had prevailed over the looser in matters of church order.
The newer view had prevailed over the older in that of
the perspective of doctrine and its practical application.
The united church thus reached a comparatively stable
equilibrium, which was to last for eighty years.

CHAPTER V.

By reason of the extent of the immigration from Ulster, and of the adhesion of Puritan migrants from New England, the Presbyterian Church was now one of the three largest in the country. While the Congregationalists predominated in New England, and the Episcopal Church was established in New York and in the States south of Mason and Dixon's line, in the States between the Hudson and the Potomac there were more Presbyterians than anything else. At the beginning of the War of Independence the thirteen colonies had 186 Presbyterian and 61 Reformed ministers. Taken along with the Congregationalists, who were in the friendliest relations with them, they constituted a controlling majority of the American people.

In the Southern colonies the Presbyterian churches were increasing rapidly by immigration from Ulster. The advantages of a strong organization and of vigorous synodical authority were especially shown in enabling the Synod to meet the rapidly multiplying demand for ministerial service from unorganized communities and vacant churches in the Carolinas, Virginia, western Pennsylvania, and northern New York. At least one session of each meeting of the Synod was occupied with no other business than arranging supplies, frequently by requiring the older churches to give up the services of their pastors for the time needed for a journey to the South or across the Alleghanies. Even

45

from Nova Scotia came an appeal for help, so widely diffused was confidence in the Synod's ability to overtake the demands of a growing field.

The correspondence of the time shows how much attention was aroused in New England by the effective discipline over pastors, candidates, and people which the Synod exercised. As a consequence the Puritan churches and ministers within the bounds of the middle and Southern colonies gave their adhesion to the Synod very generally. Those which lay between the Hudson River and the Connecticut line had organized themselves into a Presbytery of Dutchess County in 1752, and were admitted to the Synod in 1763.

The college at Princeton continued to surpass the hopes of its founders as a source of supply of the ministry. The presidency of Samuel Davies (1759–61), the most brilliant preacher thus far of the church, ended too quickly to realize the expectations his election had roused. In 1753–54 he and Gilbert Tennent had visited Great Britain and Ireland to secure an endowment fund from the Presbyterians and orthodox dissenters, and had met with marked success. His successor, Samuel Finley, was one of the few survivors of the *Sturm und Drang* period of the Awakening, and his academy at Nottingham had been a fruitful nursery of ministers. In his presidency (1761–66) there was a notable revival in the college. In 1768 Princeton received one of its great presidents in Dr. John Witherspoon, who had been elected in 1766. He already had made a name as the literary champion of earnest Calvinism against the moderate party in the Kirk of Scotland. He now showed no less ability as an administrator and educator, the latter as filling the new chair of divinity.

His position in church affairs in Scotland threw him into sympathetic relations with the Associate Presbytery in America; and in 1769, at their request, he moved for a committee of conference with a view to union. These negotiations continued until 1774, when it was manifest that the Associate brethren could not see their way to an agreement. Probably this final refusal was due to the stiffening received in the meantime from the Scottish Associate Synod. In 1764–68 five ministers of the Burgher branch of the Associate body had arrived in America, and applied for admission into the Associate Presbytery. As the point of difference between the two Seceder churches had no pertinence to America, the Presbytery agreed to accept them on the footing of assent to the common principles as defined in the Secession Testimony. But as the American Presbytery was subordinate to the Scotch Synod, this now felt itself compromised by being brought into fellowship with ministers who approved of the Burgher oath. Two more ministers were sent out, with instructions not to take their seat in Presbytery until the Burgher members were expelled. This was done in 1771, and they were told that " it was very sinful " in Presbytery to have admitted them.

During the period we are considering the Associate Presbytery increased to thirteen ministers, resident in Pennsylvania and New York, and in 1776 it was divided into two Presbyteries, named from those colonies. As each was directly subject to the Synod in Scotland, they were related to each other only by way of correspondence—an arrangement which resulted in the development of two distinct types of American Seceders. The Reformed Presbytery, organized in 1774, had now three ministers laboring among small " societies " in Pennsylvania.

Besides the Synod and these conservative Presbyteries there was a Presbytery of South Carolina, organized in 1723, or sooner, largely composed of Scotchmen, and claiming to represent the Kirk of Scotland. Its members seem to have been in sympathy with the Moderate party in the Kirk, as we hear of Principal Robertson and Dr. Hugh Blair selecting a minister for their Charleston church. They were not, therefore, fraternal in their relations to the zealous revivalist preachers of the Synod.

In New England the course of events had been not unlike that in the Middle States. It is true that the question on which the Presbytery of Londonderry divided in 1736 was that of their relation to the Congregationalist churches and their discipline. But it is notable that the Presbytery of Boston, organized in 1745 by the minority, threw itself with zeal into the measures of the Great Awakening, and rapidly outgrew its elder rival, which by 1765 had become extinct by depletion. By 1771 the new body began to consider the propriety of constituting a Synod, a step which was carried out in 1774, the fifteen or sixteen ministers of the Synod of New England being divided into four Presbyteries — Boston, Newburyport (afterward Salem), Londonderry, and Palmer. Nearly at the same time were organized two other Presbyteries: that of the Eastward and that of Grafton, or of the Connecticut River. The latter was composed of President Wheelock, of Dartmouth College, then newly founded, and other Congregationalist admirers of Presbyterian methods; and it held itself strictly aloof from other Presbyterian bodies. The Presbytery of the Eastward was refused recognition by the Synod, on the ground that its founder and leading spirit, John Murray, of Boothbay, Me., had no ministerial standing, as the Presbytery of Philadelphia had deposed him from the ministry little more than a year after it had ordained him. He, however, was a man of much greater vitality than any in the new Synod, and the Presbytery of the Eastward grew at its expense, the first secessions being those of the church in Boston and that in Newburyport, where George Whitefield had been buried in 1770. Its aged pastor, Jonathan Parsons, in whose house the great preacher had died, took Murray's part; and in 1776 Murray became his successor, after refusing a call to Boston. The Psalmody question also arose in New England, as in 1774 Moses Baldwin of Palmer made the first move toward a substitute for the Scotch psalter. This led some of the conservatives to turn their eyes toward the Associate Presbytery of New York.

This was the period of greatest growth of New England Presbyterianism. In New Hampshire the five churches of 1760 had grown to twenty by 1778; and the number in Maine cannot have been less. That of ministers in all three bodies is estimated at thirty-two.

The Synod of New York and Philadelphia, however, was by far the largest and most growing body. But it was not possessed of complete homogeneity and harmony. The Old Side and the New were united, but not quite reconciled, and three occasions for dissension were found: (1) The reconstruction of the Presbyteries was found easy, except in the districts covered by the two Presbyteries of Newcastle and the Old Side Presbytery of Donegal. This was the region in which the antagonisms of the old controversies had been sharpest and most personal; and the Synod found it hard to effect such a reconstruction as was demanded by the interests of the church at large. At one time a part of the Presbytery of Donegal for three years actually declined the jurisdiction of Synod rather than submit to its arrangements; and there was a constant transfer of ministers and churches from Presbytery to Presbytery for the sake of peace. (2) The especial bone of contention within the Presbyteries was the examination of candidates for the ministry. The Plan of Union forbade Presbyteries to license or ordain any one " until he give them competent satisfaction as to his learning and experimental acquaintance with religion, and skill in divinity and cases of conscience." The Old Side members contended that this meant nothing more than the requirement of the Westminster Directory, that the Presbytery shall " inquire touching the grace of God in the candidate, and if he be of such holiness of life as is requisite in a minister of the gospel." The New Side, however, would be content with nothing less than the rehearsal in Presbytery of his religious experiences, in the spirit of the Awakening. To this it was objected that beyond the profession of faith in the gospel no man or body of men had a right to inquire into the religious state of another; and that the proper means to ascertain the presence of grace in a man is not his own testimony concerning himself, but the testimony of those who have best known his life and conversation. In 1761 the Synod was on the verge of a fresh division on this issue, each party contending that it stood for the true sense of the Plan of Union, and a large majority sustaining the demand for a public rehearsal of experiences. To avoid a renewal of the schism it was agreed that the majority of each Presbytery should take whichever course it preferred; and that if the minority could not acquiesce conscientiously, they should be organized as a separate Presbytery. This was a most un-Presbyterian solution of the difficulty, as it abandoned the principle of unity in procedure in a matter of vital importance. Thus the Second Presbytery of Philadelphia, organized under this authority out of Old Side ministers and churches, had power to admit to the ministry men who in the view of the First Presbytery, and of the church at large, might be altogether unfit persons. The majority acted with more charity than prudence in thus setting what proved a fatal precedent, as Presbyteries of this structure were sure to perpetuate and intensify the differences they represented.

As a rule, however, the majority in the united Synod acted with more rigor of authority than charitable consideration for the scruples or sensibilities of the minority. Although it consisted largely of New England Puritans, who had entertained scruples as to the exercise of presbyterial and synodical authority over the churches, and of the New Brunswick party, which had tried to minimize that authority into an advisory power, it now showed little hesitation in laying down with sharp precision the lines on which the order and discipline of the church must move. This was seen (3) in the dispute as to the power of Synod and Presbytery to deal with applicants from the Presbyterian churches of Great Britain and Ireland. The Presbyterian churches of England, and a part of those of Ireland, had fallen into Arianism. Even in the Scottish Kirk a similar tendency had been shown; and since the secession of the Erskines and their friends, the Moderates had obtained complete control in the Scottish Assembly. Their indifference to both the independence of the church and to theological doctrines was rooted in a carelessness to any deeper godliness than morality of outer life. It therefore behooved the American church to guard the entrance to its ministry from these quarters, and the New Side proposed to effect this by reserving to the Synod the right to admit them finally. Before the division of 1741 it was they who had been sticklers for the rights of the Presbyteries over against the Synod—a part now adopted by the Old Side brethren in repeated protests, which also pointed out the danger of causing ministers from abroad to set up separate Presbyteries. A compromise was reached in 1774, by which the Presbyteries were admonished to exercise great care, and required to make a special report to

Synod of every case, and to transmit the credentials of the persons admitted, while Synod reserved the power to annul their admission.

Less obtrusive, but of more lasting importance, was the growing difficulty as to the psalmody of the church, and that first in the congregations which had been connected with the Synod of New York, where the disposition to a change was greatest. It was especially in the Second Church of Philadelphia, organized of those who sympathized with the Awakening, and long the pastoral charge of Gilbert Tennent, that the dissension was manifest, a minority appealing from Session to Presbytery, and from Presbytery to Synod, against "the introduction of Dr. Watts's imitation of the Psalms." The Synod had already sanctioned its use in churches which preferred it, and refused to recall that approval, while it sent Drs. Witherspoon, Rodgers, and Macwhorter to talk the recalcitrant party into a different judgment. They reported, but not in terms which indicated their success. The difficulty was made more acute by the unwise language Dr. Watts had employed in the preface to his version, denying the fitness of the Psalms for Christian use until they had been adapted to "the language of the New Testament."

The proceedings of the Synod during this period are more barren than we should have expected of references to public affairs, as it was the time of those successive and acute struggles with Great Britain over the power of taxation which finally precipitated the War for Independence. In 1766 the Synod, on motion of Dr. Alison, sent an address to the king on the repeal of the Stamp Act. Under the surface of this apparent indifference, however, lay an intense concern in the possible course of events as affecting the ecclesiastical as well as the civil status of the colonies.

Thrice in the history of the colonies preparations had

been made for the consecration of a bishop for the British colonies of America; and thrice the plan had come to naught through what the anti-prelatists of America regarded as the interpositions of Providence, viz., the fall of Archbishop Laud in 1640, the disgrace of the Earl of Clarendon in 1667, and the sudden death of Queen Anne in 1714. In George III. for the first time the new dynasty was represented by a king of English birth and sympathies, and withal a zealous churchman, while in Thomas Secker, the primate of Canterbury, and Beilby Porteus, Bishop of Chester and the king's chaplain—himself a native of Virginia—the American Episcopal Church had two zealous friends at court. To prepare the way for the new step, Dr. T. B. Chandler, of Burlington, whose great abilities certainly designated him as the occupant of the proposed see, published " An Appeal to the Public in Behalf of the Church of England in America " (New York, 1767), showing the hardships it endured for want of a bishop. No discipline was maintained over clergy or people; the rite of confirmation could be enjoyed only by those who could make the journey to England; the same journey must be undertaken by all candidates for holy orders, and by reason of wars, pestilences, and shipwrecks one in five of these never returned. He declared that American Episcopalians desired no power over their brethren of other communions. Their bishop would be supported by their own gifts, not by compulsory tithes, and he would claim no such jurisdiction as English bishops' courts (until 1857) exercised over marriages, divorces, wills, and other questions affected by canon law.

In the controversy this provoked the hardships were admitted; nor was it necessary to call into question the excellent intentions of American Episcopalians. But even they could give no security against the enactment of a

general tithe law and the establishment of prelatical jurisdiction by the British Parliament, either at once or at some
early date.

Point was given to these apprehensions by recollections
of the stratagem practiced by Governor Fletcher to effect
the establishment of episcopacy in New York. At a time
when the chaplain of the forces was the only Episcopal
minister in the colony, he induced the colonial legislature
to pass an act (1693) for the employment of " able Protestant ministers " for the different inhabited parishes. Then,
acting on the principle *Cujus regio, ejus religio,* and in the
face of the protest of the legislature, he interpreted this to
mean exclusively clergymen of the Church of England, as
no others were of the same communion with William III.!
He and his successors, and other zealous Episcopalians,
aided by the English Society for the Propagation of the
Gospel, hastened to provide episcopally ordained clergymen
even for the thoroughly Puritan churches on Long Island,
whose houses of worship they seized on the ground that
these had been erected by a public tax, and were therefore
the property of the Established Church. And in 1703 the
Episcopalian vestry of Philadelphia waited on Lord Cornbury, governor of New York, and expressed their hopes
that his cousin, Queen Anne, would extend the benefits
of his government to Pennsylvania.

These transactions emphasized to the Puritan and Presbyterian churches the dangers to religious equality attendant on the connection with England. The Ulster immigrants naturally would recall the legal establishment of
prelacy in their native province, with tithes and episcopal
courts, at a time when four out of five of its Protestant
inhabitants were Presbyterians ; and they remembered how
their fathers had been summoned before those courts on the
charge of living in fornication with their own wives, because

they had not been married with a ring by an Episcopalian
rector. These experiences fitted them to welcome independence as the final disappearance of a peril which had
overhung them ever since the young king's accession. It
is not without significance that Presbyterian Synod and
the Connecticut Association held a joint convention by
delegates from 1766 till 1776, and that the Synod of 1775
promptly accepted the leadership of the Continental Congress, expressly leaving to " that august body " the choice
of a fast-day to be held in view of " the alarming state of
public affairs." To those who have looked below the surface it is clear that ecclesiastical considerations were as
active in promoting the revolt of the colonies as were the
disputes over revenue. Connection with a " mother-country " in which church and state had a common head, and
were controlled by the same legislature, carried with it
other perils than those of fiscal exaction.

CHAPTER VI.

THE period of the War of Independence is acknowledged on all hands to have been one of disaster to the spiritual condition of the country. In part this was due to the mixture of ecclesiastical considerations in the motives of the contest. These did not raise it to the horrible dignity of a war of religion, but they brought strife into the sanctuary of peace, and they prompted to willful injuries to church property. The fact that the Congregationalists, Presbyterians, Reformed, Lutherans, and Baptists as a whole were on the patriotic side, while the Episcopalians and the Methodists in the main sided with the mother-country, which also possessed the sympathy and quiet coöperation of the majority of the Friends, was recognized in the conduct of hostilities. When the British troops entered an American town they were pretty sure to seize on the patriotic churches and convert them into barracks, hospitals, or stables, leaving them in a state of wreck at their departure. The patriot troops naturally would retaliate on the Episcopal churches as they had opportunity.

Only the Highlanders, who had settled at Cape Fear and some other places of North Carolina after the rebellion of 1745, broke the unanimity with which the Presbyterians of America—Scotch, Scotch-Irish, Welsh, and Puritan— supported the cause of independence. The Synod of 1783 congratulates the church on " the general and almost universal attachment of the Presbyterian body to the cause of liberty," as " confessed by the complaints and resentment of the common enemy." It points to " our burnt and wasted churches, and our plundered dwellings " as " an earnest of what we must have suffered " had the issue of the war been different. Dr. Inglis, the Tory rector of Trinity Church, wrote in 1776: " I do not know one Presbyterian minister, nor have I been able, after strict inquiry, to hear of any, who did not, by preaching and every effort in their power, promote all the measures of the Continental Congress, however extravagant." There was, indeed, one minister in the Synod of New England who embraced the British side of the controversy, and joined the royal army. The Synod deposed him, and suspended another of its members until he brought a certificate of his loyalty from the State of New Hampshire.

Dr. Witherspoon, along with several other Presbyterians, sat in the Continental Congress, and voted for independence. Charles Thomson, an elder in the session of the First Church, was its trusted secretary, and by his proverbial truthfulness gave additional weight to its proclamations and gazettes. George Duffield shared with William White the duties and honors of the chaplaincy. The wife of James Caldwell, of Elizabeth—the minister who brought the patriot troops an armful of psalm-books when their wadding gave out—was assassinated by a Tory, and he himself was shot by a drunken sentinel while on chaplain's duty ; and John Rosbrugh, of Allentown, " was barbarously murdered by the enemy at Trenton," in cold blood after he had surrendered. George Duffield had at least one narrow escape, and on the head of John Murray, of Boothbay, was set a reward as great as on those of Samuel Adams and John Hancock.

The Synod of 1778 met at Bedminster because Philadelphia was " in possession of the enemy." The Tories

complained that the fast-days kept by Presbyterians and
Puritans were used especially to keep alive the opposition
to English policy.   In the calls to observe these I find
constant reference to the decay of piety, the gross immoralities which so commonly attend a state of war, and the
spread of irreligion.   In the twenty years before the war
there had been a perceptible decay of religious earnestness.
The white-heat methods of the Awakening had been followed by the usual reaction, which attests how much of
the temporal and the human had been blended with what
was of God in it, and therefore was found lasting.   The
disputes with the " mother-country " had diverted attention from eternal to temporal interests.   The churches of
America were ill fit to stand the strain of a time of war,
and the temptations it offered to the malevolent passions.
Not all the patriotic ministers showed the calmness and
good-will which marked Dr. John Rodgers, of New York,
the friend and trusted adviser of Washington, who, in his
years of exile from his own charge, subordinated every
other consideration to his work in the ministry of reconciliation.

The peril was much increased by the alliance, which
brought groups of French officers into contact with the
people in every important seaport, and with the army at
large.   The frivolous and scoffing deism of the school of
Voltaire was thus naturalized in America, and an irreligious
tone began to pervade its society, especially its public
life.   Religion was valued, if at all, as a supplement to
the jail and the police ; belief in a disclosure of God to his
creatures was thought a jestworthy superstition.

Besides these gravest losses in the character and temper
of the people, the churches suffered much disorganization.
Their buildings were torn down, or diverted for a time to
other uses in a way which involved great loss.   Princeton

College was closed for years, thus interrupting the preparation of young ministers. It was almost impossible for many pastors to obtain the means of supporting their families, especially in the districts reached by the war.

Yet in the face of discouragements of all sorts, the routine of the church's work was kept up in the Presbyterian bodies, and in the Synod some forty candidates were ordained to the ministry. In the New England States, indeed, the year 1778 marks the highest point reached by Presbyterian growth, and the following decade the beginnings of decay, as but one new church was organized, while several were dissolved; and in 1782 the Synod of New England, in view of its " broken circumstances," was dissolved to form a Presbytery.

In 1781 the Synod of New York and Philadelphia organized the Presbytery of Redstone in western Pennsylvania. When the Treaty of Paris in 1762 threw open this region to undisputed settlement, the Scotch-Irish had poured across the Alleghany ranges to and beyond what is now the Ohio line. In 1766 Charles Beatty—who as a young Irish peddler had startled William Tennent at Neshaminy by offering his wares in good Latin—and George Duffield had been sent by Synod to preach to the new settlements and report on their spiritual condition. But not until 1774 was there a minister among them to stay; and two years later John Macmillan accepted a call to this field. He was a man who knew how to convert such a population into a self-supporting community in church matters, by raising up laborers at home. Largely to him and his pupils is it due that this became the most Presbyterian region of the whole country, and the most conservative in its influence on the church at large. Yet by 1781 there were but four ministers in the Redstone Presbytery, which, like Hanover, was to be a mother of Presbyteries. Not until 1790 was the first house of worship erected, congregations meeting in the woods in summer, and in private houses in winter. In 1782 Matthew Henderson, of the Associate Presbytery, settled in this region, and gathered several small congregations, who were to share in the troubles which attended the union with the Covenanters.

With the return of peace in 1783 the ecclesiastical relations of America took a new aspect. The demand was now made for absolute religious equality, such as existed in Rhode Island and Pennsylvania; and it was secured by degrees. The battle was hardest in Virginia, where the Presbytery of Hanover took the lead in demanding it, and was vigorously supported by the Baptists. The doctrine that religion needs nothing from the state but a general protection was now enunciated in terms which would have shocked the Westminster Assembly, who " did crie down " Thomas Goodwin's plea for a general toleration. The colonial system lasted longest in New England, where the " standing order " was abolished in Connecticut in 1816, and in Massachusetts in 1833.

One effect of ecclesiastical independence was the termination of the monopoly of printing the English Bible, which had been vested in the king's printers in London. The Continental Congress first proposed to have an edition printed under its auspices, and failing in that for want of type, ordered the importation of a large quantity. In 1782 Robert Aitken, of Philadelphia, an elder in the Associate Church, brought out an edition, which both Congress and Synod commended to the public.

As the ties were now severed which connected the Protestant churches of America with those of Europe, we find a general movement toward their organization as national churches. The Episcopal Church, no longer especially favored by law and influence in high places, now obtained bishops not only without opposition, but with the friendly coöperation of other Americans. The Dutch and German Reformed churches established General Synods, and declared their independence of foreign judicatories. The Methodist societies in 1784 cast off the personal control still claimed by John Wesley over all who bore the name. The Congregationalist churches of New England began to draw together into General Associations for each State, after the Connecticut model. The Separate, the Free-Will and some other branches of the Baptists began to organize into general conferences. The Roman Catholics made their first approach to a national organization by the consecration of John Carroll as Bishop of Baltimore.

The Presbyterians felt a similar impulse. It was shown first in the attempt to consolidate the two conservative bodies, the Covenanters and the Seceders. As the former promptly acknowledged the new government of the United States, and thus ceased to be " an anti-government party," it was felt that the chief obstacle to their fellowship with the Seceders had been removed. As early as 1777 a conference on the subject was begun. The Covenanters, however, had embraced a theory of civil government and its direct dependence on Christ's mediatorial headship, which justified their previous attitude toward the government of Great Britain, and this they now showed no disposition to abandon. As one of them said : " You may agree to what propositions you please, but I will agree to none but with this interpretation—that all that power and ability civil rulers have are from Christ, the Prophet of the Covenant of grace, and that all that food and raiment mankind enjoy are from Christ, the Priest of the Covenant." To these positions the Associate Presbytery of Pennsylvania refused their assent; but in 1780 the much smaller Presbytery of New York came to terms of union. Through the influence of one of its members, Robert Annan, of Wallkill, the question was called up again in the other Presbytery, and a union carried in the meeting of June, 1782, by the casting vote of the moderator, James Proudfit, thus constituting the Associate Reformed Church of America. The minority of two ministers and four elders protested, and appealed to the Scotch Associate Synod; but the majority refused, with some reason, to admit an appeal to a foreign judicature. The appeal, however, was carried to the Scotch Synod, which in 1785 recognized the protesters as the Associate Presbytery of Pennsylvania, and sent them, in Thomas Beveridge and James Anderson, able assistants, to rebuild the denomination. The latter, in 1784, prepared by direction of Presbytery their " Testimony for the Doctrine and Order of the Church of Christ," to which subscription was required. As the Scotch Reformed Presbytery equally refused to recognize the union, and took steps in 1789 to reconstitute their American churches, the transaction resulted in adding another to the number of Presbyterian subdivisions, as indeed had been predicted by some who opposed it. It did, however, establish an intermediate body between the strict conservatives and the Presbyterian Synod, and thus helped to an approach from each side. The Associate Reformed Church, indeed, had been formed out of very conservative elements, but on the principle of distinguishing between lesser and greater, essentials and inessentials, in the matters which had been reasons for division. And this character it always retained.

A complaint from the Reformed Dutch Classis of New Brunswick having opened the question of the mutual relation of the American churches of the Reformed faith and order, the Synod of New York and Philadelphia took advantage of it to secure a conference on " matters of general utility and friendship." This was extended afterward to include the Associate Reformed Synod in the conference, and to cover the suggestion of "a plan for some kind of union among them." The conference was held in October, 1785, and was free, full, and friendly, but led to nothing more than a plan for annual conferences by delegates, like that with the Connecticut Association before the war.

One obstacle to any immediate action was the prospect of an extensive change in the constitution of the Presbyterian Church. It was felt that it had outgrown an arrangement which required or assumed the attendance of the whole body of ministers at a single point, and that much was to be gained by the union of neighboring Presbyteries in subordinate synods. By erecting a delegated General Assembly, subdivided into Synods, as these were into Presbyteries, the American church would also more distinctly announce its new standing as a national church, ready to take under its care those who sought its communion in every part of the country.

The first step was taken by the Synod of 1786, which adopted a plan for rearranging the bounds of the Presbyteries. This increased their number from twelve to sixteen, and grouped these into four Synods, with a proviso as to the number of ministers and of ruling elders each Presbytery should elect annually to the General Assembly of the Presbyterian Church in the United States of America.

This Synod also ordered the preparation of "a book of discipline and government . . . accommodated to the state of the Presbyterian Church in America" by a committee of which Witherspoon was chairman, and Macwhorter, Rodgers, Duffield, Sproat, Robert Smith, Alison, and Ewing were the clerical members. For nearly a century the method of transmitting grave constitutional questions "in overture" to the Presbyteries had been in use in the Kirk of Scotland, but had not been adopted by the American Synod, as it was not a delegated body. The committee, however, were instructed to distribute three hundred copies of their Plan among the Presbyteries, and every Presbytery was required to "report its observations in writing" to the Synod of 1787. In that Synod a session was assigned for hearing these "observations": but the minutes have no record of their purport, or even of their being actually read, except that those of the Presbytery of Baltimore were presented and heard the next morning. We have no means, therefore, of ascertaining the degree of unanimity with which the Plan was received by the Presbyteries, nor could their "observations" amount to a direct vote on its acceptance or rejection. The committee itself was not quite unanimous. Dr. Matthew Wilson, although of the Old Side by training and conviction, offered a substitute which would have established congregational instead of "classical" Presbyteries. The Presbytery of Suffolk (Long Island) proposed to separate from the church, on the ground that the Plan was impracticable, and its churches would not comply with it; but it was persuaded to withdraw the proposal.

The Synod discussed the Plan in detail, made important alterations, and ordered the distribution of a thousand copies, as amended, among the Presbyteries, "for their consideration, and the consideration of the churches under their care." In the next Synod we hear of three memorials from congregations, but none from Presbyteries. After a full discussion and further amendment, the whole Plan,— embracing the Confession of Faith (amended in the matter of the civil magistrate's relation to the church), the Longer Catechism (with an amendment as to toleration), the Shorter Catechism, the Directory for Worship (radically altered and not for the better), and a Form of Government and Discipline,—was adopted and ratified finally, by what majority the minutes do not say. This final vote was taken in a Synod of thirty-five ministers and eight elders. One hundred and thirty-six ministers entitled and expected to be present were not so; and some four hundred church sessions had no ruling elder to represent them. The language of the minutes, " as now altered and amended," indicates that what was finally voted upon differed from both the first draft sent to the Presbyteries in 1786, and the revised draft sent to the Presbyteries and churches in 1787. Dr. Ashbel Green says that " many articles of the constitution as finally sanctioned remained as then agreed upon." But even the name of the General Assembly was settled in the Synod of 1788.

Yet it was enacted not only that " the Form of Government and Discipline and the Confession of Faith " should be that of the church, but that they should " continue to be our constitution and the confession of our faith and practice unalterable, unless two thirds of the Presbyteries under the care of the General Assembly shall propose alterations or amendments, and such alterations or amendments shall be agreed to and enacted by the General Assembly." Attempts to lay bonds upon the future by constitutional enactment are a weakness characteristic of Americans. But never was the attempt made by a body possessed of less prescriptive right to do so; and in this case no more was forbidden than that a national church should freely give utterance to its actual faith in authoritative form!

It has been claimed that this Presbyterian form of government was the model after which that of the United States was formed. The same claim, I believe, has been put forward for every other form of church government then in existence in America. The Synod of 1787 certainly was debating and amending the report of Witherspoon and his associates, at the time when the Constitutional Convention was discussing in the same city the best form for a new government of the country. Alexander Hamilton, James Madison, and James Wilson, the three leading debaters of the Convention, although none of them Presbyterians, may well have been familiar with the Scottish methods. And a certain vague resemblance exists between Congress, legislature, and county government on the one side, and Assembly, Synod, and Presbytery on the other. There, however, the likeness ends. These ecclesiastical bodies are not legislatures, but only courts for the interpretation of law. The legal background, also, of Presbyterian procedure is the Scottish law, which in turn rests on the Civil Law of Rome. That of the American constitution is the Common Law of England, which always was most jealous of any intrusion of the Civil Law. Each of the superior courts of the Presbyterian system possesses an authority over the lower, which the States never have conceded to the national Government. And, lastly, the democratic element in the American Constitution has no real correspondent in the Presbyterian system. Its permanent eldership, and its parochial bishops, with seats or representation in its church courts even when they have no pastoral charge, are aristocratic rather than democratic. This last practice, I may add, is unknown to the Reformed churches of Europe.

The one feature in the Constitution of the United States, which suggests a Presbyterian influence, is the method of amendment by reference to and consent of the States. This, however, was not yet in use in the American church when the Constitution was drafted. If copied at all, it must have been directly from the constitution of the Kirk of Scotland, into which it was introduced by the Barrier Act of 1695.

It is not by any external copying of features that the two plans of government are related. It is through both being the fruit of the same great national impulse to give the social life its complete expression by a polity of national dimensions and spirit.

It is not in the field of political but in that of ecclesiastical life that the Presbyterian method of synodical government attains a significance far wider than the reach of the denomination. The Presbyterian Synod of colonial times stood entirely alone. It was the only instance in which the collective wisdom and discretion of the whole body was brought to bear continuously upon the affairs of an American church. The Congregationalist churches of Connecticut, indeed, had made an approach to synodical government, but this was confined to the State. If to-day the interests and affairs of every great Protestant denomination in the land are in the hands of conference, convention, or synod of some sort, meeting periodically, and with ministerial and lay members voting equally, it may fairly be claimed that all have walked in the footsteps of the Presbyterians whose Synod is the ancestor of all these no less than of the General Assembly itself.

CHAPTER VII.

REVIVAL AND DISSENSION, 1789–1810.

GREAT as always has been the influence of the Presbyterian Church on the religious life of the country, it probably at no time has been so dominant as in the closing years of the eighteenth century. The Puritan churches were localized in New England, with a growing consciousness of their distinctness, as a group of churches and of States, from the rest of the country. The Episcopal Church, which had gone into the War for Independence one of the strongest, had come out one of the weakest, through taking the wrong side. It had lost heavily by disendowment, by desertions, and by migration to the British colonies of Nova Scotia and Canada; and it was still struggling to bring opposing tendencies into coöperation, and to perfect its own organization. The Methodist Church was still in its feeble infancy, having with Asbury retired to private life during the progress of the struggle. The Baptist churches, although they had gained heavily in both New England and the South as a consequence of the Great Awakening, had achieved their growth mainly among the poor and uneducated classes; and had accepted the ideal of a " lowly ministry " of uneducated men. The German churches were isolated from the rest of the nation by their persistence in the use of a foreign language. The newer sects, Free-Will Baptists, " Christians," Universalists, Unitarians, and Shakers, were great only in their hopes.

The Presbyterian Church was strong in a learned ministry, graduates not only of Princeton but of the Scotch and the New England universities. Its members had borne the brunt of the struggle for independence from the Hudson to the Savannah. It had shared with the Baptists the honor of the struggle for religious equality against Episcopalian privilege in the Southern States, and had sustained it alone in New York and New Jersey. It had the support of the large Scotch-Irish element in the Middle and Southern States, and of the New England overflow westward across the Hudson. It was more homogeneous and harmonious than ever before, the Old Side men and their traditions having died out, and the methods of the Great Awakening having been heartily accepted. It had shown its staying power in maintaining a unique synodical authority over its pastors and people, in holding up the standard of Calvinistic orthodoxy in an age far more alien to that mode of thought than our own, and in extending its missionary labors to newly settled districts. Not only did it flourish in the older States, but the new territories beyond the Appalachian ranges seemed especially its own.

Had the church been able to maintain this position in the nation's religious life, and had it even been able to retain in its membership the children of the great Ulster immigration and to continue to assimilate the New England overflow, it would now take rank, not as the third, but as the first, of the great Protestant communions of America. The ranks of the Baptists and the Methodists, of the Episcopalians and the Disciples, have been swollen at its expense. Of the descendants of the Ulster Presbyterians in America probably not much above a third are to-day Presbyterian. However large the membership and extensive the influence of the church, therefore, it cannot be called successful even in holding its own, much less in aggressive power.

It is in the period now under consideration that the signs of this partial failure are first beginning to show themselves, and at the same time its reasons. The first of these was the scholastic shape in which the doctrines of the church were presented in its confession and catechisms, and the influence of these upon preaching and teaching. Calvinism, as John Duncan well says, is " a sheep in wolf's clothing." It is sure to repel those who for the first time have their attention fixed on such questions, until further thought brings them to see that the difficulties which attend any and every view of God's relation to the moral universe are not to be got rid of by denying man's inmost dependence upon God. There are no truths which require more judicious and guarded statement than these ; and while the Westminster divines were not quite unaware of this, they were far more concerned to guard against logical incompleteness of statement than against the accumulation of what is mere inference of their own logic. In this respect the Scottish " Confession of Faith," drafted by John Knox in 1560, is so much superior, that its supersession by the more elaborate and less popular document was an historical calamity.

A second difficulty in the church's way was the rigidity of her polity in the matter of ministerial education. She was right in setting up a high ideal, and has benefited all the churches of America by this. She was wrong in refusing to recognize that there are times when a higher expediency demands a temporary relaxation of the rule. It was a just requirement for a fairly educated and fully intelligent community, which enjoyed the prosperity and the leisure of a country not newly settled. On the frontier, however, and among those who were enduring the hardships and privations of a new settlement, with but few opportunities for even the simplest education, the rigid exaction of a collegiate education for every candidate for the ministry was a fatal embarrassment. It is true that the Assembly and its Synods maintained a missionary system of some extent, and at times had from forty to fifty ministers and probationers at work in the outlying settlements of the South and the West. But even these were unable to overtake the demand for preachers and pastors, and the Synod of 1783 flatly refused to sanction the licensure of less educated men, a precedent followed by the General Assembly. It judged of the needs of the frontiers by the standard of Philadelphia, and insisted (the people said) on "making men gentlemen before it made them ministers." It thus left its natural adherents to the more adaptable ministrations of the Methodists and the Baptists.

At the same time, at the other extremity, on the New England frontier, the growing rigor of Presbyterian law was tending to alienate the Puritan churches. Ten years even before the adoption of the constitution of 1789 a movement was begun to effect a reorganization of these churches in New Jersey and New York, which should avoid equally the slackness of Congregationalism and the rigidity of Presbyterianism. Between 1780 and 1807 four "Associated Presbyteries" were formed on this footing, with a confession of eighteen articles only, and claiming for Presbytery no more than power to advise the churches under its care. But the movement shared the general fate of eclectic compromises. One principle or the other was sure to get the upper hand. By 1818–20 the Associated Presbyteries were broken up, leaving pastors and churches to find their proper place in either the Congregationalist or the Presbyterian bodies. The significance of the movement was as an indication that there were limits to the coöperation of the Puritan and the Presbyterian elements in the States west of the Hudson, and that the day was coming when "the New England way" would be transplanted to every part of the country.

Yet that day seemed far enough off when the General Assembly and the Connecticut Association adopted the famous Plan of Union in 1801. Its terms showed that the Assembly was not inclined to unreasonable rigidity on this side, possibly because it had taken warning from the establishment of the Associated Presbyteries. It practically made the constituent parts of the two systems interchangeable. Churches of either body might call a pastor from the other, and when any dispute arose the appeal might be to either the Presbytery or a council chosen from both bodies. Presbyterian churches might be represented in Associations by ruling elders and Congregational churches in Presbyteries by messengers chosen in church meeting. A practical test of the spirit in which the Plan was regarded by its authors occurred in 1808, when the Middle Association of Congregationalists in New York State was invited to become a subordinate division of the Synod of Albany, with the approval of the Assembly, and accepted the invitation rather than unite with others to form a State Association.

This "Presbygational" system, as it afterward was nicknamed, received the approval of the Vermont, New Hampshire, and Massachusetts Associations, and had respect especially to the settlement of western New York from New England; but during the half-century that it lasted it was extended to Ohio, and to States still farther west. It brought into the Presbyterian Church a large number of pastors and churches which were more or less in touch with the doctrinal movements of New England, and thus helped to impart to American Presbyterianism that dual character which resulted in the division of 1837.

The severest test to which the Presbyterian order and

doctrine were subjected was associated with the happiest events of this period. From the close of the War for Independence spiritual influences appeared to lose their hold on the popular mind. Unbelief became the fashion of the day. There was a decay of zeal in the churches, and in the eastern part of Massachusetts a rapid spread of Socinianism. The first signs of a change came in 1792, when extensive revivals occurred, especially in western New England. Then the frontier settlements of the new States of Kentucky and Tennessee were deeply moved. Immorality, irreligion, and skepticism abounded in this region. In 1793 the Kentucky legislature voted to dispense with prayers in its sessions. The churches and ministers were few, and fewer still those in whom was manifest " the power of an endless life." From 1798, when the revival began on the Red River, there hardly was a year unblessed; but in 1801 the movement culminated in the Southwest, and reached nearly every part of the country, on a scale which recalls the Great Awakening. The movement overflowed the limits of the places of stated worship, and took an open-air character, which recalled the labors of Whitefield and his associates. To meet the needs of a scattered population great " camp meetings " were held at central places— the first of their kind. At these the lasting conversions were many, but the infectious influence of excitements upon great multitudes found unhappy illustrations. Especially in the frontier communities of the Southwest, where the Scotch-Irish were the chief settlers, the tension of newly awakened feeling was so great as to lead to manifold extravagances and nervous disturbances, resulting in convulsive physical movements, the " falling exercise," " the jerks," and so forth. In some cases hundreds were flung prostrate, like a grain-field swept by a hurricane, or the ground was torn up by their convulsive stampings.

While Presbyterians were in the majority among both preachers and people, the Methodists also were on the ground. The former generally labored to check and restrain these physical manifestations; the latter are said to have encouraged them as a means of grace. The believers in predestination insisted on rational conviction as essential to a right conversion. The believers in freewill accepted as satisfactory conversions effected by processes which set both will and reason aside in trances or in physical convulsions. The hunger for preaching went far beyond the power of the ministers to meet it. Laymen, even children, were heard eagerly, and with powerful effect.

In these circumstances the Presbytery of Transylvania, and then the Cumberland Presbytery, which in 1802 had been set off from it, took the step of licensing as preachers a number of zealous young men, who neither had obtained the required amount of academic training nor were able to give an entire assent to the teaching of the Westminster Confession, especially on the subjects of predestination and perseverance. Against this course a minority of the Cumberland Presbytery protested and appealed to the Synod of Kentucky, which took the unfortunate step of empowering a commission to deal with the case. This body assumed to itself powers and performed acts which the General Assembly of 1807 declared to be " at least of questionable regularity." It suspended the majority of the Presbytery and all its licentiates. The Synod stood by its commission and went still further. But the Presbytery compromised its case by refusing to appeal in due form to the General Assembly, although this course was suggested twice by the Assembly itself, which disclaimed the possession of original jurisdiction. This, together with the manifest irregularities in its proceedings, so much weakened its friends in the Assembly of 1809 as to lead to an acceptance of the

Synod's explanations as fully satisfactory. A year later the Presbytery had become a separate denomination, which grew rapidly in numbers, in sobriety of method, and in demand for an educated ministry. The Synod of Cumberland, organized in 1813, the next year adopted a revision of the Westminster Confession, from which "fatalism," or what it judged such, was eliminated. Thus was constituted the left wing of American Presbyterianism, the Cumberland Presbyterian Church.

The conservative bodies on the right wing were growing steadily in numbers and influence.

(1) The Reformed Presbytery, reconstituted in 1798, obtained some notable accessions of the younger generation. One of these, Alexander McLeod, in 1800 declined a call to a New York church on the ground that some of its members were slave-holders. This at once fixed attention upon the subject, and the Presbytery required that the members of the church should emancipate their slaves. This decision was conveyed to the churches in the South by James McKinney and Samuel B. Wylie, and with a single exception the membership complied with it. By 1809 the Presbytery had become a Synod, and the three local "committees" into which it had been divided became Presbyteries. As reorganized the body dissented from the Constitution of the United States on the ground that it contained no recognition of the mediatorial authority of Christ over the nations; and its membership therefore abstained from voting. In exposition of these views they published a doctrinal and historical Testimony in 1806.

(2) The Associate Presbytery (or Seceders) had grown by immigration in both the Middle and the Southern States, and in 1801 a Synod was organized in subordination to the General Synod in Scotland—a relation not terminated until 1818. In James Anderson, of western Pennsylvania,

whom they elected professor of theology in 1792, they found an able and laborious, though somewhat tedious, trainer of their ministry. With them also the question of slavery was brought up in 1800, and again in 1808, by memorials. The Associate Synod, however, did not adopt the heroic remedy the Reformed Presbytery had applied. They, in 1811, advised emancipation, but left open an alternative, which deprived the act of much of its force.

(3) The Associate Reformed Church, formed by the union of 1780–82, was growing more rapidly than either of these bodies. To the three Presbyteries the Synod embraced was added, in 1794, the Presbytery of Londonderry, embracing most of the Presbyterian churches that were left in New England. But within a year after this union the Synod began to hear unsatisfactory reports of the behavior of these churches in the matter of their Psalmody, and their communion with other churches and Christians. As no satisfaction was obtained on this point, the Synod in 1801 " disclaimed all responsibility " for the New England Presbytery. The same year witnessed a secession in the other direction. The Synod had refused to publish a " subordinate Testimony," and had adopted the Westminster Confession and Catechisms with qualifying declarations as to the jurisdiction of the civil magistrate in matters of religion. On this and like accounts two ministers withdrew, and organized in 1801 the Reformed Dissenting Presbytery, which perpetuated its existence for more than half a century. The body was called the Warwickites, from the more influential of the two. The next year the Synod made provision for the election of a General Synod, with four provincial Synods. This scheme proved too elaborate and cumbersome for the strength of the church, and had the further effect of isolating the subdivisions from each other. The eastern wing of the church,

led by the eloquent John M. Mason, of New York, diverged from the West and the South, and approximated the position of the General Assembly.

It is only from the statistics the General Assembly began to append to its minutes that we are able to obtain an idea of the rate at which the main body of Presbyterians grew. Those of 1789 show a total of 419 churches with 177 ordained ministers and 11 probationers. The returns for the following years are all defective, until we reach 1798 and 1799. In the latter year we find the Presbyteries have grown from 17 to 25, with 449 churches, served by 266 ministers and 35 licentiates. The reports are again defective until 1803, when the ingatherings from the great revival are indicated in 31 Presbyteries and 511 churches, supplied by 322 ministers and 48 licentiates. It was after 1807 that the report of communicants is attempted, but always with from 2 to 9 Presbyteries marked as having made " no report." The minutes of 1810, the last of the present period, show that 32 of the 36 Presbyteries reported 28,901 communicants gathered in 772 churches, and supplied by 434 ordained ministers and 51 licentiates.

The extent to which the churches outnumbered the ministers and licentiates suggested strenuous efforts, to which the Assembly called the Presbyteries, to increase the number of candidates. It was from the Presbytery of Philadelphia that the suggestion came for the establishment of a theological school. The work of circulating good books had been promoted even in colonial times. By a pamphlet called " Glad Tidings," describing the widespread revivals, and by establishing an " Assembly's Magazine," the church now entered the field of publication on its own account, while it formally approved of new editions of the Scriptures, and of the formation of Bible Societies. It declined to adopt the program of immediate, compulsory emancipation of the slaves held by its own members ; but it repeated its disapproval of slavery, and gladly welcomed to the ministry two colored men, who labored among their own people. It required its home missionaries not to neglect the Indians in their fields of labor, and found in Gideon Blackburn, of Tennessee, a worthy successor to the Brainards, in his labors among the Cherokees (1792–1810).

Besides the differences growing out of the revivals in the Southwest, the church had few matters of dispute to distract it. Adam Rankin came across the Alleghanies to convince the Assembly of 1789 of the wrongfulness of allowing Watts to supersede Rouse in the matter of Psalmody, and went back to cast in his lot with the Associate Reformed Church in Kentucky, and to give them also trouble enough. In 1802 Dr. Dwight's enlargement and revision of Watts, with an appendix of hymns, was adopted by the Assembly without resistance.

The only doctrinal discussions of the time grew out of the influence of the views of theology put forward by Dr. Samuel Hopkins, of Newport, in 1793. In 1798 Hezekiah Balch, of Greenville, Tenn., was heard on appeal from the Synod of the Carolinas ; and while the Assembly, on hearing his explanations, exonerated him from the charge of heresy, it yet had admonished him for making " disinterested benevolence " the test of a gracious state, and for failing to trace our innate depravity to our membership in a fallen race. These well-known points of Hopkinsian teaching he had absorbed during a visit to New England, which he took to raise funds for Greenville College. He submitted himself to the admonition of the Assembly, but remained a Hopkinsian to his death, as was his associate and successor in the college's presidency, Dr. Charles Coffin, and others.

CHAPTER VIII.

THE ERA OF NEW METHODS, 1810–30.

IT was not until some twenty years after the organization of the General Assembly that the methods of practical administration were really adjusted. There were years of outreaching and of experiment in various directions, under the influence of a spirit which was at work in every branch of the Presbyterian brotherhood, in the other Protestant churches of America, and in the churches, both established and free, of Great Britain. It was indeed in these last that the first steps in the new direction were taken, and from thence that the new methods of procedure made their way to America.

The Great Awakening, which all these churches had shared, was characterized by a disposition to subordinate everything to immediate practical efficiency. It rearranged the theology of Protestantism in a new perspective of doctrines, with reference to the conversion of sinners, laying stress upon those points only which seemed to contribute to that end. Much more in the field of practical administration it placed no value upon traditional methods or principles, when newer plans of action promised larger results. The authority of bishops, the independency of local churches, and the initiative of Synods and Presbyteries alike must yield to this; or else see those who once had accepted the new maxims form themselves into entirely new communions, in which the principle of immediate utility dominated all methods. Those who clung to the older communions, but acquiesced in the new ideas, compromised by setting up a new order alongside the old, and working the two in such harmony as was attainable.

The Presbyterian Church had to give up less in yielding to the new demands than did either of the two rival systems. It placed its aggressive work, indeed, in the hands of boards chosen annually, and administered by permanent officials—the method with which we now are so familiar, but which seemed so novel a century ago. It allowed these to adopt the policy of big meetings, with eloquent speakers to enforce the claims of the annual report upon audiences heated by eloquence. But by keeping the selection of these boards in the hands of the church's courts, it avoided the evils of a nominally popular election, by which a few persons might perpetuate indefinitely their tenure of office. To this extent the stricter Presbyterians were right in their preference for boards thus created and controlled, to those created by voluntary societies—a preference which became one of the fighting issues of the approaching era of division. A thoroughly effective board, however, must take responsibilities of action which are not reconcilable with the authority of initiative which our theory of church government vests in the General Assembly.

It was the inception of missions to the heathen, so long neglected by the Protestant churches, which introduced the new method. In America this began with the organization of the American Board of Commissioners of Foreign Missions in 1810, by the Congregationalists of Massachusetts, in response to the desire of certain candidates for the ministry, to be sent to the foreign field. The General Assembly in 1812 commended the Board to the support of its churches, and afterward refused to establish a Foreign Mission Board of its own, although urged to do so by the American Board itself. Within the church, and in coöperation with the members of kindred churches, were formed local missionary societies. These, however, confined their labors to the pagan Indians of our own country; and in 1826 even these were consolidated with the American Board.

Parallel with this rise of foreign missions, there arose a new interest in the work of home missions. The valley of the Mississippi was now open to white settlement, and the first settlers were giving painful illustration of the influence of such a migration on moral habits and feeble Christian character. In 1813 Samuel J. Mills, who had held with two others the prayer-meeting under the haystack in the meadow near Williams College, which led to the formation of the American Board, and who had been debarred from the foreign field by ill-health, visited the new settlements, in company with John F. Schermerhorn, to investigate and report upon their condition. Their account of the profanity, drunkenness, gambling, and indifference they witnessed was an eloquent and effective appeal to the Calvinistic churches, leading to the organization of home missionary societies, and to the transfer of the General Assembly's home mission work to a Board of Home Missions, with ampler powers, in 1816. It was now seen that steps must be taken to occupy the home field more effectively than had been done by sending out a few itinerants, to spread their labors over a wide field, and to form small churches, which soon perished of neglect.

Another department of home mission work was entered in 1819 by the establishment of the Board of Education. This was the time of the rise of the great national societies: the American Bible Society, organized by delegates of local societies in 1816; the American Sunday-school Union in 1824, and the American Tract Society in 1825. In the smaller Presbyterian churches home missionary work was still conducted by purely synodical methods, and none of them engaged as yet in foreign missions; but individuals, such as Dr. Alexander Proudfit, gave support to the American Board.

Hardly less important in its effects was the change now begun in the education of the church's ministry. In the colonial period such training as was given in addition to the academic course of study was generally obtained by the candidate's residence at the home of a working pastor of recognized theological attainments. It was chiefly instruction in dogmatic theology by the preparation of prescribed essays and sermons, and practical training in pastoral work in the homes of the minister's people. In New England, pastors like Joseph Bellamy and Nathaniel Emmons were especially sought out. The next step in the Presbyterian churches was to designate a fit man to exercise such oversight, and to pay him a small salary in recognition of his additional toil, rather than in compensation for it. So the Reformed Dutch Church selected Dr. John Livingston, of New York, in 1784; the Associate Presbyterian Church in 1792 appointed Dr. John Anderson, of Beaver County, Pa.; the Associate Reformed Church secured Dr. John M. Mason, of New York, in 1804, and gave him a colleague in 1809; and the Reformed Presbyterian Church appointed Dr. Samuel B. Wylie, of Philadelphia, in 1808. In the Presbyterian Church, study under pastors, especially those who, like Tennent and Blair, had founded classical academies, came first. After Witherspoon's acceptance of the presidency at Princeton in 1768, the occupant of that office was expected and paid to give instruction in sacred literature and in theology. But men of eminence as pastors and teachers, like Robert Smith, of Pequa, continued to attract students for preparation in theology.

The insufficiency of both means to meet the rapidly increasing demand for ministers was felt especially after the great revivals of 1799–1804; and the notable success of the Congregationalist seminary recently established at Andover suggested a new step. The president of Princeton College, it was found, could spare but two hours a week to carry his students of theology over the entire field. In 1809 the General Assembly submitted to the Presbyteries a plan to establish either one, two, or several theological schools. As many of the Presbyteries having voted generally for a single school, as for any other plan, steps were taken for its endowment, and in 1812 Dr. Archibald Alexander, a native of Virginia, who had first suggested the plan to the Assembly, and had left the presidency of Hampden-Sidney College for a Philadelphia pastorate, was called to be the first professor of theology, with nine students. Next year Dr. Samuel Miller was associated with him, as professor of ecclesiastical history and church government; and in 1820 Charles Hodge was employed to teach Hebrew and Greek, becoming professor of oriental and biblical literature in 1822. The seminary owed much, in its inception and early years, to the gifts and efforts of devout women in the church.

As the Middle States were still comparatively poor, and as New England was occupied with the endowment of Andover Seminary and its struggling colleges, it was hard to get an endowment for Princeton. Devout women not a few gave and collected for this purpose. John Seargent gave a fortnight's fees, and others contributed up to the measure of their ability.

The Assembly having left the Synods free to establish synodical seminaries, if they chose, the Synod of Virginia established Union Seminary at Hampden-Sidney, with one professor and an instructor; and in 1828 it obtained the support of the Synod of North Carolina. In 1821 Auburn Seminary was opened, under control of the Synod of Geneva, with its three professorships, filled by James Richards, M. L. R. Perrine, and Henry Mills. Rather on the old footing of the colonial academy was the Southern and Western Theological Seminary, set on foot by Isaac Anderson, at Maryville, Tenn., a man equally great as teacher and preacher, and Hopkinsian in his views of theology. The theological seminaries at Columbia in South Carolina (1828), and Alleghany in western Pennsylvania (1826), were synodical institutions.

This new method of training ministers represented both a loss and a gain. It could not secure that direct familiarity with the pastor's work among his people which was possible in what we may call the clerical apprenticeship of the older method. It also made it possible for the teachers to become scholastic and abstract in their methods, as working pastors were not likely to be. And by concentrating the whole work of training the ministry in the hands of a few closely associated scholars, it created the opportunity to stamp the peculiarities of some single mind upon the teaching of the church at large, so as to narrow its range of theological thought to one or a few types, and exaggerate some points of doctrinal teaching far beyond their true importance. The gain was in the greater thoroughness with which the scientific parts of theology could be mastered and imparted by teachers set free from other labors, and with the field of theology shared between several. At the same time this opened vistas of grave possibilities as to the effect of the investigations of theological science upon minds pledged to teach the views formulated in the standards of the church.

It was again the problem of clerical education that developed those differences between the two elements in the personal composition of the Presbyterian Church which afterward led to their disunion. The spiritual needs of the colored people had suggested in 1818 the establishment of an "African School" to train preachers of their own color. The proposal to place its teachers under the same special pledge to the standards, as is given by professors in Princeton Seminary, was resisted by the New England element which controlled the Synods adjacent to those States. And this disagreement probably caused its suspension in 1826.

Parallel with the new departure in ministerial education was a general effort to increase the number of theological students. The General Assembly urged the Presbyteries to press the claims of the work upon gracious young men. To aid needy students two education societies were formed, one to coöperate with the American Education Society, centered in Boston, and the other to act under the authority of the General Assembly. The former proposed to assist young men during their academic career only, giving as a reason that the church was too much divided on doctrinal questions to allow of united action as regards theological training! This only could mean dissatisfaction with the theological character of Princeton, as representing a Calvinism unaffected by the "improvements" which Edwards, Hopkins, and Emmons had introduced in New England.

At this time the especial views of Dr. Samuel Hopkins, of Newport, enjoyed a great vogue in both New England and the adjacent States. Samuel Whelpley, of New York, defended them with great vigor and some acrimony in "The Triangle" (1816); Edward Dorr Griffin, at Newark (1801–09), Gardiner Spring of the Brick Church, in New York, Samuel Hanson Cox, a young convert from Quakerism, and others, held them. James Richards, who succeeded Griffin in Newark, and was afterward professor of theology in the seminary at Auburn, erected in 1819 by those who thought Princeton too narrow, was rather an Edwardean than a Hopkinsian, and dissented strongly from the peculiar views of Dr. Emmons, which he found prevalent in western New York.

Equally decided, but in different degrees, was the opposition to this Hopkinsian drift. Dr. Ezra Stiles Ely, a New Englander, but then a hospital chaplain in New York, made himself the spokesman of extreme opposition by his " Contrast between Calvinism and Hopkinsianism " (New York, 1811), whose sharpness gave offense even in Philadelphia. He was called in 1813 to succeed Dr. Archibald Alexander in the Pine Street Church, but his settlement was resisted by a strong minority, which after a time withdrew to form a Sixth Church.

In 1817 the Synod of Pennsylvania, in a Pastoral Letter composed by Dr. Ely, congratulated the churches on the vigor shown by its Presbyteries in " resisting the introduction of Arian, Socinian, Arminian, and Hopkinsian heresies, which are some of the means by which the enemy of souls would, if possible, deceive the very elect." The stigma thus affixed to a school whom Dr. Ashbel Green had described to Mr. Balch as " the most laborious students, faithful pastors, successful preachers, and instructive writers in all New England," arrested the attention of the committee on the records of that Synod, and they reported a commendation of its zeal with an expression of regret that it had been " manifested in such a manner as to be offensive to other denominations." This was due probably to the chairman of the committee, Dr. Samuel Miller, whose friendship for Dr. Griffin did not prevent his being a decided opponent of what Dr. Rice called " those Hopkinsian crudities." It is said that he had suggested to Dr. Ely the writing of the " Contrast," but regretted the tone he took.   In his view, which time has justified, the Hopkinsian peculiarities were a temporary phase of thought, which at last would vanish into the limbo of forgotten theories.   He believed that more was to be gained by courteous discussion and patience than by judicial condemnations.   There were those who differed from this Gamaliel-like policy, and two protests against the report received the signatures of twelve of the one hundred and one members of that Assembly.

As has been pointed out by Dr. Augustus Strong, the root of all the theological peculiarities of New England theology, from Hooker and Sheppard to our own times, may be traced to the extravagant individualism which has characterized her social and intellectual life.   These short-lived " improvements " of the Calvinistic theology were but so many attempts to bring Calvinism into harmony with a principle which found its final expression in Emerson's " supremacy of the individual conscience " over all law and all forms of institutions.   In her opposition to congregational independency and her maintenance of synodical authority, the Presbyterian Church held to the principle of an organic social life in both the race and the church.   And the instinct which led her to regard these " improvements " with repugnance was historically just and theologically sound.   Here again, however, we must regret that the Westminster standards, as adopting the Covenant or " Federal " theology of the Cocceian school, presented the opposite principle in an inadequate and extremely artificial shape, and represented the primal unity of the race, and that of the redeemed with Christ, as a forensic fiction rather than a spiritual reality.   Nor did the Princeton theology at any time rise to a perception of the difference between the form of statement found in the standards and the principle really at stake.   Among the

Covenanters, who cherished the older traditions of Scottish Calvinism, there was complaint that Princeton mistook theologic fact for forensic fiction, and laid no stress on the dignity of the Saviour as the living head of his redeemed people, in explaining the connection of his righteousness with their salvation.[1]

More easy and unresisted was the encroachment of Puritan individualism in the practical life of the church. The New England men among its ministry brought with them elements of the Independent conception of the church, which differed widely from historic Presbyterianism, but which have nearly replaced it. Their demand for "a regenerate church-membership" not only set aside "the judgment of charity" of the Reformed churches, but introduced the fashion of speaking of the adult communicants as the only "members of the church," and of treating its baptized children as outside pagans, exempt even from its discipline. For the Presbyterian usage of baptizing the children of the baptized came in the Congregationalist rule that baptism should be confined to the children of communicants, i.e., of those who could give credible evidence of their conversion. Thus Dr. Gardiner Spring, on coming from New England to the pastorate of the Brick Church, set aside the usage established by Dr. Rodgers, Dr. McKnight, and Dr. Samuel Miller, and confined baptism to "those children one of whose parents was a professed Christian."[2] From the same root grew the

[1] See Dr. S. B. Wylie in "The American Christian Expositor," vol. i., pp. 419–425, and pp. 445–453. One of Dr. Wylie's former students had been challenged for his views on this point on applying for admission to the Presbyterian ministry, but had been admitted after explanations.

[2] See his "Life and Times," New York, 1865, vol. i., pp. 124–126. Dr. Spring appeals to the language of the Confession and the Longer Catechism as justifying this restriction. But his eminent predecessors in the pastorate had interpreted the language of the standards in accordance with the historic sense; he, in accordance with the language of the Great Awakening. Dr. Charles Hodge always stood by the older interpretation.

practice of establishing elaborate covenants and articles of belief in each congregation, to which every member was asked to give assent, instead of receiving them on a confession of the simplest essentials of Christian faith. The requirement was natural enough among Congregationalists, but manifestly out of harmony with Presbyterianism.

Besides these in the more public aspects of the church, there were important changes in the Congregational life of this time. The position of the ministry became less separate and formal. Even late in the eighteenth century they commonly appeared on the streets in their black gowns. In 1795, and probably later, they wore them on their way to church on Sundays. Dr. Milledoller speaks of passing Dr. Samuel Miller frequently on Sunday mornings, " both dressed in full canonicals, not omitting the three-cornered hat," and says they were called " the boy ministers." With the new century the gown was laid aside on the street, and gradually disused even in the pulpit—a symbol of the abandonment of that position of factitious reverence which the ministry had occupied. In 1801 Dr. Archibald Alexander, on a visit to New England, knew he had crossed the Connecticut State line and had entered Rhode Island from the cessation of all public deference to his ministerial character. The manners of Rhode Island were now to become national.

The labors of the ministry were arduous. Intolerance of read sermons compelled the practice of memorizing after writing, and public taste exacted a stately and elaborate style, such as John M. Mason and Edward Dorr Griffin especially exemplified, from the occupants of important pastoral charges. Long, even life-long pastorates were still the rule, and changes the exception, so that the preacher commonly spent his whole labor on a single flock, and had no opportunity to use old material in a new

pulpit. Official visitation at least twice a year was expected of them. And while the general introduction of
Sunday-schools during this period somewhat lightened
their labors among the young of their flock, where the
older tradition lingered they were expected to meet and
catechize the children of their charge every week on
Wednesday or on Saturday, with the help of some of the
elders, or, if she were a notable woman, of the pastor's
wife. The Lord's Supper was administered four times
a year; and the Edwardean test for communicants, once
rejected even by Gilbert Tennent, now came into very
general acceptance. People came not so much to get
grace, as to profess that they had got it. At the same
time the Zwinglian theory of a simple commemoration
became more common, and reliance was placed simply
upon "the hallowed associations" of the rite, and its
adaptation for enforcing truth by a striking symbol.

Between the General Assembly and the other Presbyterian bodies, except the Cumberland Presbyterians, the
breach was now complete in the matter of Psalmody.
These others still clung to the use of the Scotch Psalter
of 1649, and made the use of uninspired hymns a ground
for refusing communion. In spite of repeated efforts
toward a better collection, Dr. Dwight's "Psalms and
Hymns" remained the only book the churches of the
General Assembly were allowed to substitute for the
Scotch Psalter until 1831. It contained the whole of Dr.
Dwight's revision of Dr. Watts's Psalms.

Of the smaller Presbyterian bodies, the Associate Reformed Church had the most memorable history during
this time. From the first its origin, though a union on
the principle of preferring essentials to lesser peculiarities,
seemed to affect its position and tendencies. The leadership of Dr. John M. Mason corresponded to this initiative.

In 1811 we find the General Synod treating Psalmody as a question for forbearance rather than strictness; and five years later Dr. Mason's "Plea for Sacramental Union on Catholic Principles" showed how far he had advanced toward a comprehensive Presbyterianism. In 1820 the General Synod received overtures for a union from the General Assembly. This was accepted by a small majority at the next session, although it had been voted down in the Presbyteries, and the union thus irregularly agreed to was consummated. Three Presbyteries only united with the General Assembly; but among the ministers received were John M. Mason, Erskine Mason, George Junkin, and William Engles. In the meantime the stricter Presbyteries and churches of the West had withdrawn from the General Synod, and organized a Synod of the West, and even opened negotiations for union with the Associate Church; and in 1821 the Presbyteries and churches of the South had seceded chiefly because of the hostility to slavery shown by the Northern part of the church. Even the Synod of New York perpetuated its organization, retaining most of its churches and ministers, and finally, in 1836, recovering the library of the Newburg Seminary, which had been removed to Princeton after the union of 1822. The seminary itself was resuscitated in 1829, while the Western Synod had established another at Pittsburg in 1825.

The Associate Church, which became independent of the Scottish Synod in 1818, moved on more quietly, extending its membership South and West by home mission labors. Although slavery was declared "a moral evil" in 1811, slave-holders were not debarred from communion until 1830. In 1825 it issued a special testimony against Unitarianism and Hopkinsianism, describing the latter as a revival of Pelagianism. It declined a union with even the stricter Associate Reformed Synod of the West, standing until 1840 by the unaltered Westminster Confession and its doctrine of the civil magistrate, while rejecting the " political dissent " which the Covenanters had first adopted toward the government of Great Britain and now applied to that of America.

Among the Covenanters themselves there was not entire harmony on this point, and what there was tended to diminish as time went on. During the War of 1812–15 Dr. Alexander MacLeod was the foremost among American preachers in vindication of the policy of the national government; and this sympathetic attitude was reflected by the Synod of 1812, which proposed that its members should take what was virtually an oath of allegiance to the United States, but with no mention of the Constitution.[1] The stricter view was represented by Dr. James R. Willson, of Albany, who did not sympathize with Dr. MacLeod's purpose " to render our system less exclusive." He enjoys the distinction of being the first American writer on the history of doctrine, through his " Historical Sketch of Opinions on the Atonement " (Philadelphia, 1817).[2] The church grew steadily, if not rapidly, a General Synod with two subordinate Synods taking the place of the Synod in

[1] This oath ran: " I, A. B., do solemnly declare, in the name of the Most High God, the searcher of hearts, that I abjure all foreign allegiance whatsoever, and hold that these States and the United States are, and ought to be, sovereign and independent of all other nations and governments; and that I will promote the best interests of this empire, maintain its independence, preserve its peace, and support the integrity of the Union to the best of my power." The Synod declare their disapprobation of the constitution is " a matter of conscience, and wholly founded on the omission " of a recognition of " the sovereignty of Messiah over all persons and things." Dr. MacLeod's sermons on " The Character, Causes, and Ends of the Present War," preached in 1814, and published the year following, made a stir locally, as New York City and most of its preachers were unfriendly to the war. They were praised by Jefferson, and Secretary Stanton is said to have read them once a year during the War for the Union.

[2] Pages 123–215 are devoted to America, and contain some valuable notices. But the whole book is badly digested.

1823. As their decided opposition to slavery made their continuance in the South uncomfortable, a general migration to the States north of the Ohio was planned, their first settlement being at Eden, in southern Illinois, on whose name Mr. Dickens fastened in his " Martin Chuzzlewit."

The population of the nation during this period increased from $7\frac{2}{8}$ to $12\frac{7}{8}$ millions, extending by isolated groups as far west as the Missouri River, but moving more abundantly north of the Ohio River than south of it. But the growth of the American churches was far more rapid. This was due largely to a series of widespread revivals during the years of commercial depression and general distress, which followed the Peace of 1816. By 1819, it may be said, the skeptical tendencies which came in with the Revolution were finally overcome. The compact organization of the churches, the recognized ability of their leaders, and the efficiency of the new and centralized methods of religious work had created a new prestige for positive religion, while skepticism, under the name of free thought, became a sect whose feebleness and purposelessness were advertised by its attempts at organization and agitation. So the churches grew and multiplied, now by the fervor of revivals, now by the steady weekly ministrations of the gospel. The General Assembly began to report its statistics of membership in 1807, when it had 598 churches and 365 pastors and licentiates on its rolls. In 1820 the returns showed a communicant roll of 72,096 in over 1299 churches, supplied by 741 pastors and 108 licentiates—three Presbyteries sending no report. In 1830 the communicant membership was 173,329 in 2158 churches, ministered to by 1491 ministers and 220 licentiates.

The most rapid growth had been in the new settlements in western New York and in Ohio. It had been a saying that the Sabbath was unknown west of the Genesee River. But the Synod of Genesee and the two adjacent now contained more members of the church than the whole General Assembly could have claimed at the opening of the century.

All this cost heroic toil on the part of devoted men, who generally gave up the comforts of life in the older States, that they might save the newer for Christ and his church. They rode on long circuits through the pathless forests or over unbroken prairies, where the bending of the stalks of grass showed the " trail." They slept at night under a tree, beside a fire kept alight to scare off beasts of prey ; or they shared the rude shelter and rough fare of the settler. If they found homes for their families it was in rude shanties of two rooms, where they eked out existence far from schools, physicians, and stores, often laboring with their own hands. They met every form of resistance, from stolid indifference to avowed infidelity. They encountered drunkenness, lewdness, horse-racing, gambling, and Sabbath-breaking in the newer settlements. But nothing disheartened them or broke down their faith in God and the gospel, and bit by bit they saw better influences becoming pervasive, and the order of a Christian civilization replacing the wild lawlessness of an earlier day.

CHAPTER IX.

THE NEW AGE.

WITH the opening of the fourth decade of the nineteenth century—as of the eighteenth—there dawns a new age for the churches of America. As the date of the Great Awakening marks the transition from the Puritan to the Methodist or "Evangelical" period, so the new date stands for the transition to a period we might call the historical or the churchly, or by half a dozen related names. In this case the new influence reaches America from Great Britain, pervading different portions of our Christian community with different degrees of rapidity. It was the Protestant Episcopal Church here which, like its mother-church abroad, was the first to recognize what was congenial to its own spirit in the new atmosphere of thought and feeling.

The characteristic note of the new era is its apprehension of Christianity, not especially as doctrinal truth or devout emotion, but as historical fact. It turns away from systems to the Scriptures, especially to the Gospels. It takes up Lessing's challenge—to show how historical fact can be religious truth—and meets it by placing the Incarnation in the forefront of Christian teaching. It values all the ties of office and sacrament and worship which in any way bind our own time to that wonderful Life, and to the church which first grew out of it. It finds in these the manifestation, in forms essentially beautiful, of that which

95

is the core of Christianity—the personal presence of Christ
with his church, as her king and the source of her united
life.

This new age is especially the social age. Puritanism,
by its excessive individualism, broke up society into its
constituent elements, leaving each " face to face with God
in the wilderness." By its stress on the nice points of
doctrinal distinction on which men more easily differ than
agree, it tended to sunder them into antagonistic parties
and sects, rather than bring them into unity and brotherhood. Methodism did not overcome this Puritan tendency, but rather adopted it, as it set before the church
as its goal the salvation of the largest number of individual souls rather than the establishment of God's kingdom
through the redemption of society. It went even further
than did Puritanism in ignoring the historic continuity of
the church and sweeping aside whatever was not seen to
be directly useful to the ends it recognized.

The new age is characterized throughout by the social
stress. Beginning with the questions, " What is the church?
Where is it? What are the essentials of its organization?
What is the proper expression of its life in worship, in
organization?" it has gone on to investigate the relation
of the church to social problems of every kind. Moral
reforms, the study of the poor, the demands of social
revolutionists, the ideal of a truer human brotherhood
among men, are but the newer phases of the questions
put by the leaders of the Oxford Movement. In America
they were first propounded to the church by Stephen
Colwell in his " New Themes for the Protestant Clergy "
(Philadelphia, 1851), a book which now would cause hardly
a ripple of interest, but was then received almost as a
proposal of apostasy from the pure gospel. They now are
pressed with the vehemence and exaggeration which char-

acterize all reactions, and which frequently hide the old truth by the obtrusion of the new into the foreground.

To the Presbyterian churches, with their theocratic traditions inherited from their founders, this reaction to a more social view of religious problems should be especially welcome. The individualism of both Puritanism and Methodism is alien to their oldest and best traditions, which call for the realization of God's kingdom in this present world through the influence of Christian discipline and teaching. The Geneva of John Calvin corresponds more nearly to the new aspirations which are stirring in the churches of America than does anything else in modern history. The great Scottish kirkmen from Knox to Henderson give us suggestions for the problems of to-day. While the past cannot be restored, and its methods are no longer in place, its ideals have a lasting value for us.

Yet the first attitude of these churches toward the new tendency was one of indifference and even hostility. This was partly because it presented itself in shapes less congenial to Presbyterian tradition, and partly because Presbyterians were dominated by the ideals of the Awakening. It is true that it was two Presbyterians, Edward Irving and Sir Walter Scott, who first gave expression to the new spirit, as Dr. Newman points out in one of his Oxford pamphlets. But the seed they sowed fell into an Anglican glebe, where it brought forth a harvest of ecclesiasticism and æstheticism mainly. Not that both were not akin to the new spirit. The idea of the church needed to be impressed upon a generation which had grown indifferent to it; and the more receptive minds among us, such as James W. Alexander, did not fail to discern the significance of the truth which underlay the Tractarian extravagances. Equally necessary was the restoration of the beautiful to its place in the service of God and the order of his house.

As M. Lanfrey says, our age is one which is characterized by imagination rather than reason. Men feel the force of historical associations, or the subtle attraction of form, as they did not for centuries past. Powers no less human than reason and emotion have been called into a new activity, and demand satisfaction. To give them a noble direction, to effect their consecration to a divine service, is one of the problems of our time. It is not a question between recognition of the beautiful and indifference to it. It is whether the new recognition of the beautiful shall be Christian or pagan.

Certainly there was sore need of an æsthetic reform in the churches of sixty years ago. Methodism, with its rough-and-ready utilitarianism and directness, had swept away the last vestige of care for a fitting environment of the congregation's worship and life. The churches of that era were as ugly and cheerless as they were uncomfortable. Only the imposing mass of the pulpit symbolized the absorption of all other functions in that of the preacher. There was an angularity and a stiffness about every line, within and without, which stood in sharpest contrast to any glimpses of natural form within reach of the eye. The interlacing of the branches of a tree outside a window must have suggested to any sensitive mind the difference between the constructive methods of our Maker and those of the builders of houses for his worship. God had filled the world with beauty of form and color; but those who professed to know his mind best, to have acquired that knowledge from a book as full of beautiful form as it was of deep meanings, showed an entire indifference to anything but a practical utility conceived in the narrowest way.

Most unfortunately the new message came to Christians generally in association with narrow ecclesiastical pretensions, fitly symbolized by the chill and mechanical copies of medieval Gothic, which commonly—not always—constituted their outer expression of it. To Mr. Ruskin, who confesses his great obligations to Presbyterian training, we owe the emancipation of imaginative truth from the monopoly of a party.

As of the church edifices, so of the worship seen in them. There was no doubt a vast amount of living conviction as to the great realities on which the church is built, and an intense earnestness of personal feeling in the approach to God. The barest place of worship was often glorified to the worshiper by a beatific vision of the High and Holy One. The baldest forms were found to be an access into the holiest of all. The most prosaic songs of praise lifted the heart on wings of thanksgiving. But in all this, if the Bible be our guide in such matters, there was a lack of adaptation of the outer to the inner which was not, indeed, vital, yet unfit and unnatural. Holiness has its own beauty, and the worship which is to meet man's need must embrace the aroused activities of his whole nature.

One reason for this sordidness was found in the low ideas of the Christian sacraments which generally prevailed. Puritanism always tended to the Zwinglian view of the Lord's Supper, as seeing no need for this social fellowship in communion with Christ; and to Anabaptism, as failing to conceive of the organic tie which binds generation to generation. John Wesley's churchmanship did not save Methodism from the same conclusions, especially as the historic "means of grace" were replaced by the "more efficient" anxious bench and class-meeting. So both tendencies coöperated to diminish the importance of the great transactions of congregational life.

In some quarters, among the older-fashioned Presbyterian bodies, the venerable ceremonial which came down from the times of the Covenanters still sustained the sense of a solemn spiritual mystery and an awful presence in the communion. The element of awe, indeed, was excessive and oppressive, surpassing that of Roman or Anglican ritual in its effect upon sensitive minds. By a reaction from this the churches generally had passed to a sordid " simplicity," in which the presence of the sacramental elements seemed an incongruity. The long white communion-tables had vanished from the aisles. The season of preparation had been minimized. The "fencing of the tables" had been replaced by an address, solemn or cheerful, as the mood of the minister might be. No doubt the great end of the sacrament was attained in innumerable instances, but it often was rather by what the single worshiper brought to the rite, than by any help beyond the most meager which was offered him in the manner of the service. And at best there was the great fault of the Awakening—private and individual devoutness without the life of social communion.

In all these things we have changed much in the last sixty years, as have all the American churches. Nor are we at the end of the change. Presbyterians, as the most conservative of American churches, naturally do not move rapidly in such cases, nor is it desirable that they should. But as an historic church, with roots in centuries past, it is not for them to accept the brief and narrow traditions of a recent date as limiting their action : John Calvin and John Knox were born before John Wesley.

The same duty of progress in the light of their own history arises in view of the social problems of the economic and political field. In dealing with social reforms the utilitarian spirit of the Awakening is a constant danger. The shortest, quickest, readiest means are preferred to every other, often to the sacrifice of interests not less important than those we are seeking to promote. At the same time the reaction against the excessive individualism of the Awakening plunges men into excesses of feeling and statement which obscure the valuable truths in Puritanism and Methodism. Soon we may come to the extravagances of the French theorist, who declared that society is the only concrete moral reality, that the individual is an abstraction merely, and that conscience is a purely social function.

Now whatever else the doctrine of election may stand for, it is the assertion of the permanent worth of the individual before the greatest of all standards, the judgment of God. Our fathers prized it as a truth which counteracted the mere corporate religiousness of Rome, as that proffered a certain assurance of salvation on condition of complying with the terms laid down by the corporation. They thus brought into view the great truth which Puritanism exaggerated, and yet they laid equal emphasis on the organic character of Christian society in family, state, and church. The problem of to-day is the reconciliation of these two tendencies—the social and the individual. The spirit of an age that is passing away laid excessive stress on the individual life. That of the age on which we have entered is exaggerating equally the social life. It is our problem to rise above the Spirit of the age, and, as Jean Paul says, to enter into "the Spirit of all ages," and speak his language of sobriety and reconciliation.

CHAPTER X.

YEARS OF STRIFE, 1831–36.

THE opening of the new age upon American Presbyterianism was not peaceful.   It found elements of fermentation and discord at work which precipitated division.   The years 1830–50, indeed, were a time of controversies throughout the churches of America.   Public debates and heated newspaper discussions were heard on all sides, and the effective controversialist was a man of weight and influence in the councils of his denomination.   Both within and between the several churches lines of division were sharply drawn, and a large share of personal energy was given to border warfare along them.

The first sundering of church bonds came about among the Covenanters.   For many years two tendencies had been manifest as regards the attitude of political dissent from the American government.   Some were disposed to sharpen it; others to return to the attitude of 1777, when the Covenanters acknowledged the new American government as entitled to their allegiance, in view of the strongly Christian language of the public papers of the Continental Congress.   The absence of any expression of Christian loyalty in the national Constitution of 1787, and the ratification by the Senate and the President of a treaty in which a Moslem power was assured that "the United States is not a Christian nation," naturally strengthened the hands of the conservatives.   At last the matter came to open debate in the General Synod of 1831, and at its next meeting, two years later, resulted in a division. The cause was found largely in the altered political situation of the country. The extension of the suffrage without regard to property qualification had gone on simultaneously with the rise of political issues, such as antislavery and antimasonry, in which Covenanters felt an intense interest. Then, as now, conservative Covenanters worked to influence the votes of others, while refusing to vote themselves. The party of movement felt this to be an inconsistency, and several of them were naturalized and cast their votes in the presidential election of 1832. At a special meeting of the Eastern Sub-Synod, in which the conservatives had control, five ministers were suspended for subscribing and publishing a paper which declared that " since the commencement of Christianity, no government on earth has had fairer claims to recognition as the ordinance of God than that of the United States." The ministers thus suspended refused to recognize the sentence, as a piece of party strategy, since it was inflicted less than a month before the meeting of the General Synod in Philadelphia. One of them, Rev. S. W. Crawford, was the retiring moderator, and as he insisted on preaching the sermon the conservatives withdrew and constituted the General Synod in another church. The division thus consummated was in part one between town and country, the conservatives predominating in the latter. The comparative strength of the two parties was matter of dispute, but it seems probable that the conservatives were slightly the more numerous. In a lawsuit for the property of the church in Pittsburg they were unsuccessful, a result due in great measure to the able defense made by a young lawyer named Edwin M. Stanton.

Besides the objections to the Constitution and the treaty with Algiers, the strict Covenanters complained that the

national government " gives a legal security to gross heresy, blasphemy, and idolatry, under the notion of liberty
of conscience," and " makes no provision for the interest
of true religion," while " the major part of the States
recognize the principle of slavery." Yet a few among
them thought them not sufficiently loyal to the Covenanter
principle. After petitioning for several years, in 1840 Rev.
Robert Lusk and David Steele withdrew, and with three
elders constituted the Reformed Presbytery of North
America. This small body, the extreme right wing of
Presbyterianism, required its members to abstain from
association with others for any moral purpose, besides insisting on the maintenance of several old usages, such as
"lining out the Psalms" before singing and proclaiming the
banns in marriage. At this time all Covenanters, as well
as the Associate Church, were strict in enforcing the rule
against " occasional hearing," i.e., participation in any act
of public worship with persons of another communion
than their own. Dr. John Black, of Pittsburg, belonged
to the progressive party, yet two members of his church
were placed under discipline for pausing on the sidewalk
on their way from church to hear what a Seceder minister
was saying in a communion address.

Up to about 1828 there was comparative quiet in the
Presbyterian Church. The alarm over Hopkinsianism
had died away, and never had been very extensive. The
dispute as to the African Theological School had come to
an end with the dissolution of the school. The policy of
coöperation with the American Board in foreign and Indian missions had gained ground rather than lost it. There
was a general acquiescence in the Plan of Union, even
among those who misliked its blending of Presbyterian
and Congregationalist elements in the new churches of the
West. Differences as to the strictness with which the

Westminster standards were accepted were tolerated within the church.

The rift between conservatives and progressives began in New England itself. In 1828 Dr. Nathaniel W. Taylor, professor of didactic theology in the theological school of Yale College, delivered a *concio ad clerum* in connection with the commencement exercises, which ran a new line of division among the ministry of the Connecticut churches. Hopkinsians like Dr. Strong, Dr. Griffin, and Dr. Richards repudiated the new improvements upon Calvinism no less than did the old-fashioned Calvinists like Dr. Woods, and indeed with reason, as in some respects Dr. Taylor was in agreement with the latter against Dr. Hopkins.

Next year Albert Barnes, a young graduate of Princeton Seminary, and pastor of the church in Morristown, N. J., preached a sermon on " The Way of Salvation," in which he was said to agree substantially with Dr. Taylor, as in denying " that the sinner is held to be personally responsible for the transgressions of Adam, or of any other man; or that God has given a law which man has no power to obey "; yet he affirmed " that in connection with the sin of Adam, or as a result, all moral agents in this world will sin—and, sinning, will die." He admitted that " this language . . . does not accord with that used in the Confession of Faith," but challenged those who rejected it to produce from the standards a warrant for the ordinary statement that the sin of Adam is imputed to his posterity. In his view, the Westminster divines like President Edwards were realists, holding that " a personal identity was constituted between Adam and his posterity."

A minority of the Presbytery of Philadelphia, led by Dr. Ashbel Green, regarded the sermon as justifying a refusal to install him as pastor of the First Church, to which he was called in 1830, to succeed Dr. James P. Wil-

son. They contended that the church never had heard
him preach, and seemed to have called him on the merits
of this sermon, so that it was fairly before them.   They
also pleaded their right to examine him on his doctrinal
soundness, instead of admitting him to a seat in Presbytery on his papers of dismission from the Presbytery of
Elizabethtown.   Mr. Barnes submitted a written statement of his views, and Presbytery, by a two-thirds vote,
proceeded to install him.   The minority protested and
appealed to the Synod of Philadelphia, which sustained
their appeal, and ordered Presbytery to " hear and decide
upon the objections " made to Mr. Barnes's orthodoxy,
and " take such order as is required by a regard to the
purity of the church and its acknowledged doctrines and
order."   The Presbytery, which now had an old-school
majority, might either have condemned the sermon without asserting the authorship, as the Assembly had done in a
similar case in 1810, or it might have put Mr. Barnes on
trial for heresy at the instance of some responsible prosecutor, and proved, among other things, his authorship of
the sermon.   It took neither course, but adopted a minute
assuming the authorship, and condemning the sermon as
" highly objectionable, and manifestly, in some of its leading points, opposed to the doctrines of the Confession of
Faith."   It appointed a committee, with Dr. Green as
chairman, to wait on Mr. Barnes and persuade him to retract.   He very properly refused to submit to this unconstitutional mode of procedure.

The case came before the Assembly of 1831, the largest
that had ever met, and Dr. Green alleges that no stone
had been left unturned to secure a new-school majority.
It expressed its disapprobation of " a number of unguarded
and objectionable passages " in the sermon, but declared
that the Presbytery ought to have been satisfied with the

informal explanations given by its author when the matter first came before it.

Philadelphia was now become a center of theological disturbance which affected the whole church. The meeting-place of the Assembly, which regularly held its sessions in the very church of which Mr. Barnes was pastor, it was able to affect and influence the whole church as was no other city. Dr. Green, Dr. Junkin, Mr. McCalla, Mr. Engles, made up a force on the old-school side, which Dr. Ely—now more liberal than in the days of his "Contrast"—Dr. Potts, Dr. Skinner, and Mr. Barnes hardly balanced, especially as the last was constitutionally indisposed to polemics and gentle in temper. New York was hardly more quiet. Between them lay Princeton, where the party of moderation, conservative and yet irenic, had its headquarters, with Dr. Miller and the Alexanders as its leaders. While decidedly old school in their theology, they deprecated the polemic spirit in which Mr. McCalla and some others had entered upon the matter. James W. Alexander proposed to change Philadelphia to Misadelphia, and compared some of his brethren, "who have committed themselves as partisans much in advance of their own convictions," to the Irishman in Judge Brackenridge's "Modern Chivalry," "who cast himself from his coach into a row, crying, 'Heaven direct me to the right side!'" This party was especially strong in the South, where it was represented by the saintly Dr. John H. Rice, of Union Theological Seminary. He pleaded that "the church is not to be purified by controversy, but by holy love." Twenty years before this he had done much to assuage the sharpness of party feeling by an irenic sermon at the opening of the General Assembly. But in his last visit to the North, in 1830, he wrote: "I am not gratified by anything I see in the state of the Presbyterian Church, from

Richmond to New York. Everything is cold and dead except the spirit of controversy. In Philadelphia and New York things are in a dismal condition." He labored to countervail the rage of partisan and even sectarian feeling by rousing the church to a fresh zeal for missions, and yearned for "a larger increase of holiness among ministers."

As the decade advanced, there was an increase chiefly of controversial eagerness. One symptom of this was the frequency of prosecutions for heresy. George Duffield, a grandson of the Revolutionary chaplain, was tried before the Presbytery of Carlisle in 1832, for the teachings of his book on "Regeneration" (Carlisle, Pa., 1832), in which the new-school positions were affirmed. Presbytery found against him in eight out of ten charges, but earned the censure of the Synod of Philadelphia by refusing to go further than to "warn him to guard against such speculations as may impugn the doctrines of our church." Edward Beecher, J. M. Sturdevant, and William Kirby, all of Illinois College, were arraigned before the Presbytery of Illinois in 1833, for teaching the New Haven doctrines; but Presbytery declared that they "do not teach doctrines materially or essentially at variance with the standards." Lyman Beecher, of Lane Seminary, who had originated the temperance reform, broken the power of Unitarianism in Boston, and roused eastern Christians to the spiritual needs of the western States, was prosecuted before the Presbytery and then the Synod of Cincinnati in 1835, for heresy, slander, and hypocrisy, by Dr. Joshua L. Wilson. He was acquitted even by the Synod, which was old school, by a good majority; yet they found fault with his "disposition to philosophize" in the treatment of important doctrines, and censured his use of "terms and phrases calculated to convey ideas" not orthodox, and requested him to publish the explanations which had satisfied them. Dr. Wilson appealed to the Assembly, but the accidental loss of his papers prevented further proceedings. It is surprising that Dr. N. S. S. Beman, of Troy (N. Y.), escaped a prosecution, as his " Four Sermons on the Doctrine of the Atonement " (Troy, 1825) must have been more offensive to old-school men than anything Mr. Barnes wrote. " Barnes, Beman, and Duffield " were constantly named together in the controversies of that and a later time.[1]

But, as might have been expected, the church was far more agitated by the prosecution of Albert Barnes at the instance of Dr. George Junkin before the Second Presbytery of Philadelphia, the Synod of Philadelphia, and the General Assembly of 1836. This was based on doctrinal statements contained in Mr. Barnes's " Notes, Explanatory and Practical, on the Epistle to the Romans " (Philadelphia, 1835), the second of the long series by which he placed the results of exegetical scholarship within reach of the people, and especially of Sunday-school teachers. The Second Presbytery had been constituted of Mr. Barnes's friends, on the principle of " elective affinity." This imitation of the bad precedent of 1762 had just been anticipated in the erection of a Third Presbytery of New York. The Synod of Philadelphia in 1831 had refused to take this step, even when ordered by the General Assembly; the Assembly of 1832 had to effect the erection over the Synod's head—another bad precedent. A Synod of Delaware was constituted in 1834 on the same vicious principle, and the Second Presbytery was conjoined with it. In 1835 Dr. George Junkin, now the president of La-

---

[1] Dr. Beman was a speaker well to the front in the great field-days of the Assembly. He also was an ardent Jacksonian in politics. After one Assembly he went to Washington to condole with the President as to his political troubles. "To tell you the truth, Dr. Beman, these fellows don't bother me half so much as do the dissensions in the Presbyterian Church."

fayette College, appeared before the Second Presbytery to
present charges against Mr. Barnes of teachings contrary
to the standards.   Dr. Junkin had entered the church in
1822, with the majority of the General Synod of the Associate Reformed Church.   He united to the Seceder
interest in nice points of doctrine, a clear head and a remarkable power of self-control.   He never condescended
to the asperities of controversialists like Mr. McCalla, while
he clung to the matter in hand with Scotch-Irish tenacity.
Like Dr. Wilson, he accepted frankly the responsibilities of
the prosecutor, which the old-school men generally shrank
from, trying to secure the condemnation of new-school
teachers without taking the legal steps, which exposed
them to formal censure if they failed to secure a conviction.   To avoid the odium of its use, however, he omitted
the term "heresy" from the charges, but showed some
impatience on finding Mr. Barnes and the Presbytery not
as ready as himself for the precipitation of a new struggle
of this kind.   The counts of the indictment were much
the same as in the previous arraignment of Mr. Barnes's
sermon, but they were based on a publication in which his
views had been stated more fully, and Dr. Junkin urged
them with an acuteness Dr. Green did not possess.   Yet
the Presbytery, as was expected, acquitted him upon each
and all of them, asserting that he had not taught the errors
Dr. Junkin imputed to him.

The appeal now lay to Synod, but was complicated by
the action of the Assembly of that year.   In the Assembly
of 1834 the new-school party had still held the majority,
as in every Assembly since 1831.   But the old-school
minority had presented a Memorial expressing alarm at
"the prevalence of unsound doctrine and laxity in discipline," and enumerating grievances, one of which was the
introduction of the principle of elective affinity in the con-

stitution of Synods and Presbyteries. When the Assembly refused to accede to the requests of the memorialists, these embodied them in an " Act and Testimony " against prevalent " errors," which they issued to the church with their signatures. The emphasis and definiteness of this protest greatly strengthened the old-school party, especially in the South, which was practically the arbiter between Pennsylvania and New England, and resulted in an old-school majority in the Assembly of 1835. This adopted in the main the prayers of the memorialists, and called the attention of the Presbyteries to the list of errors alleged. It also enacted that the Synod of Delaware should form a part of the Synod of Pennsylvania at and after the first meeting of the latter, but did not touch the Presbyteries which had been formed on the same principle.

When the Synod of Philadelphia met, and Dr. Junkin's appeal came up for action, Dr. Ely challenged its right to entertain the appeal, as the Presbytery and Mr. Barnes had not been subject to its jurisdiction at the time of his trial ; and on this ground the Second Presbytery refused to transmit to Synod the books and papers necessary for the continuance of the process. The Synod, however, acted on what it believed to be the intention of the Assembly, entertained and sustained the appeal, and declared that the errors charged were some of them fundamental, and all of them contrary to the standards, and that they contravened " the system of truth therein taught, and set forth in the Word of God." Then, without passing upon Mr. Barnes's denial that he had taught these errors, they proceeded to suspend him from the ministry until he should retract them.

For a year he sat, in submission to this sentence, a hearer in his own church, awaiting the decision of the next Assembly upon his appeal. The feeling now spread widely that the conservatives had abused their opportunity, and sympathy both inside and outside the church rallied to the scholar and pastor who had been subjected to this harsh sentence.   It was felt that anything less than heresy could not justify it, and the word "heresy" his prosecutors had avoided expressly because of the odium attaching to its use.   The Assembly of 1836 reflected the reaction of feeling.   Although Dr. Witherspoon, of South Carolina, was chosen moderator by the old school, over Dr. Absalom Peters, the leader of the new-school men on the floor of the Assembly and the great champion of the Plan of Union, yet the full Assembly a few days later was found to have a new-school majority.   The protest and appeal of Mr. Barnes was sustained, and the action of the Synod reversed, but with a resolution deprecating any approval of the errors charged upon him.   On the contrary, they declared their adoption of the Confession "*ex animo* on the points of doctrine in question, according to the obvious and most prevalent interpretation."

If the new-school party had stopped with this they would have strengthened their own cause.   But they also proceeded to abuse their victory by taking counsel with extremists to the alienation of moderate men.   The Assembly of 1836 had made arrangements to adopt the Western Foreign Missionary Society, established in Pittsburg in 1831, as the organ of the church for the conduct of its work for the conversion of the heathen.   The friends of the American Board now rallied to maintain what they called the Assembly's compact with that board, and repudiated that with the Pittsburg society by a small majority. An attempt was made, and only just defeated, to place the Boards of Education and of Domestic Missions in the hands of those who desired to have them also merged in voluntary and undenominational societies.   Worst of all, the elective-affinity principle, as applied to the organization of Presbyteries, which the Assembly of 1835 had set aside, was restored on appeals from the action of the Synod of Philadelphia.

The old-school men were brought into such a state of agitation by these measures that, with little delay, they began to take steps for the division of the church. No doctrinal action of the Assembly either called for or justified this procedure. While acquitting Mr. Barnes on ground of fact—on which the Synod of Philadelphia had not passed —it had condemned *in thesi* the errors charged upon him. But the other measures of the Assembly of 1836 were such as tended to undermine the constitution of the church; and even new-school men showed by their actions a decade later that they did not care to vindicate them. While much was said of doctrinal differences in the subsequent protests, the strength of the old-school policy lay in the purpose to maintain the constitutional character of the church; and many gave their support to the old school who were not made uncomfortable by the removal of Mr. Barnes's suspension.

One of the first steps taken was to seek a union of forces with the moderate party, especially as represented by Princeton Seminary. Dr. Charles Hodge, indeed, had furnished Mr. Robert J. Breckinridge with all but one of the series of "new-school errors" specified in the Act and Testimony of 1835. Yet the organ of the seminary had treated that document and the policy it represented with contemptuous disfavor. In the autumn of 1836 Drs. Cuyler, Junkin, and others met the professors in Dr. Hodge's study, to offer reasons why Princeton should make a change of front. Among the considerations employed were the perils the seminary ran of being transferred to new-school control, and the likelihood that Mr. Robert Lenox and other laymen would take steps at once to establish a distinctly old-school seminary, unless Princeton abandoned its opposition to the old-school policy. The conference did not seem to attain its end, yet from that time the venerable senior professors, Alexander and Miller, are found in hearty coöperation with the old-school party of action.

It cannot be said that the new-school men showed much desire to aid Dr. Miller and the rest in the efforts they had made to maintain Princeton in an attitude of conciliation. In January, 1836, they had founded Union Theological Seminary in New York, in a distinctly new-school and Plan-of-Union spirit, and independent of the control of the Assembly. It seemed as if they purposed to drive Princeton into the arms of the other party, where, indeed, we next find it.

CHAPTER XI.

THE DIVISION OF 1837–38.

THE old-school leaders had now resolved to divide the church, either by a voluntary secession and the organization of a True Presbyterian Church, or by the excision of those whom they regarded as un-Presbyterian in doctrine and practice. The extreme measures of the Assembly of 1836 placed the initiative in their hands, and they hastened to make use of it.

The meeting of the Assembly of 1837, in Philadelphia, was preceded by that of an old-school convention, which met a week earlier with a view to " effectual measures for putting an end to the contentions which for years had agitated the church." The South was represented largely, and moderate men like Dr. Miller took part in the preparation of a " Testimony and Memorial" to the General Assembly, exhibiting the doctrinal errors and lapses in discipline which they believed were defacing the church. The list of the former, which Dr. Miller revised, was now much longer than in the " Act and Testimony," and included even points of Hopkinsian teaching which the new school, and also New Haven, decidedly rejected.

From the first the old-school men had a decided majority in the Assembly, and the only question left was the best way to use it. To their great credit it must be said that they strove to avoid a violent disruption, by coming to terms of peaceful separation with the minority. The first step taken was to abrogate the Plan of Union of 1801, which had added much to the numerical strength of the church, while detracting greatly from its homogeneity. The Assembly of 1835, out of deference to Dr. Miller's statement that the Plan was a compact which the Assembly had proposed, had asked the General Association of Connecticut to agree to its annulment, so far as concerned churches yet to be formed. But this resolution was never transmitted to the Association. The Assembly of 1837 now voted its abrogation in a resolution which carried with it no qualifications. After adopting the Memorial of the convention, and citing to the bar of the next Assembly any Presbyteries or Synods charged with the disorders enumerated, the Assembly took up the chief question. A committee of both parties was appointed to arrange a plan for a voluntary division. They found no difficulty in agreeing as to the division of funds and institutions of the church, and the disposal of its archives, and the style and title of the proposed new-school Assembly. But the new-school men would not assent to an immediate division by the action of the Assembly then in session, and with the old-school body recognized as the historic successor of the undivided church. They required that the plan should be overtured to the Presbyteries for their approval. In this, as in other cases, they stood on the letter of Presbyterian law. But ordinary law, in the old-school view, was not adequate to the occasion. While proposing to summon to the next Assembly Synods and Presbyteries charged with irregularities in procedure, they now resolved to set all rules of procedure at defiance, rather than leave their policy to the chances of an overture.

For a time the old-school men were at a loss how to proceed, but Dr. Baxter, the successor of Dr. Rice at the head of Union Seminary (Virginia), struck out the sug-

gestion that the abrogation of the Plan of Union was re-
troactive, and that the Synods and Presbyteries organized
under that arrangement had ceased to form a part of the
church. Rev. W. S. Plumer, of Richmond, moved a declaration to this effect with regard to the Synod of the Western Reserve. After an animated discussion it was carried
by a strict party vote—132 to 105. The Synods of Utica,
Geneva, and Genesee, all in western New York, were then
exscinded in the same fashion, but by smaller majorities,
as a number of the moderate party would have preferred
a gentle course with them. Five other Synods were directed to take order with certain of their Presbyteries
which were charged with tolerating errors in doctrine or
disorders in practice. Ministers and churches within the
bounds of these Synods who were Presbyterian in order
and doctrine were directed to seek membership in whichever Presbytery of the church they found most convenient;
and orderly Presbyteries to report to the next Assembly
for direction.

The next step was to conform the methods of the church
to what the old-school men regarded as strict Presbyterianism, although it really was one of the most questionable
results of the Awakening. The Western Missionary Society was erected into the Assembly's Board of Foreign
Missions. The American Education and Home Missionary Societies were invited to cease their operations within
the bounds of the church, leaving the field to the Boards
of Education and of Domestic Missions.

Thus was consummated the division of 1837, which resulted in cutting off 533 churches and over a hundred
thousand communicants—a larger number than the whole
church body contained in 1801, when the Plan of Union
was set on foot. The surprise and indignation with which
it was received showed that the old-school leaders had

been far-sighted in refusing to risk their policy upon a reference to the Presbyteries by overture. If they had gone to the church with such a proposal there would have been a reaction greater than that of 1836. But most men easily come to accept accomplished facts, however they may dislike the manner of their accomplishment. Even the organ of Princeton, in vindicating the abstract right of the Assembly to do what it had done, declined to pass upon the wisdom of its action. Everywhere the party of action found itself thrown upon the defensive and forced to adopt an apologetic tone. Eventually, in the interest of peace in its own fold, the old-school Assembly had to declare that public disapproval of the exscinding acts was no bar to ministerial fellowship.

After the excision of the four Synods, the new-school men naturally took measures to vindicate themselves before the Christian public, and to assert their legal and constitutional rights. In August they met in convention at Auburn, N. Y., and outlined their policy. The four Synods and their Presbyteries were neither to abandon the Plan of Union and the churches formed under it, nor to recognize the action of the Assembly as having any validity. They were to send their delegations to the Assembly of 1838, and claim their seats by constitutional right. Equally important was the preparation of the Auburn Declaration, in which the charges of doctrinal unsoundness made by the old-school convention were contrasted point by point with the actual teachings of new-school men.

In accordance with this program, and acting on legal advice, the delegations from the exscinded Presbyteries presented their credentials to the Assembly of 1838, but the clerks of that body acted in accordance with a declaration they had made the year before, in refusing to place their names on the roll. Before the reading of the clerks' report on the roll, Dr. William Patton, a new-school man, whose name was on the roll, tried to offer a motion that the roll be completed by adding the names of these delegates. The retiring moderator, Dr. David Elliott, refused either to entertain the motion or to recognize an appeal from his own ruling. The clerks then reported the roll of the Assembly, and the retiring moderator made the customary call for members whose credentials had not yet been presented. Dr. Erskine Mason now rose, holding in his hand the commissions of delegates from the Presbyteries of the four Synods, which the clerks had rejected, and moved that the roll be completed by adding these. Dr. Elliott again declared out of order the motion, and also an appeal from his decision. Rev. Miles P. Squier, representing an exscinded Presbytery, made a personal demand that his name be added to the roll, but was declared to have no standing in the court. Rev. John P. Cleveland then moved that Dr. Beman, of Troy, act as temporary moderator, as Dr. Elliott had refused to discharge his constitutional duty, and took the vote on his own motion after it was seconded. The new-school delegates voted for it, the old-school mostly remaining silent. Dr. Beman did not attempt to take possession of the chair, but, standing in the aisle of the church, he entertained motions to organize the Assembly by the choice of a moderator and clerks, and to adjourn its meetings to the First Church. On these motions the new-school men alone voted, and they alone met at the place thus designated. They proceeded to declare the repeal of the exscinding acts, and they elected six trustees of the General Assembly to displace old-school men then in office.

These six brought suit before the courts of the commonwealth of Pennsylvania for possession of the property held by the Assembly's trustees, since the charter of incorporation had been granted by it. The general doctrine of the American state is that an ecclesiastical body is a voluntary association, and that its constitution partakes of the nature of a civil contract between the body at large and each of its members. In case of a violation of this contract the civil courts will grant redress upon proper complaint. This view, however, made its way more slowly into the practice of Pennsylvania than that of the sister-commonwealths, probably because of the long and continuous control of its supreme bench by Presbyterian elders of Scotch-Irish stock. These were so strong in their conviction of the right of a church to manage its own affairs, independently even of constitutional restrictions, that they inclined to regard the highest court of the church as possessing an authority coördinate with their own, even where civil rights were in question. In the former view of the law the new-school case was a very strong one, and Chancellor Kent, of New York, told Dr. Gardiner Spring that if the case had been tried in his own commonwealth it would have been decided in their favor. As it was, the verdict of a Supreme Court jury, under instructions from Judge Rogers, spread dismay among the old-school men, as it was against them; but the court in banc set aside the verdict on grounds which made a fresh trial useless. It was ruled by Chief-Justice Gibson, supported by Judges Huston and Kennedy (Rogers dissenting), that the Plan of Union " was evidently not intended to be permanent," and as it had been enacted, so it might be " repealed, by an ordinary act of legislation "; and that "those who built up Presbyteries and Synods on the basis of it had no reason to expect that their structures would survive it." This may be law—it is not history.

When the separation was complete it was found that the new school embraced about four ninths of the ministry and membership of the church, mostly lying in the Northern States. It coincided in the main with the lines of discrimination between Scotch-Irish and New England elements, as it grew largely out of the incompatibility of their tempers. In the three exscinded Synods of New York, only six churches and about four hundred members went over to the old school. The new-school Assembly had the adhesion also of the Synods of Michigan and eastern Tennessee, and of majorities in the Synods of New York, Albany, and Illinois, as well as half the Synods of New Jersey and Indiana, and strong minorities in those of Ohio and Cincinnati. Elsewhere the line of severance ran sharply through Presbyteries and even congregations.

The moderate men in some cases went with the old school from theological sympathy, yet under protest; and in others they sided with the new school from a sense of the injustice that had been done them. Their greatest strength appeared in the Synod of New York, which divided between new and old school at its session of 1838 in Newburg. Forty-nine protested against any division, claiming to be the undivided Synod, and got the name of the High School, from their place of meeting. Finally the new school as a body united with them on this footing, and the Synod adhered to the new-school Assembly. The Synod of Ohio, while adhering to the old school, recorded upon their minutes that the exscinded Synods were still constitutionally a part of the church. Gardiner Spring, Ichabod Spencer, and Daniel Lord protested formally against the excision before their old-school Presbytery.

The division was effected most slowly in the South, outside the area in which Hezekiah Balch and his disciples had diffused Hopkinsian ideas. Elsewhere the interest in the controversies had been limited to a few, and many

had to take time to make up their minds. The suggestion
to withdraw from both parties and organize a Southern
Presbyterian Church was made in South Carolina, and
probably was an echo of the nullification excitement of a
few years before. In a similar way the repugnance of the
South to the centralization of authority in the national
government suggested an opposition to the assumption of
authority by the national Assembly of the church. But
altogether less than a fourth cast in their lot with the new
school. It was alleged as early as 1838 [1] that the prevalence of antislavery sentiments among the new-school
men, as in New England, was one of the reasons for the
coöperation of the South in the policy of division. This
is not borne out by the facts. It is true, as Dr. Miller
said in 1823, that the South had become " very sensitive,
extremely, perhaps excessively sensitive on this subject "
long before this. As far back as 1796 we find the Presbytery and the Synod of South Carolina enjoining upon
James Gililand, pastor of Broadaway, that he abstain from
preaching in favor of emancipation. We see prominent
ministers like Thomas D. Baird and David Nelson leaving
the South to find a home in the free States, out of dislike
for an institution for whose abolition they were not free to
plead. We find William Maxwell, of Norfolk, the friend
and biographer of Dr. Rice, threatened in 1827 with a coat
of tar and feathers for publishing a very temperate plea
for emancipation. But we also find him and Mr. Baird,
in the Assembly of 1837, among the most zealous on the
old-school side. It is possible that Dr. Baxter, as a de-

[1] By Rev. Zebulon Crocker, in " The Catastrophe of the Presbyterian
Church " (New Haven, 1838). He was the delegate from the Connecticut
Association to the Assembly of 1837, and his work has value as an account
of the contemporary controversy in Connecticut. He says slavery was not a
principal cause of the division, but a secondary one, and he points to the
fact that Dr. Baxter, who presided over the old-school convention, had written in defense of slavery as a Scriptural institution.

fender of slavery, may have felt more comfortable in a
church which had fewer Northern men in it; and he certainly used language in 1837 which showed that the abolition problem to his own mind was part of the reasons for
a division. But even he knew, or ought to have known,
that the Scotch-Irish of the Middle States were furnishing
many of the most determined enemies of human bondage,
and that the church, by the action of 1818, had declared
slavery " inconsistent with the law of God, and totally
irreconcilable with the gospel of Christ." He must have
known that in 1833, when the Synod of Kentucky refused
to declare against slavery, Robert J. Breckinridge rose and
left the church, exclaiming, " Since God has forsaken the
Synod of Kentucky, Robert J. Breckinridge will desert
it too!" Also that a year later the Synod came to a
better mind, condemned slavery as a source of degradation,
ignorance, cruelty, and licentiousness, and urged gradual
emancipation of the slave. Of the committee which reported that action, Dr. Ashbel Green had been chairman,
and Dr. Baxter a member. The question had come up
again in 1835, through memorials asking the Assembly to
act in accordance with its previous deliverances in working for emancipation. It had been referred to a committee
of five, of whom two were from the South, with Dr. Miller
as chairman. The majority report to the Assembly of
1836, in which the new-school men had control, deprecated action. A minority report by Rev. James H. Dickey
—afterward the founder of Ashmun Institute, now Lincoln
University—was in harmony with the deliverance of 1818.
The subject was indefinitely postponed after an excited
discussion. If antislavery had been a distinctive feature
of the new school they would have secured action on this
as on other questions they cared for. In that case there
would have been no new-school church in the South.

Theologically the division of 1837 grew out of panic and alarm, rather than any more solid reason. There was no evidence that the New Haven theology had extensively pervaded, or was likely to pervade, the church. Its peculiarities were nothing but a temporary phase in the theological speculation of New England, and in some respects a distinct approach to Calvinistic orthodoxy, as compared with Hopkinsianism. It might have been treated with the wise patience which the earlier Assemblies had shown toward that form of speculation, without real prejudice to any theological or spiritual interest. Even to prove "Taylorism" upon men like Mr. Barnes and Mr. Duffield, it was necessary to hold them responsible not only for what they actually said, but for what their critics held to be necessary inferences from their words. And in some cases what was alleged to be essential to the Calvinistic orthodoxy of the Confession had never been heard of until the seventeenth century. Thus "the federal headship of Adam," and "the covenant of works" made with him, which Dr. Junkin exalted into a shibboleth, were nothing but Dutch "improvements upon Calvinism," designed to break somewhat the force of the conception of irresponsible sovereignty. In truth the heated atmosphere of church controversy was shown to be the worst possible for weighing the exact significance of a disputed formula. Nor were even the ministry of that time so well equipped in a knowledge of historical theology as to be able to distinguish between the original and essential features of Calvinistic teaching and the later accretions. In Princeton Seminary, indeed, the subject of church history, to say nothing of the history of doctrine, never was treated as an important theological discipline until our own time.

It was on the ecclesiastical side that the old-school policy was most capable of defense. Yet even here, as the subsequent developments showed, a little patience would have secured all that was sought and fought for. The very drift of thought and feeling, which had made men like Drs. Green and Miller far more Presbyterian in their old age than in their youth, was to affect the new-school men just as decidedly. " High-church " sentiment was developing rapidly in the Presbyterian Church as in the others, in this new age of churchliness. The right of the church to create and control its own agencies was obtain-ing a strong and instinctive recognition. It was also felt that under the operation of the Plan of Union the church was becoming a dual body, with two sets of agencies for its work, two conceptions of ecclesiastical order. The tone taken by the friends of the Plan, especially by Dr. Absalom Peters in his " Plea for Union in the West," was most of-fensive to all decided Presbyterians, and soon became so to the new-school men themselves. On the other hand, the success of the Board of Domestic Missions, created in 1816 out of the Standing Committee of 1802, and vested with enlarged powers in 1827, was such as to awaken a desire for a similar independence and energy in other fields, especially the foreign. Dr. Rice, from his death-bed, wrote to ask the Assembly of 1831 to declare that " the Presbyterian Church in the United States is a mis-sionary society, and every member of the church is a life-member of said society." His last visit to the North had satisfied him that the two denominations were drawing farther apart, and that Presbyterians as a body could not be brought " to unite under what is thought to be a Congre-gational Board." The Assembly took no action on his sug-gestion, but it led to the organization of the Pittsburg society.

As might be expected, this decade of strife was not characterized by extensive growth of the church. The

undivided church reports 182,017 in its communion in
1831. Its old-school in 1840 reports 126,583; the new
school, 102,060. This was the more remarkable as the
opening years of the decade had been a time of intense
revival excitement under the use of the new measure, and
it is estimated that between 1826 and 1832 not less than
two hundred thousand had thus been added to the evangelical churches. It also was noteworthy that the business
depression of 1837 and the years following had been attended by the usual awakening of religious interest in the
centers of population, where the depression was most severely felt. Up to 1835 Rev. Charles G. Finney was in full
career as a new-measure revivalist, and much of his work
was among the Presbyterians of central New York.

In fact, what John Howe calls " the carnality of religious
contention " was abroad in the church, and furnished an
obstacle to the movement of the spiritual life. It was all
the more a snare because the baser self in us loves to be
busy about the surface of spiritual things, and to show
great fervor for religion when no immediate demand for
the life of faith is pressed upon it. " Set Jehu to pulling
down idols, and see how zealous he can be," writes an old
Puritan.

It was a poor compensation for these losses that the
great debates in Presbytery, Synod, and Assembly attracted attention as never before, and familiarized a large
part of the outside community with niceties of Presbyterian
doctrine and law. Henry Clay pronounced the oratorical
display in the Assemblies finer than anything Congress had
to show. The power of Calvinistic training to develop
strong men found ample illustration, even though the
strength was not given the highest direction. The old
school were happy in the support of representatives of
the church's past in the much-loved and kindly Archibald

Alexander, the courtly and diplomatic Samuel Miller, the masterful Ashbel Green. Of the younger generation, the South furnished the two Breckinridges—John a saint of unsurpassed eloquence, Robert a type of Kentuckian chivalry; George Addison Baxter, lucid in exposition, resourceful in council; John Witherspoon the younger; and William S. Plumer, a most impressive speaker even to the latest years of a long life. The North furnished in George Junkin a representative of the Scotch-Irish strength and tenacity; in John McDowell a well-rounded, practical nature; in Charles Hodge a Johannine character, yet, like John, capable of an intense theological fervor; and in William L. McCalla a rough tongue, which lent itself to telling epigram and kept its owner all his life in hot water.

The new-school men, like progressive parties generally, impress us rather more by their intellectual quality than by strength of character, although in Thomas H. Skinner we find a singularly simple and unworldly character. Samuel Hanson Cox, a convert from Quakerism, possessed an eloquence which would have found no superior if it had been better sustained. George Potts ill spared for debate the time taken from an exceptionally devoted pastorate. Nathaniel S. S. Beman had a restless intellect and an aggressive temper, which earned him the title of the "War-horse of the New School," but is now best remembered for his services to hymnology. Erskine Mason, with far less than his great father's eloquence, acquired a wonderful influence over his people, and left a fragrant memory of personal holiness and good works. Thomas McAuley, the first president of the (new) Union Seminary, carried his Irish wit and pathos to the support of a party which embraced few of his countrymen. Judge Jessup, the father of the eminent missionaries, brought great forensic abilities to the same side, his defense of Mr. Barnes in the Assembly of 1836 being reckoned his greatest triumph as a speaker.

This unhappy decade was to witness yet another division among Presbyterians, and the most unmeaning yet. Simply through disaffection to an act of discipline three Presbyteries of the Associate Church in New York and Vermont withdrew in 1838 from the Associate Synod, under the leadership of Drs. Peter Bullions and Andrew Stark. Thus the Seceder family, like the Presbyterians and the Covenanters, found it a day of strife and of division.

CHAPTER XII.

THE twenty years which preceded the war for the Union were years of great agitation and ferment in the intellectual, social, and spiritual life of America. The new age began to declare itself and its character by a thousand signs. The spirit of the nation found expression as never before in literature and art, in social-reform movements and political agitation. A new criticism, a new philosophy, a new scholarship arose to multiply the objects of public interest, and to add to the complexity of existence. No longer content with reproducing English and Scottish thought, America flung herself boldly into contact with the culture of the civilized world, and was reinforced in this by the more varied immigration from all the countries of northern Europe.

These agitations reached the spiritual life of the country largely through new sects or agitations within the existing churches. Millerism, and its offspring, Adventism, might be traced, along with sober Premillenarianism, to the interest in Scripture prophecy which first awoke in the group of which Edward Irving was the center. Connected with the same interest in the future were the various theories of annihilation or conditional mortality, which now competed with the older Universalism as substitutes for the orthodox eschatology. Spiritualism owed its strength to an instinctive desire to pierce the veil which sunders the dead from the living, and know more definitely " the to-

morrow of death." Campbellism stood for a revolt from
the Methodism of the Great Awakening, which had pervaded all the churches more or less largely.   Socialism, in
various phases, especially Fourierism in 1842–49, sought
a reconstruction of society as the cure for the evils attending the industrial revolution which was in progress.   The
broad-church tendency, in the writings first of Coleridge
and then of Thomas Erskine, of Linlathen, sought a deeper
Scriptural and spiritual basis for the essential truths of
Christianity ; while Tractarianism, affecting chiefly the Episcopal Church, but challenging all, insisted that that foundation must be sought in Christian tradition, by going back
to the church of the first centuries.   Perfectionism, a tendency no longer confined to the Quaker and Methodist
bodies, urged the perfecting of holiness as the central principle and first duty of Christianity.

Along with these ran the great social agitations which
are characteristic of our age.   That for the abolition of
war had taken its start just after the Peace of 1815, and
was no longer a Quaker peculiarity.   The temperance
agitation may fairly be dated from Dr. Lyman Beecher's
"Six Sermons on Intemperance," preached in 1825 at
Litchfield, Conn., and published the next year.   About
the same time Albert Barnes formed at Morristown, N. J.,
the first temperance society, whose members were pledged
to limit their consumption of " apple-jack " to a pint a day,
the usual allowance being a quart.   The demand of the
movement rose rapidly to total abstinence from intoxicants
by 1836, and even to the legal suppression of the traffic
in them, and such laws had been enacted in fourteen
States between 1850 and 1856.   Among many others, Rev.
Thomas P. Hunt, a brilliant and eccentric preacher, gave
both wit and eloquence to the cause.   Dr. Robert Baird
carried the propaganda to Europe.   The immigration of

Irish and German Romanists produced a violent agitation against that church, resulting in riot and arson in several cities. Dr. Thomas Brainerd, of Philadelphia, was one of those who offered a courageous opposition to the extravagances of this excitement,[1] while Robert J. Breckinridge and Nicholas Murray (" Kirwan ") were especially prominent in antagonizing the pretensions of American Romanism.

More quiet were the labors for the extension of the Sunday-school system to the neglected portions of the country, and for the universal diffusion of the Scriptures. To both Presbyterians gave large support. John McCullagh in the South and Benjamin W. Chidlaw in the North will live forever in the history of the American Sunday-school. To the Bible Society Presbyterians have given of men and means beyond any other American church. The care of the poor, especially in the great cities, took a fresh impulse toward wisdom and kindliness from the visit of a Scotchman who had studied Dr. Chalmers's work in Glasgow and described it to Americans. He was reinforced in this by Dr. Alexander Duff during his memorable visit of 1854, which did so much, in Dr. Tyng's words, " to awaken enlarged desires and views in reference to the propagation of the gospel among the unevangelized nations of the earth." The care for the young men of our great cities through the Young Men's Christian Associations, begun in London in 1844, reached America seven years later. In this work Presbyterians were amply represented by William E. Dodge, George H. Stuart, John Wanamaker, and a host of others.

But it was especially the antislavery agitation which

---

[1] " Our Country Safe from Romanism. A Sermon delivered at the Opening of the Third Presbytery of Philadelphia, April, 1841," Philadelphia, 1841.

affected the churches. That had originated with the Christian people of both North and South, and among Presbyterians as much as any. A type of these was James G. Birnie, of Alabama, who emancipated his slaves, came North, and devoted his life to the cause of emancipation, becoming in 1840 and 1844 the first antislavery candidate for the Presidency. Another was Dr. David Nelson, of Tennessee, who emancipated his own slaves, denounced slave-holding as a sin, and refused to commune with those who practiced it. On one occasion his friends had to hide him from a Missouri mob for proposing to his congregation a subscription to buy and colonize slaves. Two years later, in 1837, Rev. Elijah P. Lovejoy was murdered in Alton, Ill., by another Missouri mob for the offense of publishing in his paper moderate articles against slavery. He was a graduate of Princeton Seminary, and a member of the Presbytery of Illinois.

The indifference or hostility of many ministers and Christians to the cause of emancipation had the effect of alienating some badly based opponents of slavery from the churches, and of leading to the association of abolition with infidelity and come-outer-ism. Those who yielded to this drift naturally lost influence with the people at large ; and while the noisiest in talk and the extremest in their demands, they actually contributed little to the final result. They denounced both church and state, copying the " political dissent " of the Covenanters, and carrying it to an extreme. As Albert Barnes said of them, " If a just cause could have been killed by the folly of its friends, the cause of African liberty would have been so by the spirit and methods of the abolitionists." These words are the weightier as coming from one who fearlessly followed his own convictions of duty in this matter. " His book on American slavery," says Professor Phelps, " was a thesaurus to the abolitionists for twenty years. . . . He preached the substance of his book to his people at a time when millions of property sat along the aisles of his church, coined out of slave-labor on cotton and rice plantations. He did it with the air of one who did not for a moment conceive it possible to do anything else. His more timid friends trembled for the result, but not he."

Among the Presbyterian churches there was a great difference of attitude toward slavery, and this formed one of the obstacles to their union. The smaller and stricter bodies, with the exception of the Associate Reformed Synod of the South, now occupied the ground taken by the Covenanters at the opening of the century, in excluding slave-holders from their communion. And those who passed over from them to the old-school church naturally carried with them a strong repugnance to human bondage.

Neither of the two Assemblies which grew out of the division of 1837-38 was ready to take any decided ground, as might be inferred from the fiasco of 1836. Both, indeed, had inherited from the Assembly of 1818 an authoritative denunciation of slavery, which plainly involved the duty of slave-holders in the membership of the church to take steps toward emancipation, or of rigorous discipline in that of the church's judicatories, even although the Assembly proceeded, in that deliverance, to pronounce against immediate emancipation, as " adding a second injury to the first," since it added that this consideration should not be made " a cover for the love and practice of slavery, or a pretense for not using efforts that are lawful and practicable to extinguish the evil."

The deliverance, however, remained a dead letter as regards the practice of the church. It was even defied form ally and openly. The Presbytery of Harmony, S. C., in 1836 resolved, in flat contradiction to the General Assembly, that " the existence of slavery is not opposed to the will of God "; and the Synod of Virginia declared that " the General Assembly had no right to declare that relation sinful which Christ and his apostles teach to be consistent with the most unquestionable piety."

In the meantime the legal status of the slave and his social condition grew worse instead of better.   The emancipation societies, founded by the Quaker, Benjamin Lundy, in 1815–26, which had been counted by the score in the South, passed out of existence; and the policy of silence as to the licentiousness and cruelties attendant on the system was enforced upon all.   The slave States passed laws of constantly increasing severity, declaring the slave to be a chattel and not a person, and forbidding even his owner to have him taught to read.   For religious instruction he was shut up to oral teaching at white mouths, and some colored preachers did manage to acquire in this way a moderate acquaintance with the Scriptures. A domestic slave-trade sprang up between the border States and the States farther South, where the cotton, rice, and sugar plantations furnished a market.   Husbands and wives, parents and young children, were thus severed for life, and the abomination of temporary marriage was actually sanctioned by some Christian ministers.

Here certainly was a large field for reformatory action on the part of conservative men.   Those who disbelieved in immediate emancipation, or even in emancipation at any date, might have united to demand the removal of these gross iniquities.   Those who sought in the Old Testament for a Scriptural justification of slavery might very well have insisted that the merciful provisions of the Mosaic legislation should find something like a counterpart in that of free America.   The church both North and South might have been a unit in insisting that its members should keep themselves unspotted from these evils, and that the Word of God should be made accessible to black as well as white. Strong and united action even within these limits—as Dr. Charles Hodge pointed out—would have taken the sting out of the abolitionist argument, and prepared the way for peaceful and gradual emancipation. It was the unfaithfulness of the American churches, and not least of the Presbyterian churches, to the plain requirements of duty, which suffered the evil to grow and gather head, until its end came in a deluge of human blood.

Of the two Assemblies, the new-school naturally was the more faithful to the deliverance of 1818, which it repeated in substance in 1846 and 1849. Yet not until 1850 did it take the first step toward reducing doctrine to practice, declaring slave-holding a matter of discipline when not excusable by special circumstances. In 1853 the Assembly called upon its Southern Presbyteries to report what had been done to purge the church of this evil. The Presbytery of Lexington responded that ministers and members of its churches were slave-holders by choice and on principle. As the Assembly met this deliverance by a decided condemnation, the Southern part of the new-school church, numbering six Synods, twenty-one Presbyteries, fifteen thousand communicants, seceded and formed the United Synod of the Presbyterian Church. It at once made overtures of union to the old-school Assembly, meeting in New Orleans; but as these required a condemnation of the exscinding acts of 1837, and would have plunged the church afresh into the controversy over slavery, they were declined. This was the last of a series of ecclesiastical divisions over slavery, which presaged the secession of the slave States. The Associate Reformed Presbyterians had divided on this line in 1821; the Methodists and Baptists in 1844; the " Christian " Connection in 1866.

The old-school Assembly preserved its unity until the eve of the war by moving in the other direction. There is a wide gap between the deliverance of 1818 and those of 1845 and 1849. The Assembly of 1845 went no further than to decline to deny " that there is evil connected with slavery," or to " approve those oppressive and defective laws by which, in some of the States, it is regulated." Nor would it by any means " countenance the traffic in slaves for the sake of gain; the separation of husbands and wives, parents and children, for the sake of ' filthy lucre ' or for the convenience of the master; or cruel treatment of slaves in any respect." But it recognized no responsibility on the part of the church to secure the removal of such evils, except by preaching the duty masters owed to their slaves, and had not a word to say of the duty of emancipation, or of the sin of refusing the slave access to the Scriptures. The deliverance was adopted by a vote of 168 to 13. In this view slavery was no longer an evil contrary to the law of God and the gospel of Christ, but an institution which had come to be associated with certain remediable evils, about which the church need not greatly concern herself. Yet the Assembly of 1846 declared that the church had " always held and uttered *substantially* the same sentiments " on this subject. In 1849 the Presbytery of Chillicothe, O., memorialized the Assembly, asking that slavery be declared a sin and the lower courts be enjoined to exercise discipline to remove it from the church. The Assembly, without a division, voted that it was " inexpedient and improper for it to attempt or propose " measures of emancipation. Four members of the Assembly protested, declaring that the deliverance of 1845, " instead of benefiting the slave, it is feared has given relief to the consciences of slave-holders, which had already begun to cry out against their wrong."

One result of this new policy was to throw the old-school church upon the defensive in its correspondence with foreign churches. The Irish Presbyterian Church and the Free Church of Scotland both recognized the old-school church as the rightful representative of Presbyterian orthodoxy in America. In their correspondence by letter between the Assemblies, the Irish and Scotch indulged in the language of strong remonstrance, and were told, in pious and diplomatic phrase, to mind their own business, as the American Assembly declined to discuss the subject with them. As a consequence the correspondence came to an end, only to be resumed by delegates after the war.

Another result was a small secession from both the old and the new school churches. The new-school Presbytery of Ripley, O., had already withdrawn, when the deliverance of 1845 led a minority of the old-school Presbytery of Mahoning, Pa., to take the same course. The two organized the Synod of the Free Presbyterian Church in 1847, which finally united during the war for the Union with the new-school Assembly, because of its increased faithfulness in dealing with slavery. By that time the Free Church extended west to Iowa, embracing five Presbyteries and forty-three ministers.

The relations of the old and new school churches were naturally distant and unfriendly at the first. It was not until 1862 that they got so far as to exchange greetings by delegates. By that time both parties had come to discover that the distance between them had always been less than it seemed in the heated atmosphere of controversy, and that it actually was growing less through mutual approximation.

On the new-school side there was a decided growth of
Presbyterian feeling, which drew them and their Congregationalist allies farther apart.   They were becoming dissatisfied with the management of home missions and the
education of the ministry by voluntary societies of an
interdenominational character.   Church boards, with the
style of permanent committees, were established in 1852
to take charge of their home missions and their publication work.   Even with the American Board methods on
the foreign field there was a growth of discontent.   The
rules prescribed for the organization of the native converts
into churches tended to give those churches a Congregationalist character.   The policy of Dr. Rufus Anderson,
the very able but arbitrary secretary of the board, in forc-
ing upon the missionaries in India the abandonment of
Dr. Duff's educational methods of evangelization, roused
a lively resentment both in India and at home.   It was
felt that those missions were detached from a basis common to all Presbyterians in the foreign field, and in harmony with the principles of the Presbyterian polity. R. G.
Wilder, of the Kolapoor mission, renounced his connection
with the American Board rather than become Puritanized
in this way, and was supported thereafter by Presbyteries
and churches which sympathized with his action.

Theologically the new-school church did not fulfill any
of the prognostications of its unfriendly critics.   It did
not run headlong through a descending career of Taylorism, Arminianism, and Socinianism.   It retracted none of
the positions laid down in its Auburn Declaration of 1837.
It held fast to the assertion that Christ died for all, elect
and non-elect alike.   It denied the legal equivalence of
our Lord's sufferings to the pains due to us for sin.   It
refused to make the Cocceian " federal headship of Adam "
a test of orthodoxy ; and while it traced the common hu-

man depravity to his fall, it declined to call this sin before it resulted in sinful acts. It asserted the natural ability of the sinner to do what God's law requires of him, seeing in him only the moral inability which consists of voluntary inclination to evil.

On the other hand, a new theological atmosphere had begun to pervade the church, thanks especially to the influence of Professor Henry B. Smith, of Union Seminary, whom Dr. Archibald Hodge declared to be the greatest theologian of the American Presbyterian Church.[1] Himself a New Englander, he did much to destroy the hegemony of New England in American theology, by bringing it into relation with the deeper thought of the conservative and constructive minds of Europe, and by giving this a shape fitted to American needs. A somewhat similar standpoint was reached by those who, like Dr. Jonathan F. Stearns, went back to the first fount of Protestant teaching in the writings of Luther and Calvin, and learned to appreciate the worth of their thought.[2]

At the same time the old-school church was unable to maintain the rigidity it had put on before and during the division of the church. One of the points especially at issue in the controversies of that time had been the nat-

[1] Dr. J. H. Good, of the (German) Reformed Church, is my authority for this. He had it from Dr. Hodge himself.

[2] See Dr. Stearns's sermon on Justification by Faith, preached before the Synod of New York and New Jersey, October 20, 1852, and published by direction of the Synod. " I know it will be alleged that great improvements have been made in the nineteenth century, and why not in theology ? It has been claimed that our own branch of the church deserves to be held in *honor*, as having made valuable modifications of the ancient theology. But, my brethren, I must confess, I stand greatly in doubt of those modifications. Some of them, I apprehend, are but *adaptations* or *adjustments* to a superficial style of thinking among us, which is neither sound nor destined to stand the test of the more penetrating style of thinking which a better age will ere long bring into favor. I am sure we have no modifications sufficient to erect a *school* upon, which will not *peril* the soundness of our foundations." Dr. Stearns quotes Edwards and Hopkins with great respect, and confesses his obligations to Archdeacon Hare.

ure or extent of the subscription required to the doctrinal standards of the church. The old-school men made no discrimination in their discussions which would indicate any latitude of dissent from even less important statements. Dr. Junkin, in prosecuting Mr. Barnes, repudiated the very idea. That a new-school man had expressed a conviction that differed from what the Confession said was enough to justify his condemnation as unfaithful to his ordination vows. In the Assembly of 1858, however, Dr. Robert J. Breckinridge introduced a motion to have the Board of Publication bring out a commentary on the Scriptures, which should conform to the teachings of the Westminster standards. Dr. Charles Hodge, in reviewing the proposal, wrote of the Confession of Faith:

"We could not hold together a week if we made the adoption of all its propositions a condition of ministerial communion." "Who is to tell the church's sense of the Confession? It is notorious that as to that we are not agreed. In the second place, even as to the points in which the sense of the Confession is plain, there is want of entire concurrence in its reception."

In justifying this statement he distinguished three modes of subscription, the first being for substance of doctrine, the second covering every statement, and the third including the truths held (1) by all Christians; (2) by all Protestants; (3) by Calvinists over against Lutherans, Arminians, and other Protestants. It is worth while to compare with this Mr. Barnes's statement of 1836: "The system of truth contained in the Confession, as distinguished from all other systems—the Socinian, the Pelagian, the Arian, the Arminian, etc.—has appeared to me to be the true system, and, without hesitation or fluctuation, I have received it."

Next to doctrinal conformity to the Westminster standards, in the controversies of 1831–37, the greatest stress had been laid on the necessity of the ruling eldership to the right constitution of a congregation. The four Synods had been exscinded not because of any defect in the standing of their ministry, but because they admitted to seats in Synod and Presbytery men who had never been ordained to the eldership, and who were no more than elected representatives of congregations. A prolonged debate in the old-school Assemblies of 1842–44 brought out the fact that no agreement had ever been reached as to the nature of the office, its relation to the pastorate, the necessity of the presence of elders in the courts of the church, and the forms by which they should be set apart to their office. Dr. Hodge, over against his colleague, Dr. Miller, and all the Scottish and Irish authorities, supported the lower view of the office, denying it to be of the same order with the pastorate, defining the elder as a lay representative of the people, and refusing him ordination by laying on hands. In that view the committee-men of 1831–37 could hardly be ruled out as unfit to sit in Synod or Assembly.

A third point of dissension had been the right of church boards as an essential feature of Presbyterian polity, over against voluntary societies. But in the Assemblies of 1854 and 1860, Dr. James Henry Thornwell, of the Columbia (S. C.) Seminary, attacked the boards, with equal truth of logic and of history, as an excrescence upon synodical government, which had no warrant in Scripture or the standards of the church. In his defense of the boards Dr. Hodge took much lower ground than had been held in 1837. He simply asserted the right of the church to govern her action by expediency in the selection or organization of her agencies.

In contrast to the old-school church, the new-school showed its Puritan affinities by a moral rigorism in discipline, and an exaction of theological subscription from its entire membership. Elaborate and exacting covenants and confessions were prescribed by their sessions for those who were admitted to communicant membership. Promiscuous dancing, card-playing, and other " worldly amusements" were sharply dealt with. While both churches proclaimed their acceptance of revival methods, there was some foundation for the claim that the new-school church was preëminent in this respect, as being more thoroughly pervaded by the spirit of the Awakening, and less affected by the earlier Presbyterian tradition.

Of the two churches it was the old-school which made the most rapid progress during the period of their separate existence. It was slightly in the majority at the time of the separation, and decidedly so at the outbreak of the war. This was due in part to the greater vigor and efficiency of its agencies in the home field, and their control by the church itself. Much more was due to the altered attitude of the Congregationalists. They also had felt the impulse to make more of their historic past, and to draw more firmly the lines of denominational distinction. They were dissatisfied with seeing their membership outside of New England absorbed by Presbyterian churches, and their churches by Presbyteries. In the new and growing States of the Northwest they now fought to their own hand, building up State Associations of their own churches, and in some cases reclaiming from the new school those who belonged to them by birthright. At last, in 1852, a national convention of the Congregationalist churches met at Albany, N. Y., and voted the discontinuance of the Plan of Union, thus drawing the denominational line firmly and permanently.[1] Thus the two systems drew apart ecclesi-

---

[1] Over against the losses to Congregationalism by the Plan of Union might be placed the losses to Presbyterianism of nearly all its New England

astically just at the time when their theological contact was coming to an end through the development of a more independent activity in the Presbyterian churches.

Until after the division of 1837, American Presbyterianism made no important addition to the literature of theology. Able preachers there were—Davies, Tennant, Mason, Griffin, Kollock, Larned, John Breckinridge, and others—and sound practical writers, such as Dickinson, Green, Miller, and the Alexanders. But there was no such succession of notable names as New England contributed to the history of theology from the time of President Edwards—perhaps I should say of Hooker and Shepard—onward.

It was in the year 1841 that Edward Robinson, of the new Union Seminary, published his " Biblical Researches," which, as Carl Ritter said, " opened the second great era of our knowledge of the Promised Land." It constitutes, along with his " Later Researches " (1856) and his " Physical Geography of the Holy Land " (1865), the greatest contribution to biblical literature America has made, as Dr. William M. Thomson's " The Land and the Book " (1859 and 1882–86) furnishes the best popular work on the same subject. Dr. Robinson's name is associated with one of those revisions to which the text of the English Bible has been frequently subjected since King James's time, as he was a member of the Committee on Versions, supervising the work, which was executed by Dr. Jas. W. McLane, of Brooklyn. Without touching the translation itself, this eliminated from the headings of the chap-

churches, through the operation of a legal code created for the benefit of Congregationalism. As the laws of the New England States recognized no higher ecclesiastical authority than that of the local congregation, as soon as any disagreement with Presbytery occurred, a disaffected majority in the congregation, however much in the wrong, could vote itself from under that jurisdiction, and set up as a Congregationalist parish, perhaps in opposition to all or a majority of the communicants.

ters expressions which amounted to a comment on the text, conformed the New Testament to the Old in the spelling of proper names, and got rid of manifest errors in the use of capitals, italics, and punctuation marks. Slight as was the revision embodied in this standard text (1851), it was attacked as a breach of faith on the part of the society by Dr. A. C. Coxe—now Bishop Coxe—in 1856. On the motion of Dr. R. J. Breckinridge the old-school Assembly condemned the revision and directed its Board of Publication to print a Bible with the unrevised text of 1611. By this action the Bible Society was obliged to return to the old text.[1]

On the old-school side biblical scholarship was finely represented by Professor Addison Alexander, of Princeton —a man of sound judgment and remarkable openness to the results of modern scholarship. The notes of George Bush on the Old Testament—written before he became a Swedenborgian—and of Melanchthon W. Jacobus on the New, like those of Mr. Barnes, were for popular rather than scholarly readers.

In dogmatic theology Dr. Charles Hodge exerted the greatest influence, indoctrinating several generations into the "Princeton theology." The graciousness of his personal influence compensated the deficiencies of his historical training and the lack of coherence at times in his logical demonstrations. His commentaries may be regarded as subsidiary to his dogmatics, which as yet reached the

---

[1] In this discussion, and those over the radical Revision of later days, great stress is laid upon the phrase " Authorized Version." By whom was it authorized ? Not by King James, nor by the convocation or episcopate of the Church of England; not the Kirk of Scotland, which authorized the Genevan version, and never any other. In Presbyterian law the version of 1611 is an unwarranted innovation, for which nothing but prescription and acquiescence can be pleaded. But the old-school church, in the case of the Plan of Union, ruled that prescription and acquiescence imparted no validity to the act of the Assembly of 1801, since that act was *ultra vires.* Much less can they serve as an authorization in the absence of any formal act.

public only through the " Princeton Review." In this he carried on a vigorous polemic with Professor Edwards A. Park, of Andover. Of Professor H. B. Smith's work at Union I have spoken already. A worthy third was Professor James H. Thornwell, of Columbia (S. C.) Seminary, who combined with the glowing eloquence of a Southern orator a strength of reasoning second to none of his day. Dr. Samuel J. Baird, in " The Elohim Revealed " (1860), set forth the older realistic Calvinism, in contrast to both Princeton and the new school. Dr. Robert J. Breckinridge in his " Knowledge of God, Objectively and Subjectively Considered " (1857–59), presents a philosophical theology of the most decided old-school orthodoxy, but without marked originality.

In the field of church history Dr. Schaff, then in the German Reformed Church, was breaking new ground in the face of much ultra-Protestant criticism and opposition. Presbyterians were attempting little, having hardly awakened to the importance of the subject. Some biographies, such as that of Dr. Rogers by Dr. Miller, and autobiographies, like those of Addison Alexander, Thomas Cleland, and Ashbel Green, constituted valuable contributions to American church history. But the plan of the General Assembly to secure and publish a history of each of its Synods and Presbyteries had fallen through, although some of these were actually prepared. Most important were Dr. William B. Sprague's " Annals of the American Pulpit " (9 vols., 1857–69), which lay the church historians of America under inestimable obligations. Dr. Robert Baird's " Religion in America " (1843–44 and 1856), although prepared with a view to European readers, was a really excellent account, historical and statistical, of the American churches. The works of Dr. Hodge (1839–40), Dr. William Hill (1839), and Mr. Webster (1858), Dr. Archi-

bald Alexander's "Log College" (1845), Dr. William Henry
Foote's "Sketches of North Carolina and of Virginia" (3
vols., 1846–55), and Dr. Davidson's " History of the Church
in Kentucky " (1847) are all books of lasting importance.

In the field of practical theology the number of writers
was very great, but not so that of those whose books have
achieved a permanent place.   The introspective character
imparted especially to this literature by the Awakening
makes it less acceptable to our own generation.   The best-
known books were David Nelson's " Cause and Cure of
Infidelity " (1836); Thomas H. Skinner's "Aids to Preaching and Hearing " (1839); Dr. Charles Hodge's " The Way
of Salvation " (1841); Ichabod S. Spencer's " A Pastor's
Sketches " (1850–53); Dr. James W. Alexander's " Consolation " (1852); Dr. Erskine Mason's " A Pastor's Leg-
acy " (1853); and Albert Barnes's " The Atonement"
(1859).   In the adjacent field of hymnody the beginning
made by President Davies was followed up by Dr. James
W. Alexander in his fine renderings from the German (collected, 1861); by Professor Henry Mills, of Auburn, in rendering from both Latin (1840) and German (1845 and 1856);
and by Drs. N. S. S. Beman and Edwin H. Hatfield, Rev.
George Duffield and Thomas S. Hastings, with original
hymns.   American Presbyterians, however, as hymn-writers, were and are both less notable and less productive
than the Congregationalists, Episcopalians, Baptists, or
Unitarians.   They contributed little to the rapid development of poetry and imaginative prose which characterized
the national life at this time.

The smaller Presbyterian bodies experienced important
changes during this period.   There was the usual tale of
petty strifes and divisions, but, along with these, most cheering evidence that the Spirit of wisdom, unity, and a sound
mind had not deserted the church.   In 1843 discontent

with the action in a disciplinary case caused a short-lived secession from the Associate Synod, which called itself the "Free Presbytery of Miami," but went to pieces in two years. Longer lived was the secession of 1844 from the Associate Presbytery of Philadelphia, which took the name of that Presbytery, but was popularly known as the Websterite party. The cause of the division was partly the refusal of the Associate Presbytery and Synod to condemn that true saint, Dr. Thomas P. Cooper, for teaching that the Holy Spirit acts immediately in regeneration, and not by means of the Word, and partly dissatisfaction with the changes in the Westminster Confession made by the Synod in 1840. This new body was dissolved in 1858, some of its ministers returning to the Seceders, while others went to the Covenanters (N. S.). The Reformed Dissenting Presbytery, which had withdrawn from the Associate Reformed Synod in 1801, found a home in the Associate Synod in 1852. The Bullions secession of 1840 from the Associate Church came to an end in 1854, when its four Presbyteries, with over twenty-five hundred communicants, returned to the Associate Synod. The death of Mr. Lusk in 1845 dissolved for a time the little Reformed Presbytery of North America, as it left David Steele alone in its ministry. But it afterward was revived.

The most important and happy change was the union of the great body of the American Seceders in a single General Assembly. As early as 1837 the Reformed Presbyterians (N. S.) asked for conference with the Associate and Associate Reformed Churches with a view to organic union. This wing of the Covenanters, having abandoned "political dissent," seemed to feel that the precedent of 1782, which brought the Associate Reformed Church into existence, might well be followed. The Associate Reformed Church, however, like the Presbyterian Church, had altered the statements of the Confession of Faith as regards the functions of the civil magistracy, and it now refused to go back to the very strong statements of the Westminster divines as to the power of civil rulers for the reformation of the church, the maintenance of sound doctrine, and the punishment of heresy. The other two churches had not made the change, nor could the Covenanters (N. S.) be induced to do so. The Associate Synod in 1840 agreed to the alteration, and by 1844 a plan for a United Presbyterian Church was in readiness for adoption. It was not found acceptable, yet the conferences continued until 1849. Even after they ceased the two Seceder churches continued correspondence on the subject, and in 1857 the Associate Synod proposed a basis of union which was adopted by the other Synod. This provided for a common modification of the Confession and a "judicial testimony" against prevalent errors, including slave-holding, oath-bound secret societies, open communion, and hymn-singing. It was approved by the Presbyteries of both, with the exception of the Associate Presbytery of northern Indiana. Thus was formed the United Presbyterian Church of North America. A small minority of the Associate Synod entered protest, declined the union, and, later in the same year, reorganized the Associate Synod. Similarly a small minority of the Associate Reformed Synod refused to enter the union, and organized the Associate Reformed Synod of New York, with two Presbyteries and sixteen ministers.

During the negotiations with the Seceders a strong desire for organic union with them was developed in the Covenanter Church, which had taken the first step. The approach of the union of 1858 awakened the hope that all three churches would be included. A conference was held at Chambersburg before the meeting of the General

Synod, at which the leading men resolved against union. As one of them expressed it, they resolved that " the Reformed Presbyterian Church should march into the millennium with banners displayed." This decision contributed to the subsequent disorganization of the body.

Among these smaller bodies, with the exception of the Reformed Presbytery, there was a gradual and partial relaxation of the disciplinary rigidity of earlier times. The rule against "occasional hearing" was generally abandoned among the Seceders, and plays no part in the union of 1858; and it disappeared also among the (N. S.) Covenanters. The stricter Covenanters, now known as those of the Synod in contrast to the General Synod, found it hard to maintain the rule in the cities. Thus in Philadelphia in 1859 young people of their churches would go to hear Mr. Grattan Guinness preach. They submitted passively to the discipline inflicted by the sessions, and then went again. Discontent also was shown with the rule forbidding funeral services.

CHAPTER XIII.

THE WAR FOR THE UNION AND TWO SECESSIONS, 1861–70.

THIS decade, 1861–70, was as memorable in the history of the Presbyterian Church as in that of the nation. It opened with a division and closed with a reunion which constitute the last notable changes in the contour of American Presbyterianism.

When the old-school Assembly met in Philadelphia in May, 1861, eight of the Southern States had declared their severance from the federal Union, and the war between their Confederate government and that of the nation had been in progress for about a month, though chiefly in the way of preparation for active hostilities. No one, who did not live through it, could realize the swift change from uncertainty and irresolution to enthusiastic decision which had passed over the country in a few days. After the first shot fired on the national flag, men had looked into each other's eyes to find reflected there a passion of patriotism of which they had not thought themselves capable. This united all parties for the time, and the least military of peoples was rapidly converting itself into an army.

Naturally this atmosphere could not be excluded from the ecclesiastical assemblages of that and the following years. Even the Peace Society had to pronounce for " vigorous police measures " for the maintenance of the national authority. Especially those bodies which had held an ambiguous position in relation to the South were expected to show on which side they stood, just as the mobs who swept the streets of the great cities after Fort Sumter was fired on made special demand for the hoisting of the flag over churches and hotels which had been believed to be in sympathy with the seceding States. The old-school Assembly, from its large affiliations with the South, much more than from its utterances with regard to slavery —as that, in the North, was not yet an issue of the struggle —was among the bodies which were expected to speak out against a movement the American people regarded as morally wicked no less than politically ruinous. Mr. McCormick, the inventor of the reaper and the founder of the Northwestern Seminary, was accustomed to speak of the old-school church and the Democratic party as "the two hoops which held the Union together." The saying reflected the popular feeling that that church had a political importance, and the new administration in Washington is said to have intimated that a declaration for loyalty would strengthen the hands of the national government, especially in Maryland, Kentucky, and Missouri. It was equally certain that such a declaration would be especially irritating to the Confederate authorities, as showing that the unexpected enthusiasm for the maintenance of the national unity had pervaded even the bodies least liable to be actuated by any slight or passing emotion.

The border-State Presbyteries were fully represented in the Assembly, and there were a few delegates, also, from the States which had declared themselves out of the Union. These were men like Dr. E. Thompson Baird, of Mississippi, who held to the hope that the church might maintain its unity in spite of political separation. Many in the Northern delegations agreed with them in deprecating all discussion and action with regard to the political situation.

These made a strong party, yet they were decidedly in the minority.

The first note was struck by the venerable Dr. Gardiner Spring, for more than half a century the pastor of the Brick Church in New York. The retiring moderator, Dr. Yeomans, asked him to offer prayer before the annual sermon, and the old man poured out his heart for the preservation of the Union. The party of silence scored a point in the selection of Dr. John C. Backus, of Baltimore, to the moderatorship, as will appear in the contrast between the action of the Assembly and the report of its committee. As the session proceeded it was seen that all the former leaders of the body were following the policy of silence, and a number of the less prominent men invited Dr. Spring to prepare and offer a resolution. He was among the most conservative men in the church, and his utterances on the slavery question mostly had been in the shape of denunciations of the abolitionists. He had united with thirty-five leading ministers of his own way of thinking in an appeal to the ministers and churches of the South, just after South Carolina had adopted the Act of Secession, assuring them of fraternal love and confidence, and inviting them to united prayer to " avert the horrors of fratricidal war." But when the war came, after he had heard a Southern Senator declare there were no terms on which the South would consent to stay in the Union, he thought himself obligated by his duty to the country to work for its preservation from destruction by the hands of its own children.

It certainly was not with the intention of obtaining extreme or radical action that the majority put their case into Dr. Spring's hands. Nor was his proposal offensive in its manner or extreme in its matter. On the sixth day of the session, after repeated failures to have the subject referred to a special committee to prepare a deliverance, he offered a preamble and Resolutions providing for a day of fasting and prayer that God might " turn away his anger from us and speedily restore to us the blessings of an honorable peace." It proceeded, " in the spirit of Christian patriotism," to " acknowledge and declare our obligations to promote and perpetuate, so far as in us lies, the integrity of these United States, and to strengthen, uphold, and encourage the Federal Government in the exercise of all its functions under our noble Constitution; and to this Constitution, in all its provisions, requirements, and principles, we profess our unabated loyalty."

The source from which the proposal came added so much to its weight that the advocates of silence secured the postponement of the discussion for two days. These Dr. Henry A. Boardman and others employed in urging Dr. Spring to withdraw or modify the paper, but without effect. After three days of heated debate, the paper, with two substitutes for it, was referred to a committee of nine, who reported—eight to one—for the policy of silence. Dr. William C. Anderson, of San Francisco, who constituted the minority, reported back Dr. Spring's Resolutions with a slight modification; and these, after renewed debate, were adopted finally by a vote of 156 to 66, with a rider offered by Dr. Jonathan Edwards, of Philadelphia. This declared that by the term " Federal Government " nothing else was meant than " the central Administration, which, being at any time appointed and inaugurated according to the form prescribed in the Constitution of the United States, is the visible representative of our national existence."

To outsiders in that heated time it seemed as though the Assembly had " roared as gently as a sucking dove." But the dignified, deliberate terms of the Resolutions expressed exactly what the best mind of the church was, without a word of bitterness or denunciation toward the South, and therefore they had the greater effect in helping to draw the line of secession below, and not above, the border States. To the minority, however, the action was as unacceptable as possible. Dr. Charles Hodge, a Republican in politics from the formation of that party until his death, presented a Protest, which was signed by himself and fifty-seven others, including the moderators of that and the previous Assemblies, and the sixteen delegates in attendance from the seceded States. It admits, of course, the right of the Assembly to enjoin upon the ministers and churches the duty of loyalty and subjection to the powers that be. It denies its right, in case of a dispute, to decide as to which or what authority has the primary claim to allegiance, and it asserts that the General Assembly had made allegiance to the Union, whatever the action of the State, a term of communion.

Those who stood by the Spring Resolutions had the whole history of the church, the teaching of the Confession, and the authority of God's Word on their side. The Protest implied a condemnation of Knox and of Calvin, of the Golden Assembly of 1638, of the Westminster Assembly of Divines, of the Revolution Assembly of 1690, and of the American Synods of 1772–82. It is impossible to see how Presbyterianism could have perpetuated its existence on either side of the Atlantic if the Kirk had acted on the theories of the Hodge Protest, and had renounced her claim to " treat in an ecclesiastical way of greatest and smallest matters, from the king's throne, that should be established in righteousness, to the merchant's balance, that should be used in faithfulness." The document was another index of the extent to which the pietism of the Awakening had displaced the theocratic conception which lies so near the core of historic Presbyterianism.

That good men in the South honestly believed it their duty to stand by their State against the nation was no more bar to a deliverance upon the matter than was the fact that good men had held it their duty to stand by the Stuart kings in the exercise of a brutal Erastian tyranny, or by the Pretender in his assertion of his right to the British throne, or by the British government in its claim to deal with the American colonies in a fashion which would have extinguished both civil and religious liberty. The most conscientious conviction may be but the conviction of an unenlightened conscience, and while the church may not " intermeddle with civil affairs which concern the commonwealth," the Confession makes an exception : " By way of advice for the satisfaction of conscience."

That there was need of such advice in the present case shows how weakening, on the social side, had been the influence of the Awakening. It had made even good men tolerant of the political atheism of the Rousseau and Jefferson school, which saw in a nation nothing higher than a human contrivance for secular ends, to be formed on such terms, and dissolved in such emergencies, as its constituent elements pleased. To those who see in God the giver of national life and order, the attempt to destroy these, on whatever pretense, must seem criminal. The readiness, however, of later Presbyterians to make almost any difference of opinion an excuse for ecclesiastical separation had tended so much to lower the feeling of the sacredness of church unity, that it could not but react upon our political life in an unhappy way.

During the summer and autumn of 1861 the Southern Presbyteries of the old-school church generally adopted resolutions renouncing the authority of the General Assembly. In pursuance of an invitation issued by a convention held at Atlanta, Ga., in August, delegates from ten

Synods, including forty-seven Presbyteries, met in Augusta, Ga., and constituted the first General Assembly of " the Presbyterian Church in the Confederate States of America." It chose as moderator Dr. Benjamin M. Palmer, whose Fast-day Sermon of 1860 had placed him in the front rank of the advocates of secession, and of whom a Confederate general said that " his services were worth more to the cause than a soldiery of ten thousand men."

It has been asserted, and no doubt sincerely, that opposition to the Spring Resolutions, on the grounds presented in Dr. Hodge's Protest, was the efficient cause of this separation. But the whole manner, scope, and circumstances of the transaction show that its causes were purely political. It was a secession from the minority as well as the majority of the General Assembly—from Drs. Hodge, Backus, and Yeomans, no less than from Drs. Spring, Anderson, and Edwards. No offer of coöperation and union was held out to those who had protested against the Spring Resolutions. On the contrary, the title taken by the new body ruled them out of its communion with the utmost distinctness. That title crystallized the new church along the lines of a political division, not those of ecclesiastical principle. It excluded even the churches and Presbyteries of the border States, so long as it remained the style of the Southern church. When the United Synod cast in its lot with that church, its Presbytery of Lexington, Ky., was left out necessarily, and sought readmission to the new-school Assembly.

Neither did the Spring Resolutions afford any reasonable ground for separation. They enunciated no new doctrine and subverted no principle of Presbyterian order. They merely passed upon a question of social duty according to the best light the Assembly had, whether right or wrong; and such a deliverance *in thesi* has no binding force upon the consciences of either members or judicatories of the church. Dr. Hodge and his co-protesters, indeed, declared that they had erected a new term of communion, and Dr. Palmer denounced them as "virtually exscinding" the Southern churches; but both wrote unadvisedly and under the influence of excitement.

If the policy of silence had been followed by the General Assembly, the question of a separation could have been put off only for a brief time. Political separation always has carried ecclesiastical division with it in the sphere of Protestantism. Even the Protestant Episcopal Church, in which the policy of silence was systematized, went apart while the war lasted. As soon as the seceding States satisfied themselves that their experiment was a success and that their Confederacy was to last, they would have adjusted their ecclesiastical arrangements to the new lines. That assurance they reached so early that it is doubtful if the Spring Resolutions even hastened the action of the Southern Presbyterians. This first Southern Assembly itself said: "It is desirable that each nation should contain a separate and independent church, and the Presbyteries of the Confederate States need no apology for bowing to the decree of Providence, which, in withdrawing their country from the government of the United States, has, at the same time, determined that they should withdraw from the church of their fathers." [1]

1 From the very frank and able "Address by the General Assembly of the Presbyterian Church in the United States of America to all the Churches of Jesus Christ throughout the Earth, unanimously adopted at their sessions in Augusta, Ga., December, 1861." It was prepared by Dr. Thornwell, and is reprinted in his works. It also says :

"We frankly admit that the mere unconstitutionality of the proceedings of the last Assembly is not, in itself considered, a sufficient ground of separation. It is the consequences of these proceedings which make them so offensive. It is the door they open for the introduction of the worst passions of human nature into the deliberations of church courts."

"The Northern section of the church stands in the awkward predicament

It was the collapse of the Confederate States which gave those Resolutions permanent significance as a reason for maintaining the separation of 1861 within the bounds of the same nation. But for that they would now have little more than an antiquarian interest, and for that purpose they are badly overworked. That the Southern church did not plant itself upon the ground taken in the Hodge Protest was shown by deliverances, far more explicit than the Spring Resolutions, in frankest support of the Confederate States. Thus, to quote one of several, the Southern Assembly of 1862, in its " Narrative of the State of Religion," says: " All the Presbyteries which have reported dwell upon the absorbing topic of the war in which we are now engaged. . . . All the Presbyterial narratives, without exception, mention the fact that their congregations have evinced the most cordial sympathy with the people of the Confederate States in their efforts to maintain their cherished rights and institutions against the despotic power which is attempting to crush them." The Assembly of 1864, besides adopting a report which contained an unmistakable condemnation of protection and approval of free trade, in its " Narrative of the State of Religion " says: " The long-continued agitations of our adversaries have wrought within us a deeper conviction of the divine appointment of domestic servitude, and have led to a clearer comprehension of the duties we owe to the African race. We hesitate not to affirm that it is the peculiar mission of

of maintaining, in one breath, that slavery is an evil which ought to be abolished, and of asserting, in the next, that it is not a sin to be visited by exclusion from communion of the saints. The consequence is that it plays partly into the hands of the abolitionists and partly into the hands of the slave-holders, and weakens its influence with both. It is a prevaricating witness whom neither party will trust."

" In our ecclesiastical capacity we are neither the friends nor the foes of slavery; that is to say, we have no commission either to propagate or to abolish it."

the Southern church to conserve the institution of slavery, and to make it a blessing to both master and slave."

The new church at once adopted a vigorous home and foreign missionary and educational policy. It took charge of the missionary work among those tribes in the Indian Territory whom General Albert Pike had persuaded to cast in their lot with the Confederacy, through their sympathy with it as slave-holders. Following out the policy defended by Dr. Thornwell before the division, it dispensed with "boards," and placed its work in charge of executive committees invested with less discretionary power and more directly responsible to the synodical bodies which constitute Presbyterian government.

In 1863 it received the Independent Presbyterian Church, a body of thirteen churches and four ministers, all in South Carolina. This had been formed in 1811 by William C. Davis and his followers. He had been deposed for the heresies contained in his book, " The Gospel Plan " (1809), by the Presbytery of Orange in 1811 ; and as both Synod and Assembly had already condemned the teachings of his book, he withdrew without appeal. In 1833 the General Assembly had censured those in its own jurisdiction who held communion with him, as he was a deposed minister. On their profession of their acceptance of the Confession, the Southern Assembly admitted them without reordination of their ministers.

The next year a union was formed with the United Synod (N. S.). This was on the basis of a doctrinal statement which covered the grounds of difference of 1837 ; and the new-school men of the South, by accepting it, showed that either they had shifted their ground in the meanwhile, or else that they never were in agreement with those who drafted the Auburn Declaration. This, however, is denied by some of them to this day.

Presbyterians of both Scotch-Irish and New England stock had their full share in the burdens and achievements of the war on both sides.   The first blood shed was that of Surgeon (afterward General) Crawford, who was wounded in the face during the bombardment of Fort Sumter. He was a son of Dr. S. Wylie Crawford, of the Covenanter (N. S.) Church.   In the South, the men of the Scotch-Irish race occupied the Appalachian chain and its upland valleys, where the plantation was unknown and slave-holders rare.   They were therefore out of sympathy with the policy of their wealthier neighbors, and in general attached strongly to the Union.   In West Virginia they cut loose from the Confederacy, and reëntered the Union as a new State.   In western North Carolina, eastern Tennessee, and adjacent parts of South Carolina, Georgia, and Alabama they offered resistance to the measures taken to draft them into the Confederate army.   Hence it was that, next to the opening of the Mississippi, the seizure of Chattanooga in eastern Tennessee was the chief strategic point of the war, as it gave the national army a basis of operations among a friendly people, from which the line of the coast States could be cut in any direction.   But, for the reasons already stated (pp. 69–71), only a fraction of this Scotch-Irish population had remained in the Presbyterian communion.

Like almost all wars, that for the Union brought with it elements of demoralization and spiritual decline.   The great cities especially suffered in the injury to public order which attends the preparation and conduct of hostilities. The churches in many cases suffered in the diversion of their attention and energies to " things seen and temporal "; and the duties of loyalty were often preached in a way which lowered the tone of the church, while it alienated many who had not acquired the new enthusiasm for

the Union, and, in later years, that for the suppression of
slavery. In a host of cases Presbyterian churches were
divided for this reason, the seceding minority commonly
organizing as an Episcopalian congregation. That church,
by a reverse of policy, gained more members in the War
for the Union than it had lost in that for Independence.

But there were compensations. There was a distinct
deepening of tone in the public utterances of the time, an
ampler and more sincere recognition of the authority of
God as the Ruler of nations, a new sense of the sacredness of the public order and unity of the nation as the gift
of God. It was felt that war itself was a solemn appeal
to the divine arbitration, and even the blasphemies of
General Hooker but emphasized for thoughtful soldiers
the solemn lessons of the hour of judgment in which they
stood.

The armies themselves were in many cases schools of
the new life to those who entered them. In that of the
Confederate States there was a revival in 1863–64, which
fairly outran the power of the chaplains and volunteer
workers to deal with it. In the army of the United States
the chaplains, with a few unworthy exceptions, were picked
men, whose labors were fruitful of good both while the
war lasted and ever since. They were aided by the labors
of the Christian Commission, in which all the orthodox
churches coöperated in sending preachers, nurses, supplies
for well and wounded, libraries and religious literature
both to the armies in action and to the winter-quarters and
hospitals. The soldiers were kept in touch with home and
under home influences, and were encouraged and helped
to keep up correspondence and to send home a part of
their pay. This kind of work was begun by John Patterson, a Presbyterian elder of Philadelphia, by George S.
Griffith, of the German Reformed Church in Baltimore,

and by Rev. Benj. W. Chidlaw in the West. It soon crystallized into a national organization, called into existence
by the national convention of the Young Men's Christian
Associations, which placed George Hay Stuart, who combined practical business abilities with great personal enthusiasm, at the head. Of the Presbyterians associated with
him, Dr. Charles Hodge, Stephen Colwell, William E. Dodge,
and Joseph Patterson deserve mention here, though not
more notable than the representatives of other denominations.

While the New Side Covenanters gave a leader to this
work of Christian benevolence, the Old Side found it hard
to maintain the attitude of "political dissent" in circumstances which so strongly enlisted their sympathies on the
side of the nation. No American church was more pronounced in its abhorrence of slavery; none cherished so
strong a sense of the sacredness of national life. Their
Synod declared: "It is seldom in the history of war that
the right is so entirely on one side, and wrong on the other,
as in the present case. . . . In this great struggle for the
preservation of law and order against disloyalty and trea-
son, we may readily distinguish between the welfare of
the country on the one hand and the sinful character of
the Constitution, and its imperfect administration, on the
other." But so long as an oath of allegiance to the Constitution was imposed upon the soldier, they could but
offer prayers and sympathy, while the fighting instincts of
Drumclog and Pentland Hills were hot within them. The
Synod of 1863 made a proffer to the government of a form
of oath pledging the recruit to be "faithful to the United
States" and yield "all due obedience to military orders."
Against this ten voted; and two entered protest against
approval of a war whose "declared purpose" was "the
maintenance and defense of the Constitution." As the

oath of allegiance ceased to be required of the soldiers, the matter was dropped, and the Synod's approval was rescinded. Secretary Stanton, through his employment in the Pittsburg lawsuit of 1848 (p. 103), understood their difficulties, and did all in his power to facilitate their serving in the army.

. The close of the war brought with it the necessity for a change in the style of the Southern church, which now took the name the " Presbyterian Church in the United States." It had suffered heavily, as had the South, from the devastations of the war, and the loss of both men and means. Churches, in some cases, had broken up, never to gather again. Wounds and the diseases of camp and march had thinned out its membership. Many wealthy families had been reduced to complete poverty by the loss of their slaves and other property. But, like the South generally, it took up the burdens of rebuilding with spirit and energy.

It was soon to be reinforced largely by accessions of Presbyteries and churches in the border States, who had suffered less, or not at all, in the years of war. The people of these States, so far as slavery was concerned, generally were in sympathy with the South, but were opposed to the dissolution of the Union, as that, indeed, would have imperiled their interests by reopening the African slave-trade. For a time they tried to maintain a neutral attitude, but ultimately they found themselves within the national military lines. After the war had ended they felt themselves aggrieved by the abolition of slavery through the thirteenth amendment to the Constitution, which affected only them. They also had had to bear a large share of the severely repressive measures which the administration had thought necessary for the effective conduct of the war.

Most unfortunately, some of these measures had been of a character which involved the churches both needlessly and wrongfully. The officers commanding the military districts undertook to suppress anything that seemed an ecclesiastical expression of sympathy with the Confederate cause, and that often with more vehemence than discretion.

The first case which attracted general attention was that of Dr. S. B. McPheeters, pastor of the Pine Street Church in St. Louis. He had twice taken the oath of allegiance to the national government, and had abstained strictly from what he called "political preaching and praying." He had defended the policy of silence on civil questions in the Assembly of 1862 against Dr. Robert J. Breckinridge, and he practiced it for himself. He had people of both ways of thinking in his congregation, and he labored to give offense to neither.

Unfortunately, one of his congregation presented a child for baptism, and gave the name of a Confederate commander, who was especially detested by the Unionists of the State on account of his raids across its southern border. Dr. McPheeters, under the Constitution of the church, had no choice but to give the child that name, as he also must have done if the name specified to him had been Abraham Lincoln or Charles Sumner. The transaction, however, was like a spark in a powder-magazine, as things then stood. Some of the Unionists of the congregation made their appeal to the provost-marshal general of the Department of the Missouri, alleging against their pastor no more than this act, and that he prayed for "kings and all in authority," and not specifically for the President of the United States. Thereupon General F. A. Dick issued an order (December 19, 1862) banishing Dr. McPheeters and his wife out of the military district on the plea of "unmistakable evidence of sympathy with the

Rebellion," forbidding his discharge of ministerial functions in the meantime, and requiring that they leave the State in ten days, and "take up their residence within the free States north of Indianapolis and west of Pittsburg." At the same time the "edifice, books, and papers" of the Pine Street Church were handed over to "the control of three loyal members, . . . who shall see that its pulpit be filled by a loyal minister of the gospel."

Dr. McPheeters, within a week after, went to Washington and laid the case before Mr. Lincoln. The President at once ordered a modification by which Dr. McPheeters and his family were allowed to continue in Missouri, and a few days later (January 2, 1863) he wrote to General Curtis, commanding in the district, that "the United States government must not, as by this order," relating to Dr. McPheeters, "undertake to run the churches. When an individual in the church or out of it becomes dangerous to the public interest he must be checked; but the churches, as such, must take care of themselves. It will not do for the United States to appoint trustees, supervisors, or other agents for the churches." This letter he meant as disposing of the case in the sense Dr. McPheeters desired, and in principle it did so. But the military authorities of the district seem to have resolved that nothing less than a specific and categorical order, naming him by name, was obligatory upon them. He remained under their ban, forbidden to attend his Presbytery or Synod, shut out of his pulpit, and refused leave even to officiate at a marriage or a funeral, until the President wrote a second letter, nearly a year later (December 22, 1863), reinforcing the first. "I have never," he said, "interfered, or thought of interfering, as to who shall or shall not preach in any church; nor have I knowingly or believingly tolerated any one else so to interfere by my authority."

Nearly four months after this, however, General Rose-crans, the new commander of the district, issued an order (March 8, 1864) requiring every ecclesiastical body within the district to ascertain whether any of their number had not taken the oath of allegiance within a time specified, and to exclude those who had not, under penalties of martial law. It was believed, on what evidence I cannot learn, that this action had been instigated by ministers and elders of the church, by way of badgering those of their brethren who differed from them in politics. Nor can I find any evidence that Mr. Lincoln's attention was ever called to it by those who had benefited by his letter.

Dr. McPheeters, and those who agreed with him as to the relations of church and state, abstained from attending under the circumstances, leaving the Presbytery of St. Louis in the hands of a minority—eighteen out of sixty members—which proceeded to dissolve the pastoral relation existing between him and the Pine Street Church. Complaints against this action went up to the General Assembly of 1864, from Dr. McPheeters, his session, and a majority of the ministers and sessions of the Presbytery, on the ground that the meeting of Presbytery was invalid, its proceedings irregular and unwarranted. Most unhappily, the Assembly treated the matter of military interference as a "side issue," and by 117 to 49 voted not to sustain the appeal, "because the proceedings in the Presbytery of St. Louis appear constitutional and regular," "and, being on the ground, and conversant with all the facts of the case, they seem most competent to undertake and decide upon what" action was required by "the disturbed state of the church" in Pine Street, St. Louis. This was done in the face of the opposition of passionate Unionists like Dr. George Junkin, who declared that the independence and spirituality of the church were at stake.

This action naturally left a very bad taste in the mouths of many in the border States. It was not removed by the deliverances and decisions of the Assembly of 1865, meeting in Pittsburg a month after the assassination of President Lincoln, with the sores of the war still unhealed, and its fruits still ungathered. All the Christian world has praised the magnanimity with which the American people dealt with the States that had attempted to destroy the unity of the nation. But the hour for magnanimity had not yet struck, nor did the Assembly anticipate it by its action. It stigmatized secession as a crime, and the withdrawal of the Southern churches as a schism. It offered recognition and restoration to such Southern ministers as would apply for it, and would declare their acceptance of the deliverances on slavery. It directed the Board of Domestic Missions to treat the South as missionary ground, and to employ loyal ministers without requiring a Presbyterial recommendation, where this could not be obtained. It proceeded to make loyalty, or a confession of repentance for disloyalty, and a rejection of the theory that slavery is "a divine institution," tests to be exacted both of ministers and members who sought to enter the church.

There came before this Assembly a complaint from Robert P. Farris, of Charles City, Mo., that he and his elder had been prevented from taking part in the organization of the Synod of Missouri at its last meeting. The moderator had decided that, in the view of ecclesiastical law, these gentlemen were members of the Synod, but that in view of the order of General Rosecrans, with which they had not complied, he could not allow them to participate in its proceedings! This decision was reversed after the Synod had been organized, and the two were allowed to sit. But it was made a test case, and the Assembly declared that it was "not called upon to decide anything in regard to the propriety or impropriety of the military order referred to," and dismissed the appeal on technical grounds.

The Protest of Dr. Samuel R. Wilson and other border-State delegates, in which they spread the Rosecrans Order on the minutes of the Assembly, was the first step toward a movement to carry the churches of those States over to the Southern Assembly, whose jurisdiction was no longer circumscribed by its title. Following the precedent set in 1835, Dr. Wilson drafted a " Declaration and Testimony " against all the deliverances of the old-school Assembly— from the Spring Resolutions of 1861 to those of recent date—which bore upon political questions, especially the deliverances on slavery in 1864 and 1865, which it very truthfully declared to be in contradiction to the deliverance of 1845. It denounced the union of church and state which had been reached in the prosecution of the war; the personal proscription of men like Dr. McPheeters; and the virtual excommunication of the whole Southern church by the Assembly of 1865. It pledged the signers to recognize no authority in ecclesiastical decisions unwarranted by the Scriptures, especially the decisions of the last two Assemblies on slavery and loyalty, " and with reference to the conducting of missions in the Southern States, and with regard to the ministers, members, and churches in the seceded and border States." This was signed by fifty-four ministers and one hundred and seventy-three ruling elders, chiefly in the border States, and was formally adopted by the Presbytery of Louisville, Ky., one minister alone dissenting. On the other hand, a convention of ministers and elders for prayer and conference was held at St. Louis, at the suggestion of Dr. Robert J. Breckinridge, to counteract the effect of the Declaration and Testimony. It prepared a Memorial, urging the Assembly to stand firmly by its deliverances, and this was

signed by eighty-four ministers and one hundred and
thirty-four elders, of whom not a score were from the border States.

The Assembly of 1866 approved the Memorial and ordered it to be printed, and then took up the gauntlet of
the Declaration and Testimony people in much the spirit
in which it had been flung down. It condemned that
document as "a slander on the church, schismatical in
character and aims," summoned its signers to the bar of
the next Assembly, excluded them from sitting in church
courts in the meantime, and declared any Presbytery
"*ipso facto* dissolved" that should enroll them, authorizing
the ministers and elders of that Presbytery who adhered
to the Assembly to take charge of the records, retain the
name, and exercise the authority of the Presbytery. This
"Gurley Order" was adopted by 196 votes to 37. Several
protests were entered, but one by Dr. Henry A. Boardman was rejected as disrespectful to the Assembly.

This action, as must have been expected, ran the line of
division through the Presbyteries in the Synods of Kentucky and Missouri. The signers of the Declaration and
Testimony stood by their action; and twelve Presbyteries
divided on the issue of admitting them to seats, and sent
rival delegations to the Assembly of 1867. The Assembly, after hearing two of the signers in their own defense,
by a vote of 261 to 4 admitted the delegations from the
Presbyteries which had acted as the Assembly of 1866 had
directed. Thus two Synods were cut off from connection
with the Assembly, and suits for church property began.
The case of the Walnut Street Church in Louisville was
made a test. The courts of the State decided against the
adherents of the Assembly; but as some of them were
citizens of another State, they were able to take it before
the courts of the United States. Finally the Supreme

Court of the United States decided the case in favor of the adherents of the Assembly, on much the same grounds of ecclesiastical omnipotence as the Pennsylvania decision of 1839.

It was noteworthy that throughout this controversy the decided old-school men of the border States, and those who sympathized with them in other parts of the church, displayed a great liking for the arguments by which the new-school men had arraigned the Exscinding Acts of 1837. The power of the Assembly to exercise original jurisdiction, or to condemn without the formality of a trial, was stoutly denied, and the rights of Presbyteries were asserted strongly. On the other hand, I observed that the new-school men did not find so much comfort in this as might have been expected. Their sympathies went so strongly with the majority in the old-school Assembly, against a party they regarded as but half-loyal, if so much, that they generally refrained from speaking evil of the Gurley Order, and of the drastic proceedings to which it led. In the nearly thirty years which have passed a gentler spirit has come to prevail, and the acts of the Assemblies of 1865–67 are not those upon which Presbyterians generally look back with gratification.

The two Synods thus thrown upon themselves were really bound by their own principles to maintain their isolation. The lofty principles of the severance of religion from politics, of matters ecclesiastical from matters civil, on which they took their stand, were no more those of the Southern than of the national Assembly. A perusal of the minutes of the former during the years of the war would have furnished them with materials for a Declaration and Testimony quite as long and as acerb as that which had led to their excision from their own church. The Missouri Synod, indeed, seemed to feel this, as it perpetuated its separate existence until 1874. The Kentucky Presbyteries, which had had no Rosecrans Order to complain of, but had been the loudest in their protests against the confusion of church and state matters, found their way to the Southern Assembly in 1868. Once more political affinities sufficed to modify ecclesiastical convictions.

One effect of their adherence was to strengthen the work of the Southern church, especially in the home field. Another was to teach her new modes of speech with regard to public questions, and to impress upon her a conception of " the spirituality of the church," which hardly can be brought into harmony with the utterances of her Assemblies, Synods, Presbyteries, and pulpits during the war. But by withdrawing from the old-school church the element which stood nearest to the South, it put off the day of reconciliation with the Presbyterians of that section.

The Southern church obtained other accessions during this period. In 1867 the Associate Reformed Presbytery of Alabama, and in 1870 that of Kentucky, entered its communion, the ties of political sympathy proving stronger than their repugnance to hymn-singing.

CHAPTER XIV.

THE REUNION OF THE OLD AND NEW SCHOOL CHURCHES, 1869–70.

THE first effect of the spirit of the new age upon the American churches was to intensify sectarian feeling. The next was to awaken a yearning after Christian unity. Dr. Archibald Alexander, in 1841, " strongly maintained that there was less and less appearance of amalgamation among Protestant sects," although he had been watching for sixty years. It was matter of remark when an evangelist like Daniel Baker preached the gospel of love wherever he could find an opening, without reference to any advantage to his own church. And he had part of his reward in seeing two bishops of the Episcopal Church among the fruits of his Presbyterian labors.

Since 1860, however, there has been a great change of tone. The separate churches are put upon their defense to justify their separate existence. The rapid pace at which our political unity has been reached is felt to be an adverse criticism upon the persistence of old-world separations in our religious life. The war itself, by throwing men into new associations with their fellow-citizens and bringing home to them how much they had in common as men and as Christians, contributed greatly to this. The high value men learned to place on national unity naturally and easily led to hopes of a better day when sectarian lines would cease to divide us, just as sectional lines were vanishing.

In the Presbyterian Church this uniting tendency was felt very early in the war. The old-school Assembly of 1862 took the first step by proposing " a friendly interchange of commissioners" between the two Assemblies; and the new-school Assembly of 1863 responded with great heartiness. The next step came again from the same quarter. During the sessions of the old-school Assembly of 1864 a reunion conference was held and a paper adopted and published with the signatures of seventy ministers and fifty-three elders. It expressed confidence in the doctrinal soundness and ecclesiastical orderliness of both churches, and in the possibility of removing the obstacles to reunion by developing " a spirit of unity and fraternity."

Two years later both the Assemblies met in St. Louis and found on their tables memorials from their Presbyteries asking that steps be taken to reunite the churches. Again the old school took the initiative, expressing an " earnest desire for reunion at the earliest time consistent with agreement in doctrine, order, and policy, on the basis of our common standards and the prevalence of mutual love and confidence," and proposing a Joint Committee of nine ministers and six ruling elders from each body to discuss its feasibility. Assent on the part of the new school was unanimous. The men chosen on each side were not from among the professors but from the working pastors of the church. Dr. Stearns, on the new-school side, was the only scientific theologian among them. After two joint meetings they were able to report to the two Assemblies of 1869 a plan of reunion, " on the doctrinal and ecclesiastical basis of the common standards;" the Confession of Faith " to be sincerely received " in " its fair historical sense, as it is accepted by the two bodies, in opposition to antinomianism and fatalism on the one hand, and to Arminianism and Pelagianism on the other." This was followed by a number of articles for effecting the readjustments which would be required by the new condition of things. This plan they asked to have published for information and referred to the Assemblies of 1868 for action.

Without waiting for this, Dr. Charles Hodge attacked the plan in the "Princeton Review" for July, 1867, asserting that the new school never had "sincerely received in their integrity all the doctrines essential to the Reformed or Calvinistic system," and that less than this as a condition of union would be "not only inexpedient but morally wrong." Dr. H. B. Smith, in the "Presbyterian and Theological Review," met this charge with a flat contradiction. He declared that the new-school church received the Confession in precisely that "Reformed or Calvinistic sense" which Dr. Hodge demanded, and that those who opposed reunion "assumed a most serious responsibility." His superior historical learning gave great weight to his affirmations as regards what was "essential to the Reformed or Calvinistic system," while his independent attitude within the new-school church (p. 139) made his testimony to its orthodoxy especially important.

Thus far the question had been handled in rather a gingerly fashion, which seemed to show that those engaged with it were more conscious of the difficulties in the way than hopeful of overcoming them. What was needed was a clear, sharp crystallization of the sentiment in favor of reunion, and this came from an unexpected quarter. In the Reformed Presbyterian (N. S.) General Synod of 1867 a resolution was offered by George H. Stuart calling a convention of all the Presbyterian churches to consider the question of a general reunion. The Synod addressed this invitation to the other national assemblies, but it was the Presbyteries which acted on it and sent delegations. Ministers and elders to the number of 263— 162 from the old school, 64 from the new school, 12 from the United Presbyterians, 12 from the Reformed Presbyterians (N. S.), 6 from the Reformed Dutch, 6 from the Cumberland Presbyterians, and 1 from the Southern Presbyterians—assembled in the First Reformed Presbyterian Church of Philadelphia on November 8, 1867. From first to last the spirit of peace and of brotherly love seemed to brood over the proceedings. Men who knew one another only in the encounters of polemics met face to face. Drs. Hodge and Smith, fresh from their tourney over the Joint Committee's plan, found themselves associated lovingly in prayer and praise for the great object of their debate. The high tide of feeling was reached when the venerable Bishops McIlvaine and Lee, at the head of a deputation from the annual meetings of two of the great evangelical societies of their church, came to bid the convention " Godspeed " in its work, and to speak kind words of their Presbyterian brethren.

The business of the convention, to propose a basis of Presbyterian reunion, was intrusted to a committee of one minister and one elder from each of the churches represented. They brought in a unanimous report, of which the second article provided that " in the united church the Westminster Confession of Faith shall be received and adopted as containing the system of doctrine taught in the Holy Scripture." To this Dr. Smith, taking the words from Dr. Hodge's article in the " Princeton Review," proposed an addition : " It being understood that this Confession is received in its proper historical, that is, the Calvinistic or Reformed, sense." On this the delegations voted separately, the new school adopting it by 46 to 2.

This action went a great way to remove the objections many of the old school had felt. The atmosphere grew clearer, and the speedy coming of the reunion was now taken for granted.

Yet when the Joint Committee met the next year, the difficulties in the way seemed greater than ever. The old-school men wanted the Philadelphia Article. The new-school men were agreed, provided a clause were added stating that this already was the position held by both churches; or they were willing to take the original doctrinal article of 1867, either with or without Dr. Smith's amendment. The old school did not like either, but when asked for an alternative had none to offer. The evident purpose was to reach a formula, which would be open to no attack from the conservatives of the old school, while soothing the susceptibilities of the other church. These last had been roused by acrimonious resuscitations of the charges made in 1835–37. At last Dr. Gurley, of Washington, proposed to supplement the Philadelphia Article, with Dr. Smith's amendment, by another which declared :

" It is also understood that various methods of viewing, stating, explaining, and illustrating the doctrines of the Confession, which do not impair the integrity of the Reformed or Calvinistic system, are to be freely allowed in the united church, as they have hitherto been allowed in the separate churches."

This basis the Joint Committee accepted as securing to the new school theological liberty within the bounds they themselves had declared to be those they desired, while it left it free to the reunited church to deal with any whose teachings exceeded just limits and corresponded to what the conservatives of the old school declared to be the belief of radical new-school men. They reported it to the Assemblies of 1868, adding also to their previous proposals an agreement acknowledging the right—not the duty—of Presbyteries "to examine ministers applying for admission from other Presbyteries." In the new-school Assembly it was this Tenth Article which roused the most opposition, as being thoroughly un-Presbyterian in its character, and unknown to the sister-churches of both Europe and America. In the old school the opposition centered on the two qualifying amendments to the Philadelphia Article. Even that which Dr. Smith had framed in Dr. Hodge's words was felt to be not quite safe for conservatism. Who could tell how much this appeal to doctrinal history—to a region of which so little was known—might be made to cover? When the Assembly finally adopted it by a vote of 185 to 79, a strong minority offered a Protest, drafted by Dr. Charles Hodge, alleging the lists of errors in the "Memorial" of 1837 as evidence of the doctrinal unsoundness of the new-school church as a whole. The answer to this Protest was prepared by Dr. William G. T. Shedd and adopted by the Assembly. Among other things, it said:

"These very errors, charged by the signers of the Protest as allowed by the new-school Presbyterians, have already been repudiated by them. The Auburn Convention, held in 1837, under the influence and doctrinal guidance of that excellent and sound divine, the late Dr. Richards, specified sixteen doctrinal errors, which contain the very same latitudinarian and heretical tenets mentioned in the Protest, rejected them *in toto*, and set over against them sixteen 'true doctrines,' which embrace all the fundamentals of the Calvinistic creed. This Assembly regard the 'Auburn Declaration' as an authoritative statement of the new-school type of Calvinism."

It was felt, however, that the situation was critical as regards the old-school church, unless something more were done to conciliate the opposition. It was suggested that reunion on the basis of "the standards pure and simple" would meet with less resistance. A resolution proposing the omission of both the Smith and the Gurley Amendments was adopted, and sent to the other Assembly by a special delegation. Before it arrived from Albany in Harrisburg the attendance had fallen below a quorum, and no action could be taken. So the Joint Committee's basis alone went down to the Presbyteries in overture, for approval or rejection. Yet while the new-school Presbyteries voted approval of this, the old-school Presbyteries very generally voted their approval of "the standard pure and simple" basis, which had never been before the new-school Assembly for action. This was largely in pursuance of the advice given in the Pittsburg Circular, which was proposed by Dr. James Allison, of the "Presbyterian Banner," and signed by Professor A. A. Hodge, Dr. M. W. Jacobus, Dr. William M. Paxton, and others. As a result the Plan of Reunion was accepted in one branch and rejected in the other.

When the two Assemblies met in New York in 1869, the zeal of the new school for reunion was visibly cooling. The manner of procedure on the other side had been unsatisfactory, if not discourteous. The men who had carried the Joint Committee's plan through the old-school Assembly had failed to stand by it in the Presbyteries. They had shown more eagerness to soothe the feelings of those who had stirred again the bitter waters of 1835–37, than to carry out the agreement definitely reached. During the interval between the two Assemblies many unfraternal and irritating things had been said of new-school men. The names of Albert Barnes and George Duffield had been bandied about as those of convicted and condemned heretics, and security had been asked that in the future

no such men should make their way into the ministry of
the church. Even more offensive than these demands had
been the answers made to them by some who regarded
themselves as excellent friends of reunion. It was implied
that the new-school church had nothing to ask but "a
tombstone and an epitaph"; that the body negotiating
under that name was substantially an old-school church;
and that Mr. Barnes stood isolated in its ministry, an un-
venerable relic of an abandoned past. In this light, it was
said, what was the meaning of the hostility shown to the
Gurley Amendment, which assured the lesser church
against undue rigidity on the part of the larger? Why
talk of exacting pledges as unbrotherly and discourteous?
The man whose word is as good as his bond never refuses
to give his bond.

Fortunately for reunion, Dr. Stearns was the retiring
moderator of the new-school Assembly, and in his sermon
he pleaded with all his soul for what had seemed a sink-
ing cause. The churches of the city threw around the
Assembly an atmosphere more friendly to it than they
would have encountered in Philadelphia or Pittsburg.
Union prayer-meetings of the two Assemblies brought
back the lost fervor. A new Committee of Conference
brought in a unanimous report for a reunion of the two
churches on the basis of the standards simply, "each recognizing the other as a sound and orthodox body, according to the principles of the Confession common to both."
This doctrinal clause alone was to be overtured to the
Presbyteries, the other parts of the basis being converted
into "Concurrent Declarations" of the two Assemblies.
The new-school Assembly once more voted unanimous
approval. In the other Assembly the vote was 285 to 9,
the minority being five ministers and four elders.

The vote of the Presbyteries in the months following

was in much the same proportion.   Every one of the one hundred and thirteen Presbyteries of the new-school church voted to approve, and all but three of them unanimously, the minority in each case being a single member.   Of the one hundred and forty-four Presbyteries of the old-school church, all but thirteen responded to the overture.   Of these one hundred and twenty-eight voted approval, and three rejection.   Among the minority was Dr. Charles Hodge, who " rode nine miles to meet the Presbytery in Cranberry, on October 5, 1869, with the *anthrax mali-tiosissimus* on the back of his neck, for the purpose of casting his final vote against " reunion.

The two Assemblies had adjourned to meet at Pittsburg on November 10th to consummate the reunion, if it had been voted by the necessary majority of the Presbyteries. The proceedings were in the main of a formal or congratulatory character.   Each Assembly declared the Basis of Reunion to be of binding force, and declared its own dissolution, the moderators calling another Assembly to meet in the First Church in Philadelphia in May, 1870.   The members of the two bodies then met in front of the First Church, in which the old-school Assembly had been meeting, and, pairing off, marched, amid great popular enthusiasm, to the Third Church, in which the new-school Assembly had held its sessions.   Here a reunion ratification meeting was held, and a joint communion service in the afternoon.   At the former a resolution was adopted to raise $5,000,000 as a thank-offering for the restoration of peace.   Pittsburg, most Scotch-Irish of American cities, had had its share in the troubles which had divided the church.   It now witnessed and approved the transaction which brought the division to an end.

Upon the Assembly of 1870, meeting in Albert Barnes's church, devolved the duty of carrying into effect the Concurrent Declarations of 1869. Sixty General Assemblies had met in the city, forty-four of them before the division, and most of them in the same church. Of the two retiring moderators Dr. Jacobus took charge of the business procedure, and Dr. Fowler preached the sermon, in which he pleaded, on grounds of expediency, for the establishment of personal supervision over the churches, such as John Knox's superintendents had exercised. Any comfort Episcopalians might have got from the suggestion was neutralized by his reference to the "imbecile pulpit" of that denomination.

The united church was subdivided into thirty-four Synods, two of them on the mission field, and these were directed to reorganize the Presbyteries within their bounds. The Concurrent Declarations had proposed that the theological seminaries place themselves under Synodical control. As there were legal difficulties in the way, the directors of Union and Princeton Seminaries simultaneously proposed, the others assenting, that ecclesiastical control should take the shape of giving the Assembly a veto upon the election and removal of professors—an arrangement accepted promptly as solving a grave difficulty.

The consolidation of the boards was quickly effected, as the differences which had played so great a part in 1835–37 had as good as disappeared. The old school, thanks to Dr. Thornwell's criticisms and Dr. Hodge's concessions, were no longer of the mind that these organizations were implied in the apostolic commission. The new school had found that voluntary societies embracing several denominations were apt to be sources of disappointment and irritation. The Boards of Foreign and Home Missions were located in New York, as that city had not only surpassed Philadelphia in population, but had acquired greater facilities for prompt communication with both fields.

The new-school church now terminated its connection with the American Board, and effected a division of the mission fields with that body. Ten years before this that church had given expression to its discontent with an arrangement which had resulted in the existence of but one genuine Presbyterian church in the foreign field after the expenditure of millions in missionary operations. They did not charge the board with any conscious management to secure this result; yet they saw in its operations what was confirmed by the published lectures on Foreign Missions by Secretary Anderson—indications of the workings of Congregationalist ideals in the management of mission affairs. In 1859 they had asked that every facility be given for the formation of missionary Presbyteries; and although the request was granted, not one such Presbytery appears in the Minutes of 1869, while forty-five foreign missionaries, including Drs. Thomson and Jessup of Syria, Dr. Doolittle of China, Mr. Bushnell of Gaboon, Mr. Bowen of Bombay, and Mr. Wilder of Kolapoor, are distributed among the Presbyteries at home, with which their connection could not be more than nominal. These facts helped to influence the new-school church toward reunion as certain to bring with it a more consistent missionary policy. The Assembly of 1869 opened negotiations for a transfer of a fair share of the mission fields of the American Board, in view of the withdrawal of new-school support from its treasury. This finally resulted in the transfer of the Syrian and Persian missions, that in the Gaboon district of Africa, and those to four of our own Indian tribes, to the care of the reunited church. This was done with due consideration for Congregationalists laboring in these fields, but with the understanding that they should be replaced and supplemented by Presbyterian workers only.

Somewhat similar was the problem presented by the

churches organized under the Plan of Union in New York and the western States. The Concurrent Declarations of 1869 called upon " imperfectly organized churches " to perfect their organization by the election of a session within five years at latest. This made the reunion a signal for a struggle between the Presbyterians and the Congregationalists in the area organized under the Plan of Union, the former urging these Presbygational churches to become thoroughly Presbyterian, while the latter pleaded with them to assert their independence and cast in their lot with the churches of the New England order. The majority became Presbyterian, and with this decision the Plan of Union passed out of history.

The consolidation of the two Boards of Publication was effected by the removal from the catalogues of each of whatever must be offensive to the sensibilities of the other body. To facilitate matters, Mr. Barnes withdrew all his publications from the Presbyterian Publication Committee and transferred them to private publishers. Dr. Gillette revised his " History of the Presbyterian Church," though not so as to eliminate all his criticisms of the exscinding policy of 1837. The result is a tamer and less piquant book, so that the original edition is more in demand.

As one of the Concurrent Declarations enacted that " no rule or precedent which does not stand approved by both the bodies should be of any authority until reëstablished in the united body," except so far as these might affect rights of property, it was thought that this opened the way for peace with the Southern church. The controversial heats which the Declaration and Testimony had produced were cooling off. The deliverances of the old-school Assembly on that and other questions growing out of the war were now of no force except so far as they corresponded to deliverances of the new-school Assembly on the same subject. On motion of Dr. William Adams, of New York, who had been the chairman of the new-school half of the Joint Committee on Reunion, a delegation of two ministers and one elder was appointed to proceed to the Assembly meeting in Louisville, to call attention to this feature of the Basis of Reunion and propose a Joint Committee for friendly conference as to the relations of the two churches. The delegation was courteously received, and the proposed committee agreed to, but on such terms as led the united Assembly to dismiss the subject and discharge its committee. The Southern Assembly, in the tone and style of the Declaration and Testimony, charged that both branches of the reunited church "did fatally complicate themselves with the state in political utterances deliberately uttered year after year." It declared that "the union now consummated was accomplished by methods which, in our judgment, involve a total surrender of all the great testimonies of the church for the fundamental doctrines of grace. . . . Of these falling testimonies, we are the sole surviving heirs." With much more pertinence and accuracy it recalled the violent and unconstitutional expulsion of some of the members of its own body, and declared that the action then taken by the old-school church was "no mere 'rule' or 'precedent,' but a solemn sentence of outlawry," and demanded "an unequivocal repudiation of that interpretation of the law," as a condition of the restoration of official relations. The olive-branch was thus used, and not for the last time, to castigate those who offered it.

The resolution for a Reunion Thanksgiving Fund came before the Assembly, that it might define the objects properly to be embraced in the range of gifts. It did so with the aim of excluding the ordinary contributions. The sum finally reported to the Assembly of 1871 was $7,607,491.91.

Of this $5,737,545.38 went to the erection or repair of churches and manses, or the extinction of debt on them, and $1,083,478.72 to institutions of learning.

Of the other participants in the Reunion Convention of 1867, none proceeded farther in the movement toward a general reunion. Both the Assemblies in session at Pittsburg resolved to ask conference with the United Presbyterian Church with a view to union on the basis of treating the differences as to psalmody and the like as matters of forbearance. The negotiations were continued for some years, but proved fruitless. The Reformed Presbyterian (N. S.) General Synod, which had called the Philadelphia Convention, passed into control of the party of reaction at its sessions in 1868. It suspended Mr. George H. Stuart by resolution from the eldership and from membership for the offense of singing uninspired hymns and meeting Christians of other names at the Lord's table. As both these offenses had been avowed before the Synod of 1856, and had been condoned by his reëlection to all the offices he held in the gift of Synod, this action was regarded by his friends as not only unjust but revolutionary. It subjected a large part of the ministry and membership to discipline for acts which, for twelve years, had been treated as worthy of toleration. The Presbyteries of Philadelphia, Pittsburg, and Saharunpoor suspended relations with the General Synod until Mr. Stuart should be restored, and for this they were exscinded by the General Synod of 1869. All three connected themselves with the Presbyterian Church, the two latter in 1870, and that of Philadelphia in 1881. This delay was to permit a decision on suits brought by the adherents of the Synod for church property in Phil adelphia. The Supreme Court showed a great advance on its earlier decisions in refusing to accept the decision of the General Synod as final, and deciding that it was

186 THE PRESBYTERIANS. [CHAP. XIV.

bound by its own constitution, like any other voluntary society. It therefore gave the property in two cases to Mr. Stuart's friends, and the third was compromised in consequence. In the meantime the Western Presbytery, where there was most dissatisfaction with the course taken by the General Synod in 1858, withdrew and joined the United Presbyterian Church. By these and subsequent losses the strength of the Reformed Presbyterian (N. S.) Church has been reduced to less than half that of the Old Side Covenanters.

CHAPTER XV.

WORK AND GROWTH, 1870–88.

THE reunion of the old and new school churches occurred at a time when the liveliest interest was felt in Christian work of every kind. There was a disposition to discredit any kind of Christian living or thinking which did not bear immediate fruit in some practical service. Martha, not Mary, came well to the front in the household of faith. It seemed to be thought that the day alike for theological speculation and for saintly meditation had come to an end; that the best music of the church was the clatter of machinery, and her finest history the tale of conversions through the labors of her workers.

All this was an inevitable reaction following the undue diversion of church energy into other fields than those of service in the kingdom. It was itself, however, an excess, and one especially out of keeping with the genius of a theological church, such as Presbyterian churches always have been. As Dr. A. A. Hodge said, in his extravagant humor, "Rather let us have an Inquisition and a little blood-letting than a dead apathy about religious doctrine."

For a time after the reunion the trend of feeling was all toward the practical. The strongest argument for the re union, indeed, was the opportunity it would furnish for effective work. It did make the Presbyterian Church one of the largest and wealthiest in America. The day had passed when the New England States so outranked the rest in prosperity that colleges and seminaries in the Middle

and even the Southern States looked to her Christian mer-
chants for substantial help.   That help gave Hezekiah Balch
the means of maintaining Greenville College in Tennessee,
and Dr. Rice the money to build Boston Hall in Union
Seminary (Va.).   In the industrial development which attended and followed the war Presbyterians shared at least
as much as people of any other denomination.   This development was found especially in districts which the
Scotch-Irish had preëmpted, and it called into activity
their eminent practical gifts.   In the cities the gain was
attended by some loss, through people of newly acquired
wealth coming to think that their fathers' church, like
their fathers' homes and mode of life, was not fine enough
for them.   This, however, affected only the less solid elements in the make-up of the Presbyterian churches.   The
growing responsibilities of the command of ampler means
fell more heavily upon them with every year of this period.

While no Christian church in the world—not even the
Moravian—gives up to the measure of its ability, there has
been a marked enlargement of Christian giving in all the
American churches, and the Presbyterians have had their
share of it.   The Reformed Presbyterians (O. S.) stand
foremost, with an average contribution of nearly twenty
dollars a member; and, indeed, nothing less would suffice
to maintain their vigorous work in the foreign and the
home field.   But in the exalted mood which attended reunion in the Assembly of 1870, large ideas were entertained, and few things roused more feeling than Dr. John
R. Paxson's vigorous castigation of the policy of starva-
tion followed by the old-school Board of Domestic Missions, and his praise of the new school for their greater
generosity to their home missionaries.   A plan was brought
before that Assembly for a general treasury of the church,
into which all contributions should go, for distribution by

a Committee of Benevolence and Finance. It was felt, however, that this restriction of individual choice was not in keeping with the history and genius of American Presbyterianism. Neither has any notable success attended the erection of a sustentation fund for the support of the weaker churches, somewhat after the model of that of the Free Church of Scotland. It had then been recently copied by the Presbyterian Church of Ireland in the crisis of disestablishment, which caused the withdrawal of the regium donum at the death of each of the Presbyterian ministers then receiving it. Dr. James McCosh, who had come from Belfast to become president of Princeton College in 1868, had shared in the heroic sacrifices of the Scottish disruption. He had done much to prepare. the Irish church for the not less heroic sacrifice by which all the ministers, except one or two, had capitalized their interest in the regium donum and paid it into a fund for the permanent endowment of their church. He hoped to awaken something of the same enthusiasm in America in proposing a similar sustentation policy ; but in the absence of a great emergency, custom and routine were too much for him.

In many of the Presbyterian churches the principle of the tithe is widely accepted and practiced as a means to secure something more solid as a basis of benevolent giving than the emotion awakened by pulpit appeals. More in keeping with the spirit of the New Testament would be the acceptance of the doctrine of Christian stewardship, which covers not a tenth, but the whole of a man's possessions, while it regards all rightful forms of expenditure as embraced in the service of God. In very recent years, to meet some special emergency, " weeks of self-denial " have been adopted, all that is saved by a week's careful economies being given to the object designated.

Closely connected with this growth of liberality has been the increased activity of women in every kind of church work.   This is a fact which cannot be regarded apart from the general tendency in American life to give to woman a prominence and a freedom of action which have been denied her even in Great Britain.   Fruitful as this tendency has been in extravagant demands for the effacement of proper distinctions between the sexes and their work in life, it has been right in the main, as working to the recognition of woman's essential equality with man in the very line of the general influence of Christianity upon society.

The Presbyterian Women's Board of Foreign Missions dates from the year of the reunion, being anticipated by a union movement in New York in 1861, and by a Congregationalist Women's Board in 1868, and one of the Northern Methodists in 1869.   In 1878 was formed the Women's Executive Committee for Home Mission Work, with especial reference to labor among the Southern freedmen.   Nor have the other Presbyterian bodies been much behind.   The women of the United Presbyterian Church formed their Missionary Society in 1875, and it was given rank as the Women's Mission Board by their General Assembly in 1888.   In 1878 they organized their Women's Association for Benevolent Work.   The Reformed Presbyterians (O. S.) also have a Women's Foreign Mission Board, and in 1878 they outran all the other Presbyterian churches by voting that women had a right to pray and exhort in social meetings (as now do those of the United Presbyterian Church), and, subsequently, that they might be elected to the office of deacon.

The presence and successful labors of women in the mission fields furnished a natural motive to their sisters at home to help by prayers and gifts.   In some cases, indeed, women had shown an ability for independent action not inferior to that of men. Mrs. Macfarland was for years the only representative of our Christian civilization in the neglected Territory of Alaska, and even presided over a constitutional convention called by the natives to set up a government, since the United States had let years pass without taking any step in that direction. Miss Sue McBeth, in Idaho, opened a theological seminary for the training of pastors for the Nez Percé Indians, and all the churches in the tribe are in charge of the graduates of her seminary. Through her labor and that of her sister two thirds of the tribe are in the membership of the church, and other tribes have applied to them for missionaries.

The Southern Presbyterian Church, if we may judge from those who profess to interpret her inaction, regards all this as a departure from Christian discipline, which presents a new obstacle to the ecclesiastical reunion of the two Assemblies. It is said that the millions secured to missions by these women's missionary boards are a poor compensation for the injury done to the family and social life of the nation by encouraging woman to usurp the rights and assume the duties of the superior sex.[1]

The attitude of that church toward the freedmen of the South has been the most striking feature of its home mission policy. Before the war the Southern slaves very commonly attended the same churches with their masters, being accommodated in the galleries of the churches. So

---

[1] This Southern view of the matter would probably be approved by the sister-churches of Europe. Dr. Christlieb, of Bonn, on his return from the Pan-Presbyterian Council in Philadelphia (1880), made an address in which he praised many things he had seen in America, but lamented " the want of a true Christian discipline" among us. This he illustrated by an incident. He was setting out with his host and hostess to attend an evening meeting, and when they reached the doorstep the lady said to her husband, " My dear, it's colder than I supposed. Won't you step back and bring me my shawl ?" "And," reports good Dr. Christlieb, " the man went !"

long as "the patriarchal relation" existed, the white people showed no repugnance to association with their bondmen either in church or elsewhere.   It was, indeed, their boast that they did not keep the black man at a distance to the extent this was done even by his warmest friends in the North.   But the free negro has been quite another matter, and the freedmen generally have been given to understand that they are no longer welcome in the white people's churches, but had better form churches of their own.   A new line of social separation between the races has thus resulted from the emancipation and the enfranchisement of the blacks.

In most cases the freedmen did not need much persuasion.   They naturally resented the control of their former masters in church matters, as in politics.   Great numbers of them, indeed, preferred the Baptist order, simply because it gave them the most complete freedom from white dominance, each church being free to manage its own affairs in its own way.   Many who had been kept in the Methodist, Lutheran, Presbyterian, and Episcopal Churches by the influence of their owners became Baptists as soon as they were free to go "to their own company."   This was a most unfortunate change, as it threw heavy responsibilities upon a class which had no training to bear them, placed them under spiritual leaders who had good reason, in many cases, to labor against the better education of the young, and sundered them from influences on whose closeness and continuance their moral progress must depend.

In these circumstances it was for the interest both of the South and of the nation that the Episcopalian and Presbyterian bodies should maintain as close relations as possible with that part of the colored population which still retained any affinity for those churches, and should thus encourage others to seek a communion in which so-briety in worship and moral discipline in daily life would be secured them. Unfortunately neither of them saw the matter in this light. The Cumberland Presbyterians encouraged their colored membership to withdraw and, in 1869, to organize themselves as a separate denomination, now numbering 13,439 members. The Southern Presbyterians have not taken this extreme step, but they inaugurated a policy of separation in congregation, Presbytery, and Synod, which was at once un-Presbyterian and unfortunate. Not only did colored pastors fall out of touch with their white brethren, but the Presbyteries organized for them and their churches covered too large an area for any effective supervision. Thus the State of Texas—a country considerably larger than France, and embracing one eleventh of the area of the United States—saw all its colored Presbyterian churches in connection with the Southern Assembly placed under the care of a single Presbytery. Five such Presbyteries cover the whole South, and five are to be united into an African Synod.

The Southern church, which lost most of its ten thousand colored members at the close of the war—having but 1211 in 1890—has made some honest but not extraordinary efforts to recover the ground and to do her share in the Christian training of a needy people left at her doors. In no year have her people given her $10,000 to spend for this purpose, and many of her wealthier congregations refuse to add the Executive Committee on Colored Evangelization (established in 1891) to the number for which they take collections. Since 1877 she has had an ably conducted institute for training colored ministers at Tuscaloosa, Ala., but its work has been crippled for want of adequate support.

A joint conference on coöperation in this work was

asked by the Southern Assembly in 1887. It was continued afterward at the request of the other Assembly. An agreement was reached in 1894 to unify the work by transferring it to a joint board, in which the Southern Assembly would constitute the minority, as having much the smaller colored membership and the lesser monetary interest. This, however, was rejected by that Assembly, and, indeed, would not have furnished a satisfactory solution of the problem. The churches organized within the national Assembly's Synods of Atlanta and of Texas among the freedmen—with 16,850 members in 1890—are nearly as exclusively colored churches by force of circumstances as those under care of the Southern Assembly are by choice and policy. If the two bodies are to remain apart, it would have been far better to have transferred all these churches to the care of the Southern Assembly, if this could have been done with assurance that "the color-line" is to disappear out of the house of God.

In other fields of home missionary labor the American churches of all names have been more active and zealous since the war than ever before. A constantly increasing responsibility has been thrown upon them by the influx of millions of immigrants from the continent of Europe. Many of these, it is true, naturally find their home in the Reformed, Lutheran, and other churches in which they held their membership before leaving home. Others, however, have been careless of church connections, or have become so through emigration. Many have been alienated from the church through its connection with the state in Europe, even if they have not been infected with the crude materialism which is the philosophy of European socialism and anarchism. Multitudes, especially of Roman Catholics, "never darken the door of a church" after coming to America, and allow their children to grow up in practical paganism. Among these classes the American churches are laboring for the salvation of the Republic from the irreligion and social disorder which threaten the Old World.

Presbyterian work has been mostly among the peoples who held by the Reformed Church in Europe—Dutch, Bohemians, Swiss, and especially the Germans of the lower Rhine valley. To secure workers among these last, two theological seminaries have been established: that at Dubuque, in 1860, by members of two old-school Presbyteries—Dubuque, Ia., and Dana, Wis.; and that at Newark, N. J., by the new-school Presbytery of Newark.

The announcement by President Grant, in his inaugural of 1868, of a policy by which the churches would be invited to coöperate with the national government in the civilization and Christianization of the Indians,[1] excited a very general interest in that work, and led to very extensive plans for their education. Of the Protestant churches only a few can be said to have really embraced their opportunity, the others either stopping with proposals or contenting themselves with feeble and ill-sustained efforts. Presbyterians were the first to enter the neglected territory of Alaska with missionary work, and they have had a splendid share in the transformation which has reduced steadily the quota of pagans among our Indian tribes. Two laymen of the church, Captain Pratt and General Armstrong, by founding and conducting the great gov-

---

[1] The Grant policy seems likely to be set aside as regards its main feature, through the jealousy which has been excited by the greater extent and success of the Roman Catholic schools established under it. The hierarchy of that church were in no way friendly to such labors, and gave them but little official support. Thanks, however, to the persistence of a single priest and his co adjutors, mainly laymen, the Roman Catholic Church has entered largely upon the fields neglected or abandoned by Protestants. Hence the outcry, chiefly from denominations which have done nothing, for the withdrawal of government aid to mission schools on the Indian reservations. To this outcry the Episcopal General Convention and our own General Assembly have yielded.

ernment schools at Carlisle, Pa., and Fortress Monroe, Va., have rendered a unique service in the work of assimilating our Indian wards to the rest of the nation. At the same time a fresh interest has awakened among the Presbyterians of that region in the remnant of the great Iroquois confederacy in central New York, a large part of which still cherishes pagan practices and superstitions. All these Indian missions have been transferred to the Board of Home Missions, after having been long classed as belonging to the foreign field. To the same board belongs the work among the resident Chinese on the Pacific coast and elsewhere, which has been proportionally more fruitful than the missions to the Chinese at home.

In the conduct of home mission work generally there has been an approximation to the method of personal supervision, for which Dr. Fowler invoked the authority of Knox and Melville. Men like Dr. Sheldon Jackson render a service of general oversight which is not less Scriptural than is the supervision by boards. Another gain has been in the diminution of the waste of men and money through the maintenance of too many churches in young communities. The reunion did much to abate the evil by consolidating weak congregations of the two branches. Something more has been done through an understanding with the Congregationalists that where either body has preëmpted any new field the other will wait a reasonable time before establishing a second church. The evil, however, is only abated, and it remains one of the scandals of our divided Christendom. It is estimated that fully half the money raised for home missionary work is wasted in " holding the fort " for sectarian ends, without achieving a real gain for the cause of Christianity. Worse still is the waste in this way of personal force, often animated by the loftiest enthusiasm for the kingdom of God.

Presbyterians and Congregationalists no longer are distinguished from other Christians in America by their belief in the school, the college, and the theological seminary as indispensable adjuncts of home mission work. All our Protestant bodies, even to Friends and Dunkers, have come to accept their view. Ignorance is no longer valued as a preparation for ministerial labor. Still more noteworthy has been the conversion of the general public to the belief in the higher education. The university system of training, imported into America by the churches, and sustained by them through an era of distrust and contempt, is now accepted as the necessary complement of the public-school system, especially in the newer States. Through this change and the generous gifts of private individuals for the founding of institutions outside of her control, the church's relation to the higher education, as well as the lower, has become less intimate and effective than it once was.

In the field of intermediate schools and that of colleges and universities, the churches show no disposition to abandon their activity, as they feel that the new universities founded by the States, or by individuals indifferent to the Christian influence on education, cannot be expected to furnish candidates for the ministry in sufficient numbers and fitly prepared for the theological seminary. The Presbyterians, though no longer holding the same relative position in the higher education, still hold their own and steadily extend their work. At the opening of the century there were but four institutions of the higher grade under their control. These had increased to more than a dozen at the time of the division of 1837. They now number some fifty, ranging from the long-established and richly endowed university in the East to the little Western college, which is no poorer than the university once was, and has reasonable hope of becoming as rich and prosperous through " growing up with the country." As these weaker colleges have been placed at a disadvantage by the competition of institutions of the other class, the General Assembly of 1883, after a discussion extending over several years, established a Board of Aid for Colleges, which has secured them valuable and much-needed assistance.

In the field of primary education there has been a more general acquiescence in the transfer of the work to State agencies, as being alone able to cope with the magnitude of the public needs. At the same time very little care has been exercised to secure from the state's schools that amount and kind of religious teaching which their character permits of. There is a strong and growing party which seeks to secularize entirely the teaching in the public schools, in the delusive expectation that this will make them less objectionable to Roman Catholics. It is reinforced by those denominations, such as the Baptists, who regard the state as a purely secular institution having no religious duties.

Naturally this secularist policy does not commend itself to consistent Presbyterians. In the two decades before the war there was a movement among the old-school Presbyterians to establish a system of parochial schools. The General Assembly of 1844 advised every congregation, which had the ability, to set up a school of its own, and directed the Board of Publication to prepare the necessary text-books. The pressure of other matters coöperated with the inertia of the churches to frustrate the plan, which ceased to be prominent after the resignation of Dr. Cortlandt van Rensselaer from the secretaryship of the Board of Education in 1860. His successor in that office let the matter drop. It was the assured belief of Dr. A. A. Hodge that it would come forward again. In recent years the Synod of New York made an earnest effort to counteract the secularization of the schools within its bounds. It called a convention of Christians of all classes to this end, but accomplished nothing, through the indifference and even hostility of the Christian people generally to the purpose. The rapid increase of crime which has gone hand in hand with the secularization of education may awaken them roughly to the need discerned by the Synod.

The position taken by the Presbyterian Church in the matter was defined by the reunion Assembly of 1870:

" We should regard the successful attempt to expel all religious instruction and influence from our public schools as an evil of the first magnitude. Nor do we see how this can be done without inflicting a deadly wound upon the intellectual and moral life of the nation. . . . We look upon the state as an ordinance of God, and not a mere creature of the popular will; and, under its high responsibility to the Supreme Ruler of the world, we hold it to be both its right and bounden duty to educate its children in those elementary principles of knowledge and virtue which are essential to its own security and well-being. The union of church and state is indeed against our American theory and constitutions of government; but the most intimate union of the state with the saving and conservative forces of Christianity is one of the oldest customs of the country, and has always ranked as a vital article of our political faith."

Another adjunct to home mission work has been that of the Board of Publication. No agency of the church has been subjected to more criticism than this. The need of any church agency for the publication of religious literature has been questioned, in view of the fact that private firms do so much to supply good books, and in a form and of a character suited to the public taste.   More forcible, I think, has been the objection to the quality of the publications of the board.   Our age grows daily more exacting in the matter of literary excellence and human interest in the books it reads.   A church board of publication is apt to follow a policy of caution which narrows the range of its work and results in a dull uniformity in its issues.   That this can be avoided has been shown in recent years by several agencies of this kind on either side of the ocean. But it did characterize the lists of the Presbyterian board to an extent which led the average reader to avoid any book bearing its imprint.   Through recent changes of policy and of management this evil bids fair to be removed.

Formerly the board employed agents merely to carry on the sale of its books, but latterly it directed them to seek to establish Sunday-schools in neglected districts. For this reason in 1887 the General Assembly enlarged the title of the board to include this work, and appointed a secretary to take charge of it.   It also has placed the statistics of Sunday-school membership and contributions on the same footing as those of the congregations.   This has contributed to the extension of Sunday-school teaching, but it would be an unfortunate result if it tended to draw any deep line of distinction between church and school.   The development of the latter has been sound and safe just in so far as it tends to closer relations with the congregation. The goal will be reached when the Sunday-school is recognized as the congregation in session for a specific purpose, under direction of the pastor and session, and entitled to draw upon the treasury of the congregation for its necessary expenses.   On that footing every member of the congregation will find his place in the school, and the teaching (or " doctrine ") of the apostolic church will resume its place beside the preaching of the Word.

In the field of foreign missions all the Presbyterian bodies have made progress since the war. The union of 1858 brought under the United Presbyterian Assembly the Associate Church's mission at Sialkot, in India (1844), and that of the Associate Reformed Church to the Copts of Egypt (1853), both highly successful enterprises. The Reformed Presbyterian Synod (O. S.) has a well-sustained mission work in Syria, and the General Synod (N. S.), since the loss of its Presbytery of Saharanpoor through the troubles of 1868–69 (p. 185), has taken steps to renew its labors in the same country. The fields already occupied by the old-school Assembly, and those ceded by the American Board in 1871, have been enlarged, and additions made to their number. As in many cases Presbyterian missionaries are working in the foreign field side by side with those of sister-churches in other lands, or those of American churches whose differences sink into insignificance in comparison with the great problem of the common labor, it has been thought best to effect ecclesiastical consolidation. Thus in India and China a single Presbyterian Synod is proposed for each country. In Japan and in Brazil consolidation has been accelerated by the desire of the native churches to emerge out of the mission stage of existence and to assume the self-direction which is the right of every national church. The United Church of Christ in Japan, thus organized of the Reformed and Presbyterian missions, is the strongest Christian body in the empire, has drawn up its own confession of faith, and governs itself, while enjoying the advice of the council of missionaries. Such unions help to take away the reproach of Christian disunion, which nowhere is seen in its ugliness so distinctly as on the mission field.

In other fields the relations of the Presbyterian churches to the sister-churches of other lands have been most friendly and harmonious. American help has been extended to the struggling churches of the Reformed order and faith in Italy, Bohemia, and Hungary. In 1876, largely through the labors of Drs. James McCosh and Philip Schaff, there was formed an " Alliance of the Reformed Churches throughout the World holding the Presbyterian System," with provision for holding an international council once in four years. It embraces some sixty churches, who have given their official adherence to it. The second of its councils was held in Philadelphia in 1880, and the fifth in Toronto. Thus far it has accomplished little more than the promotion of international and interdenominational comity among the churches. The efforts of Dr. Schaff to secure through it the preparation of a consensus of the Reformed churches, as a sort of ecumenical creed which should supersede the several confessions of the separate churches, did not prove successful. It met with opposition from both quarters, the liberals of Europe thinking it too long, and the conservatives of Ireland and America too short and vague.

Nor has it been found possible to satisfy all the churches which at first accepted membership in the Alliance. The psalm-singers of the United Presbyterian Church felt themselves aggrieved by the use of uninspired hymns at some of its sessions and the celebration of the communion. For this reason the General Assembly of this church withdrew from the Alliance for a time, because of the breach of the original agreement that the meetings would confine themselves to the Psalms in praise. But on receiving fresh assurance on this point, this Assembly appointed delegates to Toronto.

Within this very church, however, innovation has played its part. The Seceder and Covenanter Churches in earlier times were entirely agreed in rejecting the use of instrumental music, clearly as its use is prescribed in the Psalms, which the church—in their view—is required to use till the end of time. Partly the sense of this incongruity, and partly the desire to bring this part of worship into harmony with modern culture, caused a restlessness under the rule. At last in 1881 the General Assembly was induced to submit the question to the Presbyteries in overture, the rules requiring its adoption not only by a majority of the Presbyteries, but by a majority of their individual members taken in the aggregate. The result was its approval by a small majority of the actual voters, but just one short of a majority of the whole number present when the vote was taken. The opponents and the friends of the proposal both claimed a victory. The General Assembly of 1882, acting upon precedents already established, decided that the overture had been adopted. It declared, however, that the action taken did not authorize the introduction of instruments, but merely declared that " there is not sufficient Bible authority for an absolutely exclusive rule on the subject." This deliverance, as might have been expected, satisfied neither party. The conservatives found the previous testimony of the church set aside, with the assurance that no change in practice would follow it. The progressives found themselves virtually forbidden to do what the church had declared was not contrary to the Word of God. While most of the congregations followed the policy of inaction, a few proceeded to employ musical instruments, first in the Sunday-school and then in congregational worship. This produced an agitation on the other side which at times threatened a division of the church, the minority holding conventions to agitate against innovations.

In something of the same spirit of accommodation to the needs of the time was the revision of the old Psalm-

book of 1649, which this denomination adopted in 1870.
This also encountered resistance, but sporadic only and
personal.   The result is certainly " more smoothe," if not
" more agreeable to the Originall Texte," than the older
version.   But a lover of old English poetry might depre-
cate many of the alterations in a version beloved of Burns,
Campbell, Scott, Irving, Carlyle, and Archdeacon Hare,
on finding

> Strength's knots and gnarls all pared away,
> And varnish in their places.

The problems of Presbyterian reunion were freely discussed in various conferences between separate churches
at this time, but to no end.   The conference set on foot
with the United Presbyterians by the General Assembly
of 1870 brought to light nothing but the obstacles of which
everybody knew.   That ministers and churches of that
and the smaller Presbyterian bodies are attracted toward
the reunited church is evidenced by transfers of both to
the care of the General Assembly.   Thus in 1889 the
United Presbyterian Presbytery of Detroit, by a vote of
two to one, decided to unite with the Presbyterian Church,
leaving the minority—after a loss of six ministers and eight
churches—to continue the existence of the Presbytery.
But these very transfers only serve to put off the day of
reunion, by strengthening relatively the conservative elements they leave behind them.

In the national Assembly the extension of overtures to
the Southern Assembly has been frequently pressed by a
party which seemed to be bent on reunion at any price, not
excepting the church's self-respect.   Much was expected by
them from the joint celebration of the centenary of the first
General Assembly in 1888, when the Southern Assembly
adjourned from Baltimore to meet the other Assembly sit-

ting in Philadelphia. The Southern speakers, however, while eloquent enough as to the church's past, had nothing comforting to say of the future. Six years later their Assembly flatly refused to appoint a Conference Committee on Reunion, at the request of the national Assembly. What probably encourages the hope of reunion is the attitude of attention and criticism which the Southern church occupies toward the national Assembly. It never has succeeded in regarding it as a body to which it owes no more than the interdenominational courtesies due to a separate church. The severed limb feels its indestructible relation to the body.

During this period the Presbyterian churches were more or less affected by the agitation for a general union of all Christians on the basis of their common beliefs. As early as 1867, indeed, the Rev. William McCune, of the United Presbyterian Church, set on foot an agitation for the abolition of all lines of sectarian division between Protestants, and conducted it with an energy which brought him into conflict with his own church. Its General Assembly of that year had some difficulty in deciding that his contention involved " fundamental error," but it inflicted upon him a suspension, which led to his withdrawal from the church. He afterward found a home for a short time in the Presbyterian Church, but finally withdrew from it.

Twice during this period these churches were approached from without with invitations to return to " Catholic unity." The first came from Pope Pius IX. in 1870, on the eve of the holding of the Council of the Vatican which put the copestone on the edifice of papal authority. It was a request to the Protestant world to embrace the opportunity offered by this reunion of the true church to put an end to the schisms and divisions which the Reformation had introduced. Most of the Protestant bodies made no reply, but the General Assembly sent a courteous but decided refusal. As this was written by Dr. John Hall, there was no want of emphasis in its Protestantism.[1]

The other invitation came from the House of Bishops of the Protestant Episcopal Church, who addressed to the other denominations of our American Christendom a plea for reunion upon a basis which they defined, without defining the method by which it should be accomplished, whether by confederation or consolidation. The address was notable as the first official recognition from that quarter of the existence of other Christian churches in America. Since the beginning of the Oxford movement, and even before it, American Episcopalians had been making their appeal to individual Christians and ministers of other denominations, and not without success, as their church growth had been more largely effected in this way than by conquests from the world. Rapid as had been their increase in the cities and towns, however, it gave and gives no promise of their absorbing or even outnumbering the other churches. The hope some of them cherished that their church would prove the Aaron's rod which would swallow all the others is not likely to be realized, and the less so since other denominations have had the wisdom to adjust their worship, architecture, and the like to the demands of an age which requires beauty and detests sordidness. The address of the House of Bishops, therefore,

---

[1] A prominent American organ of the Roman Catholic Church, in noticing the fact that such an answer had been sent, said of the Presbyterians: " Their intellectual and moral worth, their philanthropy and zeal for God, the value of many most excellent works which they have written in defense of the divine revelation, we fully appreciate. That great numbers have been and are in the spiritual communion of the Catholic Church we sincerely hope. We desire that the schism which has separated them from our visible communion may be healed, not only for their own spiritual good, but also that the Catholic Church in the United States may be strengthened by the accession of that intellectual and religious vigor which such a great mass of baptized Christians contains in itself."

indicates a growth of practical good sense which is full of promise.

The three essentials to Christian unity which the address prescribes are the Catholic creeds, the two sacraments administered with the essential forms of words, and the " historic episcopate." The first two present no difficulty to Presbyterians. The third involves an assumption in favor of diocesan episcopacy, to which they cannot assent without shutting their eyes to the facts of church history. Recent investigation has shown that the word *episcopos* came into the use of the church from the sect of the Stoics, who employed it to designate a man who took a personal interest in the moral well-being of his neighbors. It was thus an approach to the Christian conception of the pastorate or " cure of souls," and was fitly employed to designate the minister of the Christian congregation. Its original sense still lingers in the pastoral staff, or crosier, borne by the bishops of the Latin and Greek Churches. It lost this sense when the assimilation of the church's polity to that of the Roman Empire took the *episcopos* (bishop) from his *paroikia* or parish (district around a house of worship) and gave him rule over a civil *dioikesis*. It has less of the original sense the farther we come from the original home of Christianity—less in the Latin Church than in the Greek, less in the Anglican than in the Latin, less in the Episcopal Church of America than in the mother-church of England. With each remove the dioceses grow larger and the work of the bishop less pastoral, until we see Dr. Kinsolving described as " Bishop of Texas," a region larger than France. It is the fewness of the bishops in the Episcopal Church that repels Presbyterians. To parochial episcopacy, even as described in the Ignatian Epistles, they have no manner of objection.

The address of the bishops would have excited much

less attention in the Presbyterian Church if it had not
found an earnest supporter in Dr. Charles W. Shields, of
Princeton College.   He even went beyond the terms of
the address and held up the Book of Common Prayer as
the basis for a reunion of all English-speaking Christians.
While there has been a marked increase in the desire for
liturgic worship among American as among British Presbyterians, Dr. Shields cannot be said to have carried many
with him in his plea.   As Professor Briggs has said, that
book does not meet the needs of our time and land as
well as they might be met by a work which should draw
freely on other sources—Greek and Latin, Lutheran and
Reformed, as well as Anglican.   Nor do the House of
Bishops, or the bishops of the whole Anglican communion,
met in conference at Lambeth, in adopting the proposal of
the American bishops as their own, suggest the adoption
of the Prayer-book as a prerequisite to communion.

Thus far the Presbyterian Church has declined to enter
upon any discussion of the proposal until there has been
an acknowledgment of the validity of Presbyterian ordination by the Episcopal Church, as in the earlier days of the
Reformed Church of England.   The refusal is natural, but
not logical, as the House of Bishops may be in possession
of further light on that subject.

CHAPTER XVI.

THEOLOGICAL AND LITERARY LIFE SINCE 1870.

IMPORTANT as are the works of Christian liberality and of evangelization, it is not possible for the Presbyterian Church to find in them the full scope for her vocation. She is, by God's calling, a theological church, set to witness for the great truths of God's grace in providence and redemption. Her theologians are not the least among her jewels, and no others of her sons exert so great an influence outside her own bounds.

Several of her ablest passed to their reward in the period we are now considering.

The Southern church had lost its greatest theologian by the death of Dr. Jas. H. Thornwell still earlier, in 1862. He had gone to visit his son, who had been wounded in the Confederate service, when death came to close a life rich in both pastoral and professional work.

The year 1877 saw Dr. Henry B. Smith gathered to his fathers, without ever having had the leisure to do justice to his thought. The inadequacy and uncertainty of his salary as a professor compelled him to spend in secondary labors the energies which should have been given to his proper work.

In this Dr. Charles Hodge was more fortunate, in that he could devote the leisure of eight years to the elaboration of his "Systematic Theology" (1871–73). It used to be said that he and Professor Park, of Andover, were each waiting for the other to publish his system, with critical intention.   Before the whole work was before the public the semi-centenary of his inauguration as professor occurred.   Of the three thousand students he had trained for the ministry, a goodly number gathered around him with grateful congratulations, and greetings came from other churches to the veteran professor.   In 1873 the Assembly, hearing that he was in Washington, adjourned thither from Baltimore to wait on him.   In 1878 he passed away, full of years and of good works.   His " Systematic Theology " probably exceeds any other body of divinity in the language in the reach of its influence.

Two years before his death his still greater son, Dr. Archibald Alexander Hodge, was called to Princeton from the Alleghany Seminary, as assistant and successor to his father in the chair of didactic theology.   While inferior to his father in serenity and judicial temper, he was a man of richer and more complex nature, larger experience of the world, more extensive historical learning, and greater speculative originality.   His playful, sometimes extravagant humor shaped his thought into epigrammatic form and a conversational audacity which often startled and offended weak brethren.   Under all lay a fervency of spiritual devotion which at times suggested the old mystics. His " Outlines of Theology " (1860 and 1878) and his " Popular Lectures on Theological Themes " (1887) are notable books ; but nothing he has written gives an adequate impression of his inspiring individuality.   He was not spared long to cultivate his new field, as he died suddenly, in 1886. The death of his brother, Dr. Caspar Wistar Hodge, in 1893, terminated the family connection with the seminary, and in his case put an end to an influence and an inspiration which has left no monument of its great worth.

In Dr. Wm. G. T. Shedd (*ob.* 1894) Union Seminary found a successor to Henry B. Smith, who represented the earlier Calvinism and at the same time had been one of the group of young Coleridgeans who gathered round Dr. James Marsh at Burlington, Vt., in 1826. Like Dr. S. J. Baird (p. 000), he defended the realistic conception of the race both in its fall and in its redemption. His " Theological Essays " (1877), " Commentary on Romans " (1879), " Sermons to the Natural Man " (3d ed., 1884), and " Sermons to the Spiritual Man " (1884) were the forerunners of his able but rigid " Dogmatic Theology " (3 vols., 1889–94). A more distinctly new-school type of doctrine is presented by Dr. E. D. Morris, of Lane Seminary, in his " Outlines of Christian Doctrine " (1880) and " Ecclesiology: a Treatise on the Church " (1885); and by Dr. Ransom B. Welch, of Auburn Seminary, in " Faith and Modern Thought " (2d ed., 1880) and his " Outlines of Theology " (1881).

The Southern church in Robert L. Dabney has a church leader who takes the place of both Thornwell and Smyth. His " Sensualistic Philosophy of the Nineteenth Century " (1875) and his " Theology, Dogmatic and Polemic " (3d ed., 1885) are the work of an able controversialist. He is still better known as the biographer of his friend and commander, General " Stonewall " Jackson, on whose staff he served.

The smaller Presbyterian bodies, despite their intense interest in dogmatic theology, have been prevented by their circumstances from adding much to its literature. A noteworthy exception to this is Rev. John M. Armour, of the Reformed Presbyterian Synod (O. S.), who in his " Atonement and Law " (1886) and other works seeks to furnish a defense, modern in spirit and method, for the most scholastic Calvinism, and who impresses every careful reader with his force of thought even when he provokes dissent.

To the same body we owe Dr. Thomas Sproull's " Prelec-
tions on Theology " (1882).

In the closely related field of Christian philosophy Princeton College possessed in Dr. James McCosh the chief American representative of the Scottish school, but an independent worker in this field. It still has Dr. Charles W. Shields,
whose " Final Philosophy " (2d ed., 1879) seeks to secure
to the science the place of arbitrator in pending disputes;
and Dr. Francis L. Patton, who occupies himself with the
problems of Christian theism. Dr. Laurens P. Hicock, of
Auburn Seminary and Union College, in " The Logic of
Reason " (1875) and other works, elaborates a philosophy
which touches Kant and Coleridge on one side and the
new school of experimental psychology on the other.

In apologetical theology Albert Barnes broke new ground
in his " Evidences of Christianity in the Nineteenth Century " (1868); but his " Letters to Gerrit Smith " (1869)
on the use made by Universalists of a famous passage in
one of his sermons are even more interesting and powerful
—perhaps the most characteristic of all his works. Dr.
A.W. Pitzer contributed his share of the literature provoked
by Professor Seeley's book in his " Ecce Deus-Homo "
(1867). Dr. S. H. Kellogg, in " The Light of Asia and the
Light of the World " (1885), controverted, with full knowledge and great ability, the attempts made to set Buddha,
" the light of Asia," above or beside Christ. He is a type
of the man of letters who has found the stimulus to authorship on the mission field. Beside him we place Dr. Elias
Riggs, of Constantinople, translator of the Scriptures into
Armenian, Bulgarian, and Turkish, and author of original
works in these and in modern Greek; Dr. George E. Post,
of Beirut, an authority on the natural history of the Bible,
and a contributor to Smith's Bible Dictionary; Dr. H. H.
Jessup, of Beirut, author of " The Mohammedan Mission-

sionary Problem " (1879) and " The Women of the Arabs " (1873); Dr. John C. Lowrie, author of " Missionary Papers " (1882); Dr. W. A. P. Martin, of Peking, head of the Chinese Imperial College, and author of " The Chinese: Their Education, Philosophy, and Letters "(1881); and Dr. A.W. Loomis, author of " Confucius and the Chinese Classics " (2d ed., 1882). The most prolific writer on missions is Dr. Arthur T. Pierson, editor of the " Missionary Review of the World," and author of " The Crisis of Missions " (1888) and other works calculated to stir up the church to a sense of her duty.

In the field of home missions the literary impulse is less felt. Dr. Sheldon Jackson's book on Alaska (1880) lies on the middle line between the two fields. Dr. H. W. Pierson's " In the Brush; or, Old-Time Social, Political, and Religious Life in the Southwest " (1881), gives the harvest of his observations as an agent of the Bible Society, and with unusual literary skill.

The scholarship of the church in the field of exegetical theology was tested in the selection by Dr. Philip Schaff of his co-workers on the translation of Lange's Commentary (25 vols., 1864–80). Besides the general editor, who came over from the German Reformed Church in 1864, Drs. C. A. Aiken, Charles A. Briggs, E. R. Craven, Howard Crosby, Charles Elliott, Llewellyn J. Evans, William H. Green, William Henry Hornblower, John Lillie, Samuel T. Lowrie, Dunlop Moore, Daniel W. Poor, M. B. Riddle, William G. T. Shedd, Conway P. Wing, and Edward D. Yeomans had a share in the work. So in the revision of the " Authorized " Version of the English Bible, Dr. William Henry Green presided over the Old Testament division of the American committee, to which also belonged Professors Charles A. Aiken and John De Witt, the latter then in the Reformed Church; in the New Testament committee were Drs. H. B. Smith (snatched away by death), Howard Crosby, M. B. Riddle, and Philip Schaff, while Dr. Charles Hodge was a corresponding member.

In Old Testament criticism Dr. William Henry Green is the type of conservative scholarship, and the unflinching antagonist of documentary hypotheses, of the duplication of Isaiahs, and the rest. He began his apologetic work with a reply to Bishop Colenso in 1863, and followed it up in "Moses and the Prophets" (1883), "The Hebrew Feasts" (1885), and "The Pentateuchal Question" in "Hebraica" (1890-92), besides numerous articles, especially in the "Presbyterian Review" (1880 ff.). By a sort of agreement the views of both the conservative and the liberal critics were presented in alternate numbers, Drs. Green, A. A. Hodge, and B. B. Warfield representing the former. Dr. Green's point of view is shared by Dr. Charles Elliott in his "Treatise on Inspiration" (1877) and his "Mosaic Authorship of the Pentateuch" (1884), and by many who have not given permanent shape to their pleas for the traditional theory.

On the other side, and with equal prominence, there stands a much younger man, Dr. Charles Augustus Briggs, of Union Seminary, who as early as the year of the reunion declared the traditional view of inspiration to be untenable. In his articles in the "Presbyterian Review," his book on "Biblical Study" (1883 and 1885), his "Messianic Prophecy" (1886), and his pamphlet-book, "Whither?" (1889) he made progressive advance toward the positions taken in the famous Inaugural of 1891, and his "The Bible, the Church, and Reason" (1892), and his "Higher Criticism of the Hexateuch" (1893), which led to his suspension from the ministry. Substantially in agreement with him were Professors Evans and Smith, of the Lane Seminary, while Professor Willis J. Beecher maintained with firmness and judgment an intermediate position between the two schools, standing open to hear what the new criticism had to offer, but subjecting it to a searching examination.

Of commentaries on Old Testament books the list is short. Dr. William S. Plumer, who offered the exscinding resolutions in 1837, and who cast in his lot with the Southern church, illustrates ably the old style of exegesis in his bulky book on the Psalms. Dr. Marvin R. Vincent's "Gates into the Psalm-Country" (1878 and 1883) are suggestive discourses on single points. Dr. S. H. Kellogg's "Leviticus" is the only American contribution to the Expositor's Bible. In the related field of Assyriology Professor Francis Brown, of Union Seminary, holds acknowledged rank, and is associated with Professor Briggs as American co-workers on the new dictionary of Hebrew. In that of Egyptology Rev. Alfred H. Kellogg in his "Abraham, Joseph and Moses in Egypt" (1887), has done much toward solving the problem presented by the Egyptian and Mosaic chronologies.

In the New Testament field Professor Isaac H. Hall has done scholarly work on the bibliography of the Greek text. Dr. C. René Gregory—now a Lutheran—after helping Dr. Charles Hodge in the historical portion of his "Systematic Theology," became co-worker with Professor Tischendorf on his final edition of the Greek New Testament, and since his death has completed it. Dr. Schaff, in addition to his labors in organizing the American Committee of Revisers and in arranging the terms of the publication of the Revised Version, reissued, with an Introduction, the three most scholarly treatises in advocacy of revision (Lightfoot, Trench, and Ellicott) in 1873, and published a volume giving an account of the undertaking in 1879. He also edited, with an Introduction, in 1882, the Westcott and Hort edition of the Greek text used by the revisers, and published in the same year " A Companion to the Greek New Testament and the English Version." Besides his edition of Lange, he edited, with the assistance of Dr. M. B. Riddle, and several English scholars, a popular " Illustrated Commentary on the New Testament " (1878–83), which was partially reissued as the " International Revision Commentary " in 1882 ff. In this field he was not an expert as in that of history; but he possessed a wide range of theological culture, which he made useful to the American churches.

Dr. Marvin R. Vincent's " Word-Studies in the New Testament " (1887–90) represents an effort to reach the sense of the text by analysis and comparison. President D. S. Gregory, in " Why Four Gospels? " (3d ed., 1885), gives a popular discussion of a most interesting problem. Dr. Howard Crosby (*ob.* 1891), in his " Commentary on the New Testament " (1885), as in earlier works, brought sound classical scholarship to the service of exegetics. Dr. W. S. Plumer has discussed the Epistles to the Romans and the Hebrews on the same scale as the Psalms. Dr. Shedd has written on Romans. Dr. S. T. Lowrie bases his work on Hebrews on the very able commentary of Hofmann of Erlangen. Dr. John Lillie's posthumous " Lectures on the Epistles of Peter "(1869) is the work of one whom Dr. Schaff placed among the best biblical scholars of America. Rev. W. R. Reid, of the United Presbyterian Church, has written on Revelation—a book now much less discussed than half a century ago. Dr. J. H. McIlvaine's "Wisdom of the Apocalypse "(1886) explains the book from a novel point of view.

In historical theology Dr. Schaff holds the lead with his great " History of the Christian Church," unhappily never finished. His translation and adaptation of Herzog's " Real-Encyklopädie " (1884 and 1887), his " Creeds of Christendom " (4th ed., 1884), his monographs on " Augustine, Melanchthon, and Neander " (1886), and his " Library of the Nicene and Post-Nicene Fathers " (25 vols., 1886 ff.) all contributed to familiarizing American readers with historic method in estimating the church's past. When he came to America in 1845 history was still the obedient handmaid of dogmatic theology, and histories were written in the interests of edification or orthodoxy or sect. It is to his labors, and those of Henry B. Smith and John F. Hurst—the latter a Methodist—that we owe the emancipation of the science.

Of general writers on church history the tale is as short as that of writers on special and local history is long. Rev. Samuel Macauley Jackson's " Concise Dictionary of Religious Knowledge " (1889; 3d ed., 1893) is quite strong in the departments of history and biography, and the best handbook of its kind we have. Dr. William M. Blackburn has written a popular handbook (1879) which is much superior to his earlier monographs in this field, being eminently graphic and readable. It is not possible to give the same praise to Dr. J. C. Moffat's " Church History in Brief " (1885) or " The Church in Scotland " (1882). Rev. George Slater's " Historical and Critical Essay on the *Acta Pilati* " (1879), Professor Francis Brown and President R. D. Hitchcock's "Teaching of the Twelve Apostles " (Greek and English ; 2d ed., 1885), and Dr. Schaff's translation of the same document stand for a hopeful widening of historic interest.

In the field of European Protestant history Dr. Henry M. Baird's " Huguenots of France " (2d ed., 1885) and his "Huguenots and Henry of Navarre" (1886), Dr. C. M. Baird's " Huguenot Emigration to America " (2d ed., 1885), and Dr. E. H. Gillett's " Life and Times of John Huss " (3d ed., 1870) are all creditable to American scholarship.

In the field of American Presbyterian history the palm

is due to Dr. J. B. Scouller for his careful studies of the
history of the United Presbyterian Church and its predecessors, most of which have not been published in book
form.   Dr. Charles Augustus Briggs's " American Presbyterianism: Its Origin and Growth " enriches the subject
with new documents and seeks to show the justification
history offers to liberal interpretation; but none of his
works evidence the possession of the historic spirit.   Dr.
George P. Hays's popular book, " Presbyterians," offers a
good conspectus of the past and present of the church in
its several branches.   Dr. Alfred Nevin's " Encyclopedia
of the Presbyterian Church " contains much that should
find no place in such a work, and omits much that should.
It is written with little regard to historical perspective; but
it contains information which might have been lost.   It is
confined to the national and the southern Assemblies.

Of local histories the number is very great, and the quality improving, possibly through the exhaustion of lauda-
tory commonplaces and certainly through the diffusion of
a truer interest in the historic past.   Dr. S. D. Alexander's
rather dry and matter-of-fact history of the New York
Presbyteries, Dr. Thomas Murphy's more exuberant and
enthusiastic book on the Presbytery of Philadelphia North,
Mr. Sloan's " Presbytery of Kittatining," Dr. Norton's
" Illinois," and Dr. Howe's " South Carolina " are especially worthy of mention.   So are Dr. Prentiss's " First Fifty
Years of Union Seminary " (1889) and Mr. Hageman's work
on "Princeton and its Institutions " (1879).   Dr. Conway P.
Wing's " First Church of Carlisle " (1877) and his " Presbyteries of Donegal and Carlisle " (1876), Mr. Turner's
"Neshaminy Church " (1876), and the " Centenary Memorial " of the meeting of the four Synods at Pittsburg in 1875
are all solid contributions to Presbyterian history.   As
these dates show, the national centenary of 1876 was more

fruitful than that of the General Assembly in 1888 in suggesting historical research in this field. In good biographies the period has not been rich, the best being Dr. A. A. Hodge's life of his father, Dr. Stearns's life of Dr. Henry B. Smith, Mr. George Junkin's life of his father, and Dr. Palmer's life of Dr. Thornwell. Mr. H. C. Alexander's life of Dr. Addison Alexander is much below the interest of the subject, and Mr. Grasty's life of Dr. McPheeters is one of the worst-written books in the language. The autobiographies of Dr. Gardiner Spring, Dr. Samuel Irenæus Prime, and George H. Stuart share in the charm which belongs to that species of writing. Professor Sloane's life of his father is a portrait of a man who exhibited the strong Covenanter type of character, in combination with most attractive personal qualities.

In the department of devotional theology the church is fortunate in possessing writers of more than national repute. The many articles and the less numerous books of Drs. Theodore L. Cuyler, John Hall, and J. R. Miller have nourished the spiritual life wherever the English language is spoken. Of the church's preachers Dr. T. De Witt Talmage is the most widely known, though not for qualities distinctly Presbyterian; John Hall, whose sermons gather force, where others weaken, toward the close; John De Witt, who sees so finely the points of contact between lofty principles and homely duties; Henry van Dyke, who brings the culture of the modern world to bear on his pulpit work; Charles Wadsworth, who illumined every topic with the coruscations of genius; Herrick Johnson, who presses his theme with the cogency of a great pleader; Charles H. Parkhurst, who turns the light upon the dark places alike of the human conscience and of New York society; William S. Plumer, who fused a severe theology with tender emotion; Francis L. Patton, who by sheer force of logic cuts the channels for right action and feeling; Benjamin M. Palmer, whose fervid eloquence has the polish of the Southern school of oratory; Professor W. W. Moore, who seizes on the effective points of a subject with marvelous precision—these are but a few of the notable preachers who have helped to keep the American pulpit vigorously masculine and socially powerful.

In sacred poetry Presbyterians make a much feebler showing. The Scotch-Irish race has never been imaginative, on either side of the Atlantic. Margaret Junkin Preston is a poet of unquestioned power and of the purest Presbyterian stock. Her poem on the dangerous illness of the Prince of Wales elicited thanks from his noble wife. Sidney Lanier, though dealing but seldom with sacred themes, has not written a line out of keeping with his Huguenot descent and his Presbyterian training. Mrs. Elizabeth Prentiss displays less of vigor in expression, but a boldness in tender thought, which at times recalls the mystics. Mr. Samuel W. Duffield, like his father (p. 146), had a genuine gift of song and a wide acquaintance with Latin and English hymnology. His "English Hymns: Their Authors and their History" (2d ed., 1886) is a literary commentary on Dr. Robinson's "Laudes Domini" (1884). His "Latin Hymn-Writers and their Hymns" (1889) is pronounced by Rev. John Julian "the most complete and popular account which has been published in the English language." Professor Francis A. March's "Latin Hymns with English Notes" (1874) has put the finest within the reach of a wide public. Dr. Philip Schaff's "Christ in Song" (1869) contains some beautiful translations by the editor. The "Library of Religious Poetry" (1881), edited by him and Mr. Arthur Gilman, and Dr. S. Irenæus Prime's "Songs of the Soul" (1874) are anthologies of some value.

In the development of the worship of praise Dr. Charles S. Robinson may be said to have achieved a revolution by his series of musical hymn-books, from his " Songs of the Church " (1862) and " Songs of the Sanctuary " (1865) to his last revision of " Laudes Domini " (1892). He always has been stronger and more independent in the musical than the literary character of his books; but his " Annotations upon Popular Hymns " (1893) shows a close familiarity with the hymn-writers and their work. Dr. Edwin F. Hatfield, long the clerk of the General Assembly, was himself a hymn-writer of merit. His " Church Hymn-Book, with Tunes " (1872), is carefully edited as regards both text and music, and, while keeping well within the lines of established tradition, does not ignore the new poets and musicians. In " The Poets of the Church " (1884) he furnishes a kind of biographical commentary to his own collection. The " Hymns and Songs of Praise " (1874), edited by Drs. R. D. Hitchcock, Zachary Eddy (Reformed), and Philip Schaff, is the amplest collection, and in its day the widest in range of selection. " Carmina Sanctorum," by Drs. Hitchcock and Schaff and Mr. Lewis Ward Mudge, is a smaller collection, but with much the same character. Dr. Charles Cuthbert Hall, in his " Evangelical Hymnal," shows himself a decided innovator, drawing upon the latest Anglican composers and hymn-writers very freely. In " The Church Praise-Book " (1881), edited by himself and Mr. Hubert P. Main, Dr. M. Woolsey Stryker gives a very catholic selection, enriched with ten of his own hymns. In his " Church Song " (1889) he increases this number threefold. His hymns in " The Song of Miriam " (1888) have much beauty of thought, but sometimes fall short of the simplicity and obviousness in expression required for the widest popularity. Other Presbyterian hymnodists are Dr. Hervey D. Ganse, Rev. Epher Whitaker, Rev. Aaron

R. Wolfe, Rev. Arthur T. Pierson, Mrs. Herrick Johnson, Anson D. F. Randolph, Mrs. M. H. Seward ("Agnes Burney"), and Professor Robert P. Dunn.

The efforts of the reunited church and of the Southern Assembly to secure satisfactory books of praise were not at once successful. After a preliminary balk "The Presbyterian Hymnal" (1874) appeared, understood to be the work chiefly of Dr. J. T. Duryea. In both hymns and tunes it fell decidedly below the better class of American hymnaries, but it was twenty years before its revision was effected, and then only because the more educated and exacting congregations were discarding it in favor of private compilations. Even worse in its dolefulness of spirit and general feebleness' was the Southern " Psalms and Hymns for the Worship of God " (1874), now also superseded by a better book. It is to be regretted that both churches have abandoned the Reformed tradition, and widened the breach among Presbyterians, by failing to place the Book of Psalms in the forefront of their hymnaries.

This necessarily imperfect summary shows the increasing activity of American Presbyterians in many branches of scholarly work. It is weakest on the literary side, nor can it be said that they have contributed largely to the gratifying growth of national literature during the present half-century.

The Presbyterian churches have had their share of the friction which attends the process of readjustment of old beliefs to new discoveries and theories, which has made up the intellectual history of the last half-century. Naturally conservative by temperament and theological by vocation, they have been less prompt than others to accept new views, but they often have ignored their claims instead of submitting them to a searching examination. In the readjustments of religious belief to scientific discovery and speculation their attitude has been wise and patient. When it became clear that the age of the earth and of man involved at least a reinterpretation of the Mosaic account of creation, and called in question the chronology which Ussher and Newton had extracted from the Old Testament narrative, there was a slow and quiet acquiescence in the fact. The evolutionary theory of the origin of species, and of man's animal nature, was met with toleration, except in the prosecution of Dr. James Wodrow in the Southern church. The attempt to elevate science itself to the level of a complete philosophy, with the result of reducing men to the rank of parts of nature, governed by necessary laws as nature is, and therefore destitute of any real freedom of action, was even greeted with favor by some orthodox writers, on account of its supposed coincidence with the conclusions of Calvinism.

There has been, therefore, but little ecclesiastical disturbance along the lines on which the hardest intellectual battle of the age has been fought and is not yet completed. That along the lines of literary and historical criticism falls to the next chapter. The controversies and heresy trials of this period were, therefore, of minor importance, and with one exception they attracted almost no attention outside of the church. That exception was the prosecution of Professor David Swing before the Presbytery of Chicago, in 1874, by Professor Francis L. Patton, of the Northwestern Seminary, who also was editing the "Interior" and serving a Chicago church as its pastor. In his editorial work his attention was called to the preaching and public acts of a brother-pastor, Professor David Swing. This gentleman was of German descent and of old-school training. He had come in 1866 to the pastorate of the Westminster Church (O.S.) from a chair in Miami University, and had attracted a large congregation by his original and suggestive sermons. He showed in these the mind of a prose poet rather than of a logician, while his antagonist was a logician before everything. In certain statements found in Professor Swing's published sermons Dr. Patton thought he detected contradictions of the Confession of Faith on Election, Perseverance, Original Sin, the Vicarious Sacrifice of Christ, the Trinity, the Deity of Christ, Justification by Faith, Plenary Inspiration, Biblical Infallibility, and the Call to the Ministry, besides his " giving the weight of his influence to the Unitarian denomination " by lecturing in behalf of one of their chapels. This long indictment was reached by logical inferences from Professor Swing's words, and these inferences the latter repudiated. The Presbytery, which was composed mainly of new-school men, acquitted Professor Swing, after a trial which lasted six weeks, by a vote of three to one. As an appeal was taken to the Synod of Illinois, Professor Swing at once announced his withdrawal from the church, as he had an utter distaste for polemics, and his attachment to the Presbyterian Church had been much weakened by this experience. He gathered an independent congregation, to which he preached with no diminution of his popularity or increase of his orthodoxy until his death, in 1894. Two men—the Esau of liberalism and the Jacob of orthodoxy —were always struggling to the birth in him, and this kind of midwifery greatly added to Esau's chances.

The transaction made an unpleasant impression throughout the church. Few could go with the Presbytery in its absolute acquittal of the accused, and not many were satisfied with the spirit and manner of the prosecution. Many things which were alleged to prove Professor Swing's heterodoxy would pass now without a word of comment, still less of objection. It is no longer possible to elevate the destiny of Penelope and Socrates, or the moral character of John Stuart Mill, to the level of an issue in dogmatics.

Nothing like the same interest attached to the trial of Rev. John Miller before the Presbytery of New Brunswick in 1877, although he was the son of Dr. Samuel Miller, of Princeton Seminary. It was felt on all hands that Mr. Miller had put himself outside the pale of Presbyterianism by his rejection of the doctrine of the Trinity, although he held to the proper deity of Jesus the Christ. He also asserted the annihilation of man by death until he is raised again at the resurrection; and that Christ took upon him original sin and was capable of sin. The decision reached by the Presbytery commanded the assent of the entire church.

There was not quite the same unanimity in approving the action of the Presbytery of Huntingdon, Pa., in the case of the Rev. J. W. White, in 1884. Mr. White evidently was in a state of mental reaction against the legal conception of redemption, and was striving after one in which real should replace jural relations and conceptions. He also asserted that the scope of the atonement is found defined in its effects upon redeemed men. On this point, and in his conception of the resurrection, he showed the influence of Swedenborg's teaching. The Presbytery, after condemning his teaching on these points, allowed him to withdraw from the ministry of the church. This gentleness the Synod of Pennsylvania disapproved, while applauding the Presbytery's findings on the charges.

CHAPTER XVII.

THE CONGREGATIONAL LIFE AND WORSHIP OF THE CHURCH.

In the Presbyterian view of the church, it consists of a series of assemblies, congregational, presbyterial, provincial (or synodical), national, and ecumenical. Each larger body embraces as its parts all the lesser which fall within its bounds, and possesses their functions of teaching, worship, and discipline. Thus the presbyterial church is the aggregate of all the congregational churches under its care, and more. The ministers (or bishops) resident within its bounds are members of the presbyterial church, but not of congregational churches, their ordination transferring them from the one to the other.

In the Presbyterian system in practice the Presbytery is the most important unit. It meets far more frequently than the larger bodies can; it elects the members of the Assemblies, and in the large States those of the Synods; it has supervision of a manageable area; it has the sole power of ordination and of licensure; it possesses primary jurisdiction over the ministry of the church; and, through the operation of the Barrier Act, it possesses a control of the church's constitution in which Synods and sessions do not share. In its original purpose it was to serve many uses. It was a theological school for the training of its own members by the selection of profitable themes of discussion and by friendly criticisms of the sermons preached.

The trials of students before licensure, and of licentiates before ordination, are a remnant only of this. It also exercised the most direct care over its congregations. It met with each church in turn, to take cognizance of its spiritual condition, the faithfulness of its minister, the efficiency of its eldership, the household care of the young, the freedom of the people from scandals, and their constancy in attendance on worship and the Lord's Supper. This is continued to some extent among the lesser Presbyterian bodies, but the American Presbytery generally exercises its episcopal functions at a distance, and in a very general way. It very commonly has so many churches under its care that it could not visit them once in a generation. Its meeting with any of them is but upon invitation, and the spiritual benefit (or harm) which results from the visit is through the general influence of its proceedings rather than any direct dealing with the church itself. This is still more true, of necessity, of the Synods and the General Assembly.

For these reasons the spiritual life of the church is developed almost entirely through the congregation. Each local church is what its people, its session, and especially its pastor, make of it. The predominance of the pastor in its life, and of the preaching function in its worship, is such as would not have been possible in the apostolic age, because of the difference in the conception and working of the earliest church. That was a body of great complexity, and therefore ranked high in the sociological scale. " The simplicity that is in Christ" was not a simplicity of function or of operation, as the Apostle describes these in his Epistles to the churches of Corinth and of Ephesus. All the special powers and capacities which their new life had brought to light in the members of the apostolic church were given scope and exercise in its congregational life and its labors for the advance of the gospel. The resultant unity was not that of simplicity, but of complexity—" the whole body fitly joined together and compacted by that which every joint supplieth, according to the effectual working in the measure of every part."

The modern church has undergone sociologic retrogression from complexity to simplicity. It has not been able to suppress the bestowal of gifts and the evocation of powers for service; but neither has it furnished a place for them. They have been obliged to find their scope outside the church rather than in it. Thus the modern societies for the care of the poor have taken up a work which was the glory of the early church. The Sunday-school, for the exercise of the gift of teaching or " doctrine," has been organized outside the congregation, though it gradually is making its way back into it. The prayer-meeting has been found necessary to give scope to Christian freedom in the exercise of the gifts of supplication and exhortation, because the stiff dignity and simplicity of the Sabbath services left no room for them. The Young Men's (and Women's) Christian Associations, the Temperance societies, the Christian Endeavor societies, and the rest of their kind, are but so many indications of the woful impoverishment of the life of the congregation through its simplification.

In the actual working of our Presbyterian churches generally this evil has reached an extreme development. The habit of speaking of a congregation as Dr. A's or Mr. B's church is but an expression of the fact. Practically the pastor carries the undivided work on his own shoulders, the sexton being the official next in importance. The Scriptural diaconate for men has been replaced by trustees, who have only the duties of collecting pew-rents, paying salaries and bills, and keeping the church-building in repair. The diaconate for women has disappeared altogether, or is feebly represented by Dorcas societies, ladies' aid societies, sewing-circles, mothers' meetings, and the like ; and the effort to restore it to its rightful place in the church's order was defeated by a vote of the Presbyteries, after receiving the sanction of the General Assembly of 1891, and the strong approval of the Princeton Seminary faculty.[1]

Lastly, the eldership, which has been the glory and the strength of Presbyterianism, is tending to become little more than association with the pastor in a religious committee to dispose of matters of discipline and the like. Its active and public functions ceased when the annual and formal visitation of the congregation was given up. Its members are generally too busy to do more than attend an evening meeting once a month or less, and it is exceptional to find that they regard even the visiting of the sick as one of the duties of the office. There is, consequently, a profound dissatisfaction with the present status of the eldership, both among its own members and elsewhere. Conferences are held and papers read which either describe an impossible ideal or make trifling suggestions. The sense of unexhausted possibilities in the office is not wanting, but what to do is not so evident. The purely lay character of its members, their absorption in business pursuits, their lack of personal oversight and authority in the congregation, are all in antagonism to Presbyterian history, however well these may fit into Dr. Hodge's theory that they are simply the elected representatives of the people. That theory, indeed, and the general disuse of ordination by laying on of hands, have the air of an accommodation to facts rather than the exhibition of an ideal. And the

[1] The essentially Scriptural and Protestant character of this office is well exhibited in Mr. J. M. Ludlow's little book, "Woman's Work in the Church" (Macmillans, 1865).

adoption in many churches, since 1872, of the rotary plan, by which a part of the session retires from office at the close of a specified term and is replaced by fresh election, is quite in harmony with the present status of affairs, though not with history. It was strenuously opposed by Albert Barnes when under discussion.

The equal vote of the ruling eldership with the ministry on all questions which come before the courts of the church is an essential feature of Presbyterian government, but it has become anomalous through the changed relation of the elder to the church. The elder of past days was generally a man who was not greatly inferior to his pastor in doctrinal and Scriptural knowledge. He had given close study to theological questions. He had read, if not widely, yet attentively and with reflection. He was usually as competent as his minister to pass judgment on questions which came before Synod and Presbytery. The young minister, indeed, lived in a certain fear of him and of other keen theologians of both sexes among his hearers, who were sound on "the fundamentals." This is more commonly true now of the smaller Presbyterian bodies than the larger. In ordinary cases the elder of to-day is far less fully prepared to sit in judgment upon the questions which agitate the church. He has been too busy with other pursuits to even attempt to keep abreast of the more thorough and professional training of the ministry. He either takes the safe course of voting as his minister does, or he is at the mercy of party leaders, who catch him with party watchwords, progressive or alarmist, and commit him to policies whose ultimate bearing he is too busy to understand.

In the absence of efficient assistance from his session, the pastor of our day ordinarily has his hands full to overflowing. He has to do all the preaching, all the pastoral visiting, all the presiding, all the work of administration except the financial, and often a good deal of that. While his associates in the session too generally hide their talents in a napkin, he has to trade with his beyond what their amount justifies, and the result sometimes is bankruptcy. Fitted to do one thing well, he has to do many things badly, and thus awakens the criticism which ends in a termination of the pastoral relation. Under such a system it is not wonderful that the average duration of the pastorate grows shorter. It is a striking evidence of their adaptability that our ministers hold one church as long as they do.

The evil is all the graver because of the prevalence of the notion that each church, however large, needs a single minister and no more. In our large cities it is as exceptional to find a large Episcopal congregation which has but one minister in charge, as it is to find a Presbyterian church which has more than its pastor. It is not want of means which is in the way, but the conception of the pastoral office, which exacts that each of its occupants shall show himself equal to all the multifarious requirements which have gathered around it, and that there shall be no division of labor among them. Hence the practice of multiplying small city churches beyond all need, each with its one polypragmatic pastor. For a similar reason it has been found difficult to effect any arrangement to exempt even a distinguished preacher from pastoral labor, however unfitted he may be to undertake it. In one noteworthy case the people ceased to attend church, and gave as their reason, "We want our pastor to preach to us." The pastor was a man of little note, associated with one of the greatest preachers of the age.

Closely related to this demand for simplification in the ministry has been a demand for simplicity in all that pertains to the worship and forms of the church. This assumes a Presbyterian tradition for simplicity of which his-

tory knows nothing.   The Kirk in its best days, like all
"the best Reformed churches," in all its public services
exhibited a dignity which has now disappeared.   The minister of the church still wore his gown in his pulpit ministrations, if not also on the street.   He bore himself with
the courtly manner of the old-fashioned gentleman, and
was received by his people with a deference which recognized the greatness of the office with which he was clothed.
His visits to their homes, like Edward Irving's to his Glasgow and London flocks, were not "calls" of neighborly
familiarity, but the coming and going of one who left an
atmosphere of grace and consecration in the household.
The children never heard him lightly spoken of, not for
his own sake so much as that of his office and his influence with them.

In the public services there was a lofty gravity which
became the house of God.   The congregation not only listened, but, Bible in hand, they accompanied their pastor in
his references to the teachings of the Word.   They arose
and stood in prayer, though they sat in singing.   The
elders occupied the elders' pew, close to the pulpit, as in
the Reformed churches of America still.   They were chosen
from the men of weight and spirituality of character, and
many are the testimonies to the deep impression they
made on the young of the flock by their paternal interest
in candidates for the communion or for the ministry.

Communion seasons came too seldom—generally twice
a year only—but they were times of solemnity and not
of modern simplicity.   The "token," whose history goes
back to the subapostolic ages, symbolized the communicant's pledged friendship with his Lord.   The language of
the "action-sermon," the barring or fencing of the tables,
the whole atmosphere of the rite, were more suggestive
of the presence of a great spiritual mystery than the ritual

of Canterbury or even Rome. Yet the long tables, draped with white, bore witness to the original character of the feast spread by the Master for his church, rather than to a clerical ceremonial which the people only were admitted to share in.

To-day these things are hardly to be found, except among our high-church brethren, the Covenanters. Their disappearance elsewhere has been a loss of weight in impression, and of a sense of the true purposes of worship. Man has grown more and God less in our assemblies.

The discontent with the present status of congregational worship has produced a feeling in favor of a liturgy. Drs. Greene, Miller, and Krebs among the earlier leaders of the General Assembly, and the Hodges at a later date, declined to express any disapproval of liturgic forms, although they agreed in disapproving of their imposition as a fixed order obligatory upon all, and to the exclusion of free prayer. The Hodges felt a warm interest in the movement represented by the Church Service Society of the Church of Scotland and in its Euchologion. Dr. A. A. Hodge himself prepared a book of forms for special services, which, however, does not show him to have possessed extraordinary gifts as a liturgist.

In 1855 the late Dr. Charles W. Baird formally opened the discussion of the question in his " Eutaxia; or, The Presbyterian Liturgies," in which he showed that the sister-churches of Italy, Switzerland, France, Germany, Holland, England, and Scotland, in earlier times, had been liturgic in practice. He drew from the archives of the church the liturgies which bear the great names of Calvin and Knox, and interpreted their devout accents to American ears. Dr. Charles Hodge reviewed the work in the " Princeton Review " for July, 1855, and deplored the want of a Presbyterian prayer-book to serve both as a guide in the exercise of free prayer and as a substitute for it on proper occasions.   He deplored the sometimes slovenly and frequently inappropriate fashion in which this part of worship was conducted, and especially the want of a suitable communion service, declaring that the Presbyterian Church "has suffered more than can well be estimated from these faults in the conduct of her simple services, and from failing to supply her children with those aids for religious worship which their exigencies demand" in the absence of a minister.   "If God would put it into the heart of some man of large experience in the pastoral life, familiar with the literature of the subject and with the intellectual gifts the work demands, to compile a book containing prayers for public worship, and forms for the administration of the sacraments, marriages, and funerals, he would do the church a great service, whether the book ever received the sanction of our ecclesiastical judicatures or not."

In the next decade a liturgy was actually adopted by St. Peter's Church in Rochester, and used until suppressed by the new-school Presbytery.   In 1864 Dr. Charles W. Shields, then of Philadelphia, now of Princeton College, reproduced the English Book of Common Prayer in the shape which Richard Baxter and the other English Presbyterians in 1661 declared would be satisfactory to them, and pressed its claim to supply a basis for unity in worship among Protestants.   In 1883 Professor S. M. Hopkins, of Auburn Seminary, published a liturgy for the use of Presbyterian churches.   Somewhat earlier the late John Neill, M.D., of Philadelphia, tried to establish a John Knox Society for the promotion or restoration of liturgic worship.[1]

[1] See Dr. Charles W. Baird's " Eutaxia; or, The Presbyterian Liturgies," New York, Dodd, 1855; " A Book of Public Prayer, Compiled from the Au-

Parallel with this discussion has gone forward a process of change which has put an end to uniformity in worship, and has set the Directory of 1788 aside in many, if not most, of the churches. The Lord's Prayer has been restored to the place given it by the Westminster Divines, and is repeated in unison. So are the Apostles' Creed, selections from the Psalms and other parts of Scripture. A formal offertory has taken the place of the collection. There is a silent pause after the benediction, and a free use of chants, by the choir at least. In other cases we see a free use of spontaneous symbolism, not always in the best taste, but a witness to the growing need of appeal to the imagination, no less than to the understanding and the emotions, in true worship. For no worship is really adequate to human needs whose methods leave any province of our manifold human nature out of account. God has made us the most complex of his creatures, and calls for a response to his goodness from every side of our human nature.

It is but natural that much of the change this restlessness has led to has not been for the better. The prominence given to the quartet choir in our city churches, often leading to the relinquishment of the singing to them, and the time devoted to choir pieces and organ voluntaries, constitute a censurable departure not only from Presbyterian history, but from the very idea of congregational worship. It is an importation of the methods of the concert-hall into the church, which is offensive both to good taste and to

thorized Formularies of Worship of the Presbyterian Church, as Prepared by the Reformers, Calvin, Knox, and others, with Supplementary Forms," New York, Scribner, 1868; Dr. Charles W. Shields's "The Book of Common Prayer and Administration of the Sacraments, and other Rites and Ceremonies of the Church, as Amended by the Westminster Divines in the Royal Commission of 1661, and in Agreement with the Directory for Public Worship of the Presbyterian Church in the United States," Philadelphia, 1864, New York, 1883; also his "Liturgia Expurgata," Philadelphia, 1864, third edition, New York, 1884; Professor S. M. Hopkins's "A General Liturgy and Book of Common Prayer," New York, Barnes, 1883.

devout instincts. Not so bad, but certainly not laudable, has been the introduction of an undignified and unsuitable music into the Sunday-school, the praise-service, and even, in some cases, into the stated services of worship. It is undeniable that the school of music begun by Philip Phillips and developed by Ira D. Sankey has led multitudes to sing who otherwise would not have done it. The gain, however, is attended by a loss so grave as to justify the church in setting her face against it. The power of association is nowhere more in evidence than in the influence which music exercises. The association of the greatest and most affecting truths with words commonly paltry and often vulgar, and with music often more suitable to a dance-hall than to the house of God, is a chief among the many influences which have been robbing religion of its severity and God of his awfulness. Popularity is too dearly bought at such a price.

More promising of good is the growing taste for a music at once popular and excellent in quality, which the English churches have fostered. The names of Dykes, Hullah, Wesley, Barnby, Sullivan, indicate that as yet it is an exotic in America; but its amount in the newer hymnaries is increasing steadily, and it is to be expected that a school of this character will arise among us, and will emancipate it from a certain stiffness which is alien to our national character. The good work done by Lowell Mason and Thomas S. Hastings for the American churches entitles them to lasting gratitude; but they worked for an age in which musical culture was making its beginnings in America; and, as Browning says, each age must produce its own music.

The proper spiritual life of the congregation differs from that of the past in showing neither the denominational distinctness and uniformity nor the doctrinal exactitude of former times. The lines and bounds of spiritual affinity become less distinct through greater freedom of intercourse and interchange with other Christians. Presbyterians may still commit the Shorter Catechism to memory in their childhood, but their riper years are nourished by writers of so many schools that that famous text-book of highly abstract theology generally falls into the background of the mind. They still, by force of heredity, are more interested in doctrinal questions than are their fellow-Christians generally, but in a different way from their fathers. There is a loss in this syncretism by which the thoughts of À Kempis and Pascal, Keble and Newman, Robertson and Kingsley, lie side by side with the tenets of their vernacular Calvinism. In minds of the less logical kind the result is a great deal of confusion and irresolution, with a disposition to keep open house for whatever offers itself as new. But there is a gain also in the enrichment of the spiritual life from the fruits of other fields, which are yet the Master's domain. The hymnaries of the church exemplify this gain. Were all that is not from the pen of the Calvinistic hymnodists, from Baxter to Bonar, eliminated from the selection, the result would be a great impoverishment.

A decided gain to the spiritual life of the modern churches has been in gifts bestowed upon them in this age which are not seen so distinctly in the past. One of these is the new sense of intimate personal communion with the Saviour in what some old writers call " the process of his life and death, resurrection and ascension." Beginning from the revivals of 1857–59 in both the British Islands and America, there has been a growing dissatisfaction with the merely jural conception of man's redemption in Christ, and a pressing on " to know him, and the power of his resurrection, and the fellowship of his sufferings, becoming conformed unto his death." Christians are seeking after

the deepest spiritual significance of the mysteries of death
to sin and rising again to righteousness, as made possible
to us through fellowship with him in all he was and did.
There is no resting in salvation as a judicial transaction
liberating men from the penalties of sin. The inner life
of conflict with evil, and victory through faith, is seen to
be associated with the great transactions recorded in the
Gospels in a way not to be expressed to the understanding
in the phrases of any philosophy, or even theology, that
has been formulated. Hence the welcome shown to those
mystical writers whose bold utterances express this truth
in parable and paradox.

   This new phase of Christian experience certainly deprives the law of condemnation of the prominence which
the teachers of the Great Awakening gave it in the *ordo
salutis.* Hence the complaints from the representatives of
that school that there is no such " thorough law-work "
in modern conversions as in those of past generations.
Sinners come to the rest of faith without such maddening
visions of their own depravity, such prostrating sense of
the sinfulness of sin, such readiness to accept even damnation at God's hands as their just reward, as were seen in
1735–42, or in 1800–19. This is true; but if these tre-
mendous emotions be the indispensable prerequisites of
the Christian life, there is no age of the church before the
rise of Pietism in Germany which must not be pronounced
fatally deficient. Even the apostolic age and that of the
Reformation will not satisfy these conditions. It is true
that Luther went through experiences not less harrowing
in the days of his ignorance ; but he never looked for them
in his own people, who had been brought by easier ways
into the light of the gospel. And he, like Calvin, describes
repentance for sin, not as an achievement to be got through

and done with before exercising faith, but as a lifelong and deepening experience resulting from faith.

This new view is carrying the church back into sympathy with the Reformers in the matter of the way in which men enter upon the new life. The desire grows less for sharp crises of transition from conscious enmity to conscious friendship with God. The principle of Christian Nurture enunciated by Horace Bushnell in 1847—viz., that a child brought up under Christian influence should never know a time when love to God is not an active principle in its life—is displacing the old assumption that even the offspring of the godly are the born enemies of God and must await the crisis of conversion. In this respect the church no longer presents the unity it once did in its practical theology. In some quarters the assumptions of the Awakening still control her action. In others the newer view, which is also the older, has obtained practical recognition, and the demand for conscious conversion is no longer made of the children of the church.

Another grace bestowed on the modern church, and one closely connected with this new sense of direct relation to Christ, is the spirit of helpfulness. The neighborhood of the Master is found to be no place for idlers in the vineyard. So there has been a development of spontaneous activity in the churches, which, as has been shown, finds itself badly suited with room in the church as popularly understood and organized. The new wine, in many instances, has burst the old bottles.

With this also has come a peril of doing and overdoing, without the vocation and the leading which must come before right spontaneous action. Unfortunate, too, has been the growing disposition to propose that the church shall take the whole social burden on her shoulders, and hold herself responsible for the right conduct of affairs which belong properly to the state. Into the sphere of state action—the sphere of rights and of law—the church may not enter, except as announcing the great principles of social duty. She is not made a judge or a divider between rich and poor or between labor and capital. Nor is it hers to decide by what methods the state is to deal with the problems of slavery or intemperance or the social evil, although she has the right to insist that they shall not be ignored. She can undertake these things only at the sacrifice of far higher interests, at the peril of forfeiting her proper spiritual influence.

The institutional church, which has grown up in our great cities as the result of this new interest in social problems, is a sign of good. It is a return to apostolic ideals in many respects, especially in getting rid of that severance of the spiritual from the material in ministering to human needs which stands in such contrast to all the precedents of the New Testament. It may result in a restoration of the manifold activities of the churches of the first days, and thus reclaim for the gospel the gracious activities to which it gave the first impulse. No doubt it will make many mistakes in the process, and learn by its mistakes.

The discipline of the modern church over its own members has become a matter of some difficulty, in view of the church's divisions, and the readiness of many of these to open their arms to persons whose stay in the others has become uncomfortable. In some of our religious bodies there is hardly a pretense of exercising discipline over their lay members. In others it is abandoned to the judgment of each congregation, and can rise no higher than the local and temporary sense of propriety in each. The Presbyterian churches always have confessed their responsibility, both local and collective, for seeing that the walk and conversation of their people is according to godliness. The scope of this responsibility has been narrowed and its efficiency weakened by the notion that none but the communicants in the church are its members; and even when there has been a disposition to enlarge the conception, it has been too generally by including merely " the children of the church" who, through youth or indecision, have not yet become communicants. In this respect the Congregationalist conception of the church has displaced that which is distinctively Presbyterian, to the diminution of the church's social influence, and to the injury of her non-communicant members. The present tendency to assert for the church a firmer and broader influence will help to correct this, and will bring even our Independent brethren to see that the demand for a church-membership individually assured of their conversion does not place the church in a position fitted to meet the social need, and is not in harmony with the teachings of the New Testament. Sociology promises to play havoc with ecclesiology of that type.

In view of these openings toward a new development we cannot regard the American church, either as meaning a congregation or embracing a "denomination," as an accomplished fact. Thus far, indeed, there has been little that is distinctly American in our religious life, and that little not the most laudable. All our sects, except a few to which we refuse the Christian name, are of European origin. We have been singularly barren in ecclesiastical originality, while original in nearly all other fields of national life. The national instinct, indeed, has hardly touched the churches, as yet, with its unifying power. We are still in the colonial stage, abounding in European elements of all sorts, but not yet American.

The manner in which the political unity of the nation

came about probably foreshadows the solution of the
problem of Christian unity, which already presses upon
our Protestant churches.   It will not be by sacrificing the
wealth of variety in the present order (or seeming chaos)
of our ecclesiastical life, but by some elastic method, like
our federal Union, which will leave room for variety in the
types of worship and of life, and yet prevent or avoid the
breach of unity.   We shall not leave behind us all the past
has bestowed, and attain to unity by the process of simplification in creed and worship, but by finding room and
use in mutual help for all that God has given us.   And
when that day comes, soon or late, there is no church that
will have more to bring than our own, and none that will
be welcomed more heartily into the new fellowship by its
sister-churches.

CHAPTER XVIII.

THE REVISION CONTROVERSY.

HALF a century ago the great controversies were waged between our religious households. It was church against church, or sect against sect. When a collision of opinion arose within a church, it generally resulted in a division, or in the formation of a new sect to represent the worsted principle. Our ecclesiastical politics had the simplicity and directness seen in an ancient Greek city, where the victorious party generally expelled the minority, and thus secured an effective unanimity. It was a common plea with those who expressed their dissent from the position taken by their own church, that they should leave it in peace, and either seek fellowship in some body which agreed with them, or form a new one for themselves.

This breaking up religious communions "with a light heart" is become less the habit of our American Christians. It begins to be recognized that doctrinal uniformity is not the most precious possession a church can claim, and may be bought at too high a price. What once would have been separate sects begin to be parties within the churches, and the discussions which would have been waged across sectarian lines are now carried on in a more brotherly fashion within the same body.

It is noticeable that the questions which perplex one church are those which are pressing for an answer in some shape in the others also. All the churches are feeling the strain of readjusting their theological formulas to the new conclusions of history and criticism, sociology and biology. All have to decide how far the new scholarship demands a new attitude toward the Scriptures; how far the Development theory may be accepted as explaining the origin of man and of society, without imperiling positions essential to the Christian conception of human spirituality and divine Providence. All have to say how far the newer ethics oblige us to reconsider our ethical ideals, and thus to modify our conception of God. And even when the shape taken by the discussion is one which is peculiar to the individual church, the wide sympathy excited in other churches with one or both of the parties to the controversy shows that the real issue is one which is common to the churches.

This was eminently true of the discussion as to the revision of the Westminster standards, which was sprung upon the church by the General Assembly of 1889. It can hardly be said to have been foreshadowed by any previous action on any one's part on this side of the ocean. The interest in the question of subscription, which had been fanned into life by the discussions previous to the reunion of 1869–70, had fairly died out. None of the trials for heresy, except for a brief moment that of Professor Swing, had caused it to revive. No liberal was asserting the need of larger liberty of construction; no conservative was urging greater strictness. There seemed to be, in fact, a distinct languor in reference to all such matters; and Dr. Archibald A. Hodge's course of popular lectures on theological themes had given unusual satisfaction even to those who differed from the Princeton type of doctrine. The agitation as to the "Higher Criticism," which had been going on in the pages of the "Presbyterian Review," was quite another affair, and stood in no vital relation to the question now raised.

It was in the British churches that the alteration of the church's relation to the Westminster standards was proposed. First the United Presbyterian Church of Scotland —the church which had sent its missionaries to America because unconditional subscription to the Confession of Faith was not required by the Synod of Philadelphia—adopted in 1879, after prolonged debate, a " Declaratory Act as to the Sense in which the Confession is to be Understood," which shifted the emphasis from the points peculiar to Calvinism to those in which Calvinists are in agreement with other Christians. Next the Free Church, which refused recognition to the new-school church of America as unsound in its Calvinism, was planning a similar declaration as to the sense in which it required subscription to the standards. Lastly the newly vigorous Presbyterian Church of England was adopting in 1889 briefer Articles of Faith, twenty-four in number, as a summary of the Westminster Confession of Faith, to which ministers and elders might assent at their ordination.

These examples acted the more directly upon the American church because of the closer relations which had been fostered by the Reformed Alliance, and through the vigorous theological literature created by the young Free Church ministry. For years there was a silent observation of what was happening abroad, and a feeling that the same problem must be solved in America also. Sound, but not ultra, conservatives, like Dr. Archibald A. Hodge, did not hesitate to express a willingness to go as far, at least, as the British churches were going for the relief of troubled consciences. He reprinted the Declaratory Act of the United Presbyterian Synod in his " Commentary on the Confession of Faith " (Philadelphia, 1885), and he told me that he saw no objection to the same step being taken by the American church.

The air, indeed, was growing electric, but the shock which brought down the avalanche came from the conservative Presbytery of Philadelphia. It sent a memorial to the General Assembly asking it to revise the proof-texts printed with the Shorter Catechism, which a sounder exegesis had shown to be not always the best for the purpose. To this there was no great objection from any quarter, and the work has since been done. But the memorial, by its very success, suggested a bolder step. In the General Assembly of 1889 memorials were presented from fifteen Presbyteries asking it to take steps toward a revision of the Westminster Confession. The Assembly, without a division, resolved to transmit an overture to the Presbyteries asking their sense of the propriety of attempting a revision, and what changes they thought necessary.

The constitutionality of the overture was challenged, especially by the lawyers in the conservative wing of the church. The Adopting Act of 1789 (p. 65) had declared that the Confession should be " unalterable, unless two thirds of the Presbyteries shall propose alterations or amendments, and [these] shall be agreed to and enacted by the General Assembly." It was claimed that this reserved the initiative to the Presbyteries, and that the General Assembly could not move in the matter until two thirds of the Presbyteries invited it to do so. The action, however, of the Synod of 1787 did not vitiate the overture of 1889, which proposed and sanctioned no alteration in the Confession, but merely suggested to the Presbyteries that now was the time to do it unitedly if they desired to. A much bolder course, indeed, had been taken by the Assembly of 1803, which had directed one of its committees " to consider whether any, and, if any, what, alterations ought to be made in the Confession of Faith."

The response to the overture from the Presbyteries of

the church was surprising both in the extent of the desire for a change it elicited and the emphasis with which it was expressed. Up to the opening of the question there must have been a steady growth of dissatisfaction which had found no utterance. Not only among new-school men and among the younger ministers was this shown, but in all classes. Dr. Henry J. van Dyke, who had made no secret of his sympathy with the " Declaration and Testimony " movement, Drs. James McCosh and J. T. Duffield of Princeton College, Dr. Theodore L. Cuyler, Dr. Henry C. McCook, Dr. William O. Campbell, and other old-school men, were as emphatic as Drs. Philip Schaff, Howard Crosby, E. R. Craven, Herrick Johnson, Stephen W. Dana, Charles L. Thompson, and others on the new-school side.

The opposition, however, was strong, able, and resolute. The faculty of Princeton Seminary (Drs. Green, Warfield, C. W. Hodge, etc.) were a unit in opposition, and with them stood Dr. Patton, now the president of the college. They were reinforced by Dr. Shedd, of Union Seminary, and Dr. John de Witt, of the Chicago Seminary. On the same side stood Drs. John Hall, Samuel T. Lowrie, and George P. Hays, with Judge Drake of Missouri, and a host of lawyers among the elders. Professor C. A. Briggs occupied a rather ambiguous position, as fearing that the Confession if revised might leave him less sailing-room than he then enjoyed. His pamphlet, " Whither ? " certainly throws cold water on the proposal to revise, although he finally voted for the New York Presbytery's resolution for " revision, understanding the word to be used broadly as comprehending any Confessional changes." The direction in which this last expression points was taken by twenty-one of the Presbyteries, beginning with that of Albany, which overtured the General Assembly for an entirely new

Confession of Faith. Others expressed their desire for a brief statement of the church's essential doctrine, which should not supersede, but stand beside, the Confession, after the fashion of the Scotch Declaratory Act.

The reasons given for revision were very various, but some were so generally expressed as to permit of their being stated as the mind of the church. It was said that the Confession was both defective and excessive in statement. The church had undergone great changes since the Westminster divines had been in session. It had been led into a deeper sense of the love of God to mankind, of the work of the Spirit in the hearts of men, and of the church's vocation as a missionary agency. The Confession contained no explicit recognition of the love of God to men, and no confession of the church's duty toward the nations that sit in darkness. It was explicit enough as to controversial points which were of interest to the seventeenth century. It had nothing to say of the issues of modern debate—of the great conflict, for instance, between materialistic science and spiritual religion.

On the other hand, it went beyond the teachings of Scripture in explicitly asserting the reprobation of the wicked, in refining as to the number of the elect being incapable of increase or decrease, in speaking of " elect infants " with the evident implication that some are reprobate, and in declaring the Bishop of Rome to be the Antichrist. The third chapter of the Confession, which treats " Of God's Eternal Decree," was the center of the whole debate, the conservatives insisting that every part of it was either a primary statement of the Calvinistic principle or a necessary inference from it, while the revisionists declined to regard logically necessary inferences as necessarily true. This, indeed, the conservatives conceded in refusing to admit that if there be " elect infants " there must also be

"reprobate infants." The Westminster divines, as Dr.
C. P. Krauth showed in his reply to Dr. Charles Hodge on
this point, would not have shrunk from the inference. It
shows how great the change which has taken place in our
conception of God's character, that not a single opponent
of revision would subscribe to the opinion which the authors of the Confession actually held and meant to express.
Many of them even refused to believe that the dogma of
infant damnation had ever been held by Calvinists.

The opponents of revision argued (1) that it was dangerous, as likely to lead to changes which would impair
"the integrity of the Reformed or Calvinistic system"—
Professor H. B. Smith's phrase, of which conservatives
were now less afraid than when they voted it out of the
Basis of Union. It is true that the leading advocates of
revision were pledged to resist such changes, and were
ready to have the Committee on Revision instructed to
reject them if proposed. To many, however, reprobation
or preterition belonged to that integrity, and they were
alarmed by the urgency for its excision. They also were
alarmed, and with some reason, by the wild and loose criticisms of the Confession in which some of the advocates of
revision—not the leaders, however—indulged themselves.

They also (2) objected to revision as needless, since "the
elastic formula of subscription" employed by the American
church bound its office-bearers only to "sincerely receive
and adopt the Confession, . . . as containing the System
of Doctrine taught in the Holy Scriptures." This, they
insisted, meant simply the Reformed or Calvinistic system
in its integrity, apart from the special peculiarities of statement employed by the framers of the Confession. Subscription did not carry with it unqualified and unlimited acceptance of the Confession, but only of its essential articles.
This plea, as Dr. Craven showed, was not in accordance

with the history of the church and the expression of its
mind by several General Assemblies. These identified the
Confession itself with "the system of doctrine taught in
the Holy Scriptures." The right to even public exception
to any statement in the Confession was abolished by the
Old Side at the division of 1741, and was not reasserted
by the New Side at the reunion of 1758, with the express
exception of "so much of the xxiiid Chapter as gives authority to the civil magistrate in matters of religion." That
chapter was changed in 1786–87, thus eliminating the exception. The same Synod originated the formula of assent
at ordination still in use: "Do you sincerely receive and
adopt the Confession of Faith of this Church, as containing
the System of Doctrine taught in the Holy Scriptures?"
The Synod also declared the books which made up its constitution to be "the standard of our doctrine, government,
discipline, and worship." Neither it nor the earlier Assemblies regarded it as being "the system of doctrine" or
"the standard of doctrine" mixed up with other matters.
The Assembly of 1824 described the doctrinal standards
of the church as "a summary of those divine truths which
are diffused throughout the sacred volume," and added:
"They as a system of doctrine, therefore, cannot be abandoned, in our opinion, without an abandonment of the Word
of God." They again speak of them as "the system of
doctrine which men of sound learning, full of the Holy
Ghost and mighty in the Scriptures, have devised from the
oracles of the living God." In a word, the Confession *is*
the system to which the church requires its ministers, elders,
and deacons to subscribe. That system is contained in it
in the sense in which "the Word of God is contained in
the Scriptures of the Old and New Testaments," as orthodox men understand that formula and rationalists do not.

The liberty to except whatever is not essential to the

integrity of the Reformed or Calvinistic system no more exists legally than does the liberty to except whatever is not essential to the evangelical system held by Calvinists and Arminians alike. The church has no more drawn the one line than the other. The attempt to draw the former line was defeated in 1869 by the conservatives of the old-school church. Those ministers of the church, therefore, who betrayed their lack of sympathy with the essentials of Calvinism during the debate on revision had just the same rights in the church as those who avowed their Calvinism but expressed their dissent from any of the statements of the Confession. Both were there on toleration simply—a toleration growing out of the impossibility Dr. Charles Hodge confessed (p. 140) of requiring subscription to an elaborate Confession, but never officially defined as to its limits. The debate should have opened the eyes of the conservatives to the doctrinal uncertainty of the church's position. The church's creed should be one to which the ministry could subscribe as unreservedly as the bridegroom answers in a marriage. This was what was required of her ministers and elders in the earlier period of her history. When this ceased to be possible with regard to the Confession of Faith, the remedy should have been found in an alteration of the document, and not in treating the language of the act of subscription as an " elastic formula," when the terms bear no such sense.

Much stress was laid upon the fact (3) that nobody but ministers and elders had to subscribe the Confession, as persons were received to the membership of the church upon the confession simply of their faith in Jesus Christ. This had not been the practice of the new-school churches, in which Congregationalist influences had led to the adoption of extended articles of belief and covenants as terms of communion. But it was the law of the reunited church, and there had been a general conformity of local practice to its requirements. When, therefore, the members of the church complained of any statement in the Confession, and urged a revision, it was answered that they need not trouble themselves about it, as they were not required to assent to it.

This, however, was not the whole truth of the matter. The Confession is officially described as that of the Presbyterian Church, not of its ministry and eldership. And in our country distinctions between clergy and people do not count for much. Every man is expected to stand up for the creed of his church as he does for the platform of his party. The Roman Catholic workmen in our shops and factories must have an answer ready when they are challenged as to the dogma of papal infallibility or the immaculate conception; the Baptist must have his reasons for immersion and close communion; and so along the whole line of denominational peculiarities.

The debate on revision brought the extreme statements of the Westminster standards into strong light, and threw the members of the church everywhere upon the defensive. Reprobation and infant damnation became topics of common conversation. Presbyterians had to declare where they stood on these points, without the least reference to the fact that they never had subscribed the Confession. It was felt that the whole membership of the church had a vital interest in its authoritative statements of doctrine, and that a normal confession must be one which is both intelligible and credible to the people at large.

It also was said (4) that the alleged defects of the Confession were not serious matters, as no Confession of Faith could be expected to state the whole faith of the church, but only to establish the lines of definition and defense which are essential to its doctrinal integrity. It was answered that this was true enough, and that the divines at Westminster would have done their work much better if they had borne the principle in mind. But the things to be omitted must not be such fundamental truths as the love .of God to mankind, which is nowhere stated with explicitness. Neither should the operation of the Spirit in men's hearts, apart from his comforting and sanctifying believers, have been left to inference. In truth, since the days of Jonathan Edwards, and starting, indeed, from his later theological development, there had been a shifting of the theological center from the sovereignty to the love of God. This had been the root of the larger activity of the church in the mission field and in works of charity at home. This had supplied a new theological perspective to the preaching even of Dr. Shedd and Dr. Hall. But the Confession was out of harmony with all this.

It was argued also (5) that in spite of its alleged omissions and excesses the Confession had served the church for nearly two centuries and a half of splendid growth and achievement. This argument was generally allowed to pass, but it had the least foundation of any. American Presbyterianism, in all its eleven branches, did not contain one third of the descendants of the Presbyterian immigration to America. This fact and the division and subdivision of the church were directly traceable to the scholastic and one-sidedly intellectual character, and the resulting tendency to doctrinal niceties and polemics, which the Westminster standards have imparted to Presbyterianism.

As the voting proceeded the conservatives at first were disposed to insist that nothing less than a two-thirds majority would warrant the Assembly in proceeding further. But this claim was generally abandoned, as the overture

made no specific proposal for revision, and its adoption
would effect none. The vote finally stood 134 Presbyteries for revision explicitly, and 4 substantially so, a two-
thirds majority of all being 142.

When the Assembly of 1890 met, a prolongation of the
struggle was expected. The conservatives, however, accepted the decision and proffered their assistance in effecting the revision. Princeton took the lead in this, much to
the indignation of extreme conservatives, who forgot that
a sort of opportunism is one of its fixed traditions. It suggested Dr. Warfield as its representative; but his declaration that the Confession unrevised " suited him down to the
ground " had created a prejudice against him as a reviser.
Dr. Green was appointed instead, and a committee was
created out of both parties, which distinctly did not represent the state of feeling in the church on the subject. The
result was a great disappointment, as its report, while con-
ceding much that had been asked, did not make that on
which the revision movement hinged. The offensive statements as to preterition were touched so slightly as to leave
that matter much where it had stood before.

The Assembly of 1891 sent down the report to the
Presbyteries for further suggestions, which were forwarded
to the committee. The conclusions finally reached were
laid before the Assembly of 1892 in twenty-eight overtures, and these were sent to the Presbyteries for their
final action.

These overtures certainly contained some of the changes
ardently desired by the majority of the church. The
statement as to the unalterable number of the elect was to
disappear; the operation of God's grace and of his Holy
Spirit in the lives and hearts of the unregenerate was enunciated; the limitation of the work of creation to six days
was changed so as to leave the question of time an open

one; the salvation of the heathen by God's grace, without
the preached Word, was admitted as possible; that of all
infants dying in infancy was clearly stated; the pope was
not to be pilloried as Antichrist, nor marriage with Roman
Catholics explicitly forbidden; and the power of ministers
to retain and remit sins was pronounced to be " ministerial
and declarative " only.   But the doctrine of reprobation
or preterition was not eliminated, as had been asked by
over a hundred Presbyteries.   On this point, it is said,
Princeton was most determined and most persuasive.   Six
of the twenty-four members of the Committee of Revision [1] recorded their dissent from the result in the case of
Chapter III.

It now fell to the advocates of revision to decide whether
half a loaf was better than none, or the contrary.   A large
number of them must have concluded that it was better to
lay the whole subject on the shelf for the time than adopt
a truncated revision, which might stand in the way of one
more perfect.   At the same time there was a decided feeling among many that the church had taken the wrong
course, as revision would necessarily prove more irritating
to one half the church and less satisfactory to the other
than would the preparation of a new creed, less scholastic
and more practical in character.   The report of the committee offered nothing but sundry patches of new cloth on
an old garment, and the whole effect was incongruous in
the extreme.   A sixteenth-century document blistered

---

[1] The committee consisted of Dr. William E. Roberts, chairman; Dr.
William E. Moore, secretary; Dr. William Henry Green, Dr. Matthew B.
Riddle, Dr. Willis J. Beecher, Dr. Edward D. Morris, Dr. Herrick John-
son, Dr. William Alexander, Dr. Ebenezer Erskine, Dr. James T. Leftwich,
Dr. Samuel J. Niccolls, Dr. Edward R. Burkhalter, Dr. Robert R. Booth;
Elders Hon. William Strong, Hon. Samuel J. R. Macmillan, Hon. Alfred
Hand, Hon. Emerson E. White, Hon. Henry B. Sayler; and Messrs. Win-
throp S. Gilman, Barker Gummere, William Evarts, George Junkin, and
Charles M. Charnley.

over with nineteenth-century amendments could not form a homogeneous whole.

This state of feeling was indicated in the final vote. The vote of 147 Presbyteries was needed to adopt any of the overtures. The highest number received by any was 114, and this number was given for four. The rest, with four exceptions, ranged from 105 to 113, while the explicit vote in the negative ranged from 61 to 68. But the latter were reinforced by fifteen Presbyteries (mostly on the mission field) which made no report; thirteen others (two on the mission field) which reported no action on the overtures; and seventeen which refused to act on them as doubting their constitutionality. Fifteen out of these three groups had voted for revision in 1890.

The support of the overtures did not come by any means from those Presbyteries alone which had supported the original proposal. The twenty-four Presbyteries of the Cherokee nation, Chillicothe, Dubuque, Ebenezer, Huntingdon, Kingston, La Crosse, North Laos, North Texas, Palmyra, Peoria, Platte, Portsmouth, Redstone, Rock River, Sacramento, St. Louis, San Francisco, Shenango, Springfield, Trinity, Washington, Wooster, and Zanesville, all had voted with the minority in 1890. They now voted for all or nearly all the overtures—as did Pittsburg for sixteen of them, Philadelphia for nineteen, and New Brunswick for twenty-one—and would have carried them if the revisionists had kept their ranks. But in addition to the fifteen abstentionists already referred to, the thirty-one Presbyteries of Albany, Chemung, Chippewa, East Oregon, Freeport, Grand Rapids, Indianapolis, Iowa City, Jersey City, Larned, Logansport, Mahoning, Mankato, Maumee, Milwaukee, Montana, New York, North River, Otsego, Petoskey, Puget Sound, Rochester, St. Clairsville, St. Lawrence, Solomon, Southern Oregon, South Florida, Stockton,

Syracuse, West Jersey, and Whitewater, all of which had voted for revision in 1890, now voted against the overtures about as evenly as the conservative Presbyteries above mentioned voted for them. This in a few cases may have been the result of a shift of control of the Presbytery from one party to another, but it cannot have been true in most cases. These Presbyteries wanted revision, or something like it, as much as ever, but not after this fashion.

The four overtures which fell below the average of support were the first, third, fourth, and the second half of the fifteenth. The first proposed to insert into the list of the things which " move us to a high and reverend estimate of the Scriptures " a statement of the *external* evidences. This belated bit of apologetics received but 97 votes. The third was the restatement of the doctrine of reprobation, which represented Princeton's ultimatum. It was rejected by 107 votes against it to 67 in its favor. The fourth eliminated the " six days' " limit out of the statement of creation, and it received 100 votes to 74 in the negative. The second half of the fifteenth, on which a separate vote was asked, was offensive to the conservatives. Drs. Green, Patton, Alexander, and Leftwich, and Messrs. Junkin and Stratton had appended an expression of their dissent from it to their signatures to the report. It enlarged the statement of the Confession as to the regeneration of elect persons in the absence of the ordinary means from " all other elect persons, who are incapable of being outwardly called by the ministry of the Word," to " all other elect persons, who are not outwardly called by the Word." It also was in the minority by 92 negative to 81 affirmative votes. The overture just preceding, which would have struck out the language as to " elect infants," received but 105 votes to 68.

The Assembly of 1893 received over sixty memorials

asking the preparation of a new and shorter creed, but voted to lay the matter aside. In this decision there was a general acquiescence. The church was weary of the discussion. It was felt that the whole subject had been taken up by the wrong handle, with the result of obtaining the maximum of irritation and the minimum of relief.

Here the matter has rested, but cannot continue to do so for many years. The discussion placed the church permanently in such a relation to its own Confession as makes it impossible for it to retain the place it had held before 1889. The work of the Westminster divines has been challenged as inadequate in its statement of the gospel of divine grace, and as presumptuous in its handling of divine mysteries. This has been done not by some obscure and isolated group of theologians, but by men of the largest influence in every part of the church. Its statements on matters of vital importance have been declared unsatisfactory by more than a majority of the Presbyteries, and the substitution of other statements has been approved. In this the church has gone much too far to stop, but the delay will not be wasted if some attention be given to ascertaining a better mode of procedure than was adopted in 1889.

The preparation of a new Confession of Faith for the Presbyterian Church of America, with the coöperation of any of the sister-churches which can be induced to participate in it, seems the most feasible method of solving the problem. The right, even the duty, of each national church to express its own faith in its own words was recognized among the earlier Calvinists. That they had as many confessions as churches was one of the characteristics which distinguished them from the Lutherans with their Augsburg Confession, for which they claimed an ecumenical character. Holland did not copy France, nor did the

Huguenot Church of France repeat the Swiss. The church of the Pfalz drafted its own Heidelberg Catechism as its confession. The Scottish Kirk in Knox's day was well acquainted with the confessions of the continental churches, but it prepared a confession of its own, a document full of the spirit and the flavor of Scotland. No church thought of playing the rôle of theological parasite, in the fashion of the hermit-crab, as Professor Drummond describes it. It was felt that the weight and force of the collective testimony of these churches was greatly increased through each testifying, " in its own tongue " and its own terms, " the wonderful works of God." It is to this freedom of individual utterance that the British churches are now returning, for the Scottish Declaratory Acts cannot but lead to the step already taken by the Presbyterian Church of England. It will be in accord with the oldest traditions of the Reformed churches if their American representatives, laying aside the helmet of brass and the coat of mail devised by the divines of Westminster for a scholastic-polemic age, should go forth to the world with an expression of their own insight into Scriptural truth, their own statement of those great doctrines of grace which exalt God and humble man.

It is true that we are told—and Dr. Briggs seems to agree in the statement—that the modern church has not the ability to do anything half so good in that line as the Westminster divines did. That statement is extremely doubtful. They were not men of the first order of their own time. The great names which most adorn the Puritan age, with the exception of Samuel Rutherford, are all wanting from the list of the Assembly. James Ussher, Stephen Charnock, Thomas Brookes, John Owen, John Howe, Richard Baxter, Robert Leighton, were all absent. William Twiss, Herbert Palmer, Stephen Marshall, Anthony Tuckney, and John Lightfoot were the best theologians among them, and not one of them but the last survived his age in any production of his pen. Their attempt to supplement their work as an Assembly by a commentary on the Scriptures proved a failure. Even their collective repute failed to float their sapless " Annotations " into favor.

The theologians of our American church may have less scholastic training, and less faith in the adequacy of logic to meet every emergency, than had the body which met in Westminster Abbey. They may make but little of the nice distinctions and discriminations which seemed so precious to the divines who debated across that green-baize table in the Jerusalem Chamber. But they have had the advantage of two centuries of deepening knowledge of God's Word and deepening experience of his guidance of his church. And what they would offer for the service of God in the assertion of his truth, and for the upbuilding of his kingdom, would be their own, and not the borrowed offering, which was always rejected from sacrifice.

CHAPTER XIX.

THE BRIGGS AND SMITH TRIALS.

A CIRCUMSTANCE which tended to strengthen the hands of the conservatives in the final vote on revision was the precipitation of a new controversy upon the church, and one even more exciting in its character. The Assembly of 1891, to which the report on revision was made, was the first which had the case of Professor Charles A. Briggs, of Union Theological Seminary, before it. This case raised the question of the church's attitude to what lay behind and above the Confession—to the Bible itself.

Two questions, frequently confounded, were involved in this case and in that of Professor Henry Preserved Smith, of Lane Seminary, which came after it. The first is that of the inerrancy of the Scriptures; the second that of the composite character of the first six books of the Old Testament and the prophecies of Isaiah. They are entirely independent questions, as any one may take the negative side on either while holding the positive on the other.

It was long contended by Christian scholars that the Bible as it stands in the original text is altogether free from errors and contradictions. Immense ingenuity was expended in showing that the figures and dates of the Old Testament in Hebrew were mathematically exact, and that the apparent discrepancies of the several Gospels presented no real contradictions. Of late years, however, this kind of harmonizing seems to have been abandoned by scholars of the most orthodox type as regards some of these alleged discrepancies, while they limit the concession to a much smaller number of instances than the negative critics allege. It is admitted that the Hebrew and Greek texts contain some errors of statement, and the problem is how these are to be accounted for without giving up the Bible as an inspired guide of human life.

The two ways which have been suggested are (1) to ascribe the errors and inaccuracies to the copyists' lack of care in transcription, or (2) to modify the conception of divine inspiration so as to leave room for human error in the inspired man with regard to matters which do not pertain to "teaching, reproof, correction, and instruction in righteousness." To minds of the conservative type the former solution of the difficulty very naturally commends itself, as apparently the safer, and as involving no modification of the usual conceptions of the divine dealings with men. It is not, however, one which finds any warrant in the Westminster Confession, which declares that " the Old Testament in Hebrew and the New Testament in Greek being immediately inspired by God, and by his singular care and providence kept pure in all ages, are therefore authentical; so as, in all controversies of religion, the church is finally to appeal to them." The authors of this statement certainly did not regard the divine efficiency as less enlisted in the preservation of the Scriptures from error during their transmission to us than in their first origination by the inbreathing of the Holy Spirit. And when they appeal in the same chapter to " the consent of all the parts " as an evidence of the " infallible truth and divine authority thereof," they leave no room to suppose that they have reference only to original copies, while the present texts have fallen from this " consent of the parts " into inconsistencies, or from this " infallible truth " into errancy

through lapse of that " singular care and providence."
Such a supposition they distinctly reject—more distinctly,
indeed, than a theory of inspiration which leaves room for
the presence of mistaken judgments in the inspired man
as regards other and lesser matters than " the goodness,
wisdom, and power of God," " the comfort of the church
against the corruption of the flesh and the malice of Satan
and the world," " the full discovery of the way of man's
salvation," " the whole counsel of God concerning all
things necessary for his own glory, man's salvation, faith,
and life," and authoritative guidance " in all controversies
of religion," which things the Confession defines, as the
content of the Bible.

Yet this theory of the inerrancy of the original texts,
along with the admitted errancy of the texts we have, not
only has obtained recognition as a permissible solution, in
the face of the Confession's teaching to the contrary, but
has been exalted to serve as a new test of orthodoxy, to
the condemnation of those who prefer the other solution,
which finds nothing like an explicit condemnation in the
Confession.   In this way the divine providence, which our
Lord declares to extend to the numbering of the hairs of
our head, is•confessed inadequate to preserving the Bible
in that state of perfection in which it was first given to the
church, and which, we are told, we must believe it once
possessed if we are to believe that its human authors were
really inspired by God.

The other question as to the origin of certain parts of
the Bible is of lesser importance.   Inspiration may use
editors as well as authors, and did so in the case of the
third evangelist, who knew nothing at first-hand of the
story he tells.   It is, indeed, another affair when the books
of the Mosaic law are represented as a series of inventions
of late date, with no root in the nation's legal traditions,

so that "The Lord spake unto Moses, saying, . . . " becomes a mere mode of speech with no historic warrant. No such significance, however, can be attached to the question of the double authorship of the Book of Isaiah, except that the notion of prophecy as prediction out of historic relation to the prophet's environment rests largely on the assumption that one Isaiah wrote the whole book.

In this case, also, the contact with the churches of Great Britain, and especially with the Free Church of Scotland, had much to do with the origination of the controversy. In 1881 Professor W. Robertson Smith had been removed from his professorship of Hebrew in the Free Church College, Aberdeen, by the Free Church Assembly, his offense being the views he presented of the origin of the Old Testament Scriptures in articles contributed to the Encyclopædia Britannica, and in his book, "The Old Testament in the Jewish Church" (Edinburgh and New York, 1881). The case attracted general attention on both sides of the Atlantic, and raised the question whether the church was likely to confirm the faith of her own members, or to exert the right influence upon the world, if she decided to expel her Thomases from the apostolate, as her Master did not.

The case was complicated by the peculiarly unconciliatory temper of Professor Smith, who combined a great deal of the *fortiter in re* with very little of the *suaviter in modo.* It was to be regretted that these difficult and delicate questions should be first pressed on the attention of the church by one who, whatever his learning, had so little reverence for opinions long cherished by his countrymen, and identified by them, rightly or wrongly, with their grasp upon the Word of God. Much the same embarrassment attended the appearance of the same problems in the American church. Professor Charles Augustus Briggs shares

Professor Robertson Smith's temper as well as his critical opinions, and goes beyond the Scotchman in his enjoyment of a spirited controversy. If we may judge from the way in which he is said to have received the remonstrances of those friends to whom he showed his Inaugural before its delivery, he prefers to say the thing which will shock his hearers, rather than to give it a shape less offensive. In none of his works is there shown that faculty of reverence which is as needful for the critic as for the pastor. He never gave the church the impression that, in his view, the great work of a professor in training the ministry to a knowledge of the Scriptures is to show them what are the elements of power which have given those books their hold on the faith, the affections, and the conscience of mankind. On the other hand, it is beyond question that he knew how to win the enthusiastic affection of his pupils, and that in some cases he had been the means of rescuing young men from a profound skepticism as regards the Bible to a practical faith in its authority.

But it was the former side of his work which was most in evidence before the church when in 1891 he was transferred from the chair of Hebrew and cognate languages in Union Seminary to the newly founded chair of biblical theology, and delivered (January 20th) his inaugural address. As early as 1870 he had repudiated publicly the traditional theory of inspiration. In his articles in the " Reformed and Presbyterian Review " and in his " Biblical Study " (1883) and " Messianic Prophecy " (1886) he had shown himself affected by the school of critics to which Professor Robertson Smith belongs, but always with reservations which kept him within the bounds of toleration. In the Inaugural he showed that he had reached a point which, conservatives thought, made it impossible to pass it over in silence. His case first came before the General

Assembly of 1891, under the agreement of Union and other seminaries to submit the election of professors to the Assembly for confirmation. His friends contended that his transfer from one chair to another did not require the Assembly's approval; but the Assembly overruled this, and by 449 to 60 votes formally refused to confirm his appointment.

His Presbytery therefore appointed a committee to consider the propriety of trying him upon charges of unsound doctrine. This committee reported charges, which the Presbytery ordered him to answer. On November 4, 1891, the Presbytery heard his answer, and by 94 votes to 39 decided to dismiss the case " in view of the declarations made by Dr. Briggs touching his loyalty to the Holy Scriptures and the Westminster standards, and of his disclaimers of interpretations put on some of his words." The prosecuting committee then took the unusual step of appealing directly to the General Assembly, while thirty-four members of the Presbytery complained in the ordinary way to the Synod of New York. The Assembly of 1892, meeting at Portland, Ore., entertained the Protest and ordered the Presbytery to try the case on its merits. The Presbytery, meeting in November, 1892, cited Professor Briggs to appear before it a month later, and to answer the list of charges, with specifications, which the Committee of Prosecution had laid before it. When the trial actually occurred, it was a matter of more than national interest. The prosecution was conducted with distinguished ability and legal acumen, though not with great exegetical learning, by Drs. G. W. F. Birch and Joseph J. Lampe, and Elder John J. McCook. The charges were that he taught (1) that men may be enlightened unto salvation by reason or through the church, apart from the Bible; (2) that the inspiration of the Bible was not such as to exclude errors as to matters of fact even from the original documents; (3) that he denied the Mosaic authorship of the Pentateuch and of the unity of authorship of the Book of Isaiah; and (4) asserted the continuance of sanctification after death. The second point was really the essential one, and cannot be said to have been handled fully and frankly by the prosecution. Appeal was made to a great number of authorities, who really held to the inerrancy of the Hebrew and Greek texts as we have them, and who would have repudiated Dr. Green's concessions as emphatically as those of Dr. Briggs. In his reply Professor Briggs showed his superiority in a professional familiarity with the subjects under discussion, and was unhappy only in the tone which characterized every reference to the prosecution and the Assembly. The Presbytery, by a somewhat diminished majority, acquitted Dr. Briggs on all the charges.

The Committee of Prosecution now appealed a second time to the General Assembly, both on the ground of exceptions taken to the Presbytery's conduct of the trial, and of the wrongfulness of the verdict reached. To this course it was objected that a committee of Presbytery could not appeal against the Presbytery, and that no appeal could be taken from a verdict of acquittal by a public prosecutor. It was pointed out that no such appeal had ever been entertained in the American church, that it was forbidden to the national courts by an amendment to the Constitution, that it was a violation of the common law inherited from England, and that it was contrary to the universal principles of equity. That such appeals had been taken by private prosecutors in the cases of Mr. Barnes and Dr. Beecher established no precedent for this case, as the public prosecutor incurs none of the personal risks which Presbyterian law attaches to the failure of the private prosecutor to make good his charges. The revised Book

of Discipline, however, allowed of an appeal being taken
by "either of the original parties," where the old book
had limited this to "a party aggrieved" by the decision.
On this point mainly the conservatives rested their case.

In the selection of members of the Assembly of 1893,
as in the case of its predecessor, pains were taken to send
up delegations whose sympathies coincided with those of
the majority in each Presbytery. This worked badly for
Professor Briggs's friends, who were the majority in very
few Presbyteries, and secured an Assembly much more
conservative than the church at large, and one whose
scholarship was not as ample as would have been obtained
with less party management. It is not always those who
have given most attention to a complex question who are
the most positive about it. Next to the report on the vote
of the Presbyteries on the twenty-eight overtures for the
revision of the Confession, the Briggs case was the most
important matter of business, and in point of popular
interest it almost wholly eclipsed that. The Assembly,
by a vote of 410 to 145, decided to entertain the appeal,
Dr. Nicholls, of St. Louis, and four other members of the
Judicial Committee objecting to this course. The trial of
the appeal then proceeded, Messrs. Lampe and McCook
stating the case for the prosecution, and Dr. Briggs reply-
ing. After hearing other members of the Presbytery and
members of the Assembly, the vote was reached, and 295
voted to sustain the appeal as a whole and 84 to sustain
in part, while 116 voted not to sustain.

Before the sentence was pronounced a subcommittee of
the special committee appointed to draft it waited on Dr.
Briggs in the hope that he would make some retraction,
which might render a stay of proceedings short of suspension possible. He replied first verbally, and then in writing, that he had nothing to retract, as he "adhered to all

the positions taken before the General Assembly." The Assembly therefore went on to declare the decision of the Presbytery of New York erroneous and its proceeding faulty, and to pronounce Professor Briggs guilty of all the charges on which he had been tried—of having " uttered, taught, and propagated views, doctrines, and teachings contrary to the essential doctrines of Holy Scripture and the standards of the Presbyterian Church, and in violation of [his] ordination vow, which said erroneous teachings, views, and doctrines strike at the vitals of religion, and have been industriously spread." On this ground it suspended him "from the office of a minister in the Presbyterian Church, until such time as he shall give satisfactory evidence of repentance to the General Assembly for the violation by him of said ordination vow."

This decision lacks the calm of the judicial temper. It is pervaded by a personal animus, which finds an outlet in many of its phrases, and especially in the conversion of the charge of unsound teaching into one of personal immorality, and in making the restoration of the offender dependent not upon the retraction of his alleged errors, but upon his " repentance " for his sin. It thus affixes a stigma to the accused, which was not warranted by any evidence before the Assembly, nor embodied in any of the charges on which he was tried. It bases this sin of unfaithfulness on each and all of the charges, thus declaring that whoever holds that there were two Isaiahs and not one, or that Moses did not write the books of the Pentateuch—a point on which the Confession of Faith has nothing to say —is guilty of a breach of his ordination vow, if he be a minister of the church.

In truth, there is no such thing as an " ordination vow " with regard to doctrine. The candidate for the ministry is admitted on the declaration of his present assent to the teachings of the Confession of Faith. He gives no promise that he will continue that assent. His utmost implied obligation is to state fully and frankly his divergences from the Confession and leave the church to judge whether they are such as require that his place in the ministry shall be abandoned. Even on the supposition that Dr. Briggs was conscious of an essential divergence of his views from those of the Confession—a supposition he denies, and no man has the right to say the denial is dishonest—he had done all that honesty and manliness required of him.

It is to be regretted that in neither of the two protests, signed respectively by 97 and 62 members of the Assembly, was this point insisted upon. The second, indeed, complained of the injustice which the Assembly had done to a " Christian scholar of acknowledged high character." The first confined itself to a protest against the new theory of an inerrant and infallible Bible which nobody had seen, but in which all must believe from this time forward. As the sentence runs the General Assembly pronounced every signer of this protest guilty of violating his ordination vow. Among them were Drs. Herrick Johnson, Samuel J. Niccolls, Charles L. Thompson, George Alexander, Charles A. Dickey, Francis Brown, Henry M. Storrs, Edward P. Sprague, William R. Taylor, J. Garland Hamner, Henry H. Stebbins, and Revs. Thomas C. Hall, Robert A. Carnahan, and C. P. H. Nason.

The case of Professor Henry Preserved Smith, of Lane Seminary, came before the Assembly in regular order through his appeal from the adverse decision of the Synod of Ohio. In March, 1891, he had read a paper on Inspiration before the Presbyterian Ministerial Association of Cincinnati, and this was printed along with a similar paper by Professor Llewellyn J. Evans, also of Lane Seminary. It was eighteen months later that the Presbytery of Cin-

cinnati referred the matter to a committee, which drafted
three charges, of two of which the Presbytery found Dr.
Smith guilty, and suspended him from the ministry until
he should renounce the errors alleged. On this he appealed to the Synod of Ohio, complaining both of the
procedure and the verdict of the Presbytery. The Synod
entertained the appeal, but, after hearing the case, voted
not to sustain any of its twelve specifications. The highest vote on any was 51 to 78. On all twelve Dr. Smith
now appealed to the General Assembly.

The case was not complicated with any of the personal
considerations or side issues which complicated that of
Professor Briggs. The appellant's manner of stating his
opinions and of conducting his case was open to no exception. He commanded the esteem even of those who had
united in condemning him. The issue simply was whether
the original manuscripts, as they came from the hands of
the inspired writers, did or did not possess an inerrancy
which they have lost in the process of transmission. But
this issue had been prejudged in the sentence on Professor
Briggs, and Dr. Smith's appeal was rejected by a vote of
396 not to sustain, against 55 to sustain and 47 to sustain in
part, the appeal. In this case the Assembly remembered
its duty to confer with the accused, but its Committee of
Conference found him unprepared to make any statement
which would modify the result. As sentence had been
pronounced already, in terms which corresponded to the
charges, by the Presbytery of Cincinnati, there was no
room for the blunder of converting a suspension for alleged
heresy into one for immoral conduct.

With these decisions the matter has rested for the present. The majority, very naturally, hold them to be final
and to constitute an interpretation of the Confession which
is binding upon all. The minority reply that this is to

fall into the second of the two heresies charged upon Dr.
Briggs, and to treat the church as an independent source
of divine illumination.   Not content with the protests
tabled in the Assembly of 1893, they met in convention
that year at Cleveland to reiterate their refusal to accept
a new dogma at the hands of the General Assembly.   In
taking this course of dissent and protest against even judicial decisions, they have on their side the authority of Dr.
Charles Hodge, who wrote, in 1866, "The right of protest, as it has always been exercised, includes the right of
dissenting from the deliverances and judgments of church
courts, on the ground of their being unwise, unjust, unscriptural. . . . The Assembly [of 1866] recognizes the
principle that adhesion to its deliverances cannot be made
a condition of Christian or ministerial communion."

But whatever may be thought of the manner of the decision, it was not possible that any other could be reached
under the circumstances.   The traditional respect for the
Bible as a perfect book, the general acceptance of the
most absolute and mechanical theories of its inspiration,
have been common features of our American churches of
every name.   These have been so long associated with the
reverence for the Bible's spiritual greatness, and recognition of its actual worth as a guide for life and a disclosure
of God, that the scholar who first broached a different
view in any quarter was certain to be regarded as "striking at the vitals of religion."   Especially must this be
expected of the most conservative and most theological of
the American churches.   Men felt as if Professor Briggs
were cutting the very ground from beneath their feet.
They were in no mood to judge calmly as to which theory
of inspiration best fitted the facts.   They were the less so
in this case, because it was presented to them in association with doubtful opinions as to the origin and composi-

tion of some of the books of Scripture, and other matters
of the higher criticism, and because the champion of the
new views was a man whose statements were often so unguarded as to convey an entirely false notion of his meaning. At times he seemed anxious to intensify the shock
which must attend his enunciation of his views even in
their mildest expression.

The judgment excited a general dissent, but a still more
general assent, in the other churches. In all quarters the
progressives regretted or ridiculed, and the conservatives
rejoiced. As America is the most conservative of Protestant countries, the satisfaction predominated. It was
said that one of the most learned of American churches
had given her decision on the side of orthodoxy, and that
with an emphasis which must help to stem the tide of
loose opinion about the Bible. It was not noticed that the
form of the decision did not place the church on that Westminster platform on which all the churches stood as late as
thirty years ago. It admitted, by unmistakable implication,
the presence of errors in the Hebrew and Greek texts. It
admitted the errancy of the Bible as we have it. It only
pronounced against one way of accounting for these, and
gave its sanction to the other. How the theory it sanctioned may be used in the interest of negative criticism
remains to be seen.

CHAPTER XX.

THE SEMINARY QUESTION, AND OTHER MATTERS.

As the Union Theological Seminary refused to accept the decision of the Assembly of 1891 with regard to Professor Briggs's professorship, there was at once a straining of the relations created by the voluntary compact of 1870 between the Assembly and the theological seminaries in a shape suggested by Union Seminary itself. After some hesitation the directors of the seminary applied to the Assembly for an abandonment of the compact by mutual agreement, on the ground that the directors of the seminary had exceeded their powers in entering into it. To this the Assembly refused to assent, but it proposed to refer the matter to arbitration, and appointed its own representatives on the proposed board of arbitration. When these met in November, in New York, and opened a correspondence with the directors of the seminary, they were told that the board, by a vote of 19 to 1, had decided to terminate the compact with the Assembly; so there was no use for the service of arbitrators. The Assembly of 1893 placed on record its protest against this action, and instructed its Committee on Theological Seminaries to receive no reports from Union Seminary while its directors maintained this attitude, disclaimed responsibility for its teachings, and directed the Board of Education to give aid only to students in the seminaries approved by the Assembly.

The same Assembly received the first report from a special committee which had been directed by the Assembly of 1892 to consider the relations of the seminaries to the Assembly, and to report what changes were necessary to secure the Assembly's authority over them. It rehearsed a part of the facts connected with the establishment of Princeton Seminary, and declared that since the creation of a separate board of trustees for that seminary in 1822 the church had abandoned its earlier and proper policy in the establishment and control of these institutions. It found the fourteen seminaries of the church, with 880 students taught by 93 teachers, in possession of over $8,000,000 in property (Union, $2,100,000; Princeton, $1,500,000; McCormick, $1,400,000; Auburn, $800,000; Alleghany, $750,000; Lane, $560,000; San Francisco, $500,000; Danville, $260,000; Omaha, $25,000; Newark, $67,000; Dubuque, $50,000), which the committee assumed to have been given by members of the church to secure such teaching as the General Assembly approved, but which the donors had seen fit to vest in self-perpetuating bodies or in bodies controlled by Synods or Presbyteries only. It was not until 1894, however, that the committee felt free to report a plan to establish the control of the General Assembly. It was to request the seminaries to so amend their charters as to secure that their funds shall be held in trust for the church at large, for the purpose of theological education according to its standards; and also to secure to the Assembly a veto upon the election of directors and trustees, and upon the election, appointment, and transfer of all professors and teachers; and to vest in the Assembly the power to proceed legally against seminaries which violate any of these provisions. After a discussion which occupied parts of three mornings, the report was adopted by a vote of 441 to 117, the seminary professors in the Assembly voting with the majority.

The Assembly had not long adjourned when it began to be seen that the action taken was hasty and ill considered. The especial advocates of a reunion with the Southern Assembly discovered that the action was distasteful in that quarter, and that its success would furnish one more of the obstacles to that policy. The Southern church deprecates centralization, and always has kept seminaries under synodical control. It also became evident that the obstacles to the changes of charter the Assembly asked were as good as insurmountable. Some of the States could give no legal recognition to a body constituted, as is the General Assembly, from citizens of all the States of the Union, and changed in its composition with every year. Nor are State legislatures so fond of ecclesiastical centralization as to place property held within their limits under control of a body meeting outside them, and thus to be invested with the control of millions of property. Probably the Alleghany Seminary would have had the least difficulty in obtaining a modification of its charter, but for a reason which would have made the change eminently undesirable. Any chartered institution which accepts fresh legislation from the legislature, since the adoption of the present Constitution of Pennsylvania, is brought thereby under the supervision and control of the State to an extent which deprives it of the autonomy it previously possessed. It is probable that this is not the only State in which such consequences would have resulted.

It also was found that the existing boards of trustees or directors could not be brought to see the matter from the Assembly's point of view. The experiences of 1830–36, and the terror of action on the part of the Assemblies then felt by the friends of Princeton Seminary, were recalled, and went to prove that the General Assembly was not always and necessarily the best safeguard of a conservative orthodoxy. Certainly Alleghany, under the exclusive control of the Synod of Pittsburg, at that time felt much more secure in its position.

At this writing the majority of the seminaries have had the Assembly's proposal under consideration, and every one of these has refused to accede to it.

The proposal would not have secured the object aimed at. What the Assembly needs for the purpose in view is the power of summary removal, not of veto upon appointments. It was this that enabled the Free Church of Scotland to get rid of Professor Robertson Smith, to whose election it made not the smallest objection. But the lack of this, as also of the powers it asked, is not distressing the church to anything like the degree that the majority of 1894 seemed to suppose. While the Assembly is in session, its members, collectively and individually, are tempted to think it the great power which moves the church, when in truth it is but the balance-wheel of the machine.

Another subject which came before the Assembly of 1894 was the plan for a federal council of the Reformed churches of America. This might be described as an attempt to form a more perfect union, within national limits, than the International Alliance of the Reformed Churches offered, and to take away the reproach of antagonism between bodies whose differences are far too trifling to justify rivalry. In another sense it is a reflex of the unifying action taken in the mission fields of Japan and Brazil and contemplated in other missionary lands.

The object of the plan is to include all the Reformed churches of America which hold the Presbyterian polity. The churches which acted by their commissioners in drafting the plan are the Presbyterian, the United Presbyterian, the Reformed Presbyterian (O. S. and N. S.), the Cumberland Presbyterian, the Associate Reformed Presbyterian, South, and the two Reformed churches formerly known as the Dutch and the German.   This includes all but the Southern Presbyterian Church and the fragments left out in the formation of the United Presbyterian Church.

The object of the plan is too good to admit of question. Whether the specific plan is the best for the object is doubted by some.   As the proposed federal council is to consist of four ministers and four elders from each of the churches, the smaller bodies would have an undue weight in influencing its decisions.   The representatives of their 125,000 communicants would all but balance those of the 1,400,000 in the larger bodies.   It is true that the scope of the powers conferred is limited, but it extends to declarations and definitions of a common policy in regard to questions of national magnitude, such as temperance, public schools, and the amendment of the national Constitution in a Christian sense.   It also is to be constituted an ecclesiastical board of arbitration in all cases of dispute between the churches embraced in the federation.

The problem which the proposal really raises is whether this plan would serve to hasten a still closer union or to retard it.   In some cases these half-way measures stand in the way of something better.   In others they give such a foretaste of its advantages as strengthens the desire for it.   This was notably true of the national Articles of Confederation under which the American people managed their affairs until the adoption of the Constitution.   The resemblance of the Plan to those Articles is so close as to suggest conscious imitation.   They also created a single deliberative body, with vaguely defined and greatly limited powers, in which each of the contracting parties had an equal vote ; they also conferred power in relation to external affairs, while jealously reserving the control of domestic matters; and they also constituted the central body an umpire in disputes between the parties to the agreement. The best service the Articles of Confederation rendered was to tide over a period of excessive colonial jealousies, and to prepare the country for " a more perfect union " on a national basis. We might well put up with the faults found with the plan under discussion if we had reasonable ground for the expectation that it would do its work equally well. The favor with which it has been received seems to promise its final adoption by the churches concerned.

One of the lesser Presbyterian bodies had its share of agitation and distress during these last years. The dissolution of the Reformed Presbytery of North America, by the death of Rev. David Steel, Sr., gives the Synod of the Reformed Presbyterian (or Covenanter) Church (O. S.) the hegemony of the extreme right wing of the Presbyterian host. It has stood for old-fashioned, theocratic Presbyterianism with a vigor and an ability which remind one of John Stuart Mill's saying that if the most capable men are found leading the van, the next so will be seen bringing up the rear.

Their attitude of requiring political dissent as a term of communion, which they inherited from the Hillmen of the western Lowlands, they have maintained for two hundred years. In that time they never have sworn an oath of allegiance to any government on earth, or held communion with any who did so. So long as slavery was tolerated within the national area this position was maintained without much difficulty. Its abolition both created a difficulty and presented an opportunity. The difficulty was that of keeping their membership apart from a political system which, in their opinion, had purged off its worst stain. The opportunity was that of enlisting the deepened national seriousness in securing such an amendment to the national Constitution as would give the government a distinctly Christian character, and thus put an end to the necessity for their political dissent.

It was with this purpose that the National Reform Association was organized in the city of Pittsburg in the year 1864, after preliminary conventions in different parts of the country. The aim to secure support outside the Covenanter Church for the Covenanter principle has had considerable success. Bishops McIlvaine, Kerfoot, Eastburn, Huntingdon, Beckwith, Bedell, Jaggar and Kip of the Protestant Episcopal Church, Bishop Nicholson of the Reformed Episcopal Church, Bishops Haven and Simpson of the Methodist Church, Bishops Weaver, Wright, and Dickson of the United Brethren Church, and *both* Bishops Escher and Dubs of the Evangelical Association, gave their adherence to the platform of the association, showing that the children of the Covenant are no longer afraid of prelates. Drs. Charles and Archibald Hodge, Cuyler, McIlvaine, Craven, Herrick Johnson, and George P. Hays of the Presbyterian Church, Drs. Pressly, Cooper, and Barr of the United Presbyterian Church, Dr. Boyce of the Associate Reformed Church, South, and Dr. Tayler Lewis of the Reformed Church, came to its support from a less distance. Among the Congregationalists President Julius H. Seelye, Joseph Cook, and Dr. George B. Cheever stepped upon its platform. Three ex-governors, nine judges, nineteen college presidents, and twelve professors were found among its officers in 1891.

The contention of the association has been that our efforts for political and social reform are ineffective and sporadic because they lack a central theocratic aim. Just as we would bid an individual sinner, who was making

efforts to cast off his sins one by one, to start right by sur-
rendering himself to God and invoking his grace, so the
nation needs to make the same sort of right start. And
as in the individual case the open confession of his new
attitude is required equally by God's law, and by the reason
of things as committing him to the right side, so should
the nation make public and formal confession of its having
entered into covenant with God to serve him in the keeping of his law.

The monetary support of the association has come chiefly
from the Covenanter body and has developed a high degree
of liberality in giving. On the other hand, it has thrown
them into close relations with the champions of social reforms of all kinds, especially that of temperance, and has
led them to give these a hearty support.

The incongruity, however, of urging others to vote for
measures for which they would not vote themselves came
to be felt among them, especially when the commonwealth
of Pennsylvania invited a vote on an amendment to the
Constitution which would have prohibited the manufacture
and sale of intoxicants within its boundaries. The year
before this the Synod had ruled that political dissent did
not forbid service on juries. Following the lead of the
Presbytery of Pittsburg, it now decided that dissent would
not be impaired by Covenanters having themselves placed
on the registration list and voting, when no explicit approval
of the Constitution was required.

To many both of the younger and progressive men, and
of the older and conservative, this seemed an abandonment
of political dissent. The members of the church were no
longer required to hold themselves aloof from the political
system. They were even permitted to incorporate themselves into it, provided they abstained from any express
approval of an objectionable document. The former con-

tended that the Synod could not stop with this, but must
go farther.   A conference was held in a church in the
East End of Pittsburg, at which some score of the younger
ministers were present, the immediate object being advice
to one of their number who found himself in an embarrass-
ing position.   Quite as an after-thought they drew up and
signed a declaration of their views—called the East End
Platform—in which they treated the matter of political
dissent as now an open question, and published this.

The Presbytery of Pittsburg responded by suspending
from the exercise of their ministry those of the signers who
belonged to its jurisdiction.   This was done on the ground
that they denied the binding force of the covenant which
the church had adopted in 1871, and which pledged its
members not to "incorporate" themselves with any political
system until they had obtained from that a recognition of
Christ's headship over the nations.   The suspended ministers appealed to the Synod, which sustained the action
of the Presbytery and proceeded to exercise the same
rigorous discipline upon the other signers, with the exception of two, against whom the Presbytery of New York
was proceeding.   That Presbytery, however, showed less
vigor than did the Pittsburg Presbytery, and the two
were allowed to withdraw from the church without formal
censure.

Most of the signers sought an ecclesiastical home in
the nearest denomination, the United Presbyterian Church.
Several of them were accompanied by large sections of
their congregations, and in two instances the church property was taken with them.   As after the division of 1833,
the adherents of the Synod sued for its possession, invoking in defense of property rights the State to which they
refuse allegiance.

One effect of this rigorous discipline has been an altered

spirit in the affairs of the National Reform Association. The part of its membership which lies outside the Covenanter Church shows some indisposition to accept the leadership of a body with whose ecclesiastical proceedings they cannot sympathize.

The closing pages of the story of American Presbyterianism are a tale of agitation and of friction. Better this, however, than stagnation and dull acquiescence in traditional beliefs and usages. Even this evidences life and looks to a future in which

> . . . Generations yet unborn
> Shall bless and magnify the Lord.

CHAPTER XXI.

RETROSPECT AND PROSPECT, 1705–1895.

NEARLY two centuries have elapsed since the meeting of the first American Presbytery announced the establishment of the synodical method of church government in the English colonies of America. There had been, previously to that, ministers and congregations whose ecclesiastical character had been determined by their opposition to the prelatic claims of the Anglican system on the one hand and the independency of " the New England way" on the other. Newbury[port] in Massachusetts (1635), Jamaica on Long Island (1677), Newark in New Jersey (1667), Snow Hill in Maryland (1682), Rehoboth in Virginia (1684), Port Royal in South Carolina (1684), and Philadelphia (1698) stand for the earliest congregational beginnings of this character in each of those colonies. The names of Francis Doughty, Richard Denton, Abraham Pierson, Matthew Hill, Samuel Davis, Francis Makemie, and William Dunlop and Archibald Stobo stand for the personal leaders of this antagonism to " the falsehood of extremes." But until the Presbyterian theory of church government found its expression in the organization of a Presbytery it could not be said to have really taken root.

The vine thus planted has come to overshadow the whole land. Not only has the little handful of Presbyterians, gathered on soil preëmpted for many years by prelacy and independency, grown to a great host, with

1,278,000 communicants in 1890, representing more than four millions of the American people, but the Presbyterian method of government has had a marked attraction for both the antagonistic forms. The prelacy of earlier Anglicanism has given way, in America, to a distinctly Presbyterian type of Episcopal government; the power of the bishop has yielded to that of the Convention and its Standing Committee to an extent which has caused some strict canonists to doubt if the Protestant Episcopal Church can be said to be episcopally governed. Modern Congregationalism is a manifest compromise between the Independent and the Presbyterian way; and since the organization of the National Council there has been a marked growth in the disposition to look to it as the authoritative arbiter in disputed matters. The Lutherans of America, laying aside the consistorial methods of their European churches, have adopted synodical government as the best suited to their needs, and associated the representatives of the people with their pastors in their local and national councils. The Methodists have been obliged to modify their highly efficient but never popular system of clerical government by the admission of lay delegates to their conferences; at the same time the "preacher" of earlier days has been converted by a like attraction into the "pastor," and obliged to assume the duties once assigned to the class-leaders. Even the Baptists, who have been the stanchest representatives of independency, have come to intrust the real management of denominational affairs to local and national associations, the former treating churches which walk disorderly as liable to the discipline of exclusion from the association.

As a whole the Protestantism of America has become Presbyterian in substance, though not in name. A hundred years ago there were no churches, outside the Reformed household, which controlled their affairs by representative councils of pastors and people. Now this is true of nearly every important church in the Protestant family.

It cannot be said that this is because Presbyterianism adheres more strictly and literally to the letter of the Scriptures than did its rivals in method. The idea of representation on which it is based was unknown to the ancient political world, and was not anticipated in the New Testament. It was developed in the rise of the Teutonic nationalities on the ruins of the Roman empire, making possible governments at once freer and more authoritative than antiquity had known.[1] It was the great merit of Calvin, À Lasco, and Knox to have perceived that this principle of representation had been providentially developed for the benefit of the church no less than of the state, so that provincial, national, and ecumenical unity could be attained without prelates, primates, and popes; and the liberties of the Christian people secured without the severance of the church into independent local churches.

It is in America, where action is least trammeled by tradition, that the common approximation to this type is most freely illustrated. The meeting of the first Presbytery in Philadelphia was therefore the beginning of a new era for the American churches, in that the modern principle of representative government there and then found its first expression as regards the Christian church of the New World.

The Presbyterian Church, as the accredited historic representative of this great principle, which has brought the collective wisdom of each religious communion to bear upon its affairs, has not discredited it by the manner in which it has applied it. It always has been a body whose

[1] See my "Divine Order of Human Society" (Philadelphia, 1891), pp. 116-120.

weight was greater than its numbers seemed to justify. While it has not escaped the peril of hasty decisions, especially through the action of theological panics on the minds of its people, these have been exceptional in its history, and with the return of calmer moods there has been a virtual confession and a practical correction of the mistake. The great moments of this church's history have been those reunions of divided forces, when the faults and bitternesses of the past have been swallowed up in fraternal joy. Next to these have been those of noble self-restraint, when the national Synod or Assembly has calmed the local or personal agitation by a wise patience, a serene temper, a discriminating decision which helped men to distinguish a difference over words from a difference in the great things of the gospel. This wiser and more Christian rôle has been the harder to play because of the church's dual composition. Scotch-Irish and New Englander, from the very outset of her history, have been blended in her ministry and her membership. The two elements have much in common, and yet also much that marks them as diverse. Both are keenly interested in doctrinal teaching, and as such they have always inclined to those conceptions of the relation of God to man which lie out of the range of superficial thought, but commend themselves to men of profounder reflection. Both incline to construe those relations not from the point of view of what is pleasing to man, but what is honoring to God. Both, therefore, are instinctive Calvinists, regarding the glory of God as the end of man's creation and of his spiritual history. And both assign to right conceptions of these great realities an influence upon character and destiny which many regard as excessive.

The contrast of the two elements is found in the active and discursive intellect of the New Englander and the

solid conservatism of the Scotch-Irish. The one has tried
to "improve" all previous statements of Calvinism; the
other to appreciate them. The one tends to a restless
spirit of change, in which the largest truths are supposed
to need a constant overhauling; the other to a dull acquiescence, in which whatever the past has given us is accepted for that very reason. These are their perils. The
fusion of the two tendencies into a spirit at once wisely
conservative and wisely progressive has been the problem
of the Presbyterian Church more than of any other in
America. It cannot be said to have been solved; our
very divisions into eleven communions of varying degrees
of liberality and conservatism are evidence to the contrary. But nothing will more help us to the right attitude
for reaching the solution than the study of our own history. That furnishes evidence enough of the grand service rendered to the religious life of the nation by Presbyterian conservatism. It stood by the most unpopular
and decried doctrines of the Bible through periods when
the public mind was least fitted for their reception, until
soberer and more profound thinking came to their vindication. It thus saved to the general religious consciousness some of the greatest principles, which otherwise it
might have taken centuries to recover. It asserted the
principle of loyalty to the whole scope of inspired teaching,
in the face of tendencies to choose and pick what was the
more pleasing to human nature, or what an English writer
calls "the pleasanter parts of Christianity." Thus the
Presbyterian Church has played the part of a check upon
change which was not progress, and has vindicated the
integrity of the gospel of God's grace, with both its goodness and its severity. It never has cut its garment according to the fashions set by the spirit of the age, which,
indeed, Richter says, is what our fathers called Antichrist.

On the other hand, history is no mere eulogist of conservatism. It exhibits everywhere the necessity of change in human conceptions and statements of divine truths, and the reality of a deeper and more vital apprehension of them under the Spirit's leading of the church. It shows that not the most conservative of to-day are able to think in the limits and find utterance in the phrases of a century ago. Whatever lives must change; only the dead perpetuates itself from age to age unaltered. The Bible itself furnishes illustrations of this on every page. Our Lord pointed to them when he said that certain things had been allowed to their fathers because they were bound by mental limitations which had passed away, and when he censured the spirit in which they asked him to repeat the act of Elijah. He thus recognized the progressiveness of revelation within the period of canonic Scripture. Nor can we fail to recognize the continuance of this progress in the Spirit's guidance of the church. Luther sees farther than Augustine; men of our age see farther than Luther did. History alike forbids us to despise the past and to rest in the past. It discredits alike the change which proceeds from the positive to mere negation, and the stolidity which excludes all change whatever. It condemns mere liberalism and mere inaction.

No history illustrates this more distinctly than does the history of the ecclesiastical life of America, and the Presbyterian Church supplies as good a point of view as any other from which to consider it. As has been indicated already, that history falls into three great periods, whose spirit has affected all the American churches, though in varying ways and different degrees.

The first was that of Puritan influence, which had three notes: intellectual interest in doctrine, Scriptural literalism, and practical individualism. In that age Christianity was so exclusively regarded as a doctrinal system that the boundary-line between the church and the school of theology was practically obliterated, and the distinction between theology and faith lost sight of. Of this the Westminster Confession is the best monument. Men had the sublimest confidence in the adequacy of logical processes to deal with divine mysteries, but lacked that element of reverence which should furnish the atmosphere of such discussion. Milton's deficiency in awe is that of his age; and Spurgeon, who best represented the Puritan thought in our own century, confessed to an equal want in himself. This orthodox rationalism needed but to cool to become negative and unorthodox; and the cooling was seen in all the British churches, especially the Presbyterian churches of England and of Ireland. In both stages it stands convicted of want of respect for the historical, which also is seen in its Scriptural literalism. It looked into the New Testament for a Book of Leviticus, and tried to construct one out of isolated passages and incidental notices. It demanded an express warrant of Scripture for every arrangement and institution, and turned its back upon the whole experience of the church since the days of the apostles. It was this feature of Puritanism which elicited Hooker's great treatise, " The Laws of the Ecclesiastical Polity " (1594–97); but the extreme advocates of the principle drove even the Westminster divines to declare that "there are some circumstances concerning the worship of God and the government of the church, common to human actions and societies, which are to be ordered by the light of nature and Christian prudence." Even this, it will be noticed, contains no concession to history. And in the same weakness of perception of the worth of the historical, and of the blessing of being ourselves embraced and molded by historic forms of society,

is to be found the reason for the excessive individualism
of Puritanism. It always tended to the purest independency, first of the local church and then of the individual
member within that church. It had an instinctive repugnance to synodical authority, and to the inclusion of infants among the baptized members of the church, as implying some religious solidarity of the family, and pointing to the organic character of the church. When most
logical it became Baptist; in its less logical forms it denied
that baptism admitted to actual membership in the church,
and therefore refused baptism to the children of any but
those who had become communicants upon giving credible evidence of their regeneration.

It would be ungracious to dwell only on these negative
sides of the Puritan spirit, to the neglect of those elements of positive strength which had root in the Calvinistic theology. Its greatness lay in an ethical strenuous-
ness which has worked itself into the fiber of Scotch and
American character, though in different ways, and which
is reflected in the literature, the social ideals, and the
finest personal types of both countries. Next to this may
be put its loyalty to the cause of human freedom, in opposition to dynastic and oligarchic rule in both church
and state. The theology which was charged with under-
mining human responsibility was in effect the most strenuous asserter of that principle. "There is no system
which equals Calvinism," says Beecher, "in intensifying to
the last degree ideas of moral excellence and purity of character. There never was a system since the world began
which puts upon man such motives to holiness, or which
builds batteries which sweep the whole ground of sin with
such horrible artillery." The view of our human nature
which has been charged with humbling man below his
deserts has stimulated him to the most resolute assertion

of his human dignity and personal rights against the encroachments of kings and nobles, popes and prelates. " It would be hard," says John Fiske, " to overrate the debt of civil liberty which mankind owes to John Calvin."

These two paradoxes find ample illustration in the history of Presbyterianism on both sides of the ocean. The latter has been amply recognized since Macaulay first fixed attention on the facts by his essay on Milton. The former has been obscured by a good deal of unfair historical writing, in which Robert Chambers, Henry Thomas Buckle, Mr. Craig-Brown, and others have represented the disciplinary work of the Scotch Presbytery and Session as consisting mainly of witch-hunting and the suppression of popular sports. Bishop Creighton, in reviewing the last writer's work, says:

" Mr. Craig-Brown is revolted by the stern aspect of Calvinism, and denounces the discipline of the Kirk Session as little better than that of the Inquisition. Yet that discipline, repugnant as it is to modern ways of thinking, did much toward forming the strong character of the Scottish people. Without it the wild borderfolk would never have been changed into the sterling, upright people with whom we are familiar. If the idea of righteousness which was enforced by Presbyterianism was narrow and not altogether lively, it still upheld a high idea of rectitude, and the Kirk did a civilizing work which there was no other agency to undertake. There can be no doubt that its discipline retained all the strength of character which had been generated in the unquiet times of border warfare; there can be little doubt that only a stern and vigorous system could have given a moral direction to that strength. The records of the Kirk Session tell us more of the process of the purification of national character than they do of religious fanaticism."

Another English writer, of Episcopalian sympathies, Mr. Richard Heath, testifies to the excellent influence of the Presbyterian discipline where it has crossed the border and established itself in the northern shires of England: " The Northumbrian peasant is largely influenced by a form of Christianity that not only recognizes that he is a man, but that, without ceasing to be a laboring man, tending the sheep or following the plow, he can be chosen, and is chosen, and found worthy to be an elder of the church." He goes on to speak of " the superior educative power of the Presbyterian to the Church of England system, as seen in the higher form of manhood and womanhood of the people under its control. The reason is clear: the one is a democratic religion, the other the most aristocratic in the world. It is this characteristic of the Church of England which is mainly responsible for the degraded condition of the English rural poor."

In our own country the task of Presbyterian discipline among the unrestrained frontiersmen of the New World was quite as difficult as along the Scottish border. For reasons already indicated, the immigrant population of the new settlements had to be followed up most energetically with church and school agencies, to maintain what was saved and retrieve what was lost of good influences in the land of their birth.

Between Puritan and anti-Puritan the Presbyterian Church held a middle position. It set its face against congregational independency by asserting the existence, visibility, and lawful authority of the larger church and its synodical government. It found in baptism the rite of admission to membership in the church, with all its privileges, including the baptism of the children of baptized persons. Acting on the judgment of charity, it admitted to the Lord's table all such as had been brought up as

Christians and were free from scandal of life. It sought thus to embrace the whole people of a Christian country within the scope of church influences and in personal contact with the means of grace. Yet it conceded to Puritanism the necessity of vindicating the polity of the church by proof-texts from the Scriptures, and it adopted a systematic theology built up by logical inference. To Puritanism, also, it conceded the relinquishment of liturgic worship.

Its losses to Puritanism were very great on both sides of the Atlantic. Its English churches became merely Independent, and afterward Arian. In America the Presbyterian colonists from England rapidly fell away from Presbyterianism into the unstable compromise with Independency called Congregationalism. The literalism which demanded an express Scriptural sanction for every feature of the church's polity was pressed with so much zeal, and reinforced so well by the example of the Plymouth separatists, that the efforts of John Eliot, the Mathers, and other opponents of Independency came to nothing. Even the later Presbyterian emigration from Ulster to New England was unable to maintain its ecclesiastical character in surroundings hostile to the Presbyterian idea, and under laws enacted in the interest of Independency. It is only in our own days, and chiefly through immigration from the seaboard provinces of Canada, that Presbyterianism has again raised its head in New England, after being long confined to a handful of feeble and imperfectly organized congregations.

The final establishment of Presbyterian order in the Middle States was like the settlement of Pennsylvania in the political sphere. As the one supplied the keystone of the arch, a community committed to neither Cavalier nor Puritan ideals of society, so the other supplied the missing link in the ecclesiastical order. It drew to itself dissatisfied elements of both the extreme systems, Puritans from New England and Episcopalians of Virginia. It at once began the fusion of the intense Presbyterians of Ulster with the New Englanders, who thus in the Middle States underwent what biologists call "reversion to type." It even threatened to extend this reversion to New England itself, as when the Connecticut churches made a marked approach to Presbyterianism in the Saybrook Platform (1708), and came to describe themselves as Presbyterians even in official documents. Thus from the first the Presbyterian Church may be said to have assumed a central position among the churches of America.

The second period opens with the Great Awakening, which began in the Dutch Reformed Church, and then spread to the Presbyterian, before the rise of English Methodism. The excessive intellectualism of Puritanism had begun to avenge itself in a chilled and chilling atmosphere around the religious life. Its disregard of history bore fruit in a weaker grasp on the great realities of the historic revelation. The Calvinistic churches seemed likely to run a downward course through the successive stages of Arminianism, Arianism, deism, and naturalism. This was more felt in America even than in the British Islands, because colonists are more likely to drift from their moorings than are the people of long-settled countries, where the conservative influence of institution and of custom is more constant. From this fate the nation was saved by the pietistic movement of 1728–44, which brought back warmth and fervency into religion, and lighted anew the fires of spiritual zeal. In all its earlier stages it was so distinctly a Calvinistic movement that its friends hailed it as the check to the drift into Arminian laxity, and Edwards challenged the Arminians of New England to reconcile such a visible display of sovereign grace with their theory that man turns himself to God.   Yet in the Calvinistic camp it bred sore divisions, of which the rending of the Presbyterian Synod in 1741 was the most striking, though not the most irreparable.   The Ulster famine of 1726 had greatly increased the immigrants in that and the following years.   These viewed with distrust a movement to which their native province offered no parallel, and they strengthened the hands of those ministers who regarded the new stress on religious emotion as likely to undermine the interest in doctrinal soundness.   And their distrust was not removed by the attitude the friends of the Awakening assumed toward those who distrusted it.   The church was rent not along the line of cleavage between Scotch-Irish and New Englander—for the most zealous revivalists were Scotch-Irish—and yet in such a way as threatened a practical severance of the two elements into two communions. It was an indication of God's good purpose for the future of the church that the two were brought together after seventeen years of separation.

The Methodism of the Awakening was no more historic than the Puritanism of the previous period had been.   It by no means sufficed to heal all the breaches of Zion.   It offered no substantial check to the Puritan individualism, but rather lent it a new sanction by making true religion a matter chiefly of isolated personal emotion, which reaches a man by a channel which has nothing to do with human kinship, social relations, or early nurture.   It thus severed it from public and social duties to an extent which threatened a return to monastic asceticism, and made a conscious conversion from enmity to friendship with God the only way of entrance into the kingdom.   It therefore could lay but little stress on the influences of the Christian home, or of the providential leading in the individual life.   Household training and catechetical instruction of the young by their pastor were both thrust into the background, or even disused, as of little value. If infant baptism were still continued—and the "Separate" churches of New England which grew out of the Awakening commonly became Baptist churches, while the converts in the Southern colonies went the same way mostly—it was rather through instinct or custom than by force of logic. The baptized child was too generally given to understand that he could be nothing but a child of Satan until a revival came to convert him, and that his chance of eternal life depended on his embracing that favored moment. This rigid "Methodism" of the Awakening, which stands in such contrast to the manifoldness of the spiritual life as exemplified in the Scriptures and the past history of the church, together with the habits of anxious introspection it fostered, tended to impart a monotony to Christian experience, and a dreariness to the literature which records it, for which a parallel must be sought among the German Pietists and the ascetic literature of the later Jesuits.

It would again be ungracious to dwell only on these weaker sides of the Awakening. In the good providence of God it saved America from irreligion and barbarism. It lifted the spiritual life of the churches out of a dull and fruitless moderation into an inspired and aggressive energy. It set the Christian people free to exhort and supplicate as in apostolic times, by supplementing the Sunday service with the prayer-meeting. It gave a distinctly Christian character to the church's praises by supplementing the Book of Psalms with Christian hymns. It carried the message of divine love into dark and neglected places of the country, and awakened the voice of thankful song along the frontier settlements and among the Indian tribes. It aroused the church to a sense of its duty to the heathen world, and thus laid the foundation of the missionary enterprise. In its later stages it adopted the Sunday-school and similar agencies into the service of the church, and created the machinery of wholesale agitation for the support of religious enterprises and moral reforms. It put down the slave-trade, prepared the way for the abolition of slavery, and set itself to the work of dealing with intemperance and other social evils. It wrought, in fact, a social revolution, whose extent is hid from us by the fact that we have always lived among its results and do not know with what a price they were bought for us. "Other men labored, and ye are entered into their labors."

Of the American churches some simply antagonized the Awakening; others gave themselves up to it completely, or even took their rise from its activity. The Presbyterian Church again fulfilled its mission by doing neither. It labored successfully to keep alive the interest in pure theology, as did also the Puritan churches of New England and the Reformed churches of the Middle States, thus counteracting the Methodist tendency to undervalue doctrine where it was not seen to be directly available for edification. It yielded much—some might say too much —to the practical theology of the movement, in accepting the revival meeting while seeking to abate its excitements, and in coming to regard a conscious conversion as the prerequisite to full communion with the church. It retained infant baptism on the ground that the Abrahamic covenant embraced the children of God's covenant people in the New Testament no less than the Old. But its ministers tacitly and very generally went over to the Congregationalist position, in confining baptism to the children of communicants. It allowed the pastor's catechetical instruction to be displaced by the labors of the Sunday-school teacher, because it had ceased to regard that instruction as leading on to communion. Yet it sought to maintain household religion and family worship, as well as the instruction of children by their parents in Bible and catechism. It also labored to support Christian schools, in which instruction in natural and historical science should not be divorced from recognition of the Creator and the Ruler of mankind. And in its attitude toward the public life of the nation it still stood for the principle that the state is the creature of God, accountable to him, obliged by his laws. It thus practically refused to accept the Methodist theory that mankind at large is to be regarded as " the world " at enmity with God, from which individuals may be brought over by conversion into churches, whose membership can give reasonable evidence of regeneration. The old " judgment of charity " lingered on as a tradition when it had fallen into oblivion as a doctrine.

Into the good works which grew out of the Methodist movement the Presbyterian Church entered with as much alacrity as was consistent with its conservative character. Without accepting the Methodist view that the expediency of immediate success is the only test of right method, it took up the new methods so far as these commended themselves to its judgment. It became a church of Sunday-schools, prayer-meetings, missionary societies, and voluntary associations for the promotion of all kinds of good works. It gave support to the great moral reforms, without losing its head over any of them, or expecting from the success of any the immediate arrival of the millennium. It felt too deeply the corruption of our human nature to share in the hopes of those who expected lightly to bring it to perfection by changes of environment or of method; and yet it worked for both with the stolid perse-

verance befitting a service done to God.   It got the blessing which rewards such a service, as did the sister-churches.
Its foreign-missionary enterprise lifted it out of a narrow
and self-satisfied occupation with its own affairs and be-
longings, into a work so large and absorbing as to keep
all its energies on the strain.   Its home-mission labor, to
keep the newer States and the Territories from falling to
a level of intellectual and spiritual life below that of the
older States, was blessed to both.   This saved the West
from barbarism and the East from miserly selfishness.   It
identified religion with generosity, and showed ways in
which the very power of accumulation might be turned to
the service of God and of the country.

Yet the Awakening also cost the Presbyterian Church
heavy losses of its natural adherents, especially in the
Southwest.   In its maintenance of the interest in Christian doctrine it was heavily handicapped by its adherence
to a Confession of Faith unsuited to the needs of the
country and the time.   The precise, scholastic statements
of the Westminster divines, and their wire-drawn distinctions, were naturally out of harmony with the revivalist
spirit, and those who preached them found no access except to congregations trained to appreciate such preaching.   The masses wanted a preacher to show warmth of
feeling, simplicity in doctrine, insight into the perplexities
and sorrows of the human heart.   These found rather a
help than a check in Puritan doctrinalism, and the majority of the children of the Ulster immigration fell away
from the church of their fathers.   The more moderate
organized a church of their own, Presbyterian in order,
and less drastic in doctrine than the Westminster standards, exhibiting a futile attempt at compromise between
popular Arminianism and traditional Calvinism.   A far
greater number found a spiritual home among the Method-

ists, the Baptists, the Disciples, the Christians, or even the
Shakers. And all this from Calvinism "putting its worst
foot foremost."

The third period in American church history began
about sixty years ago. It is that in which the historical
side of Christianity is more highly appreciated than at any
earlier time.

Puritanism appreciated strongly the intellectual side of
Christianity ; Methodism, the emotional. In neither did
the historical element come to its rights. Yet Christianity
is as distinctly history as it is doctrine and emotion. To
do justice to this third element is the problem of our own
age. To this end we must attain a truer recognition of
our vital relation to the historic fact of the Incarnation.
The years of that wonderful ministry are no part of a dead
and gone past ; nor are they related to us merely through
some change in our legal status before the divine law that
was then accomplished. They are nearer to us than our
own yesterdays, and form a substantial part of every
Christian's life.

Hence all that comes to us from that past on the lines
of history acquires a high significance to us. The church
is the witness of the gathering of all under the one Head
(ἀνακεφαλαιώσασθαι, Eph. i. 10) of all the elect of God.
The sacraments speak of his perpetual presence with the
church, to purify and nourish her life and that of her
members. They are not symbols of an absent, but witnesses of a present Christ. We are to come to them with
the faith that the heavenly element behind them is not
less real and operative than the earthly element present
to our senses. And this involves no confusion of the two
elements, as though the earthly were made divine or the
heavenly bound to the earthly. Baptismal grace and the
real presence in the sacrament were the common teaching

of all the churches of the Reformation.   These ordinances
they declared to be the means of grace—not mere witnesses
to the possibility of grace, nor mere helps, through the
law of mental association, to lift our thoughts to profitable meditation and resolution.

In this view, also, the whole course of church history
becomes instructive to us.   Whatever the sins, ignorances,
and negligences in it that require forgiveness, Christ was
in it all.   It did not cease to be his church with the death
of the apostles or of Augustine of Hippo, and begin to be
such again with Martin Luther.   Nor is the connection
between the two points to be sought in the Waldenses,
whatever their merits, but in the great central current
where we find the marks of Christ in such men as Bernard of Clairvaux, Francis of Assisi, Thomas Aquinas,
John Tauler, John Gerson, Thomas à Kempis, Nicholas of
Cusa, Savonarola, and the other great witnesses by life
and doctrine to the living presence of Christ in the world.
So the Reformers taught, having no more will to give up
the church's history to Rome than to give up the Bible.
Yet when Philip Schaff, then freshly arrived from Switzerland, enunciated this more generous view of the past, he
was assailed as a Romanizer by Dr. Berg and others.
His heresy has become almost a commonplace now, and
the theory of Waldensian continuity has given way partly
before its honest refutation by their own historical scholars.
And the result is seen in the free use of the medieval
hymns in our hymnaries, and in the high esteem in which
the " Imitation of Christ " stands.

Closely connected with this new respect for the historic
past is the appreciation of the beautiful in its spiritual
significance.   We grow impatient with the ugly, the un-
seemly, and the sordid, when we find these connected
with the church and its worship.   We acquire sympathy

with the men of the past, who spent toil and wealth on grand and graceful edifices for the divine worship. In this we enter into sympathy with the divine purpose which has molded our world, our bodies, and God's own Word with reference to beauty as well as use, and into whose temple there is a Gate Beautiful, no less than approaches through truth and emotion.

Another note of this present age is its socialism, using that term in its broadest sense, in antithesis to individualism. Our widened outlook upon the past, and our deepened sense of the social forces which have shaped the present out of it, have weakened faith in the capacity of the individual to deal satisfactorily with all questions. This feeling has combined with the reformatory and philanthropic energy transmitted from the previous period, and with the new scientific stress upon environment as molding the life of individual and species, to give a socialist character to our thought and the methods which it originates. And this has been stimulated by reaction against the more than Puritan individualism of the English political economists, until we run the risk of sacrificing the precious fruits of liberty in the pursuit of collectivist ideals.

In this new age the Presbyterian Church still holds a central position in the religious life of the nation. She is a historic church, prizing her own past, and reverencing the great historic names in her annals, without refusing that reverence to names as great, whose work was done outside her communion. As a conservative church she has helped to counteract the sudden breaks with history which each new tendency has threatened to accomplish. She moderated the extravagance of Puritanism by holding fast to elements of earlier date and historic value. She modified the urgency of the Awakening, when it would cast aside the heritage Puritanism had bequeathed, and would have disparaged every doctrine and institution which could not be proved directly useful for the conversion of sinners.   So in our own time she has to modify and restrain the tendency which would put church and sacrament and historic tradition not only beside, but above, or in place of, Christian truth and feeling.   She has to oppose those who in the name of the historic would turn their backs on all history but what suits their own tastes and likings, would cry down the Reformers and their work, treat Puritanism as an apostasy and the Awakening as an aberration, and find nothing to their liking that is not medieval or Romanist.   There are those who cannot love the Bernards and the Gregories without hating Luther and Knox, or who think that theological development came to an end with the seventh ecumenical council.   But " God wastes *no* history," as Phillips Brooks has well said.   He no more ceased to guide his church when the middle ages ended than when they began.   To doubt this, and to seek the connecting-link with that age in Laud and a handful of High-church Anglicans, is an exact parallel to the Waldensian theory as to the medieval period.   He knows not the history of the church who does not recognize the spiritual necessity for the change which sundered the Teutonic from the Romance church in the sixteenth century, or the Latin Church from the Greek in the eleventh ; who does not recognize the sobriety and conservatism with which it was effected, and does not find in its leaders the equals at least of any men God has given his church since Athanasius and Augustine.

Equally necessary is a moderating and conservative influence in the case of another tendency of our age.   As every extreme carries in it the causes of an equal reaction, so the extremes of individualism are producing the extremes of socialism.   Personal responsibility for poverty, wretchedness, and even vice is boldly questioned in these days. Society, and especially the church, is held to answer for the whole burden of human misery, which is put into such light as to fill the entire sky of social vision from horizon to horizon. All the problems of society are laid at the feet of the church, and she is required to turn aside from the ministry of the Word to serve the tables, at which the whole mass of the hungry and the thriftless are to be fed. In the past the conversion of sinners was made too exclusively the church's work. She is now to give it over, to turn to the conversion of millionaires into socialist philanthropists. She was too often characterized by an other-worldliness, which gave up the life of this time for a better life in the hereafter. She is now to drop the question of a hereafter, and to devote herself to improving the physical no less than the moral well-being of the human mass, taken in the mass.

There is both truth and justice in these charges and these demands, but there also is mischievous exaggeration. To oppose it we need a revival of the Puritan sense of personal responsibility and the Methodist sense of the adequacy of God's grace to reach and reform men in any surroundings. We need to rid our minds of the worship of environment and heredity which materialistic science has been teaching us, and to worship the living God, who says, "All souls are mine: . . . the soul that sinneth, *it* shall die." He is the greatest fact in the environment of any human spirit, and his quickening power is more than all the forces of heredity.

The Presbyterian Church, as heir to theocratic principle which was distinctive of the Reformed Church in its most illustrious era, has never sunk to mere pietistic individualism. She always has recognized her social responsibilities, and has spoken her mind on all social problems. She is

therefore less liable than the Puritan and Methodist bodies
to these violent reactions, while she responds to the new
impulse to deal with spiritual problems on their social no
less than their individual side.   The man of to-day is not
to be contented with the Methodist teaching of yesterday.
He longs for a new order of life more even than for the
good of his own soul.   He so longs because God is quickening in him desires for that social order which our Lord
called the kingdom of heaven.   But he still needs to have
the old truth pressed upon him, that he cannot enter the
kingdom until he is born from above and puts on the
childlike nature of the newly born.

The last note of the present age is the yearning for
Christian union which is awakening in the severed parts
of Christ's church.   The desire of a universal brotherhood of men simply as such, from which no man shall be
excluded except he will to be, finds expression in many
shapes, some of them fantastic enough.   The church was
founded to satisfy that yearning.   The closer we get to
its Founder, and the more we study its history, the less
content we are with a Christendom broken into fragments
by strife over secondary matters, and the more painful becomes the contrast between Christ's ideal and its imperfect
realization.

Here, I fear, it would be hard to assert any peculiar
merit for the Presbyterian bodies.   Up to the Revolution
settlement of 1690, indeed, the Kirk kept its unity unbroken.   The custom was for those who regarded anything in its practice as wrong and burdensome to their
consciences to " declare their separation from " that thing,
without breaking the unity of the church.   Thus the sharp
dissensions between the Engagers and the Resolutioners
in 1649–50 were got over without any breach of communion.

At the Revolution all the ministers who had preached in the fields, in defiance of· Stuart persecution, and had escaped the scaffold for this faithfulness, united with the Scottish church as reëstablished, claiming that Cargill, Cameron, Renwick, and the rest of the martyrs had declared against any separation "if the Lord should send deliverance to his church, and give them access to present their grievances to its judicatories with personal safety."[1] That is, however much they might dissent from the action taken on their grievances, they would no more than declare their dissent, without leaving the church. Unhappily this view did not commend itself to a part of the elders and members who had waited upon the ministry of the persecuted preachers and had shared in the perils of the killing-time. Because the Revolution settlement provided for no acknowledgment of the lasting obligation of the Covenants, they would have none of it; and through the accession of ministers who took the same view, they, after a long wait, in 1743 were able to organize themselves as a Covenanter Church. The same course was taken by the Erskines and their friends in withdrawing from the Kirk in 1733; by Gillespie and his friends in withdrawing to form the Relief Church in 1752; and by the majority in the American Synod, in 1741, in casting out the Tennents and their friends. Then came divisions within divisions, the Covenanters in Scotland dividing, in 1751, as to the soundness of a treatise by Mr. Frazer, of Brea, one of the persecuted preachers, in which he taught that Christ died for all men; and the Seceders, in 1747, on the question of the Burgher oath. Thus the Presbyterian Church, through neglect of her established principle of ecclesiasti-

---

[1] See "An Inquiry into Church-Communion; or, A Treatise Against Separation from the Revolution Settlement of this National Church, as it was Settled Anno 1689 and 1690." By Mr. Alexander Shields, Minister of the Gospel at St. Andrews. Edinburgh, 1706; 2d ed., 1747.

cal communion and dissent, was launched on a career of
division and schism which has been the scandal of the
Presbyterian name.

In America we have had, first and last, twenty-eight
Presbyterian bodies, most of them extended over the
national field, and many of them claiming to be the only
true representatives of Presbyterian principles. Of these
ten are still in existence, unless, indeed, the eleventh still
perpetuates its organization after the death of its last
minister. If we except the two Cumberland Presbyterian
churches the differences between the other eight are simply infinitesimal when compared with their agreements in
doctrine, polity, and character. Should they plant themselves on the ground occupied by the church in its most
heroic period they could find room for all within one fold,
with freedom for each to "declare its separation" from
what it regards as the shortcomings of the whole body.
And as regards even the Cumberland churches, there is
reason to believe that if this reunited church were to declare its Calvinistic faith in its own words, there would be
less difficulty in a reunion with them than is supposed.
Even that difficulty would not be in the way of a union
with the two Reformed churches, and this might be effected without requiring them to give up their older and
more historic name. But to effect all this the church
needs more of the Spirit of wisdom, unity, and a sound
mind than she yet possesses. It seems, indeed, as though
through her very divisions God were holding her back
from the temptations which come with increase of numbers and of strength until she is fitted to bear them.

This is still more true of the outlook for Christian unity,
of which Presbyterian and Reformed unity is but a lesser
branch. It would bring great perils to the nation if all
our Protestant churches were to be united into a single

effectively organized church, without their rising to a higher plane of practical wisdom and true spirituality than they have yet reached separately. The hasty and drastic fashion in which many of them have undertaken to deal with social problems, their assumption to decide not only the ends of moral reform, but the political means by which these are to be reached, are foreshadowings of these perils. The sad chapters in the earlier history of the established churches of Europe and America, before Protestant dissent and division curbed their strength, show that human nature works in much the same fashion in Protestant as in Romanist ecclesiastics, with the exception that a married clergy is less likely to devise fantastic and excessive severities than is a celibate. We therefore seem to be wisely compelled to wait for Christian union until we are fit to use it without abusing it.

Yet to wait is not to despair of it, or to give up yearning for it, or even to abandon the assurance that it is coming at no distant date. Our ecclesiastical life as a people is still in the colonial stage. It hardly has felt the touch of the great nationalizing instinct which played so great a part in the crises of our political history in 1775, in 1787, in 1832, and in 1861–65. We have inherited from Europe a state of ecclesiastical division not unlike nor unrelated to the divisions which kept colony apart from colony in the age of colonial dependence. In those earlier decades of American history it seemed as though the differences of race, of creed, and of social ideal would keep the colonies apart forever—at least it seemed impossible to bring them together in less than three confederacies, the Southern and the New England States standing apart from the others. But the good providence of God was building up a nation out of these alien elements long before the working of his hand appeared on the surface of things. By community of peril and of toil, by the friendly interchanges of commerce, by the spreading enthusiasms of the Great Awakening, by the common interest in men of national magnitude, like Franklin and Washington, by the foolish and ill-timed exactions of the British government, and by the manifest perils to religious liberty which attended the connection with England, the colonies were drawn out of their isolation, and began to be conscious of being American. When independence was achieved under an imperfect form of union, then commercial distress, industrial decay, popular turbulence, and bitter disputes between the States forced on the adoption of the Constitution. The crisis of Nullification brought the national sentiment into more lively activity, under the very rule of a party least disposed to cherish it. That of Secession finally settled the question of the permanence of the Union, by discovering to the American people, both North and South, how precious it had become to them.

All this has taken place in a sphere where no larger union is sought than that of a single people within their national boundaries. But in the sphere where the union of all men into one human brotherhood under the headship of Jesus Christ is the goal, we have accomplished as good as nothing as yet. We are not even national.

Here we have to move between two extremes. The first offers us unity in the footing of an abandonment of the past, and a reconstruction of the church out of New Testament texts, in the spirit of Puritan literalism. We have had more than one attempt of this kind, the most notable being the body called the Disciples, whose founders, Isaac and Alexander Campbell, came to America from the Associate Presbyterian Church of Ireland, and first joined the Baptists before reaching the conclusions on which they based their new organization. In this view

the history of the church since the days of the apostles
has been little more than a series of sins and blunders, of
which the less said or remembered the better. They
frankly apply to the history of the Protestant churches
the judgments which many Protestants still apply to the
middle ages: they admit the relief of the ecclesiastical
darkness by some shining names, but assert that the whole
story is a tissue of mere usurpation and wrong-doing—
creeds, polity, methods of work, all being out of the line
of what the New Testament forbids and requires.

Such a theory of the church could have originated only
in a period when historic studies were but little cultivated,
and the popular interest in the church's history as good
as absent. It was associated, however, with a disposition
to reject the subjectivity of the Awakening, and to assert
for Christianity a strongly objective character; and this
commended it to many. The history of the body shows
that the plan does not solve the problem. Divisions and
disputes have arisen within it, which have rent the bond
of charity, because this New Testament literalism does not
remove all grounds of difference in judgment.[1] Nor is the
church called upon to sacrifice her whole history to regain
her unity. These ages have not been lost, whatever their
mistakes.

The other extreme is that which proposes Christian

[1] The Disciples may be said to be the American representatives of the
Haldane movement in Scotland, by which the younger Campbell was greatly
influenced during his attendance at Glasgow University. In the Ahorey
Presbyterian congregation, where I spent a part of my boyhood, Isaac Campbell was still remembered for the strictness of the Seceder discipline he exercised when its pastor. Professor Whitsett, of the Southern Baptists, traces
the origin of Mormonism as a working-system to the literalism of the Disciples. Orson Pratt was a preacher among the Disciples, and became the
theologian of the Latter-day Saints. And the claim of the Saints is that
they alone offer a church which literally corresponds throughout to that of
the New Testament, being persecuted by the Gentiles, speaking with tongues,
working miracles, laying on hands for the bestowal of the Spirit, anointing
the sick, etc.

union on the historical basis presented by a single church, which claims to possess the only true church order or doctrine, or both.   This is a form of ecclesiastical assumption confined to no particular church.   All have made this claim at times, especially in the days of their early progress, when they thought themselves Aaron's rod, predestined to swallow up the others.   The Friends, the Methodists, the Baptists, the Lutherans, the Presbyterians—all have had their *jure divino* claims at times, when they were ready to unchurch everybody else.   At present it is the Church of Rome and the Protestant Episcopal Church which maintain exclusive claims in America.   The latter did not assume this attitude in the era of Bishop White, when it put itself more on a level with the other churches by speaking of " other denominations."   But all the changes in the legislation of the last half-century look in this direction and grow out of the dominant spirit of the church. It is now distinctly High-church of the Oxford pattern. Nor is this position abandoned at all in the action of the House of Bishops which looks toward Christian union. The notable feature of that action was that it was addressed to other bodies of American Christians, and not simply to the individuals who compose them.   It thus marks a great advance in Christian courtesy upon the style in which the High-church claim has been pressed in most cases.   But it still assumes that the elements of Christian reunion are to be sought entirely in the Episcopal Church, while it minimizes as far as possible the number of the prerequisites.   It asks of no other church for any contribution to the problem, while it proposes to open negotiations with any upon the basis it has laid down itself.   On this basis Protestants may be reunited by becoming Episcopalians to an extent there defined, while the Episcopal Church accepts and learns nothing from them.

Here again there is need of a central and moderating influence between opposed extremes, which the Presbyterian Church might very well exercise. She has more affinity with all the diverse elements of our ecclesiastical life than has any other church. She has been a Puritan church in the Puritan age, and a Methodist church in the age of the Awakening; and she is returning to what she was before the Puritan influence touched her, in adapting herself to the churchly tendencies of the present age. It would not be to the exclusion of any of these principles that she would offer herself as a mediator between them all; nor need Christian union be achieved by leaving behind the attainments of any in the past, and all becoming Presbyterians. Such a reunion, indeed, would bring all the elements of our rich and varied spiritual life into harmony and coöperation, giving us a church practically Trinitarian and at the same time more complex than is the life of any existing body.

In his address at the celebration of his semi-centenary Dr. Charles Hodge pointed to the clew furnished by the doctrine of the Trinity to the variety of spiritual life in the churches of Christ: "There are different types of religion even among true believers. The religion of St. Bernard and of John Wesley, of Jeremy Taylor and of Jonathan Edwards, although essentially the same, had in each case its peculiar character. Every great historic church has its own type of piety. As there are three Persons in the Trinity, the Father, the Son, and the Holy Ghost, so there appear to be three general forms of religion among evangelical Christians. There are some whose religious experience is determined mainly by what is taught in the Scriptures concerning the Holy Spirit. They dwell upon his inward work on the heart, on his indwelling, his illumination, on his life-giving power; they yield themselves pas sively to his influence to exalt them into fellowship with God.   Such men are disposed more or less to mysticism. There are others whose religious life is determined more by their relation to the Father, to God as God; who look upon him as a sovereign or lawgiver; who dwell upon the grounds of obligation, upon responsibility and ability, and upon the subjective change by which the sinner passes from a state of rebellion to that of obedience.   Then there are those in whom the form of religion, as Dr. Boardman has said, is distinctly Christological.   I see around me alumni whose heads are gray as my own.   They will unite with me in testifying that this is the form of religion in which we were trained.   While our teachers did not dissuade us from looking within and searching for evidences of the Spirit's work in the heart, they constantly directed us to look only unto Jesus—Jehovah-Jesus—him in whom are united all that is infinite and awful, indicated by the name of Jehovah; and all that is human and tender and sympathetic, forbearing and loving, implied in the name Jesus. If any student went to Dr. Alexander in a state of despondence the venerable man was sure to tell him, ' Look not so much within.   Look to Christ.   Dwell on his person, on his work, on his promises, and devote yourself to his service, and you will soon find peace.' "

This remarkable passage might be alleged in refutation of Dr. Hodge's famous statement in the same address : " I am not afraid to say that a new idea never originated in this seminary."   It coincides in the main with the results reached by the present writer in thirty years' study of the religious life and history of America.   The point at which the coincidence is not perfect will be indicated.

Our ecclesiastical life looks like a chaos of mere dissension and unreasonable divisions, but it is not so.   Under the seeming chaos lies an unseen order, with the promise of its ultimate visibility. The great American churches are Trinitarian in theory—they recognize in the Godhead an essential unity, and yet a threefoldness of life so distinct that the Son speaks to the Father as "thou" and of the Spirit as "he"—but in their actual life they tend to be, in some sense, Unitarians, singling out some one of the three as the object of trust and confidence.

Some, as Dr. Hodge says, have their thoughts centered upon the Father, the *fons deitatis*, "God as God," as the sovereign will which puts forth energy in creation, providence, redemption, and judgment. Here the Puritan, Calvinistic, and Reformed churches naturally belong. They regard the work of Christ mainly as putting an obstacle out of the way of the Father's will. In that will everything is embraced. This type of thought dominates the Westminster standards and all the Reformed confessions. Dr. Hodge evidently finds its truest representatives among the theologians of New England. But whatever modifications of it might come of Dr. Archibald Alexander's type of piety, and his own contact with the mediation school during his stay in Germany, this in the long run is that of Presbyterian theology.

The second type in the historic order we find in America is that of the worship of the Holy Spirit, as the Methodist era succeeds the Puritan. Here feeling counts for more than doctrine, and the inner life is accounted the greatest of all interests. Here stand our Methodists, Moravians, Friends, and other pietistic or mystical sects.

The third type is Christocentric. It regards the Incarnation as the world's redemption, and lays its stress not on the work of Christ to reconcile the Father to man, but on his very person, in which our humanity is lifted into fellowship with God. Its stress falls on the social rather than the intellectual and the emotional life, and on the sacraments around which that social life centers. The most perfect type of this is the Catholic and Apostolic Church, which was organized chiefly out of English and Scotch Presbyterians, and is now represented at some seven or eight centers in America. Next to it comes the Protestant Episcopal Church, especially since it has been permeated by the spirit of the Oxford revival.

And these three are one. Each tendency in its turn has been dominant for a time in the religious life of America. Shall not the next age be that of their unity in the manifold life of a national (and ecumenical) Trinitarian church, in which, as in our federal system of government, there shall be room for the largest variety of type in connection with an essential unity? To such a result the Presbyterian Church can contribute at least as largely as any in the land, through its friendly relations with all, through its hospitality in the past and the present to all these forms of the spiritual life.

At any rate, the last word on the subject is one of hope and of outlook. In the seeming welter of sects and parties, the hand of God is at work. Out of it, he will show forth his glory.

APPENDIX OF THE MOST IMPORTANT DOCU-
MENTS ILLUSTRATIVE OF THE HISTORY
OF THE PRESBYTERIAN CHURCH IN
AMERICA.

I. THE SCOTTISH NATIONAL COVENANT OF 1581, RENEWED IN 1638.

WEE all and every one of us underwritten, Protest, That, after long and due examination of our owne Consciences in matters of true and false Religion, [we] are now thoroughly resolved of the Truth, by the Word and Spirit of God, and, therefore, we beleeve with our hearts, confesse with our mouths, subscribe with our hands, and constantly affirm, before God and the whole World, that this only is the true Christian Faith and Religion, pleasing God, and bringing Salvation to man, which now is, by the mercy of God, revealed to the world by the preaching of the blessed Evangel.

And received, beleeved, and defended by many and sundry notable Kirks and Realmes, but chiefly by the Kirk of Scotland, the King's Majestie, and by three Estates of this Realme, as God's eternall Truth, and onely ground of our salvation; as more particularly is expressed in the Confession of our Faith, stablished and publikely confirmed by sundry Acts of Parlaments, and now, of a long time, hath been openly professed by the King's Majestie, and whole body of this Realme, both in Burgh and Land. To the which Confession and forme of Religion wee willingly agree in our consciences in all points,

as unto God's undoubted Truth and Verity, grounded
onely upon his written Word. And, therefore, We abhorre and detest all contrarie Religion and Doctrine; but
chiefly all kinde of Papistrie in generall and particular
heads, even as they are now damned and confuted by the
Word of God and Kirk of Scotland; but, in speciall, we
detest and refuse the usurped authoritie of that Roman
Antichrist upon the Scriptures of God, upon the Kirk, the
civill Magistrate, and Consciences of men; all his tyran-
nous lawes made upon indifferent things against our Christian libertie; his erroneous Doctrine against the sufficiencie
of the written Word, the perfection of the Law, the office
of Christ and his blessed Evangel; his corrupted Doctrine
concerning originall sinne, our natural inabilitie and rebellion to God's law, our justification by faith onely, our imperfect sanctification and obedience to the law, the nature,
number, and use of the holy Sacraments; his five bastard
Sacraments, with all his Rites, Ceremonies, and false Doctrine, added to the ministration of the true Sacraments
without the Word of God; his cruell judgement against Infants departing without the sacrament; his absolute neces-
sitie of Baptisme; his blasphemous opinion of Transubstan-
tiation, or real presence of Christ's body in the Elements,
and receiving of the same by the wicked, or bodies of
men; his dispensations with solemn oaths, perjuries, and
degrees of Marriage forbidden in the Word; his crueltie
against the innocent divorced; his divellish Masse; his
blasphemous Priesthood; his profane Sacrifice for the sins
of the dead and the quick; his Canonization of men, calling
upon Angels or Saints departed, worshipping of Imagerie,
Relicks, and Crosses, dedicating of Kirks, Altars, Daies,
Vowes to creatures; his Purgatorie, praiers for the dead;
praying or speaking in a strange language, with his Proces-
sions, and blasphemous Letanie, and multitude of Advocates or Mediators; his manifold Orders, Auricular Confession; his desperate and uncertaine repentence; his generall
and doubtsome faith; his satisfactions of men for their
sins; his justification by works, *opus operatum*, works of

supererogation, Merits, Pardons, Peregrinations, and Stations; his holy Water, baptizing of Bels, conjuring of spirits, crossing, saning, anointing, conjuring, hallowing of God's good creatures, with the superstitious opinion joyned therewith; his worldly Monarchy, and wicked Hierarchie; his three solemne vowes, with all his shavelings of sundry sorts; his erroneous and bloudie decrees made at Trent, with all the subscribers and approvers of that cruell and bloudie Band conjured against the Kirk of God; and, finally, we detest all his vain Allegories, Rites, Signs, and Traditions brought in the Kirk, without or against the Word of God, and Doctrine of this true reformed Kirk; to the which we joyne ourselves willingly, in Doctrine, Faith, Religion, Discipline, and use of the Holy Sacraments, as lively members of the same in Christ our Head; promising and swearing, by the GREAT NAME OF THE LORD OUR GOD, that we shall continue in the obedience of the Doctrine and Discipline of this Kirk, and shall defend the same, according to our vocation and power, all the dayes of our lives, under the paines contained in the Law, and danger both of body and soule in the day of God's fearfull Judgement; and seeing that many are stirred up by Satan and that Romane Antichrist, to promise, sweare, subscribe, and, for a time, use the Holy Sacraments in the Kirk deceitfully, against their owne consciences, minding thereby, first, under the externall cloake of Religion, to corrupt and subvert secretly God's true Religion within the Kirk, and afterward, when time may serve, to become open enemies and persecutors of the same, under vaine hope of the Pope's dispensation, devised against the Word of God, to his greater confusion, and their double condemnation in the day of the LORD JESUS.

We, therefore, willing to take away all suspition of hypocrisie, and of such double dealing with God and his Kirk, Protest, and call The Searcher of all Hearts for witnesse, that our minds and hearts do fully agree with this our *Confession, Promise, Oath, and Subscription,* so that we are not moved for any worldly respect, but are perswaded

onely in our Consciences, through the knowledge and love
of God's true Religion, printed in our hearts by the Holy
Spirit, as we shall answer to Him in the day when the
secrets of all hearts shall be disclosed; and because we
perceive, that the quietnesse and stability of our Religion
and Kirk doth depend upon the safety and good behaviour
of the King's Majestie, as upon a comfortable instrument
of God's mercy granted to this Country, for the maintaining of his Kirk, and ministration of Justice amongst us;
we protest and promise with our hearts, under the same
Oath, Hand-writ, and paines, that we shall defend his Person and Authority with our goods, bodies, and lives, in the
defence of Christ his Evangel, Liberties of our Countrey,
ministration of Justice, and punishment of iniquity, against
all enemies within this Realme or without, as we desire
our God to be a strong and mercifull Defender to us in
the day of our death, and comming of our LORD JESUS
CHRIST; to whom, with the Father, and the Holy Spirit,
be all honour and glorie eternally.

[In the renewal of 1638 there is added a rehearsal of
the Acts of the Scottish Parliament for the Confirmation
and Maintenance of the Reformed Religion, concluding
with that which prescribed the coronation oath taken by
Charles I. in 1633. It then proceeds:]

In obedience to the commandment of God, conform to
the practice of the godly in former times, and according
to the laudable example of our worthy and religious Progenitors, and of many yet living amongst us, which was
warranted also by Act of Councell, commanding a generall Band to bee made and subscribed by his Majestie's
subjects of all ranks, for two causes: One was, for de-
fending the true Religion, as it was then reformed, and is
expressed in the Confession of Faith above written, and
a former large Confession established by sundrie Acts of
lawfull Generall Assemblies and of Parlament, unto which
it hath relation set downe in publicke Cathechismes, and
which had beene for many yeeres, with a blessing from
heaven, preached and professed in this Kirk and King-

dome, as God's undoubted truth, grounded onely upon his written Word; The other cause was, for maintaining the King's Majestie his Person and Estate; the true worship of God, and the King's authoritie being so straightly joyned, as that they had the same friends and common enemies, and did stand and fall together. And, finally, being convinced in our minds, and confessing with our mouthes, that the present and succeeding generations in this Land are bound to keep the foresaid nationall Oath and subscription inviolable, Wee Noblemen, Barons, Gentlemen, Burgesses, Ministers and Commons under subscribing, considering divers times before, and especially at this time, the danger of the true reformed Religion, of the King's honour, and of the publicke peace of the Kingdome, by the manifold innovations and evils generally contained and particularly mentioned in our late supplications, complaints, and protestations, doe hereby professe, and, before God, his Angels, and the World, solemnely declare, That, with our whole hearts wee agree and resolve all the daies of our life constantly to adhere unto, and to defend the foresaid true Religion, and forbearing the practice of all novations already introduced in the matters of the worship of God, or approbation of the corruptions of the publick Government of the Kirk, or civill places and power of Kirkmen, till they bee tryed and allowed in free Assemblies, and in Parlaments, to labour by all meanes lawfull to recover the purity and libertie of the Gospel, as it was established and professed before the foresaid novations: And because, after due examination, we plainly perceive, and undoubtedly beleeve, that the Innovations and evils contained in our Supplications, Complaints, and Protestations have no warrant of the Word of God, are contrary to the Articles of the foresaid Confessions, to the intention and meaning of the blessed Reformers of Religion in this Land, to the above written Acts of Parlament, and doe sensibly tend to the re-establishing of the Popish Religion and tyranny, and to the subversion and ruine of the true Reformed Religion, and of our Liberties, Lawes, and Estates. We also

declare, that the foresaid Confessions are to bee interpreted, and ought to be understood of the foresaid novations and evils, no lesse then if everie one of them had
beene expressed in the foresaid Confessions; and that wee
are obliged to detest and abhorre them, amongst other
particular heads of Papistrie abjured therein. And, therefore, from the knowledge and conscience of our dutie to
God, to our King and countrey, without any worldly respect or inducement, so farre as humane infirmitie will
suffer, wishing a further measure of the grace of God for
this effect, We promise and sweare, by the GREAT NAME
OF THE LORD OUR GOD, to continue in the Profession
and Obedience of the foresaid Religion: That we shall
defend the same, and resist all these contrarie errours and
corruptions, according to our vocation, and to the uttermost of that power that God hath put in our hands, all
the dayes of our life: And, in like manner, with the same
heart, we declare before God and Men, That wee have no
intention nor desire to attempt anything that may turne to
the dishonour of God, or to the diminution of the King's
Greatnesse and authoritie: But, on the contrarie, wee
promise and sweare, that wee shall, to the uttermost of
our power, with our meanes and lives, stand to the defence of our dread Soveraign, the King's Majestie, his
person and authoritie, in the defence and preservation of
the foresaid true Religion, Liberties, and Lawes of the
Kingdome: As, also, to the mutuall defence and assistance, everie one of us of another in the same cause of
maintaining the true Religion, and his Majestie's authoritie, with our best counsell, our bodies, meanes, and whole
power, against all sorts of persons whatsoever. So that,
whatsoever shall be done to the least of us for that cause,
shall be taken as done to us all in generall, and to everie
one of us in particular. And that wee shall neither directly
nor indirectly suffer ourselves to be divided or withdrawn
by whatsoever suggestion, combination, allurement, or terrour, from this blessed and loyall conjunction, nor shall
cast in any let or impediment that may stay or hinder

any such resolution, as by common consent shall be found to conduce for so good ends. But, on the contrarie, shall, by all lawfull meanes, labour to further and promove the same; and if any such dangerous and divisive motion be made to us by word or writ, wee, and everie one of us, shall either suppresse it, or, if need be, shall incontinent make the same known, that it may bee timeously obviated; neither do we feare the foule aspersions of rebellion, combination, or what else our adversaries, from their craft and malice would put upon us, seeing what we do is so well warranted, and ariseth from an unfained desire to maintaine the true worship of God, the majestie of our King, and the peace of the Kingdome, for the common happiness of ourselves and posteritie. And because we cannot look for a blessing from God upon our proceedings, except with our profession and subscription we joyne such a life and conversation, as beseemeth Christians, who have renewed their Covenant with God; Wee therefore faithfully promise, for ourselves, our followers, and all others under us, both in publicke, in our particular families and personall carriage, to endevour to keep ourselves within the bounds of Christian libertie, and to be good examples to others of all Godlinesse, Sobernesse, and Righteousness, and of everie dutie we owe to God and Man. And that this our Union and Conjunction may be observed without violation, we call the living God, the Searcher of our Hearts, to witnesse, who knoweth this to be our sincere Desire, and unfained Resolution, as wee shall answer to JESUS CHRIST in the great day, and under the paine of God's everlasting wrath, and of infamie, and of losse of all honour and respect in this World. Most humblie beseeching the LORD, to strengthen us by his Holy Spirit for this end, and to bless our desires and proceedings with a happie success, that Religion and Righteousnesse may flourish in the land, to the glorie of God, the honour of our King, and peace and comfort of us all. In witnesse whereof we have subscribed with our hands all the premisses, &c.

II. A SOLEMNE LEAGUE AND COVENANT FOR REFORMA-
TION AND DEFENCE OF RELIGION, THE HONOR AND
HAPPINESSE OF THE KING, AND THE PEACE AND
SAFETY OF THE THREE KINGDOMES OF SCOTLAND,
ENGLAND, AND IRELAND. [ADOPTED 1643.]

Wee, Noblemen, Barons, Knights, Gentlemen, Citizens,
Burgesses, Ministers of the Gospel, and Commons of all
sorts, in the kingdomes of Scotland, England, and Ireland, by the providence of GOD, living under one King,
and being of one reformed religion, having before our
eyes the glory of GOD, and the advancement of the kingdome of our Lord and Saviour JESUS CHRIST, the honour
and happinesse of the Kings Majesty and his posterity,
and the true publick liberty, safety, and peace of the kingdomes, wherein every ones private condition is included:
And calling to minde the treacherous and bloudy plots,
conspiracies, attempts, and practices of the enemies of
GOD, against the true religion and professours thereof in
all places, especially in these three kingdomes, ever since
the reformation of religion; and how much their rage,
power, and presumption are of late, and at this time, increased and exercised; whereof the deplorable estate of
the church and kingdome of Ireland, the distressed estate
of the church and kingdome of England, and the dangerous estate of the church and kingdome of Scotland, are
present and publick testimonies; We have now at last,
(after other means of supplication, remonstrance, protestations, and sufferings,) for the preservation of ourselves and
our religion from utter ruin and destruction, according to
the commendable practice of these kingdomes in former
times, and the example of GODS people in other nations,
after mature deliberation, resolved and determined to enter
into a mutuall and Solemne League and Covenant, wherein
we all subscribe, and each one of us for himself, with our
hands lifted up to the most High GOD, do swear,

1. That we shall sincerely, really, and constantly, through

the grace of GOD, endeavour, in our several places and callings, the preservation of the reformed religion in the Church of Scotland, in doctrine, worship, discipline, and government, against our common enemies; the reformation of religion in the kingdomes of England and Ireland, in doctrine, worship, discipline, and government, according to the word of GOD, and the example of the best reformed Churches; and shall endeavour to bring the Churches of GOD in the three kingdomes to the nearest conjunction and uniformity in religion, confession of faith, form of church government, directory for worship and catechising; that we, and our posterity after us, may as brethren live in faith and love, and the Lord may delight to dwell in the midst of us.

2. That we shall, in like manner, without respect of persons, endeavour the extirpation of Popery, Prelacy, (that is, church-government by Archbishops, Bishops, their Chancellors, and Commissaries, Deans, Deans and Chapters, Archdeacons, and all other ecclesiasticall Officers, depending on that hierarchy,) superstition, heresie, schisme, profanenesse, and whatsoever shall be found to be contrary to sound doctrine and the power of godlinesse; lest we partake in other mens sins, and thereby be in danger to receive of their plagues; and that the Lord may be one, and his name one in the three kingdomes.

3. We shall, with the same sincerity, reality, and constancie, in our several vocations, endeavour, with our estates and lives, mutually to preserve the rights and privileges of the Parliaments, and the liberties of the kingdomes; and to preserve and defend the Kings Majesties person and authoritie, in the preservation and defence of the true religion, and liberties of the kingdomes; that the world may bear witnesse with our consciences of our loyalty, and that wee have no thoughts or intensions to diminish his Majesties just power and greatnesse.

4. We shall also, with all faithfulnesse, endeavour the discovery of such as have been, or shall be incendiaries, malignants, or evil instruments, by hindering the reforma-

tion of religion, dividing the King from his people, or one of the kingdomes from another, or making any faction or parties among the people, contrary to this League and Covenant; that they may be brought to publick triall, and receive condigne punishment, as the degree of their offences shall require or deserve, or the supreame judicatories of both kingdomes respectively, or others, having power from them for that effect, shall judge convenient.

5. And whereas, the happinesse of a blessed peace between these kingdomes, denyed in former times to our progenitors, is, by the good providence of GOD, granted unto us, and hath been lately concluded and settled by both Parliaments; we shall each one of us, according to our place and interest, endeavour that they may remaine conjoined in a firme peace and union to all posterity; and that justice may be done upon the wilfull opposers thereof, in manner expressed in the precedent article.

6. Wee shall also, according to our places and callings, in this common cause of religion, liberty, and peace of the kingdomes, assist and defend all those that enter into this League and Covenant, in the maintaining and pursuing thereof; and shall not suffer ourselves, directly or indirectly, by whatsoever combination, persuasion, or terrour, to be divided and withdrawn from this blessed union and conjunction, whether to make defection to the contrary part, or to give ourselves to a detestable indifferency or neutrality in this cause, which so much concerneth the glory of GOD, the good of the kingdomes, and honour of the King; but shall, all the days of our lives, zealously and constantly continue therein against all opposition, and promote the same according to our power, against all lets and impediments whatsoever; and, what we are not able ourselves to suppresse or overcome, we shall reveal and make known, that it may be timely prevented or removed: All which we shall do as in the sight of GOD:

And, because these kingdomes are guilty of many sins and provocations against GOD, and his Son JESUS CHRIST, as is too manifest by our present distresses and dangers, the fruits thereof; we profess and declare, before GOD and the world, our unfeigned desire to be humbled for our own sins, and for the sins of these kingdomes: especially, that we have not as we ought, valued the inestimable benefit of the gospel; that we have not laboured for the purity and power thereof; and that we have not endeavoured to receive CHRIST in our hearts, nor to walk worthy of him in our lives, which are the causes of other sins and transgressions so much abounding amongst us; and our true and unfeigned purpose, desire, and endeavour for ourselves, and all others under our power and charge, both in publick and private, in all duties we owe to GOD and man, to amend our lives, and each one to go before another in the example of a reall reformation; that the Lord may turn away his wrath and heavy indignation, and establish these churches and kingdomes in truth and peace. And this Covenant we make in the presence of ALMIGHTY GOD, the Searcher of all hearts, with a true intention to performe the same, as we shall answer at that great day, when the secrets of all hearts shall bee disclosed; most humbly beseeching the LORD to strengthen us by his HOLY SPIRIT for this end, and to blesse our desires and proceedings with such successe, as may be deliverance and safety to his people, and encouragement to other Christian churches, groaning under, or in danger of, the yoke of antichristian tyrannie, to joyn in the same or like association and covenant, to the glory of GOD, the enlargement of the kingdome of JESUS CHRIST, and the peace and tranquillity of Christian kingdomes and commonwealths.

III. THE ADOPTING ACTS OF 1647.

(a) *Approbation of the Confession of Faith.*

A Confession of Faith for the Kirks of God in the three Kingdomes, being the chiefest part of that Uniformity in Religion which by the Solemne League and Covenant we are bound to endeavour; And there being accordingly a Confession of Faith agreed upon by the Assembly of Divines sitting at Westminster, with the assistance of Commissioners from the Kirk of Scotland; Which Confession was sent from our Commissioners at London to the Commissioners of the Kirk met at Edinburgh in January last, and hath been in this Assembly twice publikely read over, examined, and considered; Copies thereof being also Printed, that it might be particularly perused by all the Members of this Assembly, unto whom frequent intimation was publikely made, to put in their doubts and objections if they had any; And the said Confession being upon due examination thereof found by the Assembly to bee most agreeable to the Word of God, and in nothing contrary to the received Doctrine, Worship, Discipline, and Government of this Kirk: And lastly, it being so necessary and so much longed for, That the said Confession be with all possible diligence and expedition approved and established in both Kingdomes, as a principall part of the intended Uniformity in Religion, and as a speciall means for the more effectuall suppressing of the many dangerous errours and heresies of these times; The Generall Assembly doth therefore after mature diliberation Agree unto and Approve the said Confession as to the truth of the matter (judging it to be most orthodox and grounded upon the Word of God) and also as to the point of Uniformity, Agreeing for our part that it be a common Confession of Faith for the three Kingdomes. The Assembly doth also blesse the Lord, and thankfully acknowledge his great mercy, in that so excellent a Confession of Faith is prepared, and thus far agreed upon in both Kingdomes; which we look upon as a great strengthening of the true Reformed Religion against the common enemies thereof. But lest our intention and meaning be in some particulars misunderstood, It is hereby expressly Declared and Provided, that the not mentioning in this Confession the severall sorts of Ecclesiasticall Officers and Assemblies, shall be no prejudice to the Truth of Christ in these particulars to be expressed fully in the Directory of Government. It is further Declared, that the Assembly understandeth some parts of the second Article of the thirty one Chapter, only of Kirks not settled or constituted in point of Government; And that although in such Kirks, a Synod of Ministers and other fit persons may be called by the Magistrates authority and nomination without any other Call, to consult and advise with about matters of Religion; And although likewise the Ministers of Christ without delegation from their Churches, may of themselves and by vertue of their Office meet together Synodically in such Kirks not yet constituted; Yet neither of these ought to be done in Kirks constituted and setled: It being alwayes free to the Magistrate to advise with Synods of Ministers and ruling Elders meeting upon delegation from their Churches, either ordinarily, or being indicted by his Authority occasionally and *pro re nata;* It being also free to assemble together Synodically, as well *pro re nata*, as at the ordinary times upon delegation from the Churches, by the intrinsicall power received from Christ, as often as it is necessary for the good of the Church so to assemble, in case the Magistrate to the detriment of the Church withhold or deny his consent, the necessity of occasionall Assemblies being first remonstrate unto him by humble supplication.

(b) The Psalm-Book.

The Generall Assembly, having considered the report of the Committee, concerning the Paraphrase of the Psalmes sent from England: And finding that it is very necessary, that the said Paraphrase be yet revised; Therefore doth appoint Master John Adamson to examine the first fourty Psalmes, Master Thomas Craufurd the second fourty, Master John Row the third fourty, and Master John Nevey the last thirty Psalms of that Paraphrase; and in their Examination they shall not only observe what they think needs to be amended, but also to set downe their own essay for correcting thereof: And for this purpose recommends to them, to make use of the travels of Rowallen, Master Zachary Boyd, or of any other on that subject, but especially of our own Paraphrase, that what they finde better in any of these Works may be chosen: and likewise they shall make use of the animadversions sent from Presbyteries, who for this cause are hereby desired to hasten their observations unto them: And they are to make report of their labours herein to the Commission of the Assembly for publike affaires against their first meeting in February next: And the Commission after revising thereof, shall send the same to Provinciall Assemblies, to bee transmitted to Presbyteries, that by their further consideration, the matter may be fully prepared to the next Assembly: And because some Psalmes in that Paraphrase sent from England are composed in verses which do not agree with the Common-tunes, Therefore it is also recommended that these Psalms be likewise turned in other verses which may agree to the Common-tunes, that is, having the first line of eight syllabs, and the second line of six, that so both versions being together, use may bee made of either of them in Congregations as shall be found convenient: And the Assembly doth further recommend, That M. Zachary Boyd be at the paines to translate the other Scripturall Songs in meeter, and to report his travels also to the Commission of Assembly, that after their Examination thereof, they may send the same to Presbyteries to be there considered untill the next Generall Assembly.

IV. THE ADOPTING ACT OF THE SYNOD OF PHILA-DELPHIA, 1729.

Although the Synod do not claim or pretend to any authority of imposing our faith upon other men's consciences, but do profess our just dissatisfaction with, and abhorrence of such impositions, and do utterly disclaim all legislative power and authority in the Church, being willing to receive one another as Christ has received us to the glory of God, and admit to fellowship in sacred ordinances, all such as we have grounds to believe Christ will at last admit to the kingdom of heaven, yet we are undoubtedly obliged to take care that the faith once delivered to the saints be kept pure and uncorrupt among us, and so handed down to our posterity; and do therefore agree that all the ministers of this Synod, or that shall hereafter be admitted into this Synod, shall declare their agreement in, and approbation of, the Confession of Faith, with the Larger and Shorter Catechisms of the Assembly of Divines at Westminster, as being in all the essential and necessary articles, good forms of sound words and systems of Christian doctrine, and do also adopt the said Confession and Catechisms as the confession of our faith. And we do also agree, that all the Presbyteries within our bounds shall always take care not to admit any candidate of the ministry into the exercise of the sacred function but what declares his agreement in opinion with all the essential and necessary articles of said Confession, either by subscribing the said Confession of Faith and Catechisms, or by a verbal declaration of their assent thereto, as such minister or candidate shall think best. And in case any minister of this Synod, or any candidate for the ministry, shall have any scruple with respect to any article or articles of said Confession or Catechisms, he shall at the time of his making said declaration declare his sentiments to the Presbytery or Synod, who shall, notwithstanding, admit him to the exercise of the ministry within our bounds, and to ministerial communion, if the Synod or Presbytery shall judge his scruple or mistake to be only about articles not essential and necessary in doctrine, worship, or government. But if the Synod or Presbytery shall judge such ministers or candidates erroneous in essential and necessary articles of faith, the Synod or Presbytery shall declare them uncapable of communion with them. And the Synod do solemnly agree, that none of us will traduce or use any opprobrious terms of those that differ from us in these extra-essential and not necessary points of doctrine, but treat them with the same friendship, kindness, and brotherly love, as if they had not differed from us in such sentiments.

All the ministers of this Synod now present, except one that declared himself not prepared, viz. Masters Jedidiah Andrews, Thomas Craighead, John Thomson, James Anderson, John Pierson, Samuel Gelston, Joseph Houston, Gilbert Tennent, Adam Boyd, Jonathan Dickinson, John Bradner, Alexander Hutchinson, Thomas Evans, Hugh Stevenson, William Tennent, Hugh Conn, George Gillespie, and John Willson, after proposing all the scruples that any of them had to make against any articles and expressions in the Confession of Faith and Larger and Shorter Catechisms of the Assembly of Divines at Westminster, have unanimously agreed in the solution of those scruples, and in declaring the said Confession and Catechisms to be the confession of their faith, excepting only some clauses in the twentieth and twenty-third chapters, concerning which clauses the Synod do unanimously declare, that they do not receive those articles in any such sense as to suppose the civil magistrate hath a controlling power over Synods with respect to the exercise of their ministerial authority; or power to persecute any for their religion, or in any sense contrary to the Protestant succession to the throne of Great Britain.

The Synod observing that unanimity, peace, and unity, which appeared in all their consultations and determinations relating to the affair of the Confession, did unanimously agree in giving thanks to God in solemn prayer and praises.

V. THE SYNOD OF PHILADELPHIA'S EXPLANATORY ACT OF 1736.

An overture of the committee upon the supplication of the people of Paxton and Derry, was brought in and is as followeth. That the Synod do declare, that inasmuch as we understand that many persons of our persuasion, both more lately and formerly, have been offended with some expressions or distinctions in the first or preliminary act of our Synod, contained in the printed paper, relating to our receiving or adopting the Westminster Confession and Catechisms, &c: That in order to remove said offence, and all jealousies that have arisen or may arise in any of our people's minds, on occasion of said distinctions and expressions, the Synod doth declare, that the Synod have adopted and still do adhere to the Westminster Confession, Catechisms, and Directory, without the least variation or alteration, and without any regard to said distinctions. And we do further declare, that this was our meaning and true intent in our first adopting of said Confession, as may particularly appear by our adopting act which is as followeth: All the ministers of the Synod now present (which were eighteen in number, except one that declared himself not prepared,) after proposing all the scruples any of them had to make against any articles and expressions in the Confession of Faith, and Larger and Shorter Catechisms of the Assembly of Divines at Westminster, have unanimously agreed in the solution of these scruples, and in declaring the said Confession and Catechisms to be the confession of their faith, except only some clauses in the twentieth and twenty-third chapters, concerning which clauses the Synod do unanimously declare, that they do not receive these articles in any such sense as to suppose the civil magistrate hath a controlling power over Synods with respect to the exercise of their ministerial authority, or power to persecute any for their religion, or in any sense contrary to the Protestant succession to the throne of Great Britain.

And we hope and desire, that this our Synodical declaration and explication may satisfy all our people, as to our firm attachment to our good old received doctrines contained in said Confession, without the least variation or alteration, and that they will lay aside their jealousies that have been entertained through occasion of the above hinted expressions and declarations as groundless. This overture approved *nemine contradicente.*

VI. THE PROTESTATION OF 1741, WHICH OCCASIONED THE DIVISION OF THE SYNOD OF PHILADELPHIA.

Reverend Fathers and Brethren,

We, the ministers of Jesus Christ, and members of the Synod of Philadelphia, being wounded and grieved at our very hearts, at the dreadful divisions, distractions, and convulsions, which all of a sudden have seized this infant church to such a degree, that unless He, who is King in Zion, do graciously and seasonably interpose for our relief, she is in no small danger of expiring outright, and that quickly, as to the form, order, and constitution, of an organized church, which hath subsisted for above these thirty years past, in a very great degree of comely order and sweet harmony, until of late—we say, we being deeply afflicted with these things which lie heavy on our spirits, and being sensible that it is our indispensable duty to do what lies in our power, in a lawful way, according to the light and direction of the inspired oracles, to preserve this swooning church from a total expiration: and after the deliberate and unprejudiced inquiry into the causes of these confusions which rage so among us, both ministers and people, we evidently seeing, and being fully persuaded in our judgments, that besides our misimprovement of, and unfruitfulness under, gospel light, liberty, and privilege, that great decay of practical godliness in the life and power of it, and many abounding immoralities: we say, besides these, our sins, which we judge to be the meritorious cause of our present doleful distractions, the awful judgment we at present groan under, we evidently see that our protesting brethren and their adherents were the direct and proper cause thereof, by their unwearied, unscriptural, antipresbyterial, uncharitable, divisive practices, which they have been pursuing, with all the industry they were capable of, with any probability of success, for above these twelve months past especially, besides too much of the like practices for some years before, though not with such barefaced arrogance and boldness:

And being fully convinced in our judgments, that it is our duty to bear testimony against these disorderly proceedings, according to our stations, capacity, and trust reposed in us by our exalted Lord, as watchmen on the walls of his Zion, we having endeavoured sincerely to seek counsel and direction from God, who hath promised to give wisdom to those that ask him in faith, yea, hath promised his Holy Spirit to lead his people and servants into all truth, and being clearly convinced in our consciences, that it is a duty called unto in this present juncture of affairs:

Reverend Fathers and Brethren, we hereby humbly and solemnly protest, in the presence of the great and eternal God, and his elect angels, as well as in the presence of all here present, and particularly to you, Reverend Brethren, in our own names, and in the names of all, both ministers and people, who shall adhere to us, as follows:

1. We protest that it is the indispensable duty of this Synod, to maintain and stand by the principles of doctrine, worship, and government, of the Church of Christ, as the same are summed up in the Confession of Faith, Catechisms, and Directory, composed by the Westminster Assembly, as being agreeable to the word of God, and which this Synod have owned, acknowledged, and adopted, as may appear by our synodical records of the years 1729, 1736, which we desire to be read publicly.

2. We protest that no person, minister or elder, should be allowed to sit and vote in this Synod, who hath not received, adopted, or subscribed, the said Confession, Catechisms, and Directory, as our Presbyteries respectively do, according to our last explication of the adopting act; or who is either accused or convicted, or may be convicted before this Synod, or any of our Presbyteries, of holding or maintaining any doctrine, or who act and persist in any

practice, contrary to any of those doctrines, or rules contained in said Directory, or contrary to any of the known rights of Presbytery, or orders made or agreed to by this Synod, and which stand yet unrepealed, unless, or until he renounce such doctrine, and being found guilty, acknowledge, confess, and profess his sorrow for such sinful disorder, to the satisfaction of this Synod, or such inferior judicatory as the Synod shall appoint or empower for that purpose.

3. We protest that all our protesting brethren have at present no right to sit and vote as members of this Synod, having forfeited their right of being accounted members of it for many reasons, a few of which we shall mention afterwards.

4. We protest that, if, notwithstanding of this our protestation, these brethren be allowed to sit and vote in this Synod, without giving suitable satisfaction to the Synod, and particularly to us, who now enter this protestation, and those who adhere to us in it, that whatsoever shall be done, voted, or transacted by them, contrary to our judgment, shall be of no force or obligation to us, being done and acted by a judicatory consisting in part of members who have no authority to act with us in ecclesiastical matters.

5. We protest that, if, notwithstanding this our protestation, and contrary to the true intent and meaning of it, these protesting brethren, and such as adhere to them, or support and countenance them in their antipresbyterial practices, shall continue to act as they have done this last year, in that case we, and as many as have clearness to join with us, and maintain the rights of this judicatory, shall be accounted in nowise disorderly, but the true Presbyterian Church in this province ; and they shall be looked upon as guilty of schism, and the breach of the rules of Presbyterial government, which Christ has established in his church, which we are ready at all times to demonstrate to the world.

Reverend and dear Brethren, we beseech you to hear

us with patience, while we lay before you as briefly as we can, some of the reasons that move us thus to protest, and more particularly, why we protest against our protesting brethren's being allowed to sit as members of this Synod.

1. Their heterodox and anarchical principles expressed in their Apology, pages twenty-eight and thirty-nine, where they expressly deny that Presbyteries have authority to oblige their dissenting members, and that Synods should go any further, in judging of appeals or references, &c., than to give their best advice, which is plainly to divest the officers and judicatories of Christ's kingdom of all authority, (and plainly contradicts the thirty-first article of our Confession of Faith, section three, which these brethren pretend to adopt,) agreeable to which is the whole superstructure of arguments which they advance and maintain against not only our synodical acts, but also all authority to make any acts or orders that shall bind their dissenting members, throughout their whole Apology.

2. Their protesting against the Synod's act in relation to the examination of candidates, together with their proceeding to license and ordain men to the ministry of the gospel, in opposition to, and in contempt of said act of Synod.

3. Their making irregular irruptions upon the congregations to which they have no immediate relation, without order, concurrence, or allowance of the Presbyteries or ministers to which congregations belong, thereby sowing the seeds of division among people, and doing what they can to alienate and fill their minds with unjust prejudices against their lawfully called pastors.

4. Their principles and practices of rash judging and condemning all who do not fall in with their measures, both ministers and people, as carnal, graceless, and enemies to the work of God, and what not, as appears in Mr. Gilbert Tennent's sermon against unconverted ministers, and his and Mr. Blair's papers of May last, which were read in open Synod; which rash judging has been the constant practice of our protesting brethren, and their irregular pro-

bationers, for above these twelve months past, in their disorderly itinerations and preaching through our congregations, by which, (alas! for it,) most of our congregations,
through weakness and credulity, are so shattered and
divided, and shaken in their principles, that few or none
of us can say we enjoy the comfort, or have the success
among our people, which otherwise we might, and which
we enjoyed heretofore.

5. Their industriously persuading people to believe that
the call of God whereby he calls men to the ministry, does
not consist in their being regularly ordained and set apart
to that work, according to the institution and rules of the
Word; but in some invisible motions and workings of the
Spirit, which none can be conscious or sensible of but the
person himself, and with respect to which he is liable to be
deceived, or play the hypocrite; that the gospel preached
in truth by unconverted ministers, can be of no saving
benefit to souls; and their pointing out such ministers,
whom they condemn as graceless by their rash judging
spirit, they effectually carry the point with the poor credu-
lous people, who, in imitation of their example, and under
their patrociny, judge their ministers to be graceless, and
forsake their ministry as hurtful rather than profitable.

6. Their preaching the terrors of the law in such a manner and dialect as has no precedent in the word of God,
but rather appears to be borrowed from a worse dialect;
and so industriously working on the passions and affections
of weak minds, as to cause them to cry out in a hideous
manner, and fall down in convulsion-like fits, to the mar-
ring of the profiting both of themselves and others, who
are so taken up in seeing and hearing these odd symptoms,
that they cannot attend to or hear what the preacher says;
and then, after all, boasting of these things as the work of
God, which we are persuaded do proceed from an inferior
or worse cause.

7. Their, or some of them, preaching and maintaining
that all true converts are as certain of their gracious state
as a person can be of what he knows by his outward

senses; and are able to give a narrative of the time and manner of their conversion, or else they conclude them to be in a natural or graceless state, and that a gracious person can judge of another's gracious state otherwise than by his profession and life. That people are under no sacred tie or relation to their own pastors lawfully called, but may leave them when they please, and ought to go where they think they get most good.

For these and many other reasons, we protest, before the Eternal God, his holy angels, and you, Reverend Brethren, and before all here present, that these brethren have no right to be acknowledged as members of this judicatory of Christ, whose principles and practices are so diametrically opposite to our doctrine, and principles of government and order, which the great King of the Church hath laid down in his Word.

How absurd and monstrous must that union be, where one part of the members own themselves obliged, in conscience, to the judicial determinations of the whole, founded on the Word of God, or else relinquish membership; and another part declare, they are not obliged and will not submit, unless the determination be according to their minds, and consequently will submit to no rule, in making of which they are in the negative.

Again, how monstrously absurd is it, that they should so much as desire to join with us, or we with them, as a judicatory, made up of authoritative officers of Jesus Christ, while they openly condemn us wholesale; and, when they please, apply their condemnatory sentences to particular brethren by name, without judicial process, or proving them guilty of heresy or immorality, and at the same time will not hold Christian communion with them.

Again, how absurd is the union, while some of the members of the same body, which meet once a year, and join as a judicatory of Christ, do all the rest of the year what they can, openly and above board, to persuade the people and flocks of their brethren and fellow members, to separate from their own pastors, as graceless hypocrites, and yet they do not separate from them themselves, but join with them once every year, as members of the same judicatory of Christ, and oftener, when Presbyteries are mixed. Is it not most unreasonable, stupid indolence in us, to join with such as are avowedly tearing us in pieces like beasts of prey?

Again, is not the continuance of union with our protesting brethren very absurd, when it is so notorious that both their doctrine and practice are so directly contrary to the adopting act, whereby both they and we have adopted the Confession of Faith, Catechisms and Directory, composed by the Westminster Assembly?

Finally, is not continuance of union absurd with those who would arrogate to themselves a right and power to palm and obtrude members on our Synod, contrary to the minds and judgment of the body?

In fine, a continued union, in our judgment, is most absurd and inconsistent, when it is so notorious, that our doctrine and principles of church government, in many points, are not only diverse, but directly opposite. For how can two walk together, except they be agreed?

Reverend Fathers and Brethren, these are a part, and but a part, of our reasons why we protest as above, and which we have only hinted at, but have forborne to enlarge on them, as we might, the matter and substance of them are so well known to you all, and the whole world about us, that we judged this hint sufficient at present, to declare our serious and deliberate judgment in the matter; and as we profess ourselves to be resolvedly against principles and practice of both anarchy and schism, so we hope that God, whom we desire to serve and obey, the Lord Jesus Christ, whose ministers we are, will both direct and enable us to conduct ourselves, in these trying times, so as our consciences shall not reproach us as long as we live. Let God arise, and let his enemies be scattered, and let them that hate him fly before him, but let the righteous be glad, yea, let them exceedingly rejoice. And may the Spirit of life and comfort revive and comfort this poor swooning and fainting church, quicken her to spiritual life, and restore her to the exercise of true charity, peace, and order.

Although we can freely, and from the bottom of our hearts, justify the Divine proceedings against us, in suffering us to fall into these confusions for our sins, and particularly for the great decay of the life and power of godliness among all ranks, both ministers and people, yet we think it to be our present duty to bear testimony against these prevailing disorders, judging that to give way to the breaking down the hedge of discipline and government from about Christ's vineyard, is far from being the proper method of causing his tender plants to grow in grace and fruitfulness.

As it is our duty in our station, without delay, to set about a reformation of the evils whereby we have provoked God against ourselves, so we judge the strict observation of his laws of government and order, and not the breaking of them, to be one necessary mean and method of this necessary and much to be desired reformation. And we doubt not, but when our God sees us duly humbled and penitent for our sins, he will yet return to us in mercy, and cause us to flourish in spiritual life, love, unity, and order, though perhaps we may not live to see it, yet this testimony that we now bear, may be of some good use to our children yet unborn, when God shall arise and have mercy on Zion.

Ministers: Robert Cross, John Thomson, Francis Alison, Robert Cathcart, Richard Zanchy, John Elder, John Craig, Samuel Caven, Samuel Thomson, Adam Boyd, James Martin, Robert Jamison.

Elders: Robert Porter, Robert McKnight, William McCulloch, John McEuen, Robert Rowland, Robert Craig, James Kerr, Alexander McKnight.

VII. THE PLAN OF UNION OF 1758.

The Synods of New York and Philadelphia, taking into serious consideration the present divided state of the Presbyterian church in this land, and being deeply sensible that the division of the church tends to weaken its interests, to dishonour religion, and consequently its glorious Author; to render government and discipline ineffectual, and finally to dissolve its very frame; and being desirous to pursue such measures as may most tend to the glory of God and the establishment and edification of his people, do judge it to be our indispensable duty to study the things that make for peace, and to endeavour the healing of that breach which has for some time subsisted amongst us, that so its hurtful consequences may not extend to posterity; that all occasion of reproach upon our society may be removed, and that we may carry on the great designs of religion to better advantage than we can do in a divided state; and since both Synods continue to profess the same principles of faith, and adhere to the same form of worship, government, and discipline, there is the greater reason to endeavour the compromising those differences, which were agitated many years ago with too great warmth and animosity, and unite in one body.

For which end, and that no jealousies or grounds of alienation may remain, and also to prevent future breaches of like nature, we agree to unite and do unite in one body, under the name of the Synod of New York and Philadelphia, on the following plan.

I. Both Synods having always approved and received the Westminster Confession of Faith, and Larger and Shorter Catechisms, as an orthodox and excellent system of Christian doctrine, founded on the word of God, we do still receive the same as the confession of our faith, and also adhere to the plan of worship, government, and discipline, contained in the Westminster Directory, strictly enjoining it on all our members and probationers for the ministry, that they preach and teach according to the form of sound words in said Confession and Catechisms, and avoid and oppose all errors contrary thereto.

II. That when any matter is determined by a major vote, every member shall either actively concur with, or passively submit to such determination; or, if his conscience permit him to do neither, he shall, after sufficient liberty modestly to reason and remonstrate, peaceably withdraw from our communion without attempting to make any schism. Provided always, that this shall be understood to extend only to such determinations as the body shall judge indispensable in doctrine or Presbyterian government.

III. That any member or members, for the exoneration of his or their conscience before God, have a right to protest against any act or procedure of our highest judicature, because there is no further appeal to another for redress; and to require that such protestation be recorded in their minutes. And as such a protest is a solemn appeal from the bar of said judicature, no member is liable to prosecution on the account of his protesting. Provided always, that it shall be deemed irregular and unlawful, to enter a protestation against any member or members, or to protest facts or accusations instead of proving them, unless a fair trial be refused, even by the highest judicature. And it is agreed, that protestations are only to be entered against the public acts, judgments, or determinations of the judicature with which the protester's conscience is offended.

IV. As the Protestation entered in the Synod of Philadelphia, *Ann. Dom.* 1741, has been apprehended to have been approved and received by an act of said Synod, and on that account was judged a sufficient obstacle to an union; the said Synod declare, that they never judicially adopted the said Protestation, nor do account it a Synodical act, but that it is to be considered as the act of those only who subscribed it; and therefore cannot in its nature be a valid objection to the union of the two Synods, especially considering that a very great majority of both Synods have become members, since the said Protestation was entered.

V. That it shall be esteemed and treated as a censurable evil, to accuse any member of heterodoxy, insufficiency, or immorality, in a calumniating manner, or otherwise than by private brotherly admonition, or by a regular process according to our known rules of judicial trial in cases of scandal. And it shall be considered in the same view, if any Presbytery appoint supplies within the bounds of another Presbytery without their concurrence; or if any member officiate in another's congregation, without asking and obtaining his consent, or the session's in case the minister be absent; yet it shall be esteemed unbrotherly for any one, in ordinary circumstances, to refuse his consent to a regular member when it is requested.

VI. That no Presbytery shall license or ordain to the work of the ministry, any candidate, until he give them competent satisfaction as to his learning, and experimental acquaintance with religion, and skill in divinity and cases of conscience; and declare his acceptance of the Westminster Confession and Catechisms as the confession of his faith, and promise subjection to the Presbyterian plan of government in the Westminster Directory.

VII. The Synods declare it is their earnest desire, that a complete union may be obtained as soon as possible, and agree that the united Synod shall model the several Presbyteries in such manner as shall appear to them most expedient. Provided nevertheless, that Presbyteries, where an alteration does not appear to be for edification, continue in their present form. As to divided congregations it is agreed, that such as have settled ministers on both sides be allowed to continue as they are; that where those of one side have a settled minister, the other being vacant, may join with the settled minister, if a majority choose so to do; that when both sides are vacant they shall be at liberty to unite together.

VIII. As the late religious appearances occasioned much

speculation and debate, the members of the New York Synod, in order to prevent any misapprehensions, declare their adherence to their former sentiments in favour of them, that a blessed work of God's Holy Spirit in the conversion of numbers was then carried on; and for the satisfaction of all concerned, this united Synod agree in declaring, that as all mankind are naturally dead in trespasses and sins an entire change of heart and life is necessary to make them meet for the service and enjoyment of God; that such a change can be only effected by the powerful operations of the Divine Spirit; that when sinners are made sensible of their lost condition and absolute inability to recover themselves, are enlightened in the knowledge of Christ and convinced of his ability and willingness to save, and upon gospel encouragements do choose him for their Saviour, and renouncing their own righteousness in point of merit, depend upon his imputed righteousness for their justification before God, and on his wisdom and strength for guidance and support; when upon these apprehensions and exercises their souls are comforted, notwithstanding all their past guilt, and rejoice in God through Jesus Christ; when they hate and bewail their sins of heart and life, delight in the laws of God without exception, reverently and diligently attend his ordinances, become humble and self denied, and make it the business of their lives to please and glorify God and to do good to their fellow men; this is to be acknowledged as a gracious work of God, even though it should be attended with unusual bodily commotions or some more exceptionable circumstances, by means of infirmity, temptations, or remaining corruptions; and wherever religious appearances are attended with the good effects above mentioned, we desire to rejoice in and thank God for them.

But on the other hand, when persons seeming to be under a religious concern, imagine that they have visions of the human nature of Jesus Christ, or hear voices, or see external lights, or have fainting and convulsion-like fits, and on the account of these judge themselves to be truly converted, though they have not the Scriptural characters of a work of God above described, we believe such persons are under a dangerous delusion. And we testify our utter disapprobation of such a delusion, wherever it attends any religious appearances, in any church or time.

Now as both Synods are agreed in their sentiments concerning the nature of a work of grace, and declare their desire and purpose to promote it, different judgments respecting particular matters of fact, ought not to prevent their union; especially as many of the present members have entered into the ministry since the time of the aforesaid religious appearances.

Upon the whole, as the design of our union is the advancement of the Mediator's kingdom; and as the wise and faithful discharge of the ministerial function is the principal appointed mean for that glorious end, we judge, that this is a proper occasion to manifest our sincere intention, unitedly to exert ourselves to fulfil the ministry we have received of the Lord Jesus. Accordingly, we unanimously declare our serious and fixed resolution, by divine aid, to take heed to ourselves that our hearts be upright, our discourse edifying, and our lives exemplary for purity and godliness; to take heed to our doctrine, that it be not only orthodox but evangelical and spiritual, tending to awaken the secure to a suitable concern for their salvation, and to instruct and encourage sincere Christians; thus commending ourselves to every man's conscience in the sight of God; to cultivate peace and harmony among ourselves, and strengthen each other's hands in promoting the knowledge of divine truth, and diffusing the savour of piety among our people.

Finally we earnestly recommend it to all under our care, that instead of indulging a contentious disposition, they would love each other with a pure heart fervently, as brethren who profess subjection to the same Lord, adhere to the same faith, worship, and government, and entertain the same hope of glory. And we desire that they would improve the present union for their mutual edification, combine to strengthen the common interests of religion, and go hand in hand in the path of life; which we pray the God of all grace would please to effect, for Christ's sake. Amen.

The Synod agree, that all former differences and disputes are laid aside and buried; and that no future inquiry or vote shall be proposed in this Synod concerning these things; but if any member seek a Synodical inquiry, or declaration about any of the matters of our past differences, it shall be deemed a censurable breach of this agreement, and be refused, and he be rebuked accordingly.

VIII. THE BASIS OF UNION OF 1782, ON WHICH THE ASSOCIATE REFORMED CHURCH WAS FORMED.

Article 1. Election, redemption, and the application thereof, are of equal extent, and for the elect only.

Art. 2. Magistracy is derived from God as the Almighty Creator and Governor of the world, and not from Christ as Mediator.

Art. 3. Whereas magistracy proceeds from God as the Creator and Governor of the world, and the profession of the true religion is not essential to the being of civil magistrates: and whereas protection and allegiance are reciprocal, and as the United States of America, while they protect us in life and property, at the same time do not impose any thing sinful on us, we therefore judge it our duty to acknowledge the government of these states, in all lawful commands, that we may lead quiet and peaceable lives in all godliness and honesty.

Art. 4. The above proposition is not to be understood in an opposite sense to that proposition relative to civil government, on which the union between the Associate Presbytery of New York and the Reformed Presbytery have agreed; but only as a plain and undisguised explication of one point of truth, in which we have the best reason to believe the whole body are united.

Art. 5. As no opposition of sentiment, relative to the important duty of covenanting, appears on either side; it is mutually agreed, that the consideration of it be referred to the councils and deliberations of the whole body.

Art. 6. Though no real or practical subordination to the Associate Synod of Edinburgh, in a consistency with Presbyterian principles, can be pled, yet from the most wise and important considerations, the former connections, whatever they have been, shall remain as before, notwithstanding of this coalescence.

IX. THE ADOPTING ACTS OF 1788.

(1) The Synod having fully considered the draught of the form of government and discipline, did, on a review of the whole, and hereby do ratify and adopt the same, as now altered and amended, as the Constitution of the Presbyterian Church in America, and order the same to be considered and strictly observed as the rule of their proceedings, by all the inferior judicatories, belonging to the body. And they order that a correct copy be printed, and that the Westminster Confession of Faith, as now altered, be printed in full along with it, as making a part of the Constitution.

RESOLVED, That the true intent and meaning of the above ratification by the Synod, is, that the Form of Government and Discipline and the Confession of Faith, as now ratified, is to continue to be our Constitution and the confession of our faith and practice unalterable, unless two-thirds of the Presbyteries under the care of the General Assembly shall propose alterations or amendments, and such alterations or amendments shall be agreed to and enacted by the General Assembly.

(2) The Synod having now revised and corrected the draught of a Directory for worship, did approve and ratify the same, and do hereby appoint the said Directory, as now amended, to be the Directory for the worship of God in the Presbyterian Church in the United States of Amer-

ica. They also took into consideration the Westminster Larger and Shorter Catechisms, and having made a small amendment of the Larger, did approve, and do hereby approve and ratify the said Catechisms, as now agreed on, as the Catechisms of the Presbyterian Church in the said United States. And the Synod order, that the said Directory and Catechisms be printed and bound up in the same volume with the Confession of Faith and the Form of Government and Discipline, and that the whole be considered as the standard of our doctrine, government, discipline, and worship, agreeably to the resolutions of the Synod at their present sessions.

ORDERED, That Dr. Duffield, Mr. Armstrong and Mr. Green, be a committee to superintend the printing and publishing the above said Confession of Faith and Catechisms, with the Form of Government and Discipline, and the Directory for the Worship of God, as now adopted and ratified by the Synod, as the Constitution of the Presbyterian Church in the United States of America, and that they divide the several parts into chapters and sections properly numbered.

[A different and somewhat fuller version of the two first paragraphs of the Adopting Act was found by Judge Drake, in 1870, in a pamphlet entitled " Acts and Proceedings of the Synod of New York and Philadelphia, A.D. 1787 and 1788 " (Philadelphia, 1788), viz. :

"The Synod took into consideration the Draught of the Form of Government and Discipline of the Presbyterian Church in the United States of America—And having gone through the same, did, on a review of the whole, ratify and adopt the said Form of Government and Discipline, as now altered and amended, as the Constitution of the Government and Discipline of the Presbyterian Church in America. And recommend to all their inferior judicatures, strictly to observe the rules laid down therein, in all ecclesiastical proceedings. And they order, that a correct copy be printed ; and that the Westminster Confession of Faith, as now altered, be printed in full along with it, as making part of the Constitution.

"Resolved that the true meaning of the above ratification by the Synod, is, that the Form of Government and Discipline, and Confession of Faith, as now ratified, is to continue to be our Constitution, and the Confession of our Faith and Practice, unalterably; unless two thirds of the Presbyteries, under the care of the General Assembly, shall propose alterations or amendments; and such alterations and amendments shall be agreed to, and enacted by the General Assembly."]

X. THE DECLARATION OF PRINCIPLES OF 1788.

The Presbyterian Church in the United States of America, in presenting to the Christian public the system of union and the form of government and discipline which they have adopted, have thought proper to state, by way of introduction, a few of the general principles by which they have been governed in the formation of the plan. This, it is hoped, will, in some measure, prevent those rash misconstructions and uncandid reflections which usually proceed from an imperfect view of any subject, as well as make the several parts of the system plain and the whole perspicuous and fully understood.

They are unanimously of opinion:

I. That " God alone is Lord of the conscience, and hath left it free from the doctrines and commandments of men, which are in any thing contrary to his word, or beside it in matters of faith or worship": therefore they consider the right of private judgment, in all matters that respect religion, as universal and unalienable; they do not even wish to see any religious constitution aided by the civil power, further than may be necessary for protection and security, and, at the same time, be equal and common to all others.

II. That, in perfect consistency with the above principle of common right, every Christian church, or union, or association of particular churches, is entitled to declare the terms of admission into its *communion*, and the qualifications of its ministers and members, as well as the whole system of its internal government which Christ hath appointed; that in the exercise of this right, they may, notwithstanding, err in making the terms of communion either too lax or too narrow; yet even in this case they do not infringe upon the liberty or the rights of others, but only make an improper use of their own.

III. That our blessed Saviour, for the edification of the visible Church, which is his body, hath appointed officers, not only to preach the Gospel *and administer the sacraments*, but also to exercise discipline for the preservation both of truth and duty; and that it is incumbent upon these *officers* and upon the whole Church in whose names they act, to censure or cast out the erroneous and scandalous; observing in all cases the rules contained in the word of God.

IV. That truth is in order to goodness, and the great touchstone of truth, its tendency to promote holiness; according to our Saviour's rule, " by their fruits ye shall know them." And that no opinion can be either more pernicious or absurd than that which brings truth and falsehood upon a level, and represents it as of no consequence what a man's opinions are. On the contrary, they are persuaded that there is an inseparable connection between faith and practice, truth and duty. Otherwise it would be of no consequence either to discover truth or to embrace it.

V. That while, under the conviction of the above principle, they think it necessary to make effectual provisions that all who are admitted as teachers be sound in the faith, they also believe that there are truths and forms with respect to which men of good characters and principles may differ. And, in all these, they think it the duty, both of private Christians and societies, to exercise mutual forbearance toward each other.

VI. That though the character, qualifications and

authority, of church officers are laid down in the Holy Scriptures, as well as the proper method of their investiture and institution, yet the election of the persons to the exercise of this authority, in any particular society, is in that society.

VII. That all church-power, whether exercised by the body in general, or in the way of representation by delegated authority, is only ministerial and declarative: *that is to say*, that the Holy Scriptures are the only rule of faith and manners; that no church judicatory ought to pretend to make laws to bind the conscience in virtue of their own authority, and that all their decisions should be founded upon the revealed will of God. Now, though it will easily be admitted that all synods and councils may err, through the frailty inseparable from humanity, yet there is much greater danger from the usurped claim of making laws than from the right of judging upon laws already made and common to all who profess the Gospel, although this right, as necessity requires in the present state, be lodged with fallible man.

VIII. *Lastly*, That if the preceding scriptural and rational principles be steadfastly adhered to, the vigor and strictness of its discipline will contribute to the glory and happiness of any Church. Since ecclesiastical discipline must be purely moral or spiritual in its object, and not attended with any civil effects, it can derive no force whatever, but from its own justice, the approbation of an impartial public, and the countenance and blessing of the Great Head of the Church Universal.

XI. THE TERMS OF SUBSCRIPTION REQUIRED OF CANDIDATES FOR ORDINATION IN THE PRESBYTERIAN CHURCH SINCE 1788.

1. Do you believe the Scriptures of the Old and New Testaments to be the word of God, the only infallible rule of faith and practice?

2. Do you sincerely receive and adopt the Confession of Faith of this Church as containing the system of doctrine taught in the Holy Scriptures?

3. Do you approve of the government and discipline of the Presbyterian Church in these United States?

4. Do you promise subjection to your brethren in the Lord?

5. Have you been induced, as far as you know your own heart, to seek the office of the holy ministry from love to God, and a sincere desire to promote his glory in the gospel of his Son?

6. Do you promise to be zealous and faithful in maintaining the truths of the gospel and the purity and peace of the Church, whatever persecution or opposition may arise unto you on that account?

7. Do you engage to be faithful and diligent in the exercise of all private and personal duties which become you as a Christian and a minister of the gospel, as well as in all relative duties and the public duties of your office, endeavoring to adorn the profession of the gospel by your conversation, and walking with exemplary piety before the flock over which God shall make you overseer?

8. Are you now willing to take the charge of this congregation, agreeably to your declaration at accepting their call? And do you promise to discharge the duties of a pastor to them as God shall give you strength?

XII. THE PLAN OF UNION OF 1801.

Regulations adopted by the General Assembly of the Presbyterian Church in America, and by the General Association of the State of Connecticut with a view to prevent alienation and promote union and harmony, in those new settlements which are composed of inhabitants from those bodies.

1st. It is strictly enjoined on all their missionaries to the new settlements, to endeavor by all proper means, to promote mutual forbearance and accommodation, between those inhabitants of the new settlements who hold the Presbyterian, and those who hold the Congregational form of Church government.

2d. If in the new settlements, any Church of the Congregational order, shall settle a minister of the Presbyterian order, that Church may, if they choose, still conduct their discipline according to Congregational principles, settling their difficulties among themselves, or by a council mutually agreed upon for that purpose. But if any difficulty shall exist between the minister and the Church or any member of it, it shall be referred to the Presbytery to which the minister shall belong, provided both parties agree to it; if not, to a council consisting of an equal number of Presbyterians and Congregationalists, agreed upon by both parties.

3d. If a Presbyterian Church shall settle a minister of Congregational principles, that Church may still conduct their discipline according to Presbyterian principles; excepting that if a difficulty arise between him and his Church, or any member of it, the cause shall be tried by the Association to which the said minister shall belong, provided both parties agree to it; otherwise by a council, one half Congregationalists and the other half Presbyterians, mutually agreed on by the parties.

4th. If any congregation consist partly of those who hold the Congregational form of discipline, and partly of those who hold the Presbyterian form, we recommend to both parties, that this be no obstruction to their uniting in one church and settling a minister; and that, in this case, the Church choose a standing committee from the communicants of said church, whose business it shall be, to call to account every member of the church, who shall conduct himself inconsistently with the laws of Christianity, and to give judgment on such conduct; and if the person condemned by their judgment be a Presbyterian, he shall have liberty to appeal to the Presbytery; if a Congregationalist, he shall have liberty to appeal to the body of the male communicants of the church; in the former case, the determination of the Presbytery shall be final, unless the Church consent to a further appeal to the Synod, or to the General Assembly; and in the latter case, if the party condemned shall wish for a trial by a mutual council, the cause shall be referred to such council. And provided the said standing committee of any church shall depute one of themselves to attend the Presbytery, he may have the same right to sit and act in the Presbytery, as a ruling elder of the Presbyterian Church.

On motion, RESOLVED, That an attested copy of the above Plan be made by the stated clerk, and put into the hands of the delegates of this Assembly to the General Association, to be by them laid before that body for their consideration; and that if it should be approved by them, it go into immediate operation.

XIII. THE EXSCINDING ACTS OF 1837.

(a) *Resolutions as to Relations existing between the Presbyterian and Congregational Churches.*

1. "That between these two branches of the American Church, there ought, in the judgment of this Assembly, to be maintained sentiments of mutual respect and esteem, and for that purpose no reasonable efforts should be omitted to preserve a perfectly good understanding between these branches of the Church of Christ.

2. "That it is expedient to continue the plan of friendly intercourse between this Church and the Congregational Churches of New England, as it now exists.

3. "But as the 'Plan of Union' adopted for the new settlements, in 1801, was originally an unconstitutional act on the part of that Assembly—these important standing rules having never been submitted to the Presbyteries —and as they were totally destitute of authority as proceeding from the General Association of Connecticut, which

is invested with no power to legislate in such cases, and especially to enact laws to regulate churches not within her limits; and as much confusion and irregularity have arisen from this unnatural and unconstitutional system of union, therefore, it is resolved, that the Act of the Assembly of 1801, entitled a 'Plan of Union,' be, and the same is hereby abrogated."

(*b*) *Excision of the Plan-of-Union Synods.*

" Resolved, That by the operation of the abrogation of the Plan of Union of 1801, the Synod of the Western Reserve is, and is hereby declared to be, no longer a part of the Presbyterian Church in the United States of America."

———

" (1) Resolved, That in consequence of the abrogation by this Assembly of the Plan of Union of 1801, between it and the General Association of Connecticut, as utterly unconstitutional, and therefore null and void from the beginning, the Synods of Utica, Geneva, and Genesee, which were formed and attached to this body under and in execution of said ' Plan of Union,' be, and are hereby declared to be out of the ecclesiastical connection of the Presbyterian Church in the United States of America, and that they are not in form and in fact an integral portion of said Church.

" (2) That the solicitude of this Assembly on the whole subject, and its urgency for the immediate decision of it, are greatly increased by reason of the gross disorders which are ascertained to have prevailed in those Synods, (as well as that of the Western Reserve, against which a declarative resolution, similar to the first of these, has been passed during our present sessions,) it being made clear to us, that even the Plan of Union itself was never consistently carried into effect by those professing to act under it.

" (3) That the General Assembly has no intention, by these resolutions, or by that passed in the case of the Synod of the Western Reserve, to affect in any way the ministerial standing of any members of either of said Synods; nor to disturb the pastoral relation in any Church; nor to interfere with the duties or relations of private Christians in their respective congregations; but only to declare and determine, according to the truth and necessity of the case, and by virtue of the full authority existing in it for that purpose, the relation of all said Synods, and all their constituent parts to this body, and to the Presbyterian Church in the United States.

" (4) That inasmuch as there are reported to be several churches and ministers, if not one or two Presbyteries, now in connection with one or more of said Synods, which are strictly Presbyterian in doctrine and order, be it, therefore, further resolved that all such churches and ministers as wish to unite with us, are hereby directed to apply for admission into those Presbyteries belonging to our connection which are most convenient to their respective locations; and that any such Presbytery as aforesaid, being strictly Presbyterian in doctrine and order, and now in connection with either of said Synods, as may desire to unite with us, are hereby directed to make application, with a full statement of their cases, to the next General Assembly, which will take proper order thereon."

XIV. THE AUBURN DECLARATION OF 1837, STATING THE "TRUE DOCTRINES" OF THE NEW-SCHOOL MEN OVER AGAINST THE "ERRORS" CHARGED ON THEM IN THE OLD-SCHOOL MEMORIAL OF THAT YEAR.

FIRST ERROR. " That God would have prevented the existence of sin in our world, but was not able, without destroying the moral agency of man; or, that for aught that appears in the Bible to the contrary, sin is incidental to any wise moral system."

TRUE DOCTRINE. God permitted the introduction of sin, not because he was unable to prevent it, consistently with the moral freedom of his creatures, but for wise and benevolent reasons which he has not revealed.

SECOND ERROR. " That election to eternal life is founded on a foresight of faith and obedience."

TRUE DOCTRINE. Election to eternal life is not founded on a foresight of faith and obedience, but is a sovereign act of God's mercy, whereby, according to the counsel of his own will, he has chosen some to salvation ; " yet so as thereby neither is violence offered to the will of the creatures, nor is the liberty or contingency of second causes taken away, but rather established ;" nor does this gracious purpose ever take effect independently of faith and a holy life.

THIRD ERROR. " That we have no more to do with the first sin of Adam than with the sins of any other parent."

TRUE DOCTRINE. By a divine constitution, Adam was so the head and representative of the race, that, as a consequence of his transgression, all mankind become morally corrupt, and liable to death, temporal and eternal.

FOURTH ERROR. " That infants come into the world as free from moral defilement as was Adam when he was created."

TRUE DOCTRINE. Adam was created in the image of God, endowed with knowledge, righteousness, and true holiness. Infants come into the world, not only destitute of these, but with a nature inclined to evil and only evil.

FIFTH ERROR. " That infants sustain the same relation to the moral government of God, in this world, as brute animals, and that their sufferings and death are to be accounted for on the same principles as those of brutes, and not by any means to be considered as penal."

TRUE DOCTRINE. Brute animals sustain no such relation to the moral government of God as does the

human family. Infants are a part of the human family;
and their sufferings and death are to be accounted for on
the ground of their being involved in the general moral
ruin of the race induced by the apostacy.

SIXTH ERROR. "That there is no other original sin
than the fact, that all the posterity of Adam, though by
nature innocent, will always begin to sin when they begin
to exercise moral agency; that original sin does not include a sinful bias of the human mind, and a just exposure
to penal suffering; and that there is no evidence in Scripture, that infants, in order to salvation, do need redemption by the blood of Christ, and regeneration by the Holy
Ghost."

TRUE DOCTRINE. Original sin is a natural bias to
evil, resulting from the first apostacy, leading invariably
and certainly to actual transgression. And all infants, as
well as adults, in order to be saved, need redemption by
the blood of Christ, and regeneration by the Holy Ghost.

SEVENTH ERROR. "That the doctrine of imputation, whether of the guilt of Adam's sin, or of the righteousness of Christ, has no foundation in the Word of God,
and is both unjust and absurd."

TRUE DOCTRINE. The sin of Adam is not imputed
to his posterity in the sense of a literal transfer of personal qualities, acts, and demerit; but by reason of the
sin of Adam, in his peculiar relation, the race are treated
as if they had sinned. Nor is the righteousness of Christ
imputed to his people in the sense of a literal transfer of
personal qualities, acts, and merit; but by reason of his
righteousness, in his peculiar relation, they are treated as
if they were righteous.

EIGHTH ERROR. "That the sufferings and death of
Christ were not truly vicarious and penal, but symbolical,
governmental, and instructive only."

TRUE DOCTRINE. The sufferings and death of Christ
were not symbolical, governmental, and instructive only,

but were truly vicarious, *i.e.* a substitute for the punishment due to transgressors. And while Christ did not suffer the literal penalty of the law, involving remorse of conscience and the pains of hell, he did offer a sacrifice, which infinite wisdom saw to be a full equivalent. And by virtue of this atonement, overtures of mercy are sincerely made to the race, and salvation secured to all who believe.

NINTH ERROR. " That the impenitent sinner is by nature, and independently of the renewing influence or almighty energy of the Holy Spirit, in full possession of all the ability necessary to a full compliance with all the commands of God."

TRUE DOCTRINE. While sinners have all the faculties necessary to a perfect moral agency and a just accountability, such is their love of sin and opposition to God and his law, that, independently of the renewing influence or almighty energy of the Holy Spirit, they never will comply with the commands of God.

TENTH ERROR. " That Christ does not intercede for the elect until after their regeneration."

TRUE DOCTRINE. The intercession of Christ for the elect is previous as well as subsequent to their regeneration, as appears from the following Scripture, viz. " I pray not for the world, but for them which thou hast given me, for they are thine. Neither pray I for these alone, but for them also which shall believe on me through their word."

ELEVENTH ERROR. " That saving faith is not an effect of the operations of the Holy Spirit, but a mere rational belief of the truth or assent to the word of God."

TRUE DOCTRINE. Saving faith is an intelligent and cordial assent to the testimony of God concerning his Son, implying reliance on Christ alone for pardon and eternal life ; and in all cases it is an effect of the special operations of the Holy Spirit.

TWELFTH ERROR. "That regeneration is the act of the sinner himself, and that it consists in change of his governing purpose, which he himself must produce, and which is the result, not of any direct influence of the Holy Spirit on the heart, but chiefly of a persuasive exhibition of the truth, analogous to the influence which one man exerts over the mind of another; or that regeneration is not an instantaneous act, but a progressive work."

TRUE DOCTRINE. Regeneration is a radical change of heart, produced by the special operations of the Holy Spirit, "determining the sinner to that which is good," and is in all cases instantaneous.

THIRTEENTH ERROR. "That God has done all that *he can do* for the salvation of all men, and that man himself must do the rest."

TRUE DOCTRINE. While repentance for sin and faith in Christ are indispensable to salvation, all who are saved are indebted from first to last to the grace and Spirit of God. And the reason that God does not save all, is not that he wants the *power* to do it, but that in his wisdom he does not see fit to exert that power further than he actually does.

FOURTEENTH ERROR. "That God cannot exert such influence on the minds of men, as shall make it certain that they will choose and act in a particular manner, without impairing their moral agency."

TRUE DOCTRINE. While the liberty of the will is not impaired, nor the established connexion betwixt means and end broken by any action of God on the mind, he can influence it according to his pleasure, and does effectually determine it to good in all cases of true conversion.

FIFTEENTH ERROR. "That the righteousness of Christ is not the sole ground of the sinner's acceptance with God; and that in no sense does the righteousness of Christ become ours."

TRUE DOCTRINE. All believers are justified, not on

the ground of personal merit, but solely on the ground of the obedience and death, or, in other words, the righteousness of Christ. And while that righteousness does not become theirs, in the sense of a literal transfer of personal qualities and merit; yet, from respect to it, God can and does treat them as if they were righteous.

SIXTEENTH ERROR. " That the reason why some differ from others in regard to their reception of the Gospel is, that they make themselves to differ."

TRUE DOCTRINE. While all such as reject the Gospel of Christ do it, not by coercion but freely—and all who embrace it do it, not by coercion but freely—the reason why some differ from others is, that *God* has made them to differ.

XV. DELIVERANCES ON SLAVERY.

(1) *The Synod of New York and Philadelphia in* 1787.

The Synod of New York and Philadelphia do highly approve of the general principles in favour of universal liberty, that prevail in America, and the interest which many of the states have taken in promoting the abolition of slavery; yet, inasmuch as men introduced from a servile state to a participation of all the privileges of civil society, without a proper education, and without previous habits of industry, may be, in many respects, dangerous to the community, therefore they earnestly recommend it to all the members belonging to their communion, to give those persons who are at present held in servitude, such good education as to prepare them for the better enjoyment of freedom; and they moreover recommend that masters, wherever they find servants disposed to make a just improvement of the privilege, would give them a *peculium*, or grant them sufficient time and sufficient means of procuring their own liberty at a moderate rate, that thereby they may be brought into society with those habits of industry that may render them useful citizens; and, finally, they recommend it to all their people to use the most prudent measures, consistent with the interest and the state of civil society, in the counties where they live, to procure eventually the final abolition of slavery in America.

(2) *The Reformed Presbytery in* 1800.

[This I have not been able to procure, but its terms made the abandonment of slave-holding a prerequisite to church communion.]

(3) *The Associate Synod in* 1811.

1. That it is a moral evil to hold negroes or their children in perpetual slavery; or to claim the right of buying and selling, or bequeathing them as transferable property.

2. That in those States where the liberation of slaves is rendered impracticable by the existing laws, it is the duty of the holders of slaves to treat them with as much justice as if they were liberated; to give them suitable food and clothing; to have them taught to read, and instructed in the principles of religion; and when their services may justly deserve it, to give them additional compensation.

3. That those slave-holders who refuse to renounce the above claim and to treat their slaves in the manner now specified, are unworthy of being admitted into or retained in the fellowship of the Church of Christ. . . .

5. That it is the special duty of sessions to see that the above regulations be faithfully acted upon.

That it is lawful for persons in our communion to purchase negroes from those who are holding them in absolute and perpetual slavery, with a view to retain them in their service until they are recompensed for the money laid out in the purchase of said slaves, provided it be done with the consent of the negroes themselves, and that, in the meantime, they be treated according to the second resolution.

But before they be acted upon by any session, care shall be taken in every congregation where the application of them is requisite, not only to have the people apprized, but instructed in the moral evil of slave-holding here contemplated.

(4) *The General Assembly in* 1818.

The General Assembly of the Presbyterian Church having taken into consideration the subject of SLAVERY, think proper to make known their sentiments upon it to the churches and people under their care.

We consider the voluntary enslaving of one part of the human race by another, as a gross violation of the most precious and sacred rights of human nature; as utterly inconsistent with the law of God, which requires us to love our neighbour as ourselves; and as totally irreconcilable with the spirit and principles of the Gospel of Christ, which enjoin that, " all things whatsoever ye would that men should do to you, do ye even so to them." Slavery creates a paradox in the moral system—it exhibits rational, accountable, and immortal beings, in such circumstances as scarcely to leave them the power of moral action. It exhibits them as dependent on the will of others, whether they shall receive religious instruction; whether they shall know and worship the true God; whether they shall enjoy the ordinances of the Gospel; whether they shall perform the duties and cherish the endearments of husbands and wives, parents and children, neighbours and friends; whether they shall preserve their chastity and purity, or regard the dictates of justice and humanity. Such are some of the consequences of Slavery,—consequences not imaginary—but which connect themselves with its very existence. The evils to which the slave is *always* exposed, often take place in fact, and in their very worst degree and form; and where all of them do not take place, as we rejoice to say that in many instances, through the influence of the principles of humanity and religion on the minds of masters, they do not—still the slave is deprived of his natural right, degraded as a human being, and exposed to the danger of passing into the hands of a master who may inflict upon him all the hardships and injuries which inhumanity and avarice may suggest.

From this view of the consequences resulting from the practice into which christian people have most inconsistently fallen, of enslaving a portion of their *brethren* of mankind—for " God hath made of one blood all nations of men to dwell on the face of the earth "—it is manifestly the duty of all christians who enjoy the light of the present day, when the inconsistency of slavery, both with the dictates of humanity and religion, has been demonstrated, and is generally seen and acknowledged, to use their honest, earnest, and unwearied endeavors, to correct the errors of former times, and as speedily as possible to efface this blot on our holy religion, and to obtain the complete abolition of slavery throughout christendom, and if possible throughout the world.

We rejoice that the church to which we belong commenced, as early as any other in this country, the good work of endeavouring to put an end to slavery, and that in the same work many of its members have ever since been, and now are, among the most active, vigorous, and efficient labourers. We do, indeed, tenderly sympathize with those portions of our church and our country, where the evil of slavery has been entailed upon them; where a *great*, and *the most virtuous part* of the *community* abhor slavery, and wish its extermination, as sincerely as any others—but where the number of slaves, their ignorance, and their vicious habits generally, render an immediate and universal emancipation inconsistent, alike, with the safety and happiness of the master and the slave. With those who are thus circumstanced, we repeat that we tenderly sympathize.—At the same time, we earnestly exhort them to continue, and, if possible, to increase their

exertions to effect a total abolition of slavery.—We exhort them to suffer no greater delay to take place in this
most interesting concern, than a regard to the public welfare *truly* and *indispensably* demands.

As our country has inflicted a most grievous injury on
the unhappy Africans, by bringing them into slavery, we
cannot, indeed, urge that we should add a second injury
to the first, by emancipating them in such manner as that
they will be likely to destroy themselves or others.   But
we do think, that our country ought to be governed in
this matter, by no other consideration than an honest and
impartial regard to the happiness of the injured party;
uninfluenced by the expense or inconvenience which such
a regard may involve.   We therefore warn all who belong to our denomination of christians, against unduly extending this plea of necessity; against making it a cover
for the love and practice of slavery, or a pretence for not
using efforts that are lawful and practicable, to extinguish
the evil.

And we, at the same time, exhort others to forbear harsh
censures, and uncharitable reflections on their brethren,
who unhappily live among slaves, whom they cannot immediately set free; but who, at the same time, are really
using all their influence, and all their endeavours, to bring
them into a state of freedom, as soon as a door for it can
be safely opened.

Having thus expressed our views of slavery, and of the
duty indispensably incumbent on all christians to labour
for its complete extinction, we proceed to recommend—
(and we do it with all the earnestness and solemnity which
this momentous subject demands)—a particular attention
to the following points.

1. We recommend to all our people to patronize and
encourage the Society, lately formed, for colonizing in
Africa, the land of their ancestors, the free people of colour
in our country.   We hope that much good may result
from the plans and efforts of this Society.   And while we
exceedingly rejoice to have witnessed its origin and organ-

ization among the *holders of slaves*, as giving an unequivocal pledge of their desire to deliver themselves and their country from the calamity of slavery ; we hope that those portions of the American Union, whose inhabitants are, by a gracious Providence, more favorably circumstanced, will cordially, and liberally, and earnestly co-operate with their brethren, in bringing about the great end contemplated.

2. We recommend to all the members of our religious denomination, not only to permit, but to facilitate and encourage the instruction of their slaves, in the principles and duties of the christian religion ; by granting them liberty to attend on the preaching of the gospel, when they have the opportunity ; by favouring the instruction of them in Sabbath Schools, wherever those Schools can be formed ; and by giving them all other proper advantages for acquiring the knowledge of their duty both to God and man. We are perfectly satisfied, that as it is incumbent on all christians to communicate religious instruction to those who are under their authority, so that the doing of this in the case before us, so far from operating, as some have apprehended that it might, as an excitement to insubordination and insurrection, would, on the contrary, operate as the most powerful means for the prevention of those evils.

3. We enjoin it on all Church Sessions and Presbyteries, under the care of this Assembly, to discountenance, and, as far as possible, to prevent, all cruelty of whatever kind in the treatment of slaves ; especially the cruelty of separating husband and wife, parents and children, and that which consists in selling slaves to those who will either themselves deprive these unhappy people of the blessings of the Gospel, or who will transport them to places where the Gospel is not proclaimed, or where it is forbidden to slaves to attend upon its institutions.—The manifest violation or disregard of the injunction here given, in its true spirit and intention, ought to be considered as just ground for the discipline and censures of the church.—And if it shall ever happen that a christian pro-

fessor, in our communion, shall sell a slave who is also in communion and good standing with our church, contrary to his or her will, and inclination, it ought immediately to claim the particular attention of the proper church judicature; and unless there be such peculiar circumstances attending the case as can but seldom happen, it ought to be followed, without delay, by a suspension of the offender from all the privileges of the church, till he repent, and make all the reparation in his power, to the injured party.

(5) *The Associate Reformed Synod in* 1830.

RESOLVED, 1. That the religion of Christ Jesus requires that involuntary slavery should be removed from the Church, as soon as an opportunity, in the providence of God, is offered to slave-owners for the liberation of their slaves.

2. That when there are no regulations of the State to prohibit it; when provision can be made for the support of the freedmen; when they can be placed in circumstances to support the rank, enjoy the rights and discharge the duties of freedmen, it shall be considered that such an opportunity is afforded in the providence of God.

3. That Synod will, as it hereby does, recommend it to all its members to aid in placing the slaves that are within the jurisdiction of this Synod in the possession of their rights as freedmen; and that it be recommended to them especially to take up annual collections, to aid the funds of the American society for colonizing the free people of color of the United States.

4. That the practice of buying or selling of slaves for gain, by any member of this Church, be disapproved, and that slave-owners under the jurisdiction of this Synod, be, as they hereby are, forbidden all aggravations of the evils of slavery, by violating the ties of nature, in the separation of husband and wife, parents and children, or by cruel or unkind treatment; and that they shall not only treat them well, but also instruct them in useful knowl-

edge and the principles of the Christian religion, and in all respects treat them as enjoined upon masters towards their servants by the apostles of our Lord Jesus Christ.

(6) *The Synod of Associate Church in* 1831.

RESOLVED, 1. That as slavery is clearly condemned by the law of God, and has been long since judicially declared to be a moral evil by this Church, no member thereof shall, from and after this date, be allowed to hold a human being in the character or condition of a slave.

2. That this Synod do hereby order all its subordinate judicatories to proceed forthwith to carry into execution the intention of the foregoing resolution, by requiring those church members under their immediate inspection, who may *be possessed of slaves*, to relinquish their unjust claims, and release those whom they may have heretofore considered as their property.

3. That if any member or members of this Church, in order to evade this act, shall sell any of their slaves, or make a transfer of them, so as to retain the proceeds of their services, or the price of their sale, or in any other way evade the provisions of this act, they shall be subject to the censures of the Church.

4. Further, that where an individual is found, who has spent so much of his or her strength in the service of another, as to be disqualified from providing for his or her own support, the master, in such a case, is to be held responsible for the comfortable maintenance of said servants.

(7) *The General Assembly (O. S.) in* 1845.

The question which is now unhappily agitating and dividing other branches of the church, and which is pressed upon the attention of the Assembly is, whether the holding of slaves is, under all circumstances, a heinous sin, calling for the discipline of the church.

The church of Christ is a spiritual body, whose jurisdiction extends only to the religious faith, and moral conduct of her members. She cannot legislate where Christ has not legislated, nor make terms of membership which he has not made. The question, therefore, which this Assembly is called upon to decide, is this: Do the Scriptures teach that the holding of slaves, without regard to circumstances, is a sin, the renunciation of which should be made a condition of membership in the church of Christ.

It is impossible to answer this question in the affirmative, without contradicting some of the plainest declarations of the word of God. That slavery existed in the days of Christ and his Apostles is an admitted fact. That they did not denounce the relation itself as sinful, as inconsistent with Christianity; that slaveholders were admitted to membership in the churches organized by the Apostles; that whilst they were required to treat their slaves with kindness, and as rational, accountable, immortal beings, and if Christians, as brethren in the Lord, they were not commanded to emancipate them; that slaves were required to be "obedient to their masters according to the flesh, with fear and trembling, with singleness of heart as unto Christ," are facts which meet the eye of every reader of the New Testament. This Assembly cannot, therefore, denounce the holding of slaves as necessarily a heinous and scandalous sin, calculated to bring upon the Church the curse of God, without charging the Apostles of Christ with conniving at such sin, introducing into the Church such sinners, and thus bringing upon them the curse of the Almighty.

In so saying, however, the Assembly are not to be understood as denying that there is evil connected with slavery. Much less do they approve those defective and oppressive laws by which, in some of the States, it is regulated. Nor would they by any means countenance the traffic in slaves for the sake of gain; the separation of husbands and wives, parents and children, for the sake of "filthy lucre" or for the convenience of the master; or cruel treatment of slaves in any respect. Every Christian and philanthropist certainly should seek by all peaceable and lawful means the repeal of unjust and oppressive laws, and the amendment of such as are defective, so as to protect the slaves from cruel treatment by wicked men, and secure to them the right to receive religious instruction.

Nor is this Assembly to be understood as countenancing the idea that masters may regard their servants as *mere property*, and not as human beings, rational, accountable, immortal. The Scriptures prescribe not only the duties of servants, but of masters also, warning the latter to discharge those duties, "knowing that their Master is in heaven, neither is there respect of persons with him."

The Assembly intend simply to say, that since Christ and his inspired Apostles did not make the holding of slaves a bar to communion, we, as a court of Christ, have no authority to do so; since they did not attempt to remove it from the Church by legislation, we have no authority to legislate on the subject. We feel constrained, further, to say, that however desirable it may be to ameliorate the condition of the slaves in the Southern and Western States, or to remove slavery from our country, these objects we are fully persuaded can never be secured by ecclesiastical legislation. Much less can they be attained by those indiscriminate denunciations against slaveholders, without regard to their character or circumstances, which have, to so great an extent, characterized the movements of modern abolitionists, which, so far from removing the evils complained of, tend only to perpetuate and aggravate them.

The Apostles of Christ sought to ameliorate the condition of slaves, not by denouncing and excommunicating their masters, but by teaching both masters and slaves the glorious doctrines of the gospel, and enjoining upon each the discharge of their relative duties. Thus only can the church of Christ, as such, now improve the condition of the slaves in our country.

As to the extent of the evils involved in slavery and the best methods of removing them, various opinions prevail, and neither Scriptures nor our constitution authorize this body to prescribe any particular course to be pursued by the churches under our care. The Assembly cannot but rejoice, however, to learn that the ministers and churches in the slave-holding States are awaking to a deeper sense of their obligation to extend to the slave population generally the means of grace, and many slave-holders not professedly religious favour this object. We earnestly exhort them to abound more and more in this good work. We would exhort every believing master to remember that his Master is also in heaven, and in view of all the circumstances in which he is placed, to act in the spirit of the golden rule: " Whatsoever ye would that men should do to you, do ye even the same to them."

In view of the above stated principles and facts—

RESOLVED, 1st. That the General Assembly of the Presbyterian Church in the United States was originally organized, and has since continued the bond of union in the Church upon the conceded principle that the existence of domestic slavery, under the circumstances in which it is found in the southern portion of the country, is no bar to Christian communion.

2d. That the petitions that ask the Assembly to make the holding of slaves in itself a matter of discipline, do virtually require this judicatory to dissolve itself, and abandon the organization under which, by the Divine blessing, it has so long prospered. The tendency is evidently to separate the northern from the southern portion of the Church; a result which every good citizen must deplore as tending to the dissolution of the union of our beloved country, and which every enlightened Christian will oppose as bringing about a ruinous and unnecessary schism between brethren who maintain a common faith.

(8) *The General Assembly* (*N. S.*) *in* 1850.

We exceedingly deplore the working of the whole system of slavery as it exists in our country and is interwoven with the political institutions of the slave-holding States, as fraught with many and great evils to the civil, political, and moral interests of those regions where it exists.

The holding of our fellow-men in the condition of slavery, except in those cases where it is unavoidable, by the laws of the State, the obligations of guardianship, or the demands of humanity, is an offence in the proper import of that term, as used in the Book of Discipline, chap. i. sec. 3, and should be regarded and treated in the same manner as other offences.

The sessions and presbyteries are, by the Constitution of our church, the courts of primary jurisdiction for the trial of offences.

That, after this declaration of sentiment, the whole subject of slavery, as it exists in the church, be referred to the sessions and presbyteries, to take such action thereon as in their judgment the laws of Christianity require.

(9) *The General Assembly (N. S.) in* 1853.

1. That this body reaffirm the doctrine of the 2d resolution adopted by the Assembly in its action at Detroit in 1850.

2. That we do earnestly exhort and beseech all those who are happily free from any personal connection with the institution of slavery, to exercise patience and forbearance toward their brethren less favoured in this respect than themselves, remembering the embarrassments of their position; and to cherish for them that fraternal confidence and love which they the more need in consequence of the peculiar trials by which they are surrounded.

3. To correct misapprehensions which may exist in many Northern minds, and allay causeless irritation, by having the real facts in relation to this subject spread before the whole church, it is recommended earnestly to request the presbyteries in each of the slave-holding States to take such measures as may seem to them most expe-

dient and proper, for laying before the next Assembly, in its sessions at Philadelphia, distinct and full statements touching the following points:—

(1) The number of slave-holders in connection with the churches under their jurisdiction, and the number of slaves held by them.

(2) The extent to which slaves are held by an unavoidable necessity "imposed by the laws of the States, the obligations of guardianship, and the demands of humanity."

(3) Whether a practical regard, such as the word of God requires, is evinced by the Southern churches for the sacredness of the conjugal and parental relations as they exist among slaves; whether baptism is duly administered to the children of slaves professing Christianity; whether slaves are admitted to equal privileges and powers in the church courts; and, in general, to what extent and in what manner provision is made for the religious well-being of the enslaved.

XVI. DOCTRINAL BASIS OF THE UNION OF 1858, FORMING THE UNITED PRESBYTERIAN CHURCH.

I. *We declare*, That God has not only in the Scriptures of the Old and New Testaments made a revelation of his will to man, as the only rule of faith and practice, but that these Scriptures, viewed as a revelation from God, are in every part the inspired word of God, and that this inspiration extends to the language, as well as to the sentiments which they express.

II. *We declare*, That our Lord Jesus Christ is not only true and Supreme God, being one in essence with the Father, but also the Son of God, in respect of his natural, necessary, and eternal relation to the Father.

III. *We declare*, That God having created man in a state of perfect holiness, and in possession of a perfect ability to obey him in all things, did enter into a covenant with him, in which covenant Adam was the representative of all his natural posterity, so that in him they were to stand or fall, as he stood or fell.

IV. *We declare*, That our first parents did, by their breach of covenant with God, subject themselves to his eternal wrath, and bring themselves into such a state of depravity as to be wholly inclined to sin, and altogether unable, by their own power, to perform a single act of acceptable obedience to God; and that all their natural posterity, in virtue of their representation in the covenant, are born into the world in the same state of guilt, depravity, and inability, and in this state will continue until delivered therefrom by the grace and righteousness of the Lord Jesus Christ.

V. *We declare*, That our Lord Jesus Christ did, by the appointment of the Father, and by his own gracious and voluntary act, place himself in the room of a definite number, who were chosen in him before the foundation of the world; so that he was their true and proper legal surety; and as such, did, in their behalf, satisfy the justice of God, and answer all the demands which the law had against them, and thereby infallibly obtain for them eternal redemption.

VI. *We declare*, That in justification there is an imputation to the believer of that righteousness, or satisfaction and obedience, which the Lord Jesus Christ, as the surety of his people, rendered to the law; and that it is only on the ground of this imputed righteousness that his sins are pardoned, and his person accepted in the sight of God.

VII. *We declare*, That the gospel, taken in its strict and proper sense, as distinguished from the law, is a revelation of grace to sinners as such; and that it contains a free and unconditional offer and grant of salvation through Christ, to all who hear it, whatever may be their character or condition.

VIII. *We declare*, That in true and saving faith there is not merely an assent of the mind to the proposition that the Lord Jesus Christ is the Saviour of sinners; but also a cordial reception and appropriation of him by the sinner as his Saviour, with an accompanying persuasion or assurance corresponding to the degree or strength of his faith, that he shall be saved by him; which appropriation and persuasion are founded, solely, upon the free, and unconditional, and unlimited offer of Christ and salvation in him, which God makes in the gospel to sinners of mankind.

IX. *We declare*, That the repentance which is a saving grace, is one of the *fruits* of a justifying faith; and, of course, cannot be regarded as a ground of the sinner's pardon, or as necessary to qualify him for coming to Christ.

X. *We declare*, That although the moral law is of perpetual obligation, and consequently does and ever will bind the believer as a rule of life, yet as a covenant, he is, by his justification through Christ, completely and forever set free from it, both as to its commanding and condemning power, and consequently not required to yield obedience to it as a condition of life and salvation.

XI. *We declare*, That the Holy Spirit, the third person of the Trinity, does, by a direct operation accompanying the word, so act upon the soul as to quicken, regenerate, and sanctify it; and that without this direct operation, the soul would have no ability to perceive, in a saving manner, the truths of God's word, or yield to the motives which it presents.

XII. *We declare*, That our Lord Jesus Christ, besides the dominion which belongs to him as God, has, as our God-man Mediator, a twofold dominion, with which he has been invested by the Father as the reward of his sufferings. These are a dominion over the Church, of which he is the living Head and Lawgiver, and the source of all that Divine influence and authority by which she is sustained and governed; and also a dominion over all created persons and things, which is exercised by him in subserviency to the manifestations of God's glory in the system of redemption, and the interests of his Church.

XIII. *We declare*, That the law of God, as written upon

the heart of man, and as set forth in the Scriptures of the Old and New Testaments, is supreme in its authority and obligations; and that where the commands of the Church or State are in conflict with the commands of this law, we are to obey God rather than man.

XIV. *We declare,* That slaveholding—that is, the holding of unoffending human beings in involuntary bondage, and considering and treating them as property, and subject to be bought and sold—is a violation of the law of God, and contrary both to the letter and spirit of Christianity.

XV. *We declare,* That all associations, whether formed for political or benevolent purposes, which impose upon their members an oath of secrecy, or an obligation to obey a code of unknown laws, are inconsistent with the genius and spirit of Christianity, and Church members ought not to have fellowship with such associations.

XVI. *We declare,* That the Church should not extend communion, in sealing ordinances, to those who refuse adherence to her profession, or subjection to her government and discipline, or who refuse to forsake a communion which is inconsistent with the profession that she makes; nor should communion in any ordinance of worship be held under such circumstances as would be inconsistent with the keeping of these ordinances pure and entire, or so as to give countenance to any corruption of the doctrines and institutions of Christ.

XVII. *We declare,* That public social covenanting is a moral duty, the observance of which is not required at stated times, but on extraordinary occasions, as the providence of God and the circumstances of the Church may indicate. It is seasonable in times of great danger to the Church—in times of exposure to backsliding—or in times of reformation, when the Church is returning to God from a state of backsliding. When the Church has entered into such covenant transactions, they continue to bind posterity faithfully to adhere to and prosecute the grand object for which such engagements have been entered into.

XVIII. *We declare,* That it is the will of God that the

songs contained in the Book of Psalms be sung in his worship, both public and private, to the end of the world; and in singing God's praise, these songs should be employed to the exclusion of the devotional compositions of uninspired men.

XVII. ADOPTING ACT OF THE UNION OF 1858.

WHEREAS, it is understood that the Testimony submitted to the General Synod of the Associate Reformed Church by the Associate Synod, was proposed and accepted as a term of communion, on the adoption of which the union of the two Churches was to be consummated; and, whereas, it is agreed between the two Churches that the forbearance in love, which is required by the law of God, will be exercised towards any brethren who may not be able fully to subscribe the Standards of the united Church, while they do not determinedly oppose them, but follow the things which make for peace, and things wherewith one may edify another:—

1. *Resolved,* That these Churches, when united, shall be called the "United Presbyterian Church of North America."

2. *Resolved,* That the respective Presbyteries of these Churches shall remain as at present constituted until otherwise ordered, as convenience shall suggest.

3. *Resolved,* That the Supreme Court of this Church shall be a General Assembly, to meet annually, to be composed of delegates from the respective Presbyteries, the number of delegates to be according to the proportion of the members constituting each Presbytery, as now fixed by the rules of the Associate Reformed Church, until a change shall be found expedient.

4. *Resolved,* That there shall be subordinate Synods, and these shall be the same as those now existing in the Associate Reformed Church, to which Synods the different Presbyteries in the Associate Church shall attach themselves for the present according to their location,

provided that the separate Synods and Presbyteries of the said Associate Reformed and Associate Churches shall also continue as at present constituted until otherwise directed.

5. *Resolved*, That the General Assembly and subordinate Synods shall be regulated according to the rules presently in force in the Associate Reformed Church, until the united Church shall see fit to alter such rules.

6. *Resolved*, That the different Boards and Institutions of the respective Churches shall not be affected by this union, but shall have the control of their funds, and retain all their corporate, or other rights and privileges, until the interests of the Church shall require a change.

7. *Resolved*, That these and other regulations found necessary, being agreed upon by the respective Synods at the present meeting in the city of Allegheny, the two Synods shall meet at such a place as shall mutually be agreed upon, and be constituted with prayer by the Senior Moderator, after which a Moderator and Clerk shall be chosen by the united Church.

XVIII. THE ACTION OF THE OLD-SCHOOL ASSEMBLY ON LOYALTY, IN 1861.

(*a*) *The Gardiner Spring Resolutions.*

Gratefully acknowledging the distinguished bounty and care of Almighty God toward this favored land, and also recognizing our obligations to submit to every ordinance of man for the Lord's sake, this General Assembly adopt the following resolutions:

Resolved, 1. That in view of the present agitated and unhappy condition of this country, the first day of July next be hereby set apart as a day of prayer throughout our bounds; and that on that day ministers and people are called on humbly to confess and bewail our national sins; to offer our thanks to the Father of light for his abundant and undeserved goodness toward us as a nation; to seek his guidance and blessing upon our rulers, and their counsels, as well as on the Congress of the United States about to assemble; and to implore him, in the name of Jesus Christ, the Great High Priest of the Christian profession, to turn away his anger from us, and speedily restore to us the blessings of an honorable peace.

Resolved, 2. That this General Assembly, in the spirit of that Christian patriotism which the Scriptures enjoin, and which has always characterized this Church, do hereby acknowledge and declare our obligation to promote and perpetuate, so far as in us lies, the integrity of these United States, and to strengthen, uphold, and encourage the Federal Government in the exercise of all its functions under our noble Constitution; and to this Constitution, in all its provisions, requirements, and principles, we profess our unabated loyalty.

And to avoid all misconception, the Assembly declare that by the terms " Federal Government," as here used, is not meant any particular administration, or the peculiar opinions of any particular party, but that central administration, which being at any time inaugurated according to the forms prescribed in the Constitution of the United States, is the visible representative of our national existence.

(*b*) *Protest of Dr. Hodge and Others.*

We, the undersigned, respectfully protest against the action of the General Assembly in adopting the minority report of the Committee on the State of the Country.

We make this protest, not because we do not acknowledge loyalty to our country to be a moral and religious duty, according to the word of God, which requires us to be subject to the powers that be; nor because we deny the right of the Assembly to enjoin that, and all other like duties, on the ministers and churches under its care; but because we deny the right of the General Assembly to decide the political question, to what government the allegiance of Presbyterians as citizens is due, and its right to make that decision a condition of membership in our Church.

That the paper adopted by the Assembly does decide the political question just stated, is in our judgment undeniable. It asserts not only the loyalty of this body to the Constitution and the Union, but it promises in the name of all the churches and ministers whom it represents, to do all that in them lies to "strengthen, uphold, and encourage the Federal Government." It is, however, a notorious fact, that many of our ministers and members conscientiously believe that the allegiance of the citizens of this country is primarily due to the States to which they respectively belong; and, therefore, that when any State renounces its connection with the United States, and its allegiance to the Constitution, the citizens of that State are bound by the laws of God to continue loyal to their State, and obedient to its laws. The paper adopted by the General Assembly virtually declares, on the other hand, that the allegiance of the citizens is due to the United States; anything in the Constitution, or ordinances, or laws of the several States, to the contrary notwithstanding.

It is not the loyalty of the members constituting this Assembly, nor of our churches and ministers in any one portion of our country, that is thus asserted, but the loyalty of the whole Presbyterian Church, North and South, East and West.

Allegiance to the Federal Government is recognized or declared to be the duty of all the churches and ministers represented in this body. In adopting this paper, therefore, the Assembly does decide the great political question which agitates and divides the country. The question is whether the allegiance of our citizens is primarily to the State or to the Union. However clear our own convictions of the correctness of this decision may be, or however deeply we may be impressed with its importance, yet it is not a question which this Assembly has the right to decide.

A man may conscientiously believe that he owes alle-

giance to one government or another, and yet possess all
the qualifications which the word of God or the standards
of the Church authorize us to demand of in our members
or ministers. As this General Assembly represents the
whole Church, the acts and deliverances of this Assembly
become the acts and deliverances of the Church. It is this
consideration that gives to the action of this Assembly in
this case all its importance, either in our own view or in
the view of others.

It is the allegiance of the Old-school Presbyterian
Church to the Constitution, the Union, and the Federal
Government, which this paper is intended to profess and
proclaim. It does, therefore, of necessity, decide the
political question which agitates the country. It pro-
nounces or assumes a particular interpretation of the Constitution. This is a matter beyond the jurisdiction of the
Assembly.

That the action of the Assembly in the premises does
not only decide the political question referred to, but
makes that decision a term of membership in the Church,
is no less clear. It is not analogous to the recommendation of a religious or benevolent institution, which our
members may regard or not at pleasure; but it puts into
the mouths of all represented in this body, a declaration
of loyalty and allegiance to the Union and to the Federal
Government. But such a declaration, made by our members residing in what are called the seceding States, is
treasonable. Presbyterians under the jurisdiction of those
States, cannot, therefore, make that declaration. They
are consequently forced to choose between allegiance to
their States and allegiance to the Church. The General
Assembly in thus deciding a political question, and in
making that decision practically a condition of membership to the Church, has, in our judgment, violated the Constitution of the Church, and usurped the prerogative of its
Divine Master.

We protest loudly against the action of the Assembly,
because it is a departure from all its previous actions.

The General Assembly has always acted on the principle that the Church has no right to make anything a condition of Christian or ministerial fellowship, which is not enjoined or required in the Scriptures and the Standards of the Church.

We have, at one time, resisted the popular demand to make total abstinence from intoxicating liquors a term of membership. At another time, the holding of slaves. In firmly resisting these unscriptural demands, we have preserved the integrity and unity of the Church, made it the great conservative body of truth, moderation, and liberty of conscience in our country. The Assembly have now descended from this high position, in making a political opinion, a particular theory of the Constitution, however correct and important that theory may be, the condition of membership in our body, and thus, we fear, endangered the unity of the Church.

In the third place we protest, because we regard the action of the Assembly as altogether unnecessary and uncalled for. It was required neither to instruct nor excite our brethren in the Northern States. It was not needed as a vindication of the loyalty of the North.

Old-school Presbyterians everywhere out of the so-called seceding States, have openly avowed and conspicuously displayed their allegiance to the Constitution and the Government, and that in many cases at great cost and peril. Nor was such action required by our duty to the country. We are fully persuaded that we best promote the interests of the country by preserving the integrity and unity of the Church.

We regard this action of the Assembly, therefore, as a great national calamity, as well as the most disastrous to the interests of our Church which has marked its history.

We protest, fourthly, because we regard the action of the Assembly as unjust and cruel in its bearing on our Southern brethren. It was, in our judgment, unfair to entertain and decide such a momentous question when the great majority of our Southern Presbyteries were, from necessity, unrepresented in this body. And it is, in our judgment, a violation of the law of love to adopt an act which must expose the Southern churches that remain in connection with our Church, to suspicion, to loss of property, to personal danger, and which tends to destroy their usefulness in their appointed fields of labor.

And finally we protest, because we believe the act of the Assembly will not only diminish the resources of the Church, but greatly weaken its power for good, and expose it to the danger of being carried away more and more from its true principles by a worldly or fanatical spirit.

(c) *The Answer to this and Other Protests, Adopted by the Assembly.*

The action of the General Assembly, in reference to which these Protests are offered, embraces two resolutions, against the former of which no objection is alleged. The whole stress of the protestation is directed upon the following sentence in the second Resolution:

" *Resolved*, That this General Assembly, in the spirit of that Christian patriotism which the Scriptures enjoin, and which has always characterized this Church, do hereby acknowledge and declare our obligation to promote and perpetuate, so far as in us lies, the integrity of these United States, and to strengthen, uphold, and encourage the Federal Government in the exercise of all its functions under our noble Constitution; and to this Constitution, in all its provisions, requirements, and principles, we profess our unabated loyalty."

The first and main ground of a protest against the adoption of this resolution, is, that the General Assembly has no right to decide purely political questions; that the question whether the allegiance of American citizens is due primarily and eminently to the State, or to the Union, is purely political, of the gravest character, dependent upon constitutional theories and interpretations, respecting which various opinions prevail in different sections of our country; that the action of the Assembly virtually determines this vexed question, decides to what Government the allegiance of Presbyterians, as citizens, is due, and makes that decision a term of communion.

That the action of the Assembly has political as well as moral bearings, is readily admitted. So had the decision of our Divine Master, when he said to the Pharisees and Herodians, " Render to Cæsar the things that are Cæsar's," Mark xii. 17; a decision still binding upon all men, and underlying this very act of the Assembly. The payment of the required tax was both a moral and a political duty.

" There are occasions," says the author of an able article on " The State of the Country," in the January number of the *Princeton Review*, " there are occasions when *political* questions *rise into the sphere of morals and religion;* when the rule of political action is to be sought, not in considerations of State policy, but in the law of God. . . . When the question to be decided turns upon moral principles; when reason, conscience, and the religious sentiment are to be addressed, *it is the privilege and duty of all who have access in any way to the public ear*, to endeavour to allay unholy feeling, and *to bring truth to bear* on the minds of their fellow-citizens." The General Assembly heartily approve these principles, and doubt not that if ever there was an occasion when political questions rose into the sphere of morals and religion, the present circumstances of our beloved country are of that character.

The protestants " deny the right of the General Assembly to decide to what Government the allegiance of Presbyterians, as citizens, is due." Strictly speaking, the Assembly has made no such decision. They have said nothing respecting the allegiance of the subjects of any foreign power, or that of the members of our mission churches in India, China, or elsewhere, who may hold connection with our denomination. The action complained of relates solely to American Presbyterians, citizens of these United States.

Even with regard to them, the Assembly has not determined, as between conflicting governments, to which our allegiance is due. We are the General Assembly of the Presbyterian Church in the United States of America. Such is the distinctive name, ecclesiastical and legal, under which we have been chosen to be known by our sister churches and by the world. In the seventy-four years of our existence, Presbyterians have known but one supreme government, one nationality, within our wide-spread territory. We know no other now. History tells of none. The Federal Government acknowledges none. No nation on earth recognizes the existence of two independent sovereignties within these United States. What Divine Providence may intend for us hereafter—what curse of rival and hostile sovereignties within this broad heritage of our fathers—we presume not to determine. Do these protestants, who so anxiously avoid political entanglements, desire the General Assembly to anticipate the dread decision of impending battle, the action of our own Government, the determination of foreign powers, and even the ultimate arbitration of Heaven? Would they have us recognize, as good Presbyterians, men whom our own Government, with the approval of Christendom, may soon execute as traitors? May not the highest Court of our Church, speaking as the interpreter of the holy law which says, "Ye must needs be subject, not only for wrath, but also for conscience' sake," Rom. xiii. 5, warn her communicants against "resisting the ordinance of God"? Rom. xiii. 2. In the language of the learned Reviewer above cited, "Is disunion morally right? Does it not involve a breach of faith, and a violation of the oaths by which that faith was confirmed? We believe, under existing circumstances, that it does, and therefore it is as dreadful a blow to the Church as it is to the State. If a crime at all, it is one the heinousness of which can only be imperfectly estimated."

In the judgment of this Assembly, "this saying is true;" and therefore the admission, on the part of the Assembly, that Presbyterians may take up arms against the Federal Government, or aid and comfort its enemies, and yet be guiltless, would exhibit that " practical recognition of the right of secession," which, says the Reviewer, would " destroy our national life."

But we deny that this deliverance of the Assembly establishes any new term of communion. The terms of Christian fellowship are laid down in the word of God, and are embodied in our standards. It is competent to this Court to interpret and apply the doctrines of the word; to warn men against prevailing sins; and to urge the performance of neglected duties. We regard the action, against which these protests are levelled, simply as a faithful declaration, by the Assembly, of Christian duty toward those in authority over us; which adds nothing to the terms of communion already recognized. Surely the idea of the obligation of loyalty to our Federal Government is no new thing to Presbyterians.

And this is a sufficient reply, also, to the second article of this Protest. Having established no new term of membership, this Assembly is not liable to the charge of having departed from the old paths.

A third ground of protest is the allegation that this action of the Assembly is uncalled for, and unnecessary. Yet, on the admission of these protestants themselves, it is " a notorious fact," that many of our ministers and members believe themselves absolved from all obligations of loyalty to our National Government—believe, in contradiction to the Princeton Reviewer, that disunion is morally right; and some are already in arms to vindicate these opinions. What, when " a crime, the heinousness of which can only be imperfectly estimated "—" striking as dreadful a blow at the Church as at the State," is already committed; when thousands of Presbyterians are likely to be seduced from their allegiance by the machinations of wicked men; when our national prosperity is overclouded; when every material interest is in jeopardy, and every spiritual energy paralyzed; when armed rebellion joins issue with armed authority on battle-fields, where tens of thousands must perish; when it remains a question, whether our national life survives the conflict, or whether our sun sets in anarchy and blood—is it uncalled for, unnecessary, for this Christian Assembly to renew, in the memories and hearts of a Christian people, respect for the majesty of law, and a sense of the obligation of loyalty? Let posterity decide between us.

That this decision of the Assembly is unjust to a portion of our Church, not now fully represented in this body, is a fourth reason of protest. We need only reply that the roll of this Assembly shows delegates from Virginia, Kentucky, Missouri, Tennessee, Mississippi, Louisiana, and Texas. All might have been as easily represented. Besides, the action has no local or sectional character. The subject is of national relations, as well as of such pressing urgency, that to have waited for a full Southern representation, in a future Assembly, would have been to lose forever the critical moment when action would be productive of good.

As to the final ground of protest, it is enough to record our simple denial of the opinions expressed. We sincerely believe that this action of the General Assembly will increase the power of the Church for good; securing, as we humbly trust it will, the favour of her exalted Head, in behalf of those who testify for a suffering truth.

XIX. ADDRESS OF THE SOUTHERN GENERAL ASSEMBLY TO ALL THE CHURCHES OF JESUS CHRIST, ADOPTED 1861.

The General Assembly of the Presbyterian Church in the Confederate States of America, to all the Churches of Jesus Christ throughout the earth, greeting: Grace, mercy, and peace be multiplied upon you:

DEARLY BELOVED BRETHREN: It is probably known to you that the Presbyteries and Synods in the Confederate States, which were formerly in connection with the General Assembly of the Presbyterian Church in

the United States of America, have renounced the jurisdiction of that body; and dissolved the ties which bound
them ecclesiastically with their brethren of the North.
This act of separation left them without any formal union
among themselves. But as they were one in faith and
order, and still adhered to their old standards, measures
were promptly adopted for giving expression to their
unity, by the organization of a Supreme Court, upon the
model of the one whose authority they had just relin-
quished. Commissioners duly appointed, from all the
Presbyteries of these Confederate States, met accordingly,
in the City of Augusta, on the fourth day of December,
in the year of our Lord one thousand eight hundred and
sixty one, and then and there proceeded to constitute
the General Assembly of the Presbyterian Church in the
Confederate States of America. The Constitution of the
Presbyterian Church in the United States—that is to say,
the Westminster Confession of Faith, the Larger and
Shorter Catechisms, the Form of Government, the Book
of Discipline, and the Directory for Worship—were unanimously and solemnly declared to be the Constitution of
the Church in the Confederate States, with no other
change than the substitution of "Confederate" for
"United" wherever the country is mentioned in the standards. The Church, therefore, in these seceded States,
presents now the spectacle of a separate, and independent,
and complete organization, under the style and title of
The Presbyterian Church in the Confederate States of
America. In thus taking its place among sister Churches
of this and other countries, it seems proper that it should
set forth the causes which have impelled it to separate
from the Church of the North, and to indicate a general
view of the course which it feels it incumbent upon it to
pursue in the new circumstances in which it is placed.

We should be sorry to be regarded by our brethren in
any part of the world as guilty of schism. We are not
conscious of any purpose to rend the body of Christ. On
the contrary, our aim has been to promote the unity of

the Spirit in the bonds of peace. If we know our own
hearts, and can form any just estimate of the motives
which have governed us, we have been prompted by a
sincere desire to promote the glory of God, and the efficiency, energy, harmony, and zeal of his visible kingdom
in the earth. We have separated from õur brethren of
the North as Abraham separated from Lot—because we
are persuaded that the interests of true religion will be
more effectually subserved by two independent Churches,
under the circumstances in which the two countries are
placed, than by one united body.

1. In the first place, the course of the last Assembly, at
Philadelphia, conclusively shows that if we should remain
together, the political questions which divide us as citizens,
will be obtruded on our Church Courts, and discussed by
Christian Ministers and Elders with all the acrimony, bitterness, and rancor with which such questions are usually
discussed by men of the world. Our Assembly would
present a mournful spectacle of strife and debate. Commissioners from the Northern would meet with Commissioners from the Southern Confederacy, to wrangle over
the questions which have split them into two confederacies, and involved them in furious and bloody war. They
would denounce each other, on the one hand, as tyrants
and oppressors, and on the other, as traitors and rebels.
The Spirit of God would take his departure from these
scenes of confusion, and leave the Church lifeless and
powerless, an easy prey to the sectional divisions and
angry passions of its members. Two nations, under any
circumstances, except those of perfect homogeneousness,
cannot be united in one Church, without the rigid exclusion of all civil and secular questions from its halls. Where
the countries differ in their customs and institutions, and
view each other with an eye of jealousy and rivalry, if
national feelings are permitted to enter the Church Courts,
there must be an end of harmony and peace. The prejudices of the man and the citizen will prove stronger than
the charity of the Christian. When they have allowed

themselves to denounce each other for their national peculiarities, it will be hard to join in cordial fellowship as members of the same spiritual family. Much more must this be the case where the nations are not simply rivals, but enemies—when they hate each other with a cruel hatred—when they are engaged in a ferocious and bloody war, and when the worst passions of human nature are stirred to their very depths. An Assembly composed of representatives from two such countries, could have no security for peace except in a steady, uncompromising adherence to the Scriptural principle, that it would know no man after the flesh; that it would abolish the distinctions of Barbarian, Scythian, bond and free, and recognize nothing but the new creature in Christ Jesus. The moment it permits itself to know the Confederate or the United States, the moment its members meet as citizens of these countries our political differences will be transferred to the house of God, and the passions of the forum will expel the Spirit of Holy Love and of Christian communion.

We cannot condemn a man, in one breath, as unfaithful to the most solemn earthly interests—his country and his race—and commend him in the next as a loyal and faithful servant of his God. If we distrust his patriotism, our confidence is apt to be very measured in his piety. The old adage will hold here as in other things, *falsus in uno, falsus in omnibus.*

The only conceivable condition, therefore, upon which the Church of the North and the South could remain together as one body, with any prospect of success, is the rigorous exclusion of the questions and passions of the forum from its halls of debate. This is what always ought to be done. The provinces of Church and State are perfectly distinct, and the one has no right to usurp the jurisdiction of the other. The State is a natural institute, founded in the constitution of man as moral and social, and designed to realize the idea of justice. It is the society of rights. The Church is a supernatural institute, founded in the facts of redemption, and is designed to realize the idea of grace. It is the society of the redeemed. The State aims at social order, the Church at spiritual holiness. The State looks to the visible and outward, the Church is concerned for the invisible and inward. The badge of the State's authority is the sword, by which it becomes a terror to evil doers, and a praise to them that do well. The badge of the Church's authority is the keys, by which it opens and shuts the Kingdom of Heaven according as men are believing or impenitent. The power of the Church is exclusively spiritual, that of the State includes the exercise of force. The Constitution of the Church is a Divine revelation—the Constitution of the State must be determined by human reason and the course of Providential events. The Church has no right to construct or modify a government for the State, and the State has no right to frame a creed or polity for the Church. They are as planets moving in different orbits, and unless each is confined to its own tract, the consequences may be as disastrous in the moral world as the collision of different spheres in the world of matter. It is true that there is a point at which their respective jurisdictions seem to meet—in the idea of duty. But even duty is viewed by each in very different lights. The Church enjoins it as obedience to God, and the State enforces it as the safeguard of order. But there can be no collision, unless one or the other blunders as to the things that are materially right. When the State makes wicked laws, contradicting the eternal principles of rectitude, the Church is at liberty to testify against them, and humbly to petition that they may be repealed. In like manner, if the Church become seditious and a disturber of the peace, the State has a right to abate the nuisance. In ordinary cases, however, there is not likely to be a collision. Among a Christian people, there is little difference of opinion as to the radical distinctions of right and wrong. The only serious danger is where moral duty is conditioned upon a political question. Under the pretext of inculcating duty, the Church may usurp the power to determine the question which conditions it, and that is precisely what she is debarred from doing. The condition must be given. She must accept it from the State, and then her own course is clear. If Cæsar is your master, then pay tribute to him; but whether the "if" holds whether Cæsar is your master or not, whether he ever had any just authority, whether he now retains it, or has forfeited it, these are points which the Church has no commission to adjudicate.

Had these principles been steadily maintained by the Assembly at Philadelphia, it is possible that the ecclesiastical separation of the North and the South might have been deferred for years to come. Our Presbyteries, many of them, clung with tenderness to the recollections of the past. Sacred memories gathered around that venerable Church which had breasted many a storm and trained our fathers for glory. It had always been distinguished for its conservative influence, and many fondly hoped that, even in the present emergency, it would raise its placid and serene head above the tumults of popular passion, and bid defiance to the angry billows which rolled at its feet. We expected it to bow in reverence only at the name of Jesus. Many dreamed that it would utterly refuse to know either Confederates or Federalists, and utterly refuse to give any authoritative decree without a "Thus saith the Lord." It was ardently desired that the sublime spectacle might be presented of one Church upon earth combining in cordial fellowship and in holy love— the disciples of Jesus in different and even in hostile lands. But, alas! for the weakness of man, these golden visions were soon dispelled. The first thing which roused our Presbyteries to look the question of separation seriously in the face, was the course of the Assembly in venturing to determine, as a Court of Jesus Christ, which it did by necessary implication, the true interpretation of the Constitution of the United States as to the kind of government it intended to form. A political theory was, to all intents and purposes, propounded, which made secession a crime, the seceding States rebellious, and the citizens who obeyed them traitors. We say nothing here as to the righteousness or unrighteousness of these decrees. What we maintain is, that, whether right or wrong, the Church had no right to make them—she transcended her sphere, and usurped the duties of the State. The discussion of these questions, we are sorry to add, was in the spirit and temper of partizan declaimers. The Assembly, driven from its ancient moorings, was tossed to and fro by the waves of popular passion. Like Pilate, it obeyed the clamor of the multitude, and though acting in the name of Jesus, it kissed the sceptre and bowed the knee to the mandates of Northern phrenzy. The Church was converted into the forum, and the Assembly was henceforward to become the arena of sectional divisions and national animosities.

We frankly admit that the mere unconstitutionality of the proceedings of the last Assembly is not, in itself considered, a sufficient ground of separation. It is the consequences of these proceedings which make them so offensive. It is the door which they open for the introduction of the worst passions of human nature into the deliberations of Church Courts. The spirit of these proceedings, if allowed to prevail, would forever banish peace from the Church, and there is no reason to hope that the tide which has begun to flow can soon be arrested. The two confederacies hate each other more intensely now than they did in May, and if their citizens should come together upon the same floor, whatever might be the errand that brought them there, they could not be restrained from smiting each other with the fist of wickedness. For the sake of peace, therefore, for Christian charity, for the honor of the Church, and for the glory of God, we have been constrained, as much as in us lies, to remove all occasion of offence. We have quietly separated, and we are grateful to God that, while leaving for the sake of peace, we leave it with the humble consciousness that we, ourselves, have never given occasion to break the peace. We have never confounded Cæsar and Christ, and we have never mixed the issues of this world with the weighty matters that properly belong to us as citizens of the Kingdom of God.

2. Though the immediate occasion of separation was the course of the General Assembly at Philadelphia in relation to the Federal Government and the war, yet there is another ground on which the independent organization of the Southern Church can be amply and scripturally maintained. The unity of the Church does not require a formal bond of union among all the congregations of believers throughout the earth. It does not demand a vast imperial monarchy like that of Rome, nor a strictly universal council, like that to which the complete development of Presbyterianism would naturally give rise. The Church Catholic is one in Christ, but it is not necessarily one visible, all-absorbing organization upon earth. There is no schism where there is no breach of charity. Churches may be perfectly at one in every principle of faith and order, and yet geographically distinct, and mutually independent. As the unity of the human race is not disturbed by its division into countries and nations, so the unity of the spiritual seed of Christ is neither broken nor impaired by separation and division into various Church constitutions. Accordingly, in the Protestant countries, Church organizations have followed national lines. The Calvinistic Churches of Switzerland are distinct from the Reformed Church of France. The Presbyterians of Ireland belong to a different Church from the Presbyterians of Scotland, and the Presbyterians of this country constitute a Church, in like manner, distinct from all other Churches on the globe. That the division into national Churches, that is, Churches bounded by national lines, is, in the present condition of human nature, a benefit, seems to us too obvious for proof. It realizes to the Church Catholic all the advantages of a division of labor. It makes a Church organization homogeneous and compact—it stimulates holy rivalry and zeal—it removes all grounds of

suspicion and jealousy on the part of the State. What is lost in expansion is gained in energy. The Church Catholic, as thus divided, and yet spiritually one, divided, but not rent, is a beautiful illustration of the great philosophical principle which pervades all nature—the co-existence of the one with the many.

If it is desirable that each nation should contain a separate and an independent Church, the Presbyteries of these Confederate States need no apology for bowing to the decree of Providence, which, in withdrawing their country from the government of the United States, has, at the same time, determined that they should withdraw from the Church of their fathers. It is not that they have ceased to love it—not that they have abjured its ancient principles, or forgotten its glorious history. It is to give these same principles a richer, freer, fuller development among ourselves than they possibly could receive under foreign culture. It is precisely because we love that Church as it was, and that Church as it should be, that we have resolved as far as in us lies, to realize its grand idea in the country, and under the Government where God has cast our lot. With the supreme control of ecclesiastical affairs in our hands, we may be able, in some competent measure, to consummate this result. In subjection to a foreign power, we could no more accomplish it than the Church in the United States could have been developed in dependence upon the Presbyterian Church of Scotland. The difficulty there would have been, not the distance of Edinburgh from New York, Philadelphia, or Charleston, but the difference in the manners, habits, customs, and ways of thinking, the social, civil, and political institutions of the people. These same difficulties exist in relation to the Confederate and United States, and render it eminently proper that the Church in each should be as separate and independent as the Governments.

In addition to this, there is one difference which so radically and fundamentally distinguishes the North and the South, that it is becoming every day more and more apparent that the religious, as well as the secular, interests of both will be more effectually promoted by a complete and lasting separation.   The antagonism of Northern and Southern sentiment on the subject of slavery lies at the root of all the difficulties which have resulted in the dismemberment of the Federal Union, and involved us in the horrors of an unnatural war.   The Presbyterian Church in the United States has been enabled by Divine grace to pursue, for the most part, an eminently conservative, because a thoroughly Scriptural, policy in relation to this delicate question.   It has planted itself upon the Word of God, and utterly refused to make slaveholding a sin, or non-slaveholding a term of communion.   But though both sections are agreed as to this general principle, it is not to be disguised that the North exercises a deep and settled antipathy to slavery itself, while the South is equally zealous in its defence.   Recent events can have no other effect than to confirm the antipathy on the one hand and strengthen the attachment on the other.   The Northern section of the Church stands in the awkward predicament of maintaining, in one breath, that slavery is an evil which ought to be abolished, and of asserting in the next, that it is not a sin to be visited by exclusion from communion of the saints.   The consequence is, that it plays partly into the hands of abolitionists and partly into the hands of slaveholders, and weakens its influence with both.   It occupies the position of a prevaricating witness whom neither party will trust.   It would be better, therefore, for the moral power of the Northern section of the Church to get entirely quit of the subject.   At the same time, it is intuitively obvious that the Southern section of the Church, while even partially under the control of those who are hostile to slavery, can never have free and unimpeded access to the slave population.   Its ministers and elders will always be liable to some degree of suspicion.   In the present circumstances, Northern alliance would be absolutely fatal.   It would utterly preclude the Church from a wide and commanding field of usefulness.

This is too dear a price to be paid for a nominal union. We cannot afford to give up these millions of souls and consign them, so far as our efforts are concerned, to hopeless perdition, for the sake of preserving an outward unity which, after all, is an empty shadow. If we would gird ourselves heartily and in earnest, for the work which God has set before us, we must have the control of our ecclesiastical affairs, and declare ourselves separate and independent.

And here we may venture to lay before the Christian world our views as a Church, upon the subject of slavery. We beg a candid hearing.

In the first place, we would have it distinctly understood that, in our ecclesiastical capacity, we are neither the friends nor the foes of slavery; that is to say, we have no commission either to propagate or abolish it. The policy of its existence or non-existence is a question which exclusively belongs to the State. We have no right, as a Church, to enjoin it as a duty, or to condemn it as a sin. Our business is with the duties which spring from the relation; the duties of the masters on the one hand, and of their slaves on the other. These duties we are to proclaim and enforce with spiritual sanctions. The social, civil, political problems connected with this great subject transcend our sphere, as God has not entrusted to his Church the organization of society, the construction of Government, nor the allotment of individuals to their various stations. The Church has as much right to preach to the monarchies of Europe, and the despotism of Asia, the doctrines of republican equality, as to preach to the Governments of the South the extirpation of slavery. This position is impregnable, unless it can be shown that slavery is a sin. Upon every other hypothesis, it is so clearly a question for the State, that the proposition would never for a moment have been doubted, had there not been a foregone conclusion in relation to its moral character. Is slavery, then, a sin?

In answering this question, as a Church, let it be distinctly borne in mind that the only rule of judgment is the written Word of God.   The Church knows nothing of the intuitions of reason or the deductions of philosophy, except those reproduced in the Sacred Canon.   She has a positive constitution in the Holy Scriptures, and has no right to utter a single syllable upon any subject, except as the Lord puts words in her mouth.   She is founded, in other words, upon express *revelation*.   Her creed is an authoritative testimony of God, and not a speculation, and what she proclaims, she must proclaim with the infallible certitude of faith, and not with the hesitating assent of an opinion.   The question, then, is brought within a narrow compass: Do the Scriptures directly or indirectly condemn slavery as a sin?   If they do not, the dispute is ended, for the Church, without forfeiting her character, dares not go beyond them.

Now, we venture to assert that if men had drawn their conclusions upon this subject only from the Bible, it would no more have entered into any human head to denounce slavery as a sin, than to denounce monarchy, aristocracy, or poverty.   The truth is, men have listened to what they falsely considered as primitive intuitions, or as necessary deductions from primitive cognitions, and then have gone to the Bible to confirm the crotchets of their vain philosophy.   They have gone there determined to find a particular result, and the consequence is, that they leave with having made, instead of having interpreted, Scripture. Slavery is no new thing.   It has not only existed for ages in the world, but it has existed, under every dispensation of the covenant of grace, in the Church of God.   Indeed, the first organization of the Church as a visible society, separate and distinct from the unbelieving world, was inaugurated in the family of a slaveholder.   Among the very first persons to whom the seal of circumcision was affixed, were the slaves of the father of the faithful, some born in his house, and others bought with his money.   Slavery again re-appears under the Law.   God sanctions it in the first table of the Decalogue, and Moses treats it as an institution to be regulated, not abolished; legitimated, and not condemned. We come down to the age of the New Testament, and we find it again in the Churches founded by the Apostles under the plenary inspiration of the Holy Ghost. These facts are utterly amazing, if slavery is the enormous sin which its enemies represent it to be. It will not do to say that the Scriptures have treated it only in a general, incidental way, without any clear implication as to its moral character. Moses surely made it the subject of express and positive legislation, and the Apostles are equally explicit in inculcating the duties which spring from both sides of the relation. They treat slaves as bound to obey, and inculcate obedience as an office of religion—a thing wholly self-contradictory, if the authority exercised over them were unlawful and iniquitous.

But what puts this subject in a still clearer light is the manner in which it is sought to extort from the Scriptures a contrary testimony. The notion of direct and explicit condemnation is given up. The attempt is to show that the genius and spirit of Christianity are opposed to it— that its great cardinal principles of virtue are utterly against it. Much stress is laid upon the Golden Rule and upon the general denunciations of tyranny and oppression. To all this we reply, that no principle is clearer than that a case positively excepted cannot be included under a general rule. Let us concede, for a moment, that the law of love, and the condemnation of tyranny and oppression, seem logically to involve, as a result, the condemnation of slavery; yet, if slavery is afterwards expressly mentioned and treated as a lawful relation, it obviously follows, unless Scripture is to be interpreted as inconsistent with itself, that slavery is, by necessary implication, excepted. The Jewish law forbade, as a general rule, the marriage of a man with his brother's wife. The same law expressly enjoined the same marriage in a given case. The given case was, therefore, an exception, and not to be treated as a violation of the general rule. The law of love has always been the law of God. It was enunciated by Moses almost as clearly as it was enunciated by Jesus Christ. Yet, notwithstanding this law, Moses and the Apostles alike sanctioned the relation of slavery. The conclusion is inevitable, either that the law is not opposed to it, or that slavery is an excepted case. To say that the prohibition of tyranny and oppression include slavery, is to beg the whole question. Tyranny and oppression involve either the unjust usurpation or the unlawful exercise of power. It is the unlawfulness, either in its principle or measure, which constitutes the core of the sin. Slavery must, therefore, be proved to be unlawful, before it can be referred to any such category. The master may, indeed, abuse his power, but he oppresses not simply as a master, but as a wicked master.

But, apart from all this, the law of love is simply the inculcation of universal equity. It implies nothing as to the existence of various ranks and gradations in society. The interpretation which makes it repudiate slavery would make it equally repudiate all social, civil, and political inequalities. Its meaning is, not that we should conform ourselves to the arbitrary expectations of others, but that we should render unto them precisely the same measure which, if we were in their circumstance, it would be reasonable and just in us to demand at their hands. It condemns slavery, therefore, only upon the supposition that slavery is a sinful relation—that is, he who extracts the prohibition of slavery from the Golden Rule, begs the very point in dispute.

We cannot prosecute the argument in detail, but we have said enough, we think, to vindicate the position of the Southern Church. We have assumed no new attitude. We stand exactly where the Church of God has always stood—from Abraham to Moses, from Moses to Christ, from Christ to the Reformers, and from the Reformers to ourselves. We stand upon the foundation of the Prophets and Apostles, Jesus Christ himself being the Chief cornerstone. Shall we be excluded from the fellowship of our brethren in other lands, because we dare not depart from the charter of our faith? Shall we be branded with the stigma of reproach, because we cannot consent to corrupt the Word of God to suit the intuitions of an infidel philosophy? Shall our names be cast out as evil, and the finger of scorn pointed at us, because we utterly refuse to break our communion with Abraham, Isaac, and Jacob, with Moses, David, and Isaiah, with Apostles, Prophets, and Martyrs, with all the noble army of confessors who have gone to glory from slaveholding countries and from a slaveholding Church, without ever having dreamed that they were living in mortal sin, by conniving at slavery in the midst of them? If so, we shall take consolation in the cheering consciousness that the Master has accepted us. We may be denounced, despised, and cast out of the Synagogues of our brethren. But while they are wrangling about the distinctions of men according to the flesh, we shall go forward in our Divine work, and confidently anticipate that, in the great day, as the consequence of our humble labors, we shall meet millions of glorified spirits, who have come up from the bondage of earth to a nobler freedom than human philosophy ever dreamed of. Others, if they please, may spend their time in declaiming on the tyranny of earthly masters; it will be our aim to resist the real tyrants which oppress the soul—Sin and Satan. These are the foes against whom we shall find it employment enough to wage a successful war. And to this holy war it is the purpose of our Church to devote itself with redoubled energy. We feel that the souls of our slaves are a solemn trust, and we shall strive to present them faultless and complete before the presence of God.

Indeed, as we contemplate their condition in the Southern States, and contrast it with that of their fathers before them, and that of their brethren in the present day in their native land, we cannot but accept it as a gracious Providence that they have been brought in such numbers to our shores, and redeemed from the bondage of barbarism and sin. Slavery to them has certainly been overruled for the greatest good. It has been a link in the wondrous chain of Providence, through which many sons and daughters have been made heirs of the heavenly inheritance. The Providential result is, of course, no justification, if the thing is intrinsically wrong; but it is certainly a matter of devout thanksgiving, and no obscure intimation of the will and purpose of God, and of the consequent duty of the Church. We cannot forbear to say, however, that the general operation of the system is kindly and benevolent; it is a real and effective discipline, and without it we are profoundly persuaded that the African race in the midst of us can never be elevated in the scale of being. As long as that race, in its comparative degradation, co-exists, side by side, with the white, bondage is its normal condition.

As to the endless declamation about human rights, we have only to say that human rights are not a fixed, but a fluctuating quantity. Their sum is not the same in any two nations on the globe. The rights of Englishmen are one thing, the rights of Frenchmen another. There is a minimum without which a man cannot be responsible; there is a maximum which expresses the highest degree of civilization and of Christian culture. The education of the species consists in its ascent along this line. As you go up, the number of rights increases, but the number of individuals who possess them diminishes. As you come down the line, rights are diminished, but the individuals are multiplied. It is just the opposite of the predicamental scale of the logicians. There comprehension diminishes as you ascend and extension increases, and comprehension increases as you descend and extension diminishes. Now, when it is said that slavery is inconsistent with human rights, we crave to understand what point in this line is the slave conceived to occupy. There are, no doubt, many rights which belong to other men—to Englishmen, to Frenchmen, to his master, for example—which are denied to him. But is he fit to possess them? Has God qualified him to meet the responsibilities which their possession necessarily implies? His place in the scale is determined by his competency to fulfil its duties. There are other rights which he certainly possesses, without which he could neither be human nor accountable. Before slavery can be charged with doing him injustice, it must be shown that the minimum which falls to his lot at the bottom of the line is out of proportion to his capacity and culture—a thing which can never be done by abstract speculation. The truth is, the education of the human race for liberty and virtue, is a vast Providential scheme, and God assigns to every man, by a wise and holy decree, the precise place he is to occupy in the great moral school of humanity. The scholars are distributed into classes, according to their competency and progress. For God is in history.

To avoid the suspicion of a conscious weakness of our cause, when contemplated from the side of pure speculation, we may advert for a moment to those pretended intuitions which stamp the reprobation of humanity upon this ancient and hoary institution. We admit that there are primitive principles in morals which lie at the root of human consciousness. But the question is, how are we to distinguish them? The subjective feeling of certainty is no adequate criterion, as that is equally felt in reference to crotchets and hereditary prejudices. The very point is to know when this certainty indicates a primitive cognition, and when it does not. There must, therefore, be some eternal test, and whatever cannot abide that test has no authority as a primary truth. That test is an inward necessity of thought, which, in all minds at the proper stage of maturity, is absolutely universal. Whatever is universal is natural. We are willing that slavery should be tried by this standard. We are willing to abide by the testimony of the race, and if man, as man, has everywhere condemned it—if all human laws have prohibited it as crime—if it stands in the same category with malice, murder, and theft; then we are willing, in the name of humanity, to renounce it, and to renounce it forever. But what if the overwhelming majority of mankind have approved it? what if philosophers and statesmen have justified it, and the laws of all nations acknowledged it? what then becomes of these luminous intuitions? They are an *ignis fatuus*, mistaken for a star.

We have now, brethren, in a brief compass, for the nature of this address admits only of an outline, opened to you our whole hearts upon this delicate and vexed subject. We have concealed nothing. We have sought to conciliate no sympathy by appeals to your charity. We have tried our cause by the word of God; and though protesting against its authority to judge in a question concerning the duty of the Church, we have not refused to appear at the tribunal of reason. Are we not right, in view of all the preceding considerations, in remitting the social, civil, and political problems connected with slavery to the State? Is it not a subject, save in the moral duties which spring from it, which lies beyond the province of the Church? Have we any right to make it an element in judging of Christian character? Are we not treading in the footsteps of the flock? Are we not acting as Christ and his Apostles have acted before us? Is it not enough for us to pray and labor, in our lot, that all men may be saved, without meddling as a Church with the technical distinction of their civil life? We leave the matter with you. We offer you the right hand of fellowship. It is for you to accept it or reject it. We have done our duty. We can do no more. Truth is more precious than union, and if you cast us out as sinners, the breach of charity is not with us, as long as we walk according to the light of the written Word.

The ends which we propose to accomplish as a Church are the same as those which are proposed by every other church. To proclaim God's truth as a witness to the nations; to gather his elect from the four corners of the earth, and through the Word, Ministries, and Ordinances, to train them for eternal life, is the great business of His people. The only thing that will be at all peculiar to us, is the manner in which we shall attempt to discharge our duty. In almost every department of labor, except the pastoral care of congregations, it has been usual for the Church to resort to societies more or less closely connected with itself, and yet logically and really distinct. It is our purpose to rely upon the regular organs of our government, and executive agencies directly and immediately responsible to them. We wish to make the Church not merely a superintendent, but an agent. We wish to develope the idea that the congregation of believers, as visibly organized, is the very society or corporation which is divinely called to do the work of the Lord. We shall, therefore, endeavor to do what has never yet been adequately done—bring out the energies of our Presbyterian system of government. From the Session to the Assembly we shall strive to enlist all our courts, as courts, in every department of Christian effort. We are not ashamed to confess that we are intensely Presbyterian. We embrace all other denominations in the arms of Christian fellowship and love, but our own scheme of government we humbly believe to be according to the pattern shown in the Mount, and, by God's grace, we propose to put its efficiency to the test.

Brethren, we have done. We have told you who we are, and what we are. We greet you in the ties of Christian brotherhood. We desire to cultivate peace and charity with all our fellow Christians throughout the world. We invite to ecclesiastical communion all who maintain our principles of faith and order. And now we commend you to God and the word of his grace. We devoutly pray that the whole Catholic Church may be afresh baptized with the Holy Ghost, and that she may speedily be stirred up to give the Lord no rest until he establish and make Jerusalem a praise in the earth.

XX. DOCTRINAL BASIS OF UNION OF THE UNITED SYNOD OF THE SOUTH (N. S.) TO THE SOUTHERN PRESBYTERIAN CHURCH (O. S.).

The General Assembly and the United Synod of the Presbyterian Churches in the Confederate States of America, holding the same system of doctrine and church order, and believing that their union will glorify God by promoting peace and increasing their ability for the edification of the Body of Christ, do agree to unite under the name of the Presbyterian Church in the Confederate States of America, and under the existing charter of the Trustees of the General Assembly of the Presbyterian Church in the Confederate States of America, on the following basis, viz. :

Article I. The General Assembly and the United Synod declare that they continue sincerely to receive and adopt the Confession of Faith and Catechisms of the Presbyterian Church, as containing the system of doctrine taught in the Holy Scriptures, and approve of its government and discipline.

XXI. THE DOCTRINAL BASIS OF THE REUNION OF THE OLD- AND NEW-SCHOOL CHURCHES IN 1869.

(1) *The Doctrinal Article Proposed by the Joint Committee in* 1867.

The Reunion shall be effected on the doctrinal and ecclesiastical basis of our common standards; the Confession of Faith shall continue to be sincerely received and adopted " as containing the system of doctrine taught in the Holy Scriptures" ; and its fair, historical sense, as it is accepted by the two bodies in opposition to Antinomianism and Fatalism on the one hand, and to Arminianism and Pelagianism on the other, shall be regarded as the sense in which it is received and adopted; and the Government and Discipline of the Presbyterian Church in the United States shall continue to be approved as containing the principles and rule of our polity.

(2) *The Article Proposed in the Presbyterian Reunion Convention of* 1867, *with Dr. Henry B. Smith's Proviso.*

The Reunion shall be effected on the doctrinal and ecclesiastical basis of our common standards; the Scriptures of the Old and New Testaments shall be acknowledged to be the inspired Word of God, and the only infallible rule of faith and practice; the Confession of Faith shall continue to be sincerely received and adopted " as containing the system of doctrine taught in the Holy Scriptures"; it being understood, that this Confession is received in its proper, historical—that is, the Calvinistic or Reformed,—sense.

(3) *The Gurley Amendment, added to the above by the Joint Committee in* 1868.

It is also understood that various methods of viewing, stating, explaining and illustrating, the doctrines of the Confession, which do not impair the integrity of the Reformed or Calvinistic system, are to be freely allowed in the united Church, as they have hitherto been allowed in the separate Churches; and the Government and Discipline of the Presbyterian Church in the United States shall be approved as containing the principles and rule of our polity.

(4) *The Basis Finally Adopted in* 1869.

Believing that the interests of the Redeemer's kingdom would be promoted by the healing of our divisions, and that the two bodies bearing the same names, having the same Constitution, and each recognizing the other as a sound and orthodox body according to the principles of the Confession common to both, cannot be justified by any but the most imperative reasons in maintaining separate and, in some respects, rival organizations; we are now clearly of the opinion that the reunion of those bodies ought, as soon as the necessary steps can be taken, to be accomplished, upon the basis hereinafter set forth.

1. The Presbyterian Churches in the United States of America, namely, that whose General Assembly convened in the Brick Church in the city of New York, on the 20th day of May, 1869, and that whose General Assembly met

in the Church of the Covenant in the said city on the same day, shall be reunited as one Church, under the name and style of the Presbyterian Church in the United States of America, possessing all the legal and corporate rights and powers pertaining to the Church previous to the division in 1838, and all the legal and corporate rights and powers which the separate churches now possess.

2. The reunion shall be effected on the doctrinal and ecclesiastical basis of our common standards; the Scriptures of the Old and New Testaments shall be acknowledged to be the inspired Word of God, and the only infallible rule of faith and practice; the Confession of Faith shall continue to be sincerely received and adopted as containing the system of doctrine taught in the Holy Scriptures; and the government and discipline of the Presbyterian Church in the United States shall be approved as containing the principles and rules of our polity.

XXII. THE CONCURRENT DECLARATIONS OF 1869.

As there are matters pertaining to the interests of the Church, when it shall have become reunited, which will manifestly require adjustment on the coming together of two bodies which have so long acted separately, and concerning some of which matters it is highly desirable that there should be a previous good understanding, the two Assemblies agree to adopt the following declarations, not as articles of compact or covenant, but as in their judgment proper and equitable arrangements, to wit:

1. All the ministers and churches embraced in the two bodies should be admitted to the same standing in the united body, which they may have held in their respective connections, up to the consummation of the union.

2. Imperfectly organized churches are counselled and expected to become thoroughly Presbyterian, as early within the period of five years as may be permitted by the highest interests to be consulted; and no other such churches shall be hereafter received.

3. The boundaries of the several Presbyteries and Synods should be adjusted by the General Assembly of the united church.

4. The official records of the two branches of the church for the period of separation should be preserved and held as making up the one history of the church; and no rule or precedent which does not stand approved by both the bodies, should be of any authority until re-established in the united body, except in so far as such rule or precedent may affect the rights of property founded thereon.

5. The corporate rights now held by the two General Assemblies, and by their Boards and Committees, should, as far as practicable, be consolidated, and applied for their several objects, as defined by law.

6. There should be one set of Committees or Boards for Home and Foreign Missions, and the other religious enterprises of the church; which the churches should be encouraged to sustain, though free to cast their contributions into other channels if they desire to do so.

7. As soon as practicable after the union shall have been effected, the General Assembly should reconstruct and consolidate the several Permanent Committees and Boards which now belong to the two Assemblies, so as to represent, as far as possible with impartiality, the views and wishes of the two bodies constituting the united church.

8. The publications of the Board of Publication and of the Publication Committee should continue to be issued as at present, leaving it to the Board of Publication of the united church to revise these issues and perfect a catalogue for the united church so as to exclude invidious references to past controversies.

9. In order to a uniform system of ecclesiastical supervision, those Theological Seminaries that are now under Assembly control may, if their Boards of Direction so elect, be transferred to the watch and care of one or more of the adjacent Synods; and the other Seminaries are advised to introduce, as far as may be, into their Constitutions, the principle of Synodical or Assembly supervision; in which

case they shall be entitled to an official recognition and approbation on the part of the General Assembly.

10. It should be regarded as the duty of all our judicatories, ministers and people in the united church, to study the things which make for peace, and to guard against all needless and offensive references to the causes that have divided us; and in order to avoid the revival of past issues by the continuance of any usage in either branch of the church, that has grown out of former conflicts, it is earnestly recommended to the lower judicatories of the church that they conform their practice in relation to all such usages, as far as is consistent with their convictions of duty, to the general custom of the church prior to the controversies that resulted in the separation.

XXIII. THE CHARGES ON WHICH PROFESSOR BRIGGS WAS TRIED, AND THE SENTENCE PRONOUNCED BY THE GENERAL ASSEMBLY.

(a) *The Charge against Dr. Briggs.*

(1) Teaching that the Reason is a fountain of divine authority to such an extent that it may and does savingly enlighten men, even such men as reject the Scriptures as the authoritative proclamation of the will of God and reject also the way of salvation through the mediation and sacrifice of the Son of God as revealed therein; all of which is contrary to the essential doctrine of the Holy Scripture, and of the Standards of the said Church, that the Holy Scripture is most necessary, and the rule of faith and practice.

(2) Teaching that the Church is a fountain of divine authority which, apart from the Holy Scripture, may and does savingly enlighten men; which is contrary to the essential doctrine of the Holy Scripture and of the Standards of the said Church, that the Holy Scripture is most necessary, and the rule of faith and practice.

(3) Teaching that errors may have existed in the original text of the Holy Scripture, as it came from its authors; which is contrary to the essential doctrine taught in the Holy Scripture and in the Standards of the said Church, that the Holy Scripture is the Word of God written, immediately inspired, and the rule of faith and practice.

(4) Teaching that Moses is not the author of the Pentateuch, which is contrary to direct statements of Holy Scripture, and to the essential doctrines of the Standards of the said Church, that the Holy Scripture evidences itself to be the Word of God by the consent of all the parts, and that the infallible rule of interpretation of Scripture is the Scripture itself.

(5) Teaching that Isaiah is not the author of half of the book that bears his name, which is contrary to direct statements of Holy Scripture and to the essential doctrines of the Standards of the said Church, that the Holy Scripture evidences itself to be the Word of God by the consent of all the parts, and that the infallible rule of interpretation of Scripture is the Scripture itself.

(6) Teaching that Sanctification is not complete at death, which is contrary to the essential doctrine of Holy Scripture and of the Standards of the said Church, that the souls of believers are at their death at once made perfect in holiness.

(b) *The Sentence Inflicted by the General Assembly of* 1893.

This appeal being regularly issued, and coming on to be heard on the judgment, the notice of appeal, the appeal, and the specifications of errors alleged, and the record in the case from the beginning, and the reading of said record having been omitted by consent, and the parties hereto having been heard before the judicatory in argument, and the opportunity having been given to the members of the judicatory appealed from to be heard, and they having been heard, and opportunity having been given to the members of this judicatory to be heard, and they having been heard, as provided by the Book of Discipline, and the General Assembly, as a judicatory sitting in said cause on appeal, having sustained the following specifications of error, to wit:

All of said specifications of errors set forth in said five grounds of appeal, save and except the first and fifth under the fourth ground of appeal, on consideration thereof, this judicatory finds said Appeal should be and is hereby sustained, and that said Presbytery of New York, the judicatory appealed from, erred in striking out said amended charges four and seven, and erred in not sustaining, on the law and the evidence, said amended charges, one, two, three, five, six and eight; on consideration whereof this judicatory finds that said final judgment of the Presbytery of New York is erroneous, and should be and is hereby reversed; and this General Assembly sitting as a judicatory in said cause coming now to enter judgment on said amended charges, one, two, three, five, six and eight, finds the appellee, the said Charles A. Briggs, has uttered, taught and propagated views, doctrines and teachings, as set forth in said charges, contrary to the essential doctrine of Holy Scripture and the Standards of said Presbyterian church in the United States of America, and in violation of the ordination vows of said appellee, which said erroneous teachings, views and doctrines strike at the vitals of religion, and have been industriously spread; wherefore, this General Assembly of the Presbyterian church in the United States of America, sitting as a judicatory in this cause on appeal, does hereby suspend Charles A. Briggs, the said appellee, from the office of a minister in the Presbyterian church in the United States of America, until such time as he shall give satisfactory evidence of repentance to the General Assembly of the Presbyterian church in the United States of America, for the violation by him of said ordination vows as herein and heretofore found.

And it is ordered that the Stated Clerk of this General Assembly transmit a certified copy of this judgment to the Presbytery of New York, to be made a part of the record in this case. It is also ordered that a copy be furnished to the appellee, the Rev. Charles A. Briggs, D.D.

XXIV. PROPOSED PLAN FOR THE FEDERATION OF THE REFORMED CHURCHES OF AMERICA, 1894.

For the glory of God, and for the greater unity and advancement of the church of which the Lord Jesus Christ is the Head, the Reformed churches in the United States holding to the Presbyterian system adopt the following Articles of Federal Union:

1. Every denomination entering into this Union shall retain its distinct individuality, as well as every power, jurisdiction, and right which is not by this Constitution expressly delegated to the body hereby constituted.

2. The acts, proceedings, and records of the duly constituted authorities of each of the denominations shall be received in all the other denominations, and in the Federal Council, as of full credit and with proper respect.

3. For the prosecution of work that can be better done in union than separately, an Ecclesiastical Assembly is hereby constituted, which shall be known by the name and style of The Federal Council of the Reformed churches in the United States of America holding the Presbyterian system.

4. The Federal Council shall consist of four ministers and four elders from each of the constituent denominations, who shall be chosen, with alternates, under the direction of their respective supreme judicatories, in such manner as those judicatories shall respectively determine.

5. The Federal Council shall promote the co-operation of the federated denominations in their Home and Foreign Missionary work, and shall keep watch on current religious, moral, and social movements, and take such action as may concentrate the influence of all the churches in the maintenance of the truth that our nation is a Protestant Christian nation, and of all that is therein involved.

6. The Federal Council may advise and recommend in all matters pertaining to the general welfare of the Kingdom of Christ, but shall not exercise authority, except such as is conferred upon it by this instrument, or such as may be conferred upon it by the federated bodies. It shall not interfere with the creed, worship, or government of the federated denominations. In the conduct of its meetings it shall respect their conscientious views. All matters of discipline shall be left to the exclusive and final judgment of the ecclesiastical authorities of the denomination in which the same may arise.

7. The Federal Council shall have the power of opening and maintaining a friendly correspondence with the highest Assemblies of other religious denominations, for the purpose of promoting union and concert of action in general or common interests.

8. All differences which may arise among the federated bodies, or any of them, in regard to matters within the jurisdiction of the Federal Council shall be determined by such executive agencies as may be created by the Federal Council, with the right of appeal to the Federal Council for final adjudication.

9. The officers of the Federal Council shall be a President, Vice-President, Clerk, and Treasurer.

10. The Federal Council shall meet annually, and on its own adjournment, at such time and place as may be determined. Special meetings may be called by a unanimous vote of the officers of the Council on thirty days' notice.

11. The expenses of the Council shall be met by a contingent fund to be provided by a *pro rata* apportionment on the basis of the number of communicants in each denomination; and the expenses of the delegates to the Council shall be paid from this fund.

12. Amendments to these Articles may be proposed by the Federal Council, or by any of the supreme judicatories of the churches in the Federation; but the approval of all those judicatories shall be necessary for their adoption.

INDEX.

417

The American Church History Series.

By Subscription, ... In Twelve Volumes, at $2.50 per Volume